The Historical Jesus and the Temple: Memory, Methodology, and the Gospel of Matthew

In this book, Michael Patrick Barber examines the role of the Jerusalem temple in the teaching of the historical Jesus. Drawing on recent discussions about methodology and memory research in Jesus studies, he advances a fresh approach to reconstructing Jesus's teaching. Barber argues that Jesus did not reject the temple's validity but that he likely participated in and endorsed its rites. Moreover, he locates Jesus's teaching within Jewish apocalyptic eschatology, showing that Jesus's message about the coming kingdom and his disciples' place in it likely involved important temple and priestly traditions that have been ignored by the quest. Barber also highlights new developments in scholarship on the Gospel of Matthew to show that its Jewish perspective offers valuable but overlooked clues about the kinds of concerns that would have shaped Jesus's outlook. A bold approach to a key topic in biblical studies, Barber's book is a pioneering contribution to Jesus scholarship.

Michael Patrick Barber is Professor of Scripture and Theology at the Augustine Institute Graduate School. He is co-author, with Brant Pitre and John Kincaid, of *Paul, A New Covenant Jew: Rethinking Pauline Theology* (Eerdmans, 2019).

The Historical Jesus and the Temple

Memory, Methodology, and the Gospel of Matthew

MICHAEL PATRICK BARBER

Augustine Institute Graduate School of Theology, Colorado

Foreword by Dale C. Allison, Jr.

CAMBRIDGE
UNIVERSITY PRESS

Shaftesbury Road, Cambridge CB2 8EA, United Kingdom

One Liberty Plaza, 20th Floor, New York, NY 10006, USA

477 Williamstown Road, Port Melbourne, VIC 3207, Australia

314–321, 3rd Floor, Plot 3, Splendor Forum, Jasola District Centre, New Delhi – 110025, India

103 Penang Road, #05–06/07, Visioncrest Commercial, Singapore 238467

Cambridge University Press is part of Cambridge University Press & Assessment, a department of the University of Cambridge.

We share the University's mission to contribute to society through the pursuit of education, learning and research at the highest international levels of excellence.

www.cambridge.org
Information on this title: www.cambridge.org/9781009210867

DOI: 10.1017/9781009210843

First published 2023
First paperback edition 2025

A catalogue record for this publication is available from the British Library

Library of Congress Cataloging-in-Publication data
NAMES: Barber, Michael Patrick, author.
TITLE: The historical Jesus and the temple : memory, methodology, and the Gospel of Matthew / Michael Patrick Barber, Augustine Institute of Theology, Colorado.
DESCRIPTION: Cambridge, United Kingdom ; New York, NY, USA : Cambridge University Press, 2023. | Includes bibliographical references and index.
IDENTIFIERS: LCCN 2022024938 | ISBN 9781009210850 (hardback) | ISBN 9781009210843 (ebook)
SUBJECTS: LCSH: Bible. Matthew – Criticism, interpretation, etc. | Jesus Christ – Historicity. | Temple of Jerusalem (Jerusalem)
CLASSIFICATION: LCC BS2575.52 .B365 2023 | DDC 226.2/06–dc23/eng/20220801
LC record available at https://lccn.loc.gov/2022024938

ISBN   978-1-009-21085-0   Hardback
ISBN   978-1-009-21086-7   Paperback

For Kim

"You surpass them all."

(Proverbs 31:29)

Contents

Foreword

Dale C. Allison, Jr.

The publication of academic books about the historical Jesus continues apace, so much so that no one can any longer keep up: we are all overwhelmed. One may, as a result, be tempted to hope that, despite all the advertising blurbs to the contrary, the new volumes must be reruns, little more than old songs in a new key. Can there really be anything new to say? Yet, as readers of Michael Barber's book will discover, there are.

The Historical Jesus and the Temple contributes to the ongoing debates in at least three major ways. First, the book matters because it exemplifies a way forward methodologically. Over the past several decades and continuing into the present, perhaps most historians have sought to distinguish fiction from history and so recover the figure behind the gospels by deploying the so-called criteria of authenticity; above all, multiple attestation, dissimilarity, embarrassment, and coherence. Scholars have been like the angels of Matt 13:24–30, 37–43: they have endeavored to uproot the fictional weeds, bind them into bundles to be ignored, and then gathered the historical wheat into their books and articles. A growing chorus of voices, however, has registered dissatisfaction with the conventional strategies. Barber has listened to them and their complaints, and he concurs that the standard criteria have too often functioned as walls that have imprisoned historical imagination.

Yet how, if the standard tools are of questionable or limited utility, can we stay in business? How do we, while recognizing that the gospels are later interpretations and expansions of social memories, carry on the quest for the historical Jesus? Barber sensibly suggests that, "rather than looking for an uninterpreted Jesus *behind* the Gospels, the historian's best way forward is to begin with a different question: *Which interpretations* of Jesus likely bring us closest to history?" (p. 234). He proposes that we undertake this task by: (1) searching for recurrent patterns in the sources; (2) contemplating those patterns in the light of what we otherwise know of Second Temple Judaism; and (3) deciding whether directly associating the historical Jesus with this or that pattern best explains the content and shape of some aspect of early Christian thought. Barber does, to be sure, occasionally endeavor to secure a place in Jesus's life for a specific saying or story; but his major conclusions do not, as he emphasizes, rest upon his ability to do that. The upshot is that these pages instruct us on how we can obtain solid results and gain valuable insights without wielding the old criteria. Indeed, in Barber's book – which consistently strives for the probable rather than the possible – the criterion of dissimilarity gets turned upside down, and time and again we see how positing continuity between Jesus and his later followers has more explanatory power than positing discontinuity.

Barber's second major contribution is to make a strong case that, in more than one area, a characteristically Matthean interpretation preserves rather than distorts the memory of Jesus. Going back to Adolf Harnack, F. C. Burkitt, and T. W. Manson, many have found the historical Jesus above all in Q and/or Mark. In their judgment, so-called M material and Matthean redaction are, almost always, sources not for Jesus but for later ecclesiastical interests and settings. Barber rejects this simple antithesis. He is right to do so.

Over the course of my own study of Matthew, I have occasionally concluded that, in this or that respect, the First Gospel represents the past better than the Second Gospel. I have decided, for example, that Matthew's law-abiding Jesus (see esp. 5:17–20) is more credible than Mark's more liberal (and perhaps Pauline?) Jesus; that Mark 8:27–30 might be a truncated version of a story better preserved in the fuller Matt 16:13–20; that Matt 18:3 ("Truly I tell you, unless you change and become like children, you will never enter the kingdom of heaven") is, on the whole, probably more primitive than Mark 10:15 ("Truly I tell you, whoever does not receive the kingdom of God as a little child will never enter it"); that the appearance of Jesus to Mary Magdalene, found in Matthew 28 but not in Mark 16, is likely historical; and that the typological comparison of Jesus to Moses, which is implicit at points in Mark but much clearer and more developed in Matthew, is rooted in Jesus's self-conception. Yet I had never, before reading Barber, thought about all these things at once, and so I had never fully shed the old habit of equating the uniquely Matthean with the undoubtedly secondary. This volume, however, has moved me to rethink things. Barber demonstrates between the covers of one book the multiple ways in which the First Gospel – in its presentation of Jesus's relationship to the temple, to Davidic motifs, and to traditions about sacrifice and priesthood – plausibly mirrors what Jesus himself taught, and shows us that, in important ways, Matthew's interpretive framework is not an obstacle in our way but a path to the historical Jesus. The latter is not buried beneath Matthew but stares at us from its surface.

The third major contribution of *The Historical Jesus and the Temple* is Chapter 7, which focuses on cultic traditions in Matthew, on imagery surrounding sacrifice, and on priestly matters. There can be no doubt that the Protestant orientation of most modern exegetes and critical historians of Jesus has led us astray here. As Barber writes: "Given the history of prejudice against ritual and cult inherited by modern biblical scholarship, it is not surprising that allusions to Israel's liturgical traditions have often been dismissed. In general, one gets the sense that contemporary exegetes have the impression that such imagery occurs sparsely" (p. 222). Yet "it is broadly attested" and is "fully consistent with Jesus's identity as a first-century Jewish teacher."

This is an eye-opening chapter and really does mark a break with our guild's tradition. There is nothing or next to nothing on Jesus and priestly motifs in the pertinent writings of Johannes Weiss or Albert Schweitzer, Rudolf Bultmann or Günther Bornkamm, C. H. Dodd or T. W. Manson, Norman Perrin or Joachim Jeremias, E. P. Sanders or John Dominic Crossan. Yet, as Barber demonstrates, there are indeed cultic and priestly motifs in Matthew as well as the other canonical gospels, and they are more than meager. Once they are spotted, the topic of their meaning and possible relationship to Jesus naturally follows. In this endeavor, Barber is a pioneer.

Having highlighted several ways in which Barber's contribution is important, I could continue; my comments hardly exhaust its significance. I am, for instance, intrigued by his suggestions about a possible divine christology in Matthew. I trust, however, that I have said enough to establish that Barber's well-informed and thought-provoking book is a genuine contribution to the study of the historical Jesus.

I

Introduction

[O]ne must quest for the historical Jesus by accounting for the interpretations of the Gospels, not by dismissing them and certainly not by fragmenting them.

–Chris Keith[1]

Could it be that some of the Matthean "systematizations" (or "nonsystematizations") of Jesus might be very close to Jesus himself, just because they are constructions of a Jew who was temporally and culturally close to him?

–Ulrich Luz[2]

In a letter to John Adams dated to October of 1813, Thomas Jefferson writes about his desire to retrieve the "very words only of Jesus" from the gospels.[3] Jefferson describes the process of recovering these "genuine"[4] sayings as picking out "diamonds from the dunghills."[5] His selection process is governed by certain assumptions. For one thing, Jefferson is convinced that Jesus's followers badly misrepresented their master's

---

[1] Chris Keith, *Jesus's Literacy: Scribal Culture and the Teacher from Galilee*, LNTS 413 (London: T&T Clark, 2011), 66.

[2] Ulrich Luz, "Matthew's Interpretive 'Tendencies' and the 'Historical' Jesus," in *Jesus Research: New Methodologies and Perceptions, The Second Princeton-Prague Symposium on Jesus Research*, ed. James H. Charlesworth with Brian Rhea and Petr Pokorný (Grand Rapids: Eerdmans, 2014), 597.

[3] Letter to John Adams (12 October 1813); quoted from M. Andrew Holowchak, *Thomas Jefferson's Bible: With Introduction and Critical Commentary* (Berlin: Walter de Gruyter, 2019), 93–94.

[4] Letter to Francis Adrian Van der Kemp (25 April 1816); quoted from Holowchak, *Thomas Jefferson's Bible*, 95.

[5] Letter to John Adams (24 January 1814); quoted from Holowchak, *Thomas Jefferson's Bible*, 94.

teachings. He talks of "paring off" the material in the gospel narratives that originated from them. In addition, Jesus is understood to be opposed to his Jewish contemporaries; Jefferson says that Jesus came to reform the "wretched depravity" of Jewish morality.[6] In all of this, Jefferson anticipates, albeit in a crude way, much of what would later be viewed as standard fare in historical Jesus research.

Jefferson's account of his historical method serves as a helpful launching point for this study. While most of those engaged in the quest for the historical Jesus no longer pit the man from Nazareth against his Jewish heritage, Jesus scholarship is still often conceived of in binary terms that are remarkably similar to Jefferson's stated goals: the historian typically seeks to sift the "authentic" material in our sources from the "inauthentic." By means of the "criteria of authenticity," tools that emerged out of form and redaction criticism,[7] historians seek to clear away the strata of later interpretive layers from our sources and dig out the "diamonds," that is, the material that represents the original, uninterpreted Jesus.[8]

The goal of this study is not to argue that traditions formerly viewed as "authentic" should be moved to the "inauthentic" category – or vice versa. Rather, this work makes a bolder claim: Jesus scholarship should rethink the very way it has used the Gospel of Matthew. In particular, this study will ask what a close analysis of Matthew's[9] overall presentation might contribute to our understanding of Jesus's relationship to the temple. The approach taken here reflects certain important developments in biblical studies that represent important shifts in scholarship.

---

[6] Letter to John Adams (12 October 1814); quoted from Holowchak, *Thomas Jefferson's Bible*, 94.

[7] See, e.g., Chris Keith, "The Indebtedness of the Criteria Approach to Form Criticism and Recent Attempts to Rehabilitate the Search for an Authentic Jesus," in *Jesus, Criteria, and the Demise of Authenticity*, ed. Chris Keith and Anthony Le Donne (London: T&T Clark, 2012), 3–37.

[8] For a recent example, see JongHyun Kwon, *The Historical Jesus's Death as "Forgiveness of Sins,"* WUNT 2/467 (Tübingen: Mohr Siebeck, 2018), who determines, e.g., that Jesus's ransom saying (Matt 20:28//Mark 10:45) is "authentic" through the use of the conventional criteria (168–174). Instead of being an "interpretive saying" (quoting Peter Stuhlmacher, *Reconciliation, Law, and Righteousness: Essays in Biblical Theology*, trans. Everett R. Kalin [Philadelphia: Fortress Press, 1986], 16), Kwon explains that "a good case can be made for its authenticity." Here, then, "authenticity," therefore, represents an "uninterpreted" saying.

[9] This study follows the convention of calling the author "Matthew" without affirming the author's apostolic identity. For discussion on the authorship of the Gospel, see the Appendix.

THE CHALLENGE OF A JEWISH JESUS AND
ANTI-TEMPLE BIASES IN SCHOLARSHIP

Critical Scholarship's History of Antisemitism

If there is one thing that all contemporary Jesus scholars agree about, it is this: the historical Jesus must be identified as a Jewish figure. This is a shift in emphasis that should be celebrated. Indeed, many scholars today remain unaware of the pervasive influence that antisemitism has had on modern biblical criticism. For example, it is rarely remembered that Julius Wellhausen, a pioneering figure in modern biblical studies, once made Jesus's un-Jewishness axiomatic, making the following outrageous and despicable assertion: "One may regard the non-Jewish in [Jesus], the human, as more characteristic than the Jewish."[10]

It would be a serious error to dismiss Wellhausen's expressions of antisemitism as inconsequential or to think that such attitudes have only been exhibited by those on the margins of critical scholarship. Other figures known for their towering influence on the field could be mentioned.[11] For instance, Gerhard Kittel, whose name is inseparable from the influential *Theological Dictionary of the New Testament* that he edited, was an active member of the Nazi Party, spoke in defense of Hitler's response to the "Jewish problem," and was even the Führer's guest of honor at a Nazi Party convention.[12] He went on to write a work detailing potential solutions to the "Jewish problem" in which he first considers – in appallingly explicit terms – the possibility of mass extermination.[13] Though he rejects this as an unviable option, his cold and objective analysis is bloodcurdling. Nowhere does Kittel raise a single moral objection to the plan;

---

[10] Author's translation. Taken from Julius Wellhausen, *Einleitung in die drei ersten Evangelien* (Berlin: Reimer, 1905), 114: "Man darf das Nichtjüdische in ihm, das Menschliche, für charakteristischer halten, als das Jüdische."

[11] See the detailed discussions in Anders Gerdmar, *Roots of Theological Anti-Semitism: German Biblical Interpretation and the Jews: From Herder and Semler to Kittel and Bultmann* (Leiden: Brill, 2009); Peter S. Head, "The Nazi Quest for an Aryan Jesus," *JSHJ* 2/1 (2004): 55–89.

[12] See Gerdmar, *Roots of Theological Anti-Semistism*, 417–530; Head, "Nazi Quest," 70–86.

[13] Gerhard Kittel, "Die Entstehung des Judentums und die Entstehung der Judenfrage," in *Forschungen zur Judenfrage. Sitzungsberichte der Ersten Arbeitstagung der Forschungsabteilung Judenfrage des Reichsinstituts für Geschichte des neuen Deutschlands vom 19. bis 21. November 1936*, Forschungen zur Judenfrage (Hamburg: Hanseatische Verlagsanstalt, 1937), 63.

it is simply deemed impractical.[14] From the outset of his career, it is clear that Kittel's work attempted to cast Jesus as a figure in conflict with his Jewish contemporaries.[15] He would go on to explain that in announcing himself as the fulfillment of God's kingdom, Jesus *"ceases to be a Jew, and his proclamation ceases to be a member of Judaism."*[16]

Wellhausen and Kittel are worth mentioning because their names are still well known in biblical scholarship. Yet many others who were influential in their own day but largely forgotten today could also be discussed here.[17] Suffice it to say, this aspect of the history of the guild is so embarrassing and uncomfortable, it is common for scholars to pass over it in silence. It can be too conveniently brushed under the rug with the term "the No Quest period."[18] The renewed emphasis on Jesus's Jewishness, then, is an important corrective that should be celebrated.

Jesus vs. the Temple?

Nevertheless, on its own, appealing to Jesus as a "Jew" only goes so far. Scholars now recognize that the Second Temple Jewish world was characterized by diverse practices and beliefs. Given this reality, insisting broadly that Jesus was "a Jew" clarifies little. As Simon Joseph explains: "The problem with the rhetorical appeal to Jesus's Jewishness, therefore, is not that it is incorrect. The problem is that it is insufficient: it does not tell us enough."[19] A more penetrating question is: *What kind of Jew was Jesus?*

James Crossley rightly observes that in recent decades the appeal to Jesus's Jewishness has become "arguably the most dominant rhetorical generalization about the historical Jesus," even to the point that it now is "something of a cliché."[20] In particular, as Crossley points out, one notes

[14] Gerhard Kittel, *Die Judenfrage* (Stuttgart: Kohlhammer, 1933), 14. See also the discussion in Gerdmar, *Roots of Theological Anti-Semitism*, 455.

[15] See, e.g., Gerhard Kittel, *Jesus und die Rabbinen*, ed. Kropatchek, Biblische Zeit- und Streitfragen, 7/IX (Berlin-Lichterfelde: Verlag von Edwin Runge, 1912), 3.

[16] Gerhard Kittel, *Die Probleme des palästinischen Spätjudentums und das Urchristentum*, ed. Rudolf Kittel, BWANT 3.1 (Stuttgart: W. Kohlhammer, 1926), 432; trans. in Gerdmar, *Roots of Theological Anti-Semitism*, 432 (emphasis in Gerdmar).

[17] See, e.g., the discussion of Karl G. Kuhn's influence in Jason Staples, *The Idea of Israel in Second Temple Judaism: A New Theory of People, Exile, and Israelite Identity* (Cambridge: Cambridge University Press, 2021), 25–39.

[18] For helpful treatments, again, see the sources in n. 11 earlier.

[19] Simon J. Joseph, "Exit the 'Great Man': On James' Crossley's *Jesus and the Chaos of History*," *JSHJ* 16 (2018): 12.

[20] James G. Crossley, *Jesus and the Chaos of History: Redirecting the Life of the Historical Jesus* (Oxford: Oxford University Press, 2015), 4.

that many attempts that seek to depict Jesus as "Jewish" end up explaining how he really was not "*that* Jewish" after all. Specifically, Crossley notes that this is often the case in regard to Jesus's attitude toward the temple.

It is important to recognize that modern biblical scholarship, which has often been dominated by Protestant voices, has typically viewed the ritual dimension of ancient Israel's faith and life as unpalatable.[21] Such prejudices can be traced back to the pioneers of the historical-critical methods themselves. For many of them, the liturgical traditions of first-century Jewish practice represented a degeneration of Israel's religion and formed the very antithesis of the gospel message proclaimed by Jesus. He therefore has been portrayed as bringing about salvation not only from sin but also from sacrifice and priestly authority.[22] Jesus's Jewishness may be celebrated, then, but only so long as he can be distanced from Jewish liturgical beliefs.

The Gospel of Matthew, however, presents a profound challenge to the notion that Jesus rejected the temple. Jesus is remembered there as endorsing the holiness of the temple's sacrifices. To cite but one example, Matthew contains the following teaching from Jesus:

> which is greater, the gift or *the altar that makes the gift holy* [*to thysiastērion to hagiazon to dōron*]? Therefore, whoever swears by the altar [*en tō thysiastēriō*], swears by it and by everything that is on it. And whoever swears by the temple [*en tō naō*], swears by it and by *the one who dwells in it*. (Matthew 23:19–21)

Here the evangelist portrays Jesus as affirming God's presence in the temple. What is more, Jesus also speaks about worship in a strikingly Jewish way. He affirms that it is the sacrificial altar *itself* that "makes the gift holy" (Matt 23:19; cf. Exod 29:37).[23] As we will see, scholars have often made the case that other statements in the gospel can be viewed as canceling out sayings like this one. We will examine them in detail later

---

[21] See the discussions in, e.g., Jonathan Klawans, *Purity, Sacrifice, and the Temple: Symbolism and Supersessionism in the Study of Ancient Judaism* (Oxford: Oxford University Press, 2006), especially 3–10; Crispin Fletcher-Louis, "Jesus as the High Priestly Messiah: Part 1," *JSHJ* 4, 2 (2006): 156.

[22] See, e.g., Ferdinand Hahn, *Der urchristliche Gottesdienst*, SBS 41 (Stuttgart: Katholisches Bibelwerk, 1970), 17–31; John A. McGuckin, "Sacrifice and Atonement: An Investigation into the Attitude of Jesus of Nazareth towards Cultic Sacrifice," in *Remembering for the Future*, ed. Y. Bauer et al., 3 vols. (Oxford: Pergamon, 1989), 1:649.

[23] All biblical studies and abbreviations in this volume follow the standards found in Billie Jean Collins, Bob Buller, and John Kutzko, eds., *The SBL Handbook of Style*, 2nd ed. (Atlanta: SLB Press, 2014).

and show that they do no such thing. In short, Matthew undermines the conclusion that Jesus rejected the temple's validity per se.

Of course, not all Jews in Jesus's day accepted the legitimacy of the temple. The Dead Sea Scrolls, for instance, indicate the existence of a community that withdrew from the Jerusalem cult. Could Jesus have agreed with Jews like them? I will have more to say about this. For now, let us simply make this observation: if Jesus was an Essene, the preceding statement regarding the holiness of the temple and its altar would be difficult to attribute to him. Those who viewed the Jerusalem sanctuary as illegitimate would hardly claim that its altar made sacrificial gifts holy, and that God dwelled in it. Yet this brings us to another key development in scholarship that informs our study: the pluriform nature of Jewishness after 70 CE.

JEWISH PARTINGS AND THE GOSPEL OF MATTHEW

Jewish Partings after 70 CE

As mentioned previously, the variegated nature of Jewishness in the Second Temple period is well recognized. In the 1980s and 1990s, this represented an advance in scholarship. Previous research had failed to appreciate the diversity that existed in this period. Now, however, another shift is taking place, this time with respect to the post-70 CE period. Shaye Cohen sums up the traditional view: "With the destruction of the Temple the primary focal point of Jewish sectarianism disappeared... For most Jews ... sectarian self-definition ceased to make sense after 70."[24] This understanding, however, has been widely abandoned. The assumption that rabbis quickly consolidated power after the temple's destruction in 70 CE and brought an end to Jewish sectarianism[25] is now receiving sharp criticism.

Daniel Schwartz writes that the latest research "minimizes rabbinic authority both before and after 70 and tends to leave the priests regnant before 70 – and, the way things are going, may soon enthrone them

---

[24] Shaye J. D. Cohen, "The Significance of Yavneh: Pharisees, Rabbis, and the End of Jewish Sectarianism," *HUCA* 55 (1984): 45.

[25] I use the term "sect" and related words (e.g., sectarian) to describe diverse forms of Jewishness without implying a normative expression existed. See the important discussion in Yonder Moynihan Gillihan, "Sectarianism," in *T&T Clark Encyclopedia of Second Temple Judaism*, ed. Daniel M. Gurtner and Loren T. Stuckenbruck, 2 vols. (London: T&T Clark, 2019), 2:718–721.

after 70, too."[26] Likewise, Anders Runesson writes, "There is a growing consensus today that the rabbis did not become dominant until the
fourth century, possibly later."[27] Jodi Magness spotlights various references in the rabbinic literature to unsettled sectarian controversies.[28]
For instance, the condemnation of the Sadducees and Samaritans in the
Mishnah suggests ongoing friction between these groups after 70 CE (cf.
m. Nid. 4:2). Similarly, the Tosefta speaks of *mînîm* – a word used to
describe Jewish groups – who gather in private houses of worship where
improper rites are performed (t. Šabb. 13:5). Joshua Burns shows that
some of the descriptions of *mînîm* bear remarkable similarities to the
Essenes, who likely did not simply vanish immediately after the temple
was destroyed.[29] Regardless of what one makes of Burns' evaluation of
the data, the broader point is hard to dispute: *Jewish divisions were not
erased in the final decades of the first century but continued to endure
long after the New Testament books were written.*

In addition, it is now widely accepted that the rabbinic literature presents us with an idealized view of the rabbis' influence over synagogues.[30]
"Rabbinic Judaism" cannot simply be equated with "the synagogue." For
one thing, synagogues were usually run by synagogue rulers, not rabbis.[31]
What is more, there was no monolithic synagogue network in the late
first century. Anders Runesson has shown that while some synagogues
served as municipal centers, others involved voluntary associations.[32]

---

[26] See Daniel R. Schwartz, "Introduction: Was 70 CE a Watershed in Jewish History? Three
Stages of Modern Scholarship, and a Renewed Effort," in *Was 70 CE a Watershed in Jewish History?: On Jews and Judaism before and after the Destruction of the Second Temple*,
ed. Daniel R. Schwartz, Zeev Weiss, and Ruth A. Clements (Leiden: Brill, 2012), 15.

[27] Anders Runesson, "Behind the Gospel of Matthew: Radical Pharisees in Post-war
Galilee?," *Currents in Theology and Mission* 37 (2010): 467.

[28] See Jodi Magness, "Sectarianism before and after 70 CE," in *Was 70 CE a Watershed in
Jewish History?*, ed. Schwartz et al., 69–89.

[29] Joshua Ezra Burns, "Essene Sectarianism and Social Differentiation in Judaea after 70
C.E.," *Harvard Theological Review* 99, 3 (2006): 247–274.

[30] See, e.g., Stuart S. Miller, "The Rabbis and the Non Existent Monolithic Synagogue,"
in *Jews, Christians, and Polytheists in the Ancient Synagogue: Cultural Interaction during the Greco-Roman Period*, ed. Steven Fine (London: Routledge, 1999), 57–70; Lee I.
Levine, "The Sages and the Synagogue in Late Antiquity: The Evidence of the Galilee,"
in *The Galilee in Late Antiquity*, ed. Lee I. Levine (New York: Jewish Theological Seminary, 1992), 201–222.

[31] See, e.g., Amy-Jill Levine, "Matthew's Portrayal of the Synagogue and Its Leaders," in
The Gospel of Matthew at the Crossroads of Early Christianity, ed. Donald Senior, C.P.
(Leuven: Peeters, 2011), 191.

[32] Anders Runesson, *The Origins of the Synagogue: A Socio-Historical Study* (Stockholm:
Almqvist International, 2001), especially, 213–235. On the positive reception of Runesson's

For example, Philo says that Essenes gathered in "sacred spots *which they call synagogues [hoi kalountai synagōgai]*."[33] Shaye Cohen explains, "Synagogues were not beholden to any central body; every community ran its synagogue in its own way."[34]

The primitive Jesus movement should be located within this variegated Jewish environment. There can be little doubt that the earliest believers saw themselves as *Jews*. In his letters, Paul insists that he is a Jew (cf., e.g., Rom 3:9; Rom 11:1, 14; Gal 2:15). Likewise, in the book of Acts, Paul maintains his identity as a Pharisee long after encountering the Risen Lord on the road to Damascus. Before the ruling council, he declares, "Brothers, *I am* a Pharisee" (Acts 23:6). He goes on later to explain that he worships the God of Israel in accord with the Torah and Prophets, "according to the Way, which they call a *sect [kata tēn hodon hēn legousin hairesin]*" (Acts 24:14). In Acts, we also learn that early believers were known as "the *sect [haireseōs]* of the Nazarenes" (Acts 24:5; cf. Acts 15:5). The same terminology of "sect" is also used in Josephus to describe the Pharisees (*Life* 10; 12; 191) and the Sadducees (*Ant.* 13, 171; 20, 199). All of this indicates that the author of Acts believed the early community was Jewish in nature.

To speak of a "parting of the ways" between "Judaism" and "Christianity" is therefore inadequate. It implies a normative understanding of Jewishness that did not exist in the first century. Even after 70 CE, there were partings *within* the Jewish world. The complexities involved are discussed in a recent collection of essays, aptly titled *The Ways That Often Parted*.[35] The editors explain: "The unifying thesis of this volume is that Christianity's eventual distinction from Judaism was messy and multiform, occurring at different paces in diverse geographies with varied literary resources, theological commitments, historical happenstance, and political maneuvering."[36] This has enormous implications for both Matthew studies and Jesus research.

---

work in recent synagogue scholarship, see Jordan J. Ryan, *The Role of the Synagogue in the Aims of Jesus* (Minneapolis: Fortress Press, 2017), 31 and sources in n. 49.

[33] *Prob.* 81 [Colson, Loeb Classical Library]; emphasis added. See, however, the discussion in Burns, "Essene Sectarianism," 261 n. 29.

[34] Shaye J. D. Cohen, *From the Maccabees to the Mishnah*, 3rd ed. (Louisville: Westminster, 2014), 225.

[35] Lori Baron, Jill Hicks-Keeton, and Matthew Thiessen, eds., *The Ways That Often Parted: Essays in Honor of Joel Marcus*, ECL (Atlanta: SBL Press, 2018).

[36] Baron, Hicks-Keeton, and Thiessen, "Introduction," in *The Ways That Often Parted*, 2.

Matthew as a Jewish Gospel

For some time now, there has been a raging debate in Matthean studies over whether or not the Gospel's original readers viewed themselves as "within Judaism" (the so-called *intra muros* view) or "outside Judaism" (the so-called *extra muros* view).[37] David Sim writes that the question of Matthew's social location "is now without question the dominant theme in Matthean studies."[38] Yet the developments in scholarship discussed above have unsettled the traditional ways scholars have approached the issue.[39] Asking whether Matthew's community is "within Judaism" or "outside of Judaism" tends to ignore the pluriform nature of Jewishness in the first century. So as not to burden the reader, I will offer a very brief treatment of the matter in this section. A more detailed discussion of the Gospel's Jewish character can be found in an Appendix at the end of the book.

To be sure, it is challenging to figure out how to speak of Matthew's audience. Although a growing number of scholars recognize that the gospels were likely written with the hope of wide circulation,[40] this does not negate the reality that specific readers were probably nonetheless especially in view.[41] In the case of the Gospel of Matthew, the implied reader is expected to possess a deep familiarity not only with the scriptures of Israel but also with Jewish culture broadly.[42] In addition, the Gospel indicates that the disciples will be punished in synagogues (Matt 10:17). This suggests that members of Matthew's audience would have

---

[37] See, e.g., Anders Runesson, "Rethinking Early Jewish-Christian Relations: Matthean Community History as Pharisaic Intragroup Conflict," *JBL* 127 (2008): 96–98; Boris Repschinski, *The Controversy Stories in the Gospel of Matthew: Their Redaction, Form and Relevance for the Relationship Between the Matthean Community and Formative Judaism*, FRLANT 189 (Göttingen: Vadenhoeck & Ruprecht, 2000), 1–28.

[38] David C. Sim, "Matthew: The Current State of Research," in *Mark and Matthew, Comparative Readings I: Understanding the Earliest Gospels in their First Century Settings*, ed. Eve-Marie Becker and Anders Runesson (Tübingen: Mohr Siebeck, 2011), 36.

[39] Rodney Reeves, "The Gospel of Matthew," in *The State of New Testament Studies: A Survey of Recent Research*, ed. Scot McKnight and Nijay K. Gupta (Grand Rapids: Baker Academic, 2019), 291; Matthias Konradt, *Israel, Church, and the Gentiles in the Gospel of Matthew*, BMSEC, trans. Kathleen Ess (Waco: Baylor University Press, 2014 [orig. 2007]), 364–365.

[40] See, e.g., the articles in Richard Bauckham, ed., *The Gospels for All Christians: Rethinking the Gospel Audiences* (Grand Rapids: Eerdmans, 1998).

[41] See Akiva Cohen, *Matthew and the Mishnah: Redefining Identity and Ethos in the Shadow of the Second Temple's Destruction*, WUNT 418 (Tübingen: Mohr Siebeck, 2016), 89–99; David Sim, "The Gospels for All Christians? A Response to Richard Bauckham," *JSNT* 84 (2001): 3–27.

[42] See the thoughtful discussion in Leroy Huizenga, *The New Isaac: Tradition and Intertextuality in the Gospel of Matthew*, NovTSup 131 (Leiden: Brill, 2009), 21–74.

understood themselves to be under synagogue authority and, therefore, as Jewish.[43] While Gentiles may be included in the readership, there can be little doubt that the Gospel exhibits a pronounced Jewish perspective. Because of these features, the Gospel "has almost always been understood in both church and academia, in one way or another, as the 'Jewish' gospel."[44]

In particular, Matthew's strong emphasis on Torah observance seems indicative of Jewish priorities. For instance, Jesus's insistence on the law's enduring value in the Sermon on the Mount appears to have programmatic significance (cf. Matt 5:17–20).[45] Likewise, unlike the other Synoptics, Matthew shows a marked preoccupation with the problem of "lawlessness [*anomia*]" (cf. Matt 7:23; 13:41; 23:28; 24:12).[46] Anders Runesson is correct – Jesus's problem with the Pharisees in the Gospel cannot be that they "keep the law or keep it too strictly. On the contrary, they simply do not keep it rigorously enough."[47] Jesus says: "Whoever therefore loosens one of the least of these commandments and teaches others to do so will be called least in the kingdom of heaven" (Matt 5:19). The implications for Jesus's stance toward the law in Matthew would seem clear; Jesus kept the Torah in all of its details.[48] Even ancient and medieval writers such as Thomas Aquinas caught this meaning. Commenting on this passage, Aquinas affirms, "*Christ conformed his conduct in all things to the precepts of the law.*"[49]

Matthew alone reports that Jesus wore a "tassel" (*kraspedon*) on his garment, a detail that suggests his attention to the Torah's precepts (Matt 14:36; cf. Num 15:38–39).[50] In addition, in following Mark's report that Jesus told the disciples to pray that their eschatological flight to

---

[43] Amy-Jill Levine, "Concluding Reflections: What's Next in the Study of Matthew?," in *Matthew within Judaism: Israel and the Nations*, ECL, ed. Anders Runesson and Daniel M. Gurtner (Atlanta: SBL Press, 2019), 454; See W. D. Davies and Dale C. Allison, Jr., *The Gospel According to St. Matthew*, ICC, 3 vols. (Edinburgh: T&T Clark, 1988–1997), 2:183.

[44] Reeves, "The Gospel of Matthew," 277.

[45] See, e.g., Donald Senior, C.P., *Matthew*, ANTC (Nashville: Abingdon, 1998), 73.

[46] John Kampen, *Matthew within Sectarian Judaism*, AYBRL (New Haven: Yale University Press, 2019), 87.

[47] Anders Runesson, *Divine Wrath and Salvation in Matthew: The Narrative World of the First Gospel* (Minneapolis: Fortress Press, 2016), 76.

[48] Theodore Zahn, *Das Evangelium nach Matthäus*, KNT 1, 4th ed. (repr., Wuppertal: Brockhaus, 1984 [orig. 1922]), 220.

[49] See, e.g., Thomas Aquinas, *Summa Theologiae*, III, q. 40, art. 4.

[50] James G. Crossley, "Matthew and the Torah: Jesus as Legal Interpreter," in *Matthew within Judaism*, ed. Runesson and Gurtner, 31.

the mountains would not happen during the winter, Matthew adds that they should ask that it not occur *on the Sabbath* (Matt 24:20; cf. Mark 13:18). Other details also point to the evangelist's Jewish outlook. For instance, of the canonical gospels, only Matthew has Jesus mention the use of phylacteries (Matt 23:5), which we now know were likely already in use in Jesus's day.[51]

At the same time, there are passages in the Gospel that appear to be in tension with Jewish sensibilities. What more recent works are showing, however, is that many of these passages make good sense against the backdrop of the sort of Jewish partings mentioned above. For example, some have argued that the frequent appearance of the phrase "their synagogues [*tais synagōgais autōn*]" in Matthew (Matt 4:23; 9:35; 10:17; 12:9; 13:34; cf. Matt 23:34) are indicative of a break with "Judaism."[52] This assumption rests on flawed premises about the nature of first-century synagogues. Jewishness did not have a monolithic expression and there was no central authority governing the various synagogues. The phrase "their synagogues" likely points to conflict between Jesus's disciples and *certain* Jewish synagogues.[53] The term usually rendered, "church" (*ekklēsia*), is repeatedly used in Jewish sources to describe public assemblies,[54] which seems to have included synagogue gatherings.[55] Matthew's language of "church" (*ekklēsia*, Matt 16:18; 18:15, 17) cannot, therefore, be proffered as positive evidence that the community had severed all ties to synagogues. Amy-Jill Levine maintains that one must acknowledge that, for Matthew, "synagogues are a place of hostility, not hospitality."[56] This is difficult to dispute. Yet even if Matthew writes to a community that feels unwelcome in synagogues broadly, this does not

---

[51] See, e.g., Kenneth G. C. Newport, *The Sources and Sitz im Leben of Matthew* 23, JSNT-Sup 117 (Sheffield: Sheffield Academic Press, 1995), 85–88.

[52] See, e.g., George D. Kilpatrick, *The Origins of the Gospel according to Matthew* (Oxford: Clarendon, 1946), 110–112.

[53] See, e.g., Runesson, "Behind the Gospel of Matthew," 460–471.

[54] See, e.g., Judith 6:16, 21; 7:29; 14:6; 1 Macc 5:16; 14:19. In LXX Neh 5:7 it has a juridical sense. It is also simply used with the sense of a group (cf. 1 Macc 3:13; Sir 23:24). For a comprehensive study, see Ralph Korner, *The Origin and Meaning of Ekklēsia in the Early Jesus Movement*, AGJU 98 (Leiden: Brill, 2017), 81–149.

[55] See, e.g., Josephus, *J.W.* 7:412; Philo, *Spec.* 1.324–325; Korner, *Origin and Meaning*, 123–126. In addition to Korner's study, see Anders Runesson, Donald Binder, and Birger Olsson, *The Ancient Synagogue from Its Origins to 200 C.E.: A Source Book*, AJEC 72 (Leiden: Brill, 2008), 11–12.

[56] See Levine, "Concluding Reflections," 552. See also the important discussion in Levine, "Matthew's Portrayal," 177–193.

necessarily mean that it saw itself as non-Jewish. It only confirms something we already know: "Jewishness" was contested.

Similarly, Jesus's harsh words in Matthew about the Pharisees and other Jews who reject his message cannot be taken as proof of "anti-Judaism." As John Kampen observes, similar denunciations of Israel are found in the Dead Sea Scrolls.[57] Those who were not part of the Qumran community are viewed as being under the power of Belial (CD-A [Damascus Document] 4:12–13). They too, it is said, will face destruction (CD-A 8:1–2). In short, Jesus's teaching in Matthew sits comfortably alongside the kind of intramural polemics we find in other ancient Jewish sources. These divisions did not disappear by the late first century, the period in which most scholars believe Matthew's Gospel was written.

Other features of Matthew that have been held up as evidence of the Gospel's supposed non-Jewish character have similarly been debunked. For instance, that the evangelist interprets the oracle concerning the royal figure in Zechariah 9 as depicting two animals is not clear evidence of his ignorance of Hebrew. Jewish rabbis interpreted the passage similarly.[58] The evangelist even provides more literal renderings of the Hebrew scriptures than what is found in the Septuagint.[59] Likewise, passages that have been interpreted as indicating that the church "replaces" Israel have misconstrued Jesus's teaching (see the Appendix for a fuller discussion). Recognizing all of this, Matthean scholars generally agree that the Gospel is best situated "within Judaism," acknowledging its variegated nature.[60] Rodney Reeves sums up the state of Matthew studies well when he writes: "most scholars contend that Matthew's Gospel was written by a Jew for Jews."[61]

---

[57] Kampen, *Matthew within Sectarian Judaism*, 49–59, 162–164.
[58] Davies and Allison, *Matthew*, 1:28. See also the discussion in Repschinski, *Controversy Stories*, 31–33.
[59] See, e.g., Davies and Allison, *Matthew*, 2:104, 220; 3:570; Hans Hüber, "OT Quotations in the New Testament," in *ABD*, 6 vols., ed. D. N. Freedman (New York: Doubleday, 1992), 4: 1099; George M. Prabhu Soares, *The Formula Quotations in the Infancy Narrative of Matthew: An Inquiry into the Tradition History of Mt 1–2* (Rome: Biblical Institute Press, 1976), 158–159.
[60] See the recent collection of essays in Anders Runesson and Daniel M. Gurtner, eds., *Matthew within Judaism: Israel and the Nations*, ECL (Atlanta: SBL Press, 2019). Here Matthean scholars are following a trajectory similar to one emerging in Pauline studies. See, e.g., Mark D. Nanos and Magnus Zetterholm, *Paul within Judaism: Restoring the First-Century Context to the Apostle* (Minneapolis: Fortress Press, 2015).
[61] Reeves, "The Gospel of Matthew," 277.

THE GOSPEL OF MATTHEW AND THE FUTURE OF THE QUEST

The Gospel of Matthew and the Historical Jesus

Our preceding discussion has important implications for Jesus research. It is often assumed that Mark, the earliest canonical gospel, must be more reliable than Matthew. Yet, as John Kloppenborg says, "Tradition-history is not convertible with *literary history*."[62] Similarly, Mark Goodacre writes:

> [the] basic assumption, that earliest is best, is open to challenge. A truer word may be spoken by one who long post-dates the events he or she is describing than by one who writes closer to those same events.[63]

Literary priority does not necessarily equal historiographical superiority. In fact, that Matthew provides us with a more reliable portrait than Mark in certain places is not merely possible but *probable*. This is especially the case when it comes to areas involving Jewish concerns.

For instance, in narrating Jesus's debate with the Pharisees over the custom of handwashing, Mark tells us, "For the Pharisees, and *all the Jews* [*pantes hoi Ioudaioi*], do not eat unless they wash their hands, holding the tradition of the elders" (Mark 7:3). Mark, however, is probably overgeneralizing here. Contrary to what the evangelist says, it is unlikely that "all Jews" washed their hands before meals. Josephus tells us that the Sadducees did not observe the traditions of the Pharisees (*Ant.* 13.297). As Matthew Thiessen shows, handwashing was likely among the traditions unique to the Pharisees.[64] In his version of the story, Matthew omits Mark's line about what "all Jews" did.

In Mark, Jesus goes on to say: "Do you not understand that whatever goes into a person from outside is not able to defile because it enters not the heart but the stomach, and goes out into the sewer?"

---

[62] John S. Kloppenborg, *The Formation of Q: Trajectories in Ancient Wisdom Collections*, 2nd ed., SAC (Harrisburg: Trinity Press International, 2000 [1987]), 244.

[63] Mark Goodacre, *Synoptic Problem: A Way through the Maze* (London: T&T Clark, 2001), 25. See also Christopher Tuckett, "Jesus Tradition in Non-Markan Material Common to Matthew and Luke," in *The Handbook for the Study of the Historical Jesus*, ed. Tom Holmén and Stanley E. Porter, 4 vols. (Leiden: Brill, 2010), 3:1857–1858, 1860–1861.

[64] Matthew Thiessen, *Jesus and the Forces of Death: The Gospels' Portrayal of Ritual Impurity within First-Century Judaism* (Grand Rapids: Baker Academic, 2020), 190–191. Among other things, evidence from Num. Rab. 20.21 indicates that disagreements about the practice continued even after the first-century period.

(Mark 7:18). The evangelist then offers an interpretation of Jesus's saying: "Thus he declared all foods clean [*katharizōn panta ta brōmata*]" (Mark 7:19).[65] For many, Mark's statement means that Jesus has abolished the kosher laws.[66] As we will discuss later, whether this accurately captures Mark's intention is debated.[67] Either way, Matthew's decision to leave the line out is surely remarkable. At the very least, one can see how Mark's assertion would appear to conflict with a crucial emphasis of Matthew's Gospel, namely, that the Torah has enduring value. In Matthew 5, for example, Jesus proclaims, "Whoever therefore loosens *one of the least of these commandments* and teaches others to do so will be called least in the kingdom of heaven" (Matt 5:19). Scholars, therefore, routinely observe that Matthew likely intentionally omits Mark's statement that Jesus "declared all foods clean" out of the concern that it might give the impression that Jesus has come to "abolish" the law (cf. Matt 5:17).[68]

As mentioned above, however, not all are convinced that Mark intends to present Jesus as annulling the food laws. According to Matthew Thiessen, within Jesus's Jewish setting it would simply be assumed that the Torah's kosher regulations were normative. Therefore, instead of portraying him as announcing that the law's clear dietary code has suddenly been rendered obsolete, Jesus should be seen as addressing a question that was debated among Jews in the first century: Can one be defiled by consuming *clean foods* that have been touched by *unclean hands*? Jesus is not weighing in on whether Jews can start eating pork or shellfish contrary to the Torah but on whether one is defiled by consuming (kosher) foods with unwashed hands. Thiessen argues Matthew better

---

[65] Though the Greek grammar is awkward here, this should not be viewed as evidence that the line is a later interpolation. For one thing, such awkwardness is not uncommon for Mark. See Joel Marcus, *Mark*, 2 vols., AB 27–27A (New York: Doubleday, 2000, 2009), 1:455.

[66] See, e.g., David Sim, "Matthew and Jesus of Nazareth," in *Matthew and His Christian Contemporaries*, ed. David C. Sim and Boris Repschinski, LNTS 333 (New York: T&T Clark, 2008), 160.

[67] For alternate takes, see the discussion in Thiessen, *Jesus and the Forces of Death*, 187–195; James G. Crossley, *The Date of Mark's Gospel*, JSNTSup 266 (London: T&T Clark, 2004), 183–205; Jesper Svartvik, *Mark and Mission: Mark 7, 1–23 in its Narrative and Historical Contexts*, ConBNT 32 (Stockholm: Almqvist and Wiksell, 2000), 109–204.

[68] See, e.g., Matthias Konradt, *The Gospel according to Matthew: A Commentary*, trans. M. Eugene Boring (Waco: Baylor University Press, 2020), 237; Ulrich Luz, *Matthew*, 3 vols., Hermeneia (Minneapolis: Fortress Press, 2001, 2005, 2007), 2:332.

clarifies the meaning of the pericope.[69] Not only does Matthew omit Mark's potentially confusing statement that Jesus "declared all foods clean," the Matthean version concludes with a statement from Jesus that spotlights the heart of the issue: "But to eat with unwashed hands does not defile anyone" (Matt 15:20).

That Jesus should be understood as entering an intra-Jewish debate about purity rather than as simply annulling the food laws is supported by another aspect of Matthew's report: the evangelist depicts *the Pharisees and scribes* as the ones offended by Jesus's teaching (Matt 15:12). If Jesus is being portrayed as abrogating the Torah's food laws altogether, one would expect *all the Jews*, not merely the Pharisees, to be taken aback by Jesus's words. In the book of Acts, for instance, Peter is appalled at the prospect of consuming unclean food (Acts 10:14). The idea of eating nonkosher foods is presented not only as new to the fisherman but also as offensive to him. Although this comes from a different New Testament source, it further supports the idea that Jesus's Jewish disciples believed the Torah's kosher laws were to be observed. All of this reinforces the view that Matthew is clearer than Mark about how Jesus's teaching would have been heard in a Jewish milieu. W. D. Davies and Dale Allison are therefore likely correct that the Matthean report, "is probably closer to Jesus's teaching than Mark's account."[70]

Sim also makes the case that given what we know of the earliest community in Jerusalem, Matthew's depiction of Jesus's strong insistence on faithfulness to the law would seem to reflect the commitments of his initial Jewish followers.[71] This community appears to have been especially devoted to the law (cf. Gal 2:12; Acts 21:17–26). Others have also noted that features in Matthew which "re-Judaize" Jesus may well be due to the evangelist's connection to these early followers. This is tantalizing. It suggests that Matthew might help us to better understand Jesus's Jewishness, a vitally important aspect of any historical portrait of him.[72]

One example of this can be found in the way Matthew appears to downplay Mark's descriptions of Jesus's activity in gentile regions.[73]

---

[69] For what follows, see the discussion in Thiessen, *Jesus and the Forces of Death*, 190–191, 194–95.

[70] See Davies and Allison, *Matthew*, 2:517.

[71] Sim, "Matthew and Jesus," 163–167.

[72] See, e.g., Donald Senior, C.P., "Viewing the Jewish Jesus of History through the Lens of Matthew," in *Soundings in the Religion of Jesus: Perspectives and Methods in Jewish and Christian Scholarship* (Minneapolis: Fortress Press, 2012), 88; Craig S. Keener, *A Commentary on the Gospel of Matthew* (Grand Rapids: Eerdmans, 1998), 18–19.

[73] For the following, see Sim, "Matthew and Jesus of Nazareth," 156–159.

Matthew retains Mark's report of a visit by Jesus to the gentile territory beyond the Sea of Galilee (cf. Mark 8:1–10; Matt 8:34), but he edits the account. Whereas Mark tells us that Jesus entered the region of Tyre and healed a gentile woman's daughter after he "entered a house [*eiselthōn eis oikian*]" (Mark 7:24), Matthew simply indicates that a Canaanite woman "*came out* [*exelthousa*] *from that region*" to petition Jesus's help (Matt 15:22). Matthew therefore downplays the implication that Jesus went into gentile territory and visited a non-Israelite's house.[74] Without appealing to specific criteria of "authenticity," Sim argues that Matthew's sensitivities here likely better reflect Jewish concerns Jesus himself likely had.

We can also mention here other details where Matthew seems closer to historical verisimilitude. Mark tells us that the Roman soldiers mocked Jesus by dressing him in "purple [*porphyran*]" (Mark 15:17); Matthew says he was given a "scarlet cloak [*chlamyda kokkinēn*]" (Matt 27:28).[75] Though the two colors were very similar, Matthew's version better describes the garb of Roman soldiers and is therefore deemed more historically probable by Davies and Allison.[76]

This study does *not* argue that Matthew necessarily always best reflects history. Nevertheless, the long-standing assumption that the historian will discover Jesus only by distinguishing him from the beliefs of his followers overlooks what should now be recognized as a crucial oversight: *Jesus's earliest followers were Jewish.* To define Jesus as "dissimilar to Christianity" involves a fatally flawed move – it places him in opposition to the very kinds of Jews to whom he appealed the most. With this observation we come to one last issue that must be addressed: the question of methodology.

Rethinking "Authenticity"

We began with Thomas Jefferson's account of the historian's craft. In Monticello, arriving at the "genuine" sayings of Jesus meant separating them out from the larger narratives of the gospels. More contemporary Jesus scholars, however, are calling into question such a project. A few developments are worth highlighting here.

---

74 See Runesson, *Divine Wrath*, 75n.77.
75 A textual variant in Matt 27:28 that includes the reference to a *himation porphyroun* in D it (sy^s) is widely seen as influenced by the Markan account.
76 Davies and Allison, *Matthew*, 3:602.

First, while the limitations of the so-called criteria of authenticity – multiple attestation, dissimilarity, embarrassment, etc. – have long been recognized, their ability to function effectively as "critical controls" is now increasingly questioned.[77] Many now believe their weaknesses outweigh their strengths. In addition, we will look at an even more fundamental problem with their use: they typically attempt to isolate traditions from the interpretive frameworks of the gospel narratives. The goal, then, is to arrive at an uninterpreted Jesus. Yet, as recent work in memory studies has emphasized, seeking an uninterpreted past is not possible.

Dale Allison also makes an especially important observation: even material deemed "inauthentic" can preserve important impressions made by Jesus. For example, Allison discusses the Synoptic narrative of Jesus's conflict with Satan in the wilderness. For Allison, the report is "haggadic fiction."[78] Nevertheless, he insists that accounts of this encounter underscore a key aspect of Jesus's identity frequently repeated in our sources, namely, that he saw himself engaged in a conflict with demonic forces.[79] Instead of dismissing it as irrelevant, Allison insists the episode raises a valuable question: Why was Jesus remembered in *this* way? Allison suggests the temptation scene preserves impressions made by Jesus himself, that is, the perception that he was engaged in a spiritual struggle with evil powers. Allison writes, "fiction need not be pure fiction … fiction can indeed preserve the past."[80]

Similarly, Ulrich Luz examines Matthew's insistence that Jesus upheld the value of the law. Regardless of its authenticity, Luz rightly notes that it should not be written off as insignificant to the historian. Here we can return to a line from him that was quoted at the beginning of the chapter. He asks, "Could it be that some of the Matthean 'systemizations' (or 'nonsystematizations') of Jesus might be very close to Jesus himself, just

---

[77] See especially the contributions in Chris Keith and Anthony Le Donne, eds., *Jesus, Criteria, and the Demise of Authenticity* (London: T&T Clark, 2012).

[78] See Dale C. Allison, Jr., "It Don't Come Easy: A History of Disillusionment," in *Jesus, Criteria, and the Demise*, ed. Keith and Le Donne, 191. A fuller argument is found in Dale C. Allison, Jr., "Behind the Temptations of Jesus: Q 4:1–13 and Mark 1:12–13," in *Authenticating the Activities of Jesus*, ed. Bruce Chilton and Craig A. Evans, NTTS 28/2 (Leiden: Brill, 1999), 195–214.

[79] Dale C. Allison, Jr., *Constructing Jesus: Memory, Imagination, and History* (Grand Rapids: Baker Academic, 2010), 18.

[80] Allison, "It Don't Come Easy," 191. Along similar lines, see the discussion of the charge that Jesus is in league with Beelzebul in Mark 3:22 in Rafael Rodríguez, *Structuring Early Christian Memory: Jesus in Tradition, Performance and Text*, LNTS 407 (London: T&T Clark, 2010), 178–179.

because they are constructions of a Jew who was temporally and culturally close to him?"[81] This study seeks to offer a rigorous and thoughtful
reflection on the suggestion Luz makes. After looking at methodological issues (Chapter 2), our study will ask similar questions relating to
Matthew's depiction of Jesus's teachings regarding the temple. The chapters of this monograph, then, are not intended as stand-alone studies but
build upon one another.

First, we will ask whether Jesus accepted the legitimacy of the temple
and its sacrificial rites, as passages such as the one quoted from Matthew
23 earlier imply (Chapter 3). Matthew includes statements that have
been seen as canceling out the evidence that Jesus affirmed the temple's
validity. For example, Matthew has Jesus quote from the book of Hosea,
"I desire mercy, and not sacrifice" (Hos 6:6; cf. Matt 9:13; Matt 12:7).
How can material such as this sit alongside other teachings of Jesus in
Matthew that seem to affirm the temple's holiness. What might Matthew's
arrangement of this material tell us about Jesus's own outlook?

Going on, we will ask another question: If Jesus did endorse the temple's holiness, would this undermine the likelihood that he envisioned
its coming destruction (Chapter 4)? Some argue that Matthew portrays
Jesus as changing his stance toward the temple once he arrives in the
Jerusalem. I will argue that such explanations overlook key features of
Matthew's presentation. Moreover, I will make the case that Matthew's
presentation of all this has important implications for understanding the
historical Jesus.

Furthermore, Jesus's teaching about the temple in Matthew seems
related to his own self-understanding (Chapter 5). Within a Jewish framework, this makes sense. Here I contend that we once again find important
data for reconstructing a historical portrait of Jesus.

Finally, I will show that Matthew frequently depicts Jesus as applying
temple and priestly imagery to himself and to his disciples (Chapter 6).
I will then show that this is consistent with other sources (Chapter 7).
While some have used such traditions to argue that Jesus rejected the
validity of the temple, I will show that this is unlikely. Nonetheless, I will
also explain why it makes sense to think that Jesus himself employed such
imagery. In sum, Matthew's interpretive framework should not necessarily be viewed as a hurdle to the project of critically reconstructing the
historical portrait of Jesus. In certain cases, it should instead be viewed

---

[81] Luz, "Matthew's Interpretive 'Tendencies' and the 'Historical' Jesus," 597.

as providing some vital clues. At the outset of this chapter I quoted Chris Keith, who rightly observes that "one must quest for the historical Jesus by accounting for the interpretations of the Gospels, not by dismissing them and certainly not by fragmenting them."[82] This study attempts to show what such an approach to questing for Jesus looks like.

History and Surprises

Thomas Jefferson and John Adams both passed away on the same date: July 4, 1826.[83] The coincidence is remarkable. Two of America's "founding fathers" died exactly fifty years to the date of the signing of the Declaration of Independence. If this historical datum was analyzed according to the conventional canons of Jesus research, many, employing a kind of "criterion of dissimilarity," would likely assume that this convergence is the result of later American propaganda. Yet that is one of the delights of historical research – it is full of surprises.

Jesus historians must be careful evaluators of our sources about Jesus. At the same time, they should also be prepared for surprises. One of them, I propose, is that Matthew's presentation is more helpful to the quest than previously realized. The reason this has been obscured, however, is due to methodological presuppositions. As mentioned previously, scholars are now challenging the standard tools scholars have used to reconstruct the historical Jesus. We now turn, therefore, to the issue of methodology.

---

[82] Keith, *Jesus's Literacy*, 66.
[83] Gordon S. Wood, *Friends Divided: John Adams and Thomas Jefferson* (New York: Penguin, 2017), 1.

2

The Demise of "Authenticity" and the Challenge of Methodology

If we concentrate on the whole rather than the details ... we shall find that
we know quite a lot about Jesus.
                                                        – Morna Hooker[1]

It is likely that Jesus and the early church ... were substantially continuous
rather than distinct.
                                                        – Amy-Jill Levine[2]

In the past few decades, the question of historical methodology in Jesus
research has taken center stage. Some scholars, including major figures
such as Dale Allison, are insisting that the conventional use of the criteria
of authenticity should be jettisoned.[3] As should probably be expected,
these challenges have been met with different reactions. Some have dou-
bled down on the traditional tools, vigorously resisting the notion that

---

[1] Morna Hooker, "Foreword: Forty Years On," in *Jesus, Criteria, and the Demise of
Authenticity*, ed. Keith and Le Donne, xv.

[2] Amy-Jill Levine, "Introduction," in *Jesus in Context: Princeton Readings in Religion*, ed.
Amy-Jill Levine, Dale C. Allison, Jr., and John D. Crossan (Princeton: Princeton University Press, 2006), 10.

[3] See, e.g., Dale C. Allison Jr., "How to Marginalize the Traditional Criteria of Authen-
ticity," in *The Handbook for the Study of the Historical Jesus*, ed. Holmén and Porter,
1:3–30. See also other treatments by Allison in: "It Don't Come Easy," 186–199; *The
Historical Christ and the Theological Jesus* (Grand Rapids: Eerdmans, 2009), 53–60;
Jesus of Nazareth: Millenarian Prophet (Minneapolis: Fortress Press, 1998), 1–78. Keith,
Jesus's Literacy, 44–47. In addition, see the essays by Chris Keith, Morna Hooker, and
Rafael Rodríguez in *Jesus, Criteria, and the Demise of Authenticity*; Rafael Rodríguez,
"Authenticating Criteria: The Use and Misuse of a Critical Method," *JSHJ* 7 (2009):
152–167.

they need to be set aside.[4] Others have come to the opposite conclusion, declaring that discussions about methodology have brought historical Jesus research to a standstill. Chris Keith speaks of a "methodological quagmire."[5] Zeba Crook speaks of a new "No Quest" period.[6] Scot McKnight, who once wrote many works on the historical Jesus, has even gone as far as declaring that the quest is "dead."[7]

This chapter sets the stage for the rest of our study. I will attempt to offer a balanced analysis of the present debate about methodology. Having done this, I will then offer a proposal for how to move forward.

THE LIMITATIONS OF THE CONVENTIONAL CRITERIA

It is generally recognized that it was the scholars of the so-called "New Quest" – a movement inspired by Ernst Käsemann – who began to systematically refine "criteria" for Jesus studies. By 1987, one writer catalogued twenty-five different criteria proposed by just five scholars.[8] The literature on the topic is immense.[9] Suffice it to say, there has been a growing acknowledgment of the weaknesses of these tools.[10] Here we will discuss problems identified with the "major"[11] criteria: *dissimilarity, embarrassment, multiple attestation,* and *coherence.*

---

[4] John P. Meier, *A Marginal Jew: Rethinking the Historical Jesus,* AYBRL, 5 vols. (New Haven: Yale University Press, 1991, 1994, 2001, 2009, 2016), 5:8–21, 27n.28, 28n.29; Paul Foster, "Memory, Orality, and the Fourth Gospel: Three Dead-Ends in Historical Jesus Research," *JSHJ* 10 (2012): 198.

[5] Keith, "The Indebtedness of the Criteria Approach," 47.

[6] Zeba Crook, "Memory Distortion and the Historical Jesus" (paper presented at the annual meeting of the Society of Biblical Literature, Baltimore, MD, November 25, 2013), which summarized the case made in Zeba Crook, "Collective Memory Distortion and the Quest for the Historical Jesus," *JSHJ* 11, 3 (2013): 53–76.

[7] Scot McKnight, "The Jesus We'll Never Know," *Christianity Today* 54, 4 [2010]: 22.

[8] Dennis Polkow, "Method and Criteria for Historical Jesus Research," *SBL 1987 Seminar Papers,* ed. K. H. Richards (Atlanta: Scholars Press, 1987), 336–356.

[9] For some of the most important discussions, see the following as well as the sources cited therein: Meier, *A Marginal Jew,* esp. 1:167–195; 5:8–21, 27n.28, 28n.29; Chris Keith and Anthony Le Donne, eds., *Jesus, Criteria, and the Demise of Authenticity*; Allison, "How to Marginalize," 1:3–30.

[10] Especially significant is Morna Hooker, "On Using the Wrong Tool," *Th* 75 (1972): 570–581; Morna Hooker, "Christology and Methodology," *NTS* 17 (1970–1971): 480–487. On the influence of these pieces, see, e.g., Keith, "The Indebtedness of the Criteria Approach," 25–27, 48.

[11] On these three as the most important and commonly used criteria, see, e.g., Allison, *Historical Christ,* 54; Anthony Le Donne, *The Historiographical Jesus: Memory, Typology, and the Son of David* (Waco: Baylor University Press, 2009), 87–91; Stanley E. Porter,

Difficulties with "Dissimilarity" and "Embarrassment"

The older tendency to characterize Jesus as "dissimilar" to his Jewish contemporaries is now roundly criticized by scholars. Still, that Jesus's early disciples misrepresented or misunderstood their teacher remains an obvious concern for historians. This explains why the so-called criterion of *dissimilarity from "Christianity"*[12] and its close cousin, *the criterion of embarrassment*,[13] are so highly prized by researchers. In short, if it can be shown that a given tradition is unlikely to have been invented by Jesus's followers, it would seem to have a more likely claim to "authenticity." Nevertheless, even the most ardent advocates of these criteria recognize that they have important limitations.

For one thing, since we do not possess a complete knowledge of the early Jesus movement, it is difficult to render judgments about what was actually consistent with the primitive communities' beliefs.[14] Moreover, others ask an important question: How "dissimilar" or "embarrassing" could a given tradition be if our writers chose to include it? Mark Goodacre argues convincingly against the claim that the evangelists felt constrained to include traditions that were contrary to their tendencies. Such a view is "contradicted by the data"; for instance, Luke *does* omit material from Mark.[15] As Allison observes, while moderns might insist

---

The Criteria for Authenticity in Historical-Jesus Research: Previous Discussion and New Proposals (London: T&T Clark, 2000), 114.

[12] There is a growing awareness that the terms "Jewish" or "Judaism" and "Christian" or "Christianity" are fraught with difficulties. A discussion would take up too much space here. See, e.g., Matt A. Jackson-McCabe, *Jewish Christianity: The Making of the Christianity-Judaism Divide*, AYBRL (New Haven: Yale University Press, 2020). It is difficult to engage in discussions of Jesus research, however, without them given their common use (e.g., the criterion of "dissimilarity from Christianity"). Here I attempt to avoid problematic terminology as much as possible, resigning myself nonetheless to the fact that at points it is practically unavoidable. See Dale C. Allison, Jr., *The Resurrection of Jesus: Apologetics, Polemics, History* (London: T&T Clark, 2021), 25n.1. On *Ioudaios* as "Jew," see Staples, *The Idea of Israel*, 11–21.

[13] Some see *embarrassment* as another form of *dissimilarity from Christianity*. See Brian Han Gregg, *The Historical Jesus and the Final Judgment Sayings in Q*, WUNT 207 (Tübingen: Mohr Siebeck, 2006), 30; Polkow, "Method and Criteria," 341; Tom Holmén, "Doubts about Double Dissimilarity: Restructuring the Main Criterion of Jesus-of-History Research," in *Authenticating the Words of Jesus*, ed. Chilton and Evans, 76. Yet see the nuanced discussion in Meier, *A Marginal Jew*, 4:174n.125.

[14] See, e.g., Meier, *A Marginal Jew*, 1:170–171; John Meier, "The Present State of the 'Third Quest' for the Historical Jesus: Loss and Gain," *Biblica* 80 (1999): 475–476; E. P. Sanders and Margaret Davies, *Studying the Synoptic Gospels* (London: SCM Press, 1989), 316.

[15] Mark Goodacre, "Criticizing the Criterion of Multiple Attestation: The Historical Jesus and the Question of Sources," in *Jesus, Criteria, and the Demise of Authenticity*, ed. Keith and Le Donne, 167.

that these elements "must have been" problematic, the gospel writers' very inclusion of them suggests otherwise.[16]

Furthermore, as Marianne Meye Thompson rightly observes, "one should expect to find discernible lines of continuity from Jesus to the church. Indeed, it is strange to have gotten to a place in New Testament studies where such continuity is assumed to be the exception, rather than the norm."[17] *Dissimilarity from "Christianity"* by definition eliminates traditions that would have been important to the early believers; *these would have been the ones they most likely would have preserved.*[18]

Problems with "Multiple Attestation"

In its simplest form, multiple attestation holds that the historical likelihood of material increases if it is reported in more than one independent source and/or in more than one literary context. Yet, like the other criteria, multiple attestation has its own obvious weaknesses. For one thing, multiple attestation cannot exclude the possibility that a saying was created early on and quickly gained wide acceptance.[19]

Multiple attestation also rests on opinions about the relationship of our sources to one another, some of which we can be more confident about than others. For example, that Matthew and Luke used Mark rests on strong evidence and is almost unanimously accepted. Recent work has shown that it is also highly unlikely that the Gospel of Thomas is independent of the Synoptics.[20] Beyond that, however, there are serious debates that are difficult to shrug off as "mostly settled." The existence of a Q source has been questioned by leading scholars whose influence

---

[16] Allison, "How to Marginalize," 6; Meier, *A Marginal Jew*, 5:15. See also Rodríguez, "Authenticating Criteria," 165–166.

[17] Marianne Meye Thompson, *The Promise of the Father: Jesus and God in the New Testament* (Louisville: Westminster John Knox Press, 2000), 62.

[18] See Robert Stewart Barbour, *Traditio-Historical Criticism of the Gospels: Some Comments on Current Methods* (London: SPCK, 1972), 10–11.

[19] See Allison, *Jesus of Nazareth*, 2–10; Paula Fredriksen, *From Jesus to Christ*, 2nd ed. (New Haven: Yale Nota Bene, 2000), 6; Meier, *Marginal Jew*, 1:175; Craig A. Evans, "Authenticity Criteria in Life of Jesus Research," *Christian Scholar's Review* 19 (1989): 9.

[20] See, e.g., Simon Gathercole, *The Composition of the Gospel of Thomas: Original Language and Influences*, SNTSMS 151 (Cambridge: Cambridge University Press, 2012); Mark Goodacre, *Thomas and the Gospels: The Case for Thomas's Familiarity with the Synoptics* (Grand Rapids: Eerdmans, 2012). That the "momentum" belongs with those in this camp, see Markus Bockmuehl, *The Ancient Apocryphal Gospels*, Interpretation (Louisville: Westminster John Knox, 2017), 172.

on the field should not be ignored. In a work co-authored with Margaret Davies, E. P. Sanders concludes, "Of all the solutions [to the Synoptic Problem], this one, which remains the dominant hypothesis, is least satisfactory."[21] Mark Goodacre has written an especially impactful critique.[22] Many others are now also raising problems with the theory, often preferring the Farrer Hypothesis (Markan priority without Q).[23] Amy-Jill Levine writes that after completing a recent commentary on Luke she is "increasingly doubtful of the existence of Q," adding, "it strikes me as just as likely, if not more likely, that Luke had access to Matthew's Gospel."[24] Stanley Porter and Bryan Dyer can rightly say that, though the Two-Source theory remains the dominant view, "there is now a legitimate diversity of opinion" about it.[25] In addition, the position that the Fourth Gospel was written independently of the Synoptics is facing stiff resistance.[26] All of this erodes confidence in appeals to multiple attestation.

Finally, before moving on, an especially important criticism of multiple attestation raised by Dale Allison should be registered. He observes that the more widely attested a tradition is, the more congenial it seems to be with beliefs of the early community. If one holds that "discontinuity with Christianity" lends credibility to a tradition, then "multiple attestation"

---

[21] Sanders and Davies, *Studying the Synoptic Gospels*, 117.

[22] Mark Goodacre, *The Case against Q: Studies in Markan Priority and the Synoptic Problem* (Harrisburg: Trinity Press, 2002)

[23] See, e.g., John C. Poirier and Jeffrey Peterson, eds., *Marcan Priority without Q: Explorations in the Farrer Hypothesis*, LNTS 455 (London: T&T Clark, 2015); Mark Goodacre and Nicholas Perrin, eds., *Questioning Q: A Multidimensional Critique* (Downers Grove: InterVarsity, 2005).

[24] Amy-Jill Levine, *Sermon on the Mount: A Beginners Guide to the Kingdom of Heaven* (Nashville: Abingdon Press, 2020), 7.

[25] Stanley E. Porter and Bryan R. Dyer, "What Have We Learned Regarding the Synoptic Problem, and What Do We Still Need to Learn?," in *The Synoptic Problem: Four Views*, ed. Stanley E. Porter and Bryan R. Dyer (Grand Rapids: Baker Academic, 2016), 267.

[26] See, e.g., Eve-Marie Becker, Chris Keith, and Helen Bond, eds., *John's Transformation of Mark* (London: T&T Clark, 2021); James Barker, *John's Use of Matthew* (Minneapolis: Fortress Press, 2015); Ian D. Mackay, *John's Relationship with Mark: An Analysis of John 6 in Light of Mark 6–8*, WUNT 2, 182 (Tübingen: Mohr Siebeck, 2004); Benedict T. Viviano, O.P., "John's Use of Matthew: Beyond Tweaking," *RB* 111, 2 (2004): 209–237; Frans Neirynck, "John and the Synoptics: 1975–1990," in *John and the Synoptics* (Leuven: Leuven University Press, 1992), 3–62; Frans Neirynck, "John and the Synoptics," in *L'évangile de Jean: Sources, redaction, théologie*, ed. M. De Jonge, BETL 45 (Leuven: Leuven University Press, 1977), 73–106. Allison reveals that he has changed his mind on the issue and now believes John is aware of the Synoptics, citing various sources. See Dale C. Allison, Jr., *Resurrecting Jesus: The Earliest Christian Tradition and Its Interpreters* (London: T&T Clark, 2005), 118n.11.

would seem to undermine that conviction. He puts it this way: "Here the criterion of multiple attestation is in a tug-of-war with the criterion of dissimilarity: they pull the same unit in opposite directions."[27]

The Challenge of "Coherence"

The criterion of *coherence* judges "authentic" those elements which fit well with what has been established by the other criteria.[28] A key difficulty here is that such a task will inevitably involve subjective analysis: What exactly constitutes "coherence"?[29] In addition, Allison raises another issue: coherence is problematic "because human beings in general and charismatic leaders in particular are sometimes so unpredictable and inconsistent."[30] There are, for example, tensions in the writings of Paul, the earliest writer of the Jesus movement.[31]

Subjective "Weighing" of the Criteria

Anthony Le Donne correctly observes, "[A]lmost all contemporary Jesus historians who employ the traditional authenticity criteria do so with repeated reservations and qualifications."[32] Meier, perhaps the most prominent and nuanced advocate of the criteria,[33] is particularly circumspect in his discussions of these tools, recognizing virtually all of the weaknesses we have outlined, including some further challenges

---

[27] Allison, "How to Marginalize," 7. Furthermore, in a recent piece, Allison observes that the search for "independent" attestation may also be undermined by the possibility that the early Jesus communities may have had more overlap with one another than is fully appreciated. See Dale C. Allison, Jr., "Cyprus and Early Christianity: Did Everybody Know Everybody?," in *Cyprus within the Biblical World: Are Borders Barriers?*, Jewish and Christian Texts in Context and Related Studies 32, ed. James H. Charlesworth and Jolyon G. R. Pruszinksi (London: T&T Clark, 2021), 127–146.

[28] See the classic formulation in Norman Perrin, *Rediscovering the Teaching of Jesus* (New York: Harper & Row, 1967), 43.

[29] See Hooker, "On Using the Wrong Tool," 577. As a test case, see the critique of Meier's use of the criterion in Dennis Ingolfsland, "The Historical Jesus According to John Meier and N.T. Wright," *Bibliotheca sacra* 155 (1998): 460–473.

[30] Allison, *Constructing Jesus*, 93.

[31] Allison, "How to Marginalize," 4.

[32] Anthony Le Donne, "The Rise of the Quest for an Authentic Jesus: An Introduction to the Crumbling Foundations of Jesus Research," in *Jesus, Criteria, and the Demise of Authenticity*, ed. Keith and Le Donne, 3.

[33] See, e.g., Jonathan Bernier, *The Quest for the Historical Jesus after the Demise of Authenticity: Toward a Critical Realist Philosophy of History in Jesus Studies*, LNTS 540 (London: Bloomsbury, 2016), 4.

we have not even considered.[34] Yet Meier remains their staunch defender. He maintains, "one must not expect from the criteria more than they can deliver," maintaining that their use "remains more art than science."[35] In the end, Meier writes, "our judgments about authenticity deal for the most part with a range of probabilities; I do not claim that the use of the criteria I propose will generate absolute certitude."[36]

Meier's complaint about the criteria's detractors is that they seem to insist that certainty is the necessary bar we must expect our tools to be able to achieve. Yet that need not be the case. Given their inherent limitations, a growing number of scholars are coming to the conclusion that the actual degree of "probability" established by the criteria is simply too low. This is not due to a conviction that "certainty" must be the standard for the historian. Rather, it is due to the various problems their application involves. Allison, who once used the criteria himself, insists that they can too easily be manipulated to produce the conclusion desired by the historian.[37] What Meier sees as an "art," others might see as a kind of "sleight of hand." Nevertheless, the problems involved with the use of the criteria are further exacerbated by recent applications of memory research to the quest.

MEMORY RESEARCH AND THE PROBLEM OF "AUTHENTICITY"

Through the use of the criteria, scholars generally seek to separate the "authentic" from the "inauthentic" material in our sources in order to get behind their interpretive frameworks. Allison and others, however, have made the case that memory research undermines this project.

Memory Construction and the Problem of Historical Knowledge

In recent years, historians have paid increasing attention to the fruits of memory research. It is now recognized that doing history entails wrestling with the social and cognitive factors associated with remembrance. This work has emphasized that the attempt to arrive at an uninterpreted past rests on naïve assumptions. Memory does not simply involve retrieving perceptions of the past; it also entails a constructive dimension.

---

[34] See Meier, *A Marginal Jew*, 1:167–195; 5:8–21.
[35] Meier, *A Marginal Jew*, 5:19.
[36] Meier, *A Marginal Jew*, 1:186.
[37] Allison, "How to Marginalize," 9.

Anthony Le Donne[38] has highlighted the work of Michael Schudson, who identifies different types of "distortion" that are inherent in memory production:

- *Distanciation*: memories become fuzzy on details, emotional associations lessen in intensity, and broader perspectives on past events are gained.
- *Narrativization*: memories are structured into a recognizable plot.
- *Cognitivization and conventionalization*: memories of the past conform to familiar experiences and stereotypes.[39]

To these, Le Donne adds another:

- *Articulation*: memories "conform to language conventions."[40]

All of this underscores that memory involves a constructive aspect; it does not merely "recall" past images. Le Donne writes, *"All memory is distortion."*[41]

It is important to observe that the preceding forms of memory distortion are interrelated. Memories become fuzzy over time (*distanciation*) precisely as elements are lost which do not conform to familiar plots. In other words, structuring memories into a narrative involves a selection process, which either retains or eliminates details.[42] This feature of memory is a necessary part of remembering; every element cannot be retained. Furthermore, what is retained remains because it is somehow deemed more "significant" or "relevant" than other impressions. *Memory is thus unavoidably interpretive.*

This constructive quality of memory is also shaped by social factors. The "schemas" that memories conform to involve scripts that are usually socially and culturally determined.[43] Recognizing these dynamics, social

---

[38] Le Donne, *Historiographical Jesus*, 52.

[39] Michael Schudson, "Dynamics of Distortion in Collective Memory," in *Memory Distortion: How Minds, Brains, and Societies Reconstruct the Past*, ed. D. L. Schachter (Cambridge, MA: Harvard University Press, 1995), 346–364.

[40] Le Donne, *Historiographical Jesus*, 52.

[41] Le Donne, *Historiographical Jesus*, 51.

[42] Alan Kirk, *Memory and the Jesus Tradition*, RJFTC (London: Bloomsbury, T&T Clark, 2018), 216.

[43] See the discussion of scripts in Jocelyn Penny Small, *Wax Tablets of the Mind: Cognitive Studies of Memory and Literacy in Classical Antiquity* (Abingdon: Routledge, 1997), 196–197; David C. Rubin, *Memory in Oral Traditions: The Cognitive Psychology of Epic Ballads, and Counting-out Rhymes* (Oxford: Oxford University Press, 1995), 21–28.

memory theorists speak of the way in which memories are "keyed" to archetypes and familiar scripts.[44]

This has led some to despair of accurate knowledge of the past. Some hold that all perceptions of the past are wholly determined by the needs of the present. This perspective is often identified as the "presentist" model.[45] Yet this approach is not without its critics. A number of researchers insist that the historian must account for the way in which the past and present mutually influence one another. As Barry Schwartz writes, "To focus solely on memory's constructed side is to deny the past's significance as a model for coming to terms with the present."[46] Schwartz and others maintain that the presentist model ignores an important dynamic: uncomfortable and painful memories are preserved despite concerted attempts to blot them out.[47] One can easily see, for example, how the presentist approach plays into the hands of Holocaust deniers. To insist that knowledge of the past is impossible is to ignore instances of memory's resilience.

Jesus, Social Memory, and the Problem of the Criteria

What memory research underscores is that the project at the heart of the criteria approach – namely, sifting the "uninterpreted Jesus" from later "layers" of redactional interpretive strata – is simply not possible. Yet, as some scholars have argued, this need not lead the Jesus scholar to despair of doing historiography.[48] For example, Le Donne has argued that the implications of social memory theory can be harnessed by the historian.

Le Donne begins by reminding us that memory registers new perceptions by means of established archetypes and scripts. Given this awareness, he makes the case that the long-standing tendency of Jesus scholars

---

[44] See, e.g., Eric Eve, *Behind the Gospels: Understanding the Oral Tradition* (Minneapolis: Fortress Press, 2014), 95; Kirk, *Memory and the Jesus Tradition*, 28.

[45] See, e.g., John Bodnar, *Remaking America: Public Memory, Commemoration, and Patriotism in the Twentieth Century* (Princeton: Princeton University Press, 1992), 15.

[46] Barry Schwartz, *Abraham Lincoln and the Forge of National Memory* (Chicago: University of Chicago Press, 2000), ix–x.

[47] Kirk, *Memory and the Jesus Tradition*, 26–30; Eve, *Behind the Gospels*, 94; Rodríguez, *Structuring Early Christian Memory*, 62–64.

[48] For a thorough discussion of social memory research and Gospel studies, see Chris Keith, "Social Memory Theory and Gospels Research: The First Decade (Part One)," *Early Christianity* 6 (2015): 3347–3376; Chris Keith, "Social Memory Theory and Gospels Research: The First Decade (Part Two)," *Early Christianity* 6 (2015): 517–542.

to dismiss biblical intertextuality in the gospels as later innovation is inadvisable.[49] Le Donne appeals to E. P. Sanders, who wrote:

There are no absolutely certain signs that tell us when a passage in the gospels has been invented as a parallel to an earlier stage of the history of salvation, when it has been recast to emphasize an actual parallel, and when Jesus himself (or John the Baptist) intentionally created a reminiscence.[50]

Sanders goes on to say that some of these parallels may in fact be later inventions. Nevertheless, he adds, one must grant the possibility of "Jesus's own conscious imitation of scriptural types."[51] Building on this, Le Donne says, "If it can be granted ... that Jesus did evoke scriptural types during his life, such typologies might have been further developed by those who remembered him and told stories about him."[52] This seems sensible.

Le Donne maintains that the historian ought not to dismiss memory distortion as unhelpful. He prefers to speak of "refraction" rather than "distortion" since "the term *distortion* carries too many negative associations."[53] In his view, the historian should not seek to "dig for an unre-fracted memory" – which is impossible – but "to account for the earliest mnemonic refractions of a memory-story."[54] By charting out various tra-jectories in our sources, Le Donne argues that the historian can engage in "historical triangulation."[55] Le Donne's work is brilliant and, due to its pioneering application of social memory theory to the quest, represents a landmark study in the history of Jesus research. I do worry, however, that attempts to trace out the development of memories might end up resting too heavily on hypothetical theories about the relationships of our sources.

In addition, while Le Donne employs the conventional criteria, other Jesus scholars are coming to the conclusion that memory research should lead us to reject the criteria approach altogether. Chris Keith writes: "The authentic/inauthentic dichotomy is false precisely because, in memory, the past is always packaged in interpretive frameworks bor-rowed from the present."[56] He concludes, "If there is no such thing as

---

[49] See the discussion in Le Donne, *Historiographical Jesus*, 52–59.
[50] E. P. Sanders, *Historical Figure of Jesus* (London: Penguin, 1993), 85.
[51] Sanders, *Historical Figure of Jesus*, 85.
[52] Le Donne, *Historiographical Jesus*, 5.
[53] Le Donne, *Historiographical Jesus*, 51.
[54] Le Donne, *Historiographical Jesus*, 87.
[55] Le Donne, *Historiographical Jesus*, 81–86.
[56] Keith, "The Indebtedness of the Criteria Approach, 40. This is a point emphasized by Rodríguez, *Structuring Early Christian Memory*, 156–158, 178–179, 224–225.

past-without-interpretation in gospel tradition, there is no such thing as 'authentic tradition' as the criteria approach defines it, and therefore nothing for the criteria of authenticity to extricate."[57] The criteria are not merely inadequate because they fail to produce "certainty." Their use is unconvincing because they depend on a conviction that the researcher can ultimately reach an uninterpreted Jesus who can be found by separating "fact" from interpretation.

How then might we proceed? Is there a way forward that takes all of these considerations into account? I believe so.

RECURRENT ATTESTATION IN A TRIPLE CONTEXT APPROACH

Since the conventional criteria of authenticity have played such a prominent role in contemporary Jesus scholarship, those who have called for abandoning them might be perceived as advocating a rejection of critical historical methodology altogether. That, however, does not necessarily follow. After all, *historians outside the field of Jesus research do not employ the criteria of authenticity*. In fact, the insistence that historical Jesus research requires a unique set of tools probably reflects the influence of long-standing theological and philosophical convictions.[58] What, then, might a critical approach to Jesus studies that is not dictated by the conventional criteria look like? A promising model can be found in the work of Dale Allison.

Recurrent Attestation

Acknowledging the limits of our historical tools, Allison maintains that "the historicity of most – not all – of the sayings attributed to [Jesus]"[59] cannot be determined. This, however, need not lead to hyper-skepticism. Drawing on recent research, Allison shows that memory tends to be most reliable when it relates the "gist" of previous experiences.[60] When memory works well, it often involves recalling broad impressions rather than specific details. He writes, "[E]yewitnesses may disagree on the details of a

---

[57] Keith, "The Indebtedness of the Criteria Approach," 40. See also Keith, "Social Memory Theory and Gospels Research: The First Decade (Part Two)," 526–527.

[58] See, e.g., Dagmar Winter, "Saving the Quest for Authenticity from the Criterion of Dissimilarity: History and Plausibility," in *Jesus, Criteria, and the Demise of Authenticity*, ed. Keith and Le Donne, 120–121.

[59] Allison, *Constructing Jesus*, 22.

[60] See especially Allison, *Constructing Jesus*, 10–15. Allison touched on this topic in an earlier book on Jesus. See Allison, *Jesus of Nazareth*, 45.

car wreck, but all agree that there was one."[61] Ancient authors such as Thucydides, Allison points out, acknowledged this dynamic.[62] It is therefore more prudent to focus on the broader impressions of Jesus that appear throughout the tradition instead of particular details.[63] This, however, does not entail embracing naïveté. Allison concedes, "it is obvious that the traditions about Jesus are rhetorical products and rhetorical resources, and that they must contain much more than the gist of eye-witness recall."[64]

Allison goes on to invoke the notion of "recurrent attestation," a concept he draws from previous scholars, most notably, C. H. Dodd.[65] Nevertheless, it should be clarified that Allison does not view "recurrent attestation" as a tool that can be employed in the manner of the conventional criteria.[66] Recurrent attestation does not "authenticate" particular logia or episodes. Here Allison makes an important move. He insists that attempts to filter out "inauthentic" stories ignores the way even manufactured[67] traditions can provide valuable clues as to who Jesus was and the kinds of things he did. For example, as mentioned earlier, Allison discusses the narratives of Satan's temptation of Jesus in the desert. Allison views these reports as "haggadic fiction."[68] Nevertheless, he insists that these accounts are consistent with the overall portrait of Jesus painted by

---

[61] Allison, *Historical Christ*, 61. See also, Allison, *Constructing Jesus*, 12–13.

[62] Allison, *Constructing Jesus*, 28.

[63] Allison, *Constructing Jesus*, 15. As Allison points out in a footnote, he is not the first to argue along these lines. The earliest advocate of such a method, he says, is Friedrich Loofs, *What Is the Truth about Jesus Christ? Problems of Christology* (New York: Charles Scribner's Sons, 1913), 120–145. See Allison, *Constructing Jesus*, 14n.73 for a bibliography.

[64] Dale C. Allison, Jr., "Memory, Methodology, and the Historical Jesus: A Response to Richard Bauckham," *JSHJ* 14 (2016): 19.

[65] See Allison, Jr., "Memory, Methodology, and the Historical Jesus," 17, also citing C. H. Dodd, *History and the Gospel* (New York: Charles Scribner's Sons, 1938), 92–110. See also C. H. Dodd, *The Founder of Christianity* (London: Collins, 1971), 21–22. Allison also cites appeals to recurrent attestation in David E. Aune, "Oral Tradition and the Aphorisms of Jesus," in *Jesus and the Oral Gospel Tradition*, ed. Henry Wansbrough, JSNTSup 64 (Sheffield: JSOT, 1991), 240–241; Meier, *A Marginal Jew*, 2:618–619; Gerd Theissen and Annette Merz, *The Historical Jesus: A Comprehensive Guide* (Minneapolis: Fortress Press, 1998), 269.

[66] See Rafael Rodríguez, "Jesus as His Friends Remembered Him: A Review of Dale Allison's *Constructing Jesus*," *JSHJ* 12 (2014): 230.

[67] See the helpful comments offered by Crook, "Collective Memory Distortion," 65n.44, who explains why it is more precise to speak of "manufactured" instead of "invented" memories.

[68] See Allison, "It Don't Come Easy," 191. His fuller argument is found in Dale C. Allison, Jr., "Behind the Temptations of Jesus: Q 4:1–13 and Mark 1:12–13," in *Authenticating the Activities of Jesus*, ed. Chilton and Evans, 195–214.

our sources, which depict him as engaged in conflict with demonic powers.[69] For Allison, then, it is significant that certain *kinds* of stories were
told about Jesus, for example, he was remembered as the sort of figure
who struggled with diabolical forces. He was not remembered broadly
as, for instance, traveling widely; none of our early sources depict him
journeying to places like Rome. The fact that particular types of reports
emerge about him is significant. Allison writes, "fiction need not be pure
fiction ... fiction can indeed preserve the past."[70]

With recurrent attestation as a launching point, Allison begins to
advance his own reconstruction of Jesus. He zeroes in on one specific
aspect of the tradition that receives frequent attestation – the notion that
Jesus was motivated by an eschatological outlook informed by Jewish
apocalyptic traditions.[71] If our sources are wrong about this, Allison
insists, they cannot be trusted on other matters. He writes:

> our choice is not between an apocalyptic Jesus and some other Jesus; it is between
> an apocalyptic Jesus and no Jesus at all... The pertinent material is sufficiently
> abundant that removing it all should leave one thoroughly skeptical about the
> mnemonic competence of the tradition.[72]

Yet, as we will see further later, Allison's argument for an apocalyptic
Jesus is not simply based on recurrent attestation. However, before moving on, it is important to examine this aspect of Allison's approach.

Between Hyper-Skepticism and Naïvete

Allison's appeal to recurrent attestation has been met with criticism.
Remarkably, it has come from scholars who take diametrically oppos-
ing positions. Richard Bauckham, Rafael Rodríguez, and Samuel
Lamerson believe Allison is too skeptical.[73] At the same time, others

---

[69] Allison, *Constructing Jesus*, 18.
[70] Allison, "It Don't Come Easy," 191.
[71] Allison, *Constructing Jesus*, 32–43. For greater clarity on what he means by "apocalyptic," see Allison, *Jesus of Nazareth*, 154–157; Allison, "Jesus and the Victory of Apocalyptic," in *Jesus and the Restoration of Israel: A Critical Assessment of N. T. Wright's
"Jesus and the Victory of God,"* ed. Carey C. Newman (Downers Grove: InterVarsity
Press, 1999), 126–41.
[72] Allison, *Constructing Jesus*, 47.
[73] Richard Bauckham, "The General and the Particular in Memory: A Critique of Dale
Allison's Approach to the Historical Jesus," *JSHJ* 14 (2016): 28–51; Rodríguez, "Jesus
as His Friends Remembered Him," 225–227; Samuel Lamerson, Review of Dale C. Allison, Jr., *Constructing Jesus: Memory, Imagination, and History*, *JETS* 54 (2011): 839.

have criticized him for being too optimistic about the reliability of "gist" memory.[74]

In responding to those who find him too skeptical about our ability to reconstruct a portrait of the historical Jesus, Allison makes various points. First, he argues that the fallibility of human recollection is simply too well documented to be glossed over.[75] Moreover, he expresses concerns about ignoring the limits of historiography. All the researcher can acknowledge is the reality of "higher and lower levels of plausibility."[76] Determining degrees of "probability" is not an exact science. Various considerations such as contextual and cultural issues must be evaluated.[77] In the end, the historical task requires modesty. Nevertheless, to acknowledge that questions always remain does not mean that all conclusions are equally implausible. To give an example, that Jesus traveled to Rome is *possible*. It must remain unlikely or improbable, however, because this is never attested. There is no evidence to warrant such a claim.

At the same time, contrary to what some have charged, Allison's use of recurrent attestation cannot be said to depend on an overly optimistic view of the trustworthiness of "gist" memory in the abstract. Allison makes a historical argument for why, in Jesus's case, it is probable that broad impressions made by him were preserved. Among other things, he observes that our sources converge in numerous ways and notes the frequency with which certain complexes occur.[78] This suggests that the past imposed certain constraints on what could and could not be said about Jesus. He writes, "A story that had Jesus dying in Rome would never have been accepted."[79] There are, therefore, good reasons to think that the "the sense" of Jesus's basic message was remembered with some accuracy.[80]

Furthermore, Allison makes the important observation that an appeal to recurrent attestation involves acknowledging the extant data that we possess, however fragmentary it may be.[81] For instance, Allison notes

74 See Crook, "Collective Memory Distortion," 69–70n.61; Michael J. Thate, *Remembrance of Things Past?: Albert Schweitzer, the Anxiety of Influence, and the Untidy Jesus of Markan Memory*, WUNT 2/251 (Tübingen: Mohr Siebeck, 2013), 215.
75 Dale C. Allison, Jr., "Response to Rafael Rodríguez, 'Jesus as his Friends Remembered Him: *A Review of Dale Allison's* Constructing Jesus,'" *JSHJ* 12 (2014): 247.
76 Allison, *Jesus of Nazareth*, 57.
77 See Allison, *Constructing Jesus*, 255–256.
78 Allison, *Constructing Jesus*, 15.
79 Allison, *Constructing Jesus*, 161.
80 Allison, *Jesus of Nazareth*, 58.
81 Allison elsewhere makes the case that an "argument from silence" is only weighty if the silence is unexpected (*Constructing Jesus*, 69).

that the Jesus tradition is characterized by "strikingly memorable" expressions. Of course, it is entirely *possible* that a figure other than Jesus was responsible for giving the tradition this shape. Yet, Allison writes, "all the relevant items are attributed to [Jesus], not to anyone else, and I know of no explanatory advantage in assigning them to some anonymous contemporary or contemporaries of his."[82] To put it another way: the evidence we actually possess attributes this particular shape of the tradition to one person – Jesus. Unless there are good reasons to reject these data and to attribute them to someone other than Jesus, another origin for them must remain a *less probable* explanation. This is not an argument from silence. It is a matter of preferring data to speculation, *probability* to mere *possibility*. As he says elsewhere, where there are no good reasons to do otherwise, to prefer "a series of conjectures, for which there is no real evidence"[83] over the information we actually possess is usually unconvincing.[84]

Allison also raises other considerations. For one, our sources are in widespread agreement that Jesus was an itinerant teacher who had disciples who followed him from place to place.[85] The evidence for this is so compelling that scholars as different as John Meier and John Dominic Crossan agree that this aspect of our sources' testimony preserves historical memory.[86] Moreover, our sources report – in various ways – that Jesus enlisted his disciples in spreading his message even while he was alive (cf. Mark 6:7–13 and parr.). This strategy is consistent with the idea that Jesus's preaching involved an eschatological dimension.[87] That Jesus sent out followers to preach is also attested by Paul (cf. 1 Cor 9:14).[88] Allison, therefore, concludes: "it is plausible that some people were already teaching, which means in effect rehearsing, parts of the Jesus tradition before their leader was gone."[89]

On their own, these considerations do not establish the reliability of any given feature of the tradition. Allison insists that a historical argument must involve more than appealing to recurrent attestation. What does

---

[82] Allison, *Constructing Jesus*, 24.
[83] Allison, *Constructing Jesus*, 68.
[84] See, e.g., the treatment of the passion narrative in Allison, *Constructing Jesus*, 425.
[85] See Allison, *Resurrecting Jesus*, 31–32, 36–37.
[86] See Meier, *A Marginal Jew*, 3:41–47; John Dominic Crossan, *The Birth of Christianity: Discovering What Happened in the Years Immediately after the Execution of Jesus* (San Francisco: HarperCollins, 1998), 291–417.
[87] Allison, *Constructing Jesus*, 25.
[88] See Dale C. Allison, Jr., *The Jesus Tradition in Q* (Harrisburg: Trinity, 1997), 104–111.
[89] Allison, *Constructing Jesus*, 26.

such historical argumentation entail? To answer that, Allison draws on an observation made by Sanders.

A "Triple Context" Approach

For Allison, recurrent attestation is only a launching point.[90] Allison recognizes that "espying a pattern is not enough; we need to account for it sensibly."[91] He writes:

I believe that once recurrent attestation highlights a theme or motif, we should seek to interpret that theme or motif in the light of early Judaism, and in such a way that helps us make sense of what we otherwise know about Christian origins.[92]

Later, he puts it this way: "we should proceed by abduction – that is, by inference to the best explanation, always looking for a Jesus who makes the most sense of the available facts and what we otherwise know of Judaism and nascent Christianity."[93] To sum up, Allison insists that we need to (1) recognize *coherent patterns via recurrent attestation*, which should lead us to (2) examine *how such elements fit within the ancient Jewish world* as well as to (3) consider *their relationship to the effects of Jesus*.

Allison's approach is influenced by comments made by E. P. Sanders, who says:

No matter what criteria for testing the sayings are used, scholars still need to move beyond the sayings themselves to a broader context than a summary of their contents if they are to address historical questions about Jesus. Since historical reconstruction requires that data be fitted into a context, the establishment of a secure context, or framework of interpretation, becomes crucial. There are basically three kinds of information which provide help in this endeavor: [1] *such facts about Jesus as those outlined above*; [2] *knowledge about the outcome of his life and teaching*; [3] *knowledge of first-century Judaism*.[94]

Drawing attention to this passage, Brant Pitre helpfully speaks of Sanders' "triple-context approach."[95] As the preceding quotation from

---

[90] Allison, "Response to Rafael Rodríguez," 251.
[91] Allison, *Constructing Jesus*, 21.
[92] Allison, *Constructing Jesus*, 21.
[93] Allison, *Constructing Jesus*, 22.
[94] E. P. Sanders, *Jesus and Judaism* (Philadelphia: Fortress Press, 1985), 17; cited with enumeration and added emphasis from Brant Pitre, *Jesus and the Last Supper* (Grand Rapids: Eerdmans, 2015), 32. See also the comments in Sanders, *Jesus and Judaism*, 166–167.
[95] Pitre, *Jesus and the Last Supper*, 45.

him indicates, Sanders argues that the Jesus historian should consider three key factors: (1) what can be known about Jesus's life, (2) the effects of Jesus's ministry, and (3) Jesus's Jewish environment.[96] Pitre argues that Sanders' triple-context approach offers scholars a way forward through the "methodological quagmire" of the post-criteria period.[97]

Allison, however, diverges from Sanders in two important ways. First, Sanders speaks of "facts" about Jesus, using positivistic terminology that Allison assiduously avoids. Second, Sanders focuses on the deeds of Jesus (e.g., his temple action). In contrast, Allison concentrates on the broad outlines of Jesus's ministry; for example, the idea that he entertained eschatological expectations.

John Meier, perhaps the best-known advocate of the criteria of authenticity, makes three specific criticisms of Allison's approach. First, he insists that Allison's detailed catalogues of recurrently attested traditions have little force if none of them can be persuasively traced back to the historical Jesus. He writes, "In reconstructing a historical Jesus, the whole *is* the sum of the parts selected for analysis. If each item that makes up the whole is viewed with skepticism, the whole must be viewed the same way."[98] Second, without the application of the conventional criteria, Meier complains that Allison lacks a consistent historical rationale. To quote Meier: "The word 'criteria' means 'rules for making a judgment'. If you have no rules for making a judgment about material claiming to come from the historical Jesus, how do you reach any judgment about him that is not hopelessly arbitrary?"[99] Third, Meier argues that Allison allows the very criteria he opposes to "sneak back" into his work.[100]

Meier's critiques are serious and must be given careful consideration. Yet responses to them can be given. First, Meier's insistence that "the whole" depends on the "sum of the parts" raises questions. Determining what constitutes the "parts" is often exceptionally difficult. As Meier himself has shown, different logia may be recognized as variations of the same saying – or they might not be. For instance, Meier argues that the historian

---

[96] See the fuller discussion in Pitre, *Jesus and the Last Supper*, 31–46.

[97] Brant Pitre, "Beyond the Criteria of Authenticity: Where Do We Go From Here?" (paper presented at the Annual Meeting of the Society of Biblical Literature, San Diego, CA, November 23, 2015), 20, quoting Keith, "The Indebtedness of the Criteria Approach," 47.

[98] Meier, *A Marginal Jew*, 5:27n.28.

[99] Meier, *A Marginal Jew*, 5:27n.20.

[100] Meier, *A Marginal Jew*, 5:27n.20.

has a hard time determining what *the* "original saying" or *the* "original form" of Jesus's prohibition of divorce entailed.[101] Meier concedes, "Jesus probably stated his prohibition a number of times, not necessarily always in the same words."[102] Nevertheless, Meier remarks, "On the basis of this criterion alone," namely, multiple attestation, "I think there is sufficient reason for holding that the historical Jesus forbade divorce."[103] Allison also observes that Meier has written the following in regards to the portrait of Jesus as a miracle-worker: "The material seems simply too mammoth and omnipresent in the various strata of the Gospel tradition to be purely the creation of the early church."[104] Understanding how all the "parts" work together, therefore, does not always seem necessary, even for Meier. It is also not always possible. Allison discusses the difficulties of relying on theories about the Q source and its hypothetical redactional editions.[105] In sum, to insist that we must always know how to distinguish the "parts" is to be far too optimistic about the tools we possess.

Second, Meier's claim that by rejecting the criteria Allison lacks a consistent historical rationale is not a fair charge. Allison does not simply rely on recurrent attestation. In regard to the notion that Jesus's message involved an eschatological dimension, for instance, Allison goes beyond recurrent attestation to make his case. He shows that this general impression of Jesus is consistent with what we know about both his first-century Jewish context as well as the beliefs of the movement that succeeded him.[106] The fact that Jesus's teaching sounds like that of other texts exhibiting Jewish eschatology situates him well in a first-century environment. Moreover, that the early community entertained eschatological hopes is abundantly clear. These converging lines of consideration establish confidence that the overall portrait of an eschatological Jesus is no innovation. Thinking Jesus entertained eschatological expectations is not simply based on a broad overview of our sources, then. Rather, it makes the most sense of the evidence we possess.

It seems to me that part of the problem is terminology. Allison avoids the language of "criteria" due to the fact that "the use of criteria to

---

[101] Meier, *A Marginal Jew*, 4:124.
[102] Meier, *A Marginal Jew*, 4:124.
[103] Meier, *A Marginal Jew*, 4:112.
[104] Meier, *A Marginal Jew*, 2:618–619; Allison, "Memory, Methodology, and the Historical Jesus," 17.
[105] See Allison, *Constructing Jesus*, 118–125.
[106] On these points, see the discussion in Allison, *Constructing Jesus*, esp. 48–55 and 76–78.

cast a scientific aura over our questing for Jesus is not very effective, for our criteria are sufficiently pliable as to be unable to resist our biases and prior inclinations."[107] Meier himself recognizes that "one must not expect from the criteria more than they can deliver," acknowledging that their use "remains more art than science."[108] Both Meier and Allison seek to avoid historical positivism, that is, an approach that reduces history to "objective facts." Jesus research, they would both agree, is not aimed at achieving certainty, but the *most probable* historical reconstruction.[109] For reasons explained previously, Allison simply believes that the weaknesses of the conventional criteria approach outweigh its benefits. I agree.

As for Meier's final critique, it is true that the conventional criteria approach often makes valid observations. Given what we do know about the early Jesus movement, some traditions, for example, are difficult to attribute to later invention. Yet Allison does not depend upon these observations in the same way the standard criteria approach does. Chris Keith writes, "One fruitful area of future research ... is the identification of various elements in the logical structure of individual criteria of authenticity that scholars may recover and use in another methodological structure."[110] In many ways, Allison models this.

THIS STUDY'S APPROACH AND SOME QUALIFICATIONS

This study examines the question of the role of Matthew in historical Jesus research by examining in particular the Gospel's portrayal of Jesus's relationship to the temple and his use of temple traditions. Its historical approach is largely informed by Allison's work. It also accepts, for the reasons given earlier, that Jesus's teaching drew from eschatological hopes rooted in Jewish apocalypticism. Some qualifications, however, are still necessary.

Clarifications Regarding Recurrent Attestation

First, in this study, we will use Allison's version of Sanders' triple-context approach in which "recurrent attestation" serves as a starting point for the historian's investigation. To be clear, however, like Allison, we do not assume the naïve position that the "gist" of the tradition must

---

[107] Allison, "How to Marginalize," 18.
[108] Meier, *A Marginal Jew*, 5:19.
[109] Allison, therefore, rejects Sanders' use of "certain" (*Constructing Jesus*, 48). Likewise, see Meier, *Marginal Jew*, 1:130: "absolute certainty is not to be had."
[110] Keith, "The Indebtedness of the Criteria Approach," 48.

necessarily be reliable. My discussion of memory research earlier is aimed at explaining we have no access to the uninterpreted past; trying to use criteria to recover an uninterpreted Jesus is simply not possible. I am not, however, arguing that memory studies serve as a replacement methodology.[111] Following Allison, I appeal to recurrent attestation as a first step to determine whether a feature of the Jesus tradition is widely attested. I start here because I believe we ought to begin with the broad outlines of the traditions. Indeed, even Meier would seem to agree with this. He explains that he began his *A Marginal Jew* project by first examining "those large swaths of material that enjoyed broad attestation with a wide variety of literary forms and religious content."[112] He moved from here to "more difficult" issues.[113] I begin with recurrent attestation, but I emphatically agree that this must also be buttressed by other considerations, namely, whether or not memories of Jesus's teaching appear intelligible within a first-century Jewish context and given the effects of his ministry.

Second, the approach taken here should not be seen as simply employing something like three separate "criteria." This study seeks to avoid the "tug of war" issue that often results within the conventional criteria method. It does not weigh the results of different criteria *against* each other. Rather, it seeks converging lines of evidence. This does not mean that we will ignore potential problems for a particular historical reconstruction. It simply means our approach will not involve weighing "criteria" against one another.

The Relationships of Our Sources

This study also agrees with the consensus view that Matthew and Luke are literarily dependent upon Mark. Beyond that, however, it remains agnostic about the interrelationship of the canonical gospels. As for the Gospel of Thomas, I accept the arguments made by others that it has been

---

[111] This charge has been unfairly made against other Jesus scholars who have appealed to the implications of Social Memory Research. See, e.g., Chris Keith, "The Narratives of the Gospels and the Historical Jesus: Current Debates, Prior Debates and the Goal of Historical Jesus Research," *Journal for the Study of the New Testament* 38, 4 (2016): 430n.7; Keith, "Social Memory Theory and Gospels Research: The First Decade (Part Two)," 541. The former article by Keith is especially important as it responds to other common critiques, which, for space, we cannot fully respond to here.

[112] Meier, *A Marginal Jew*, 5:1.

[113] Meier, *A Marginal Jew*, 5:1.

shaped by the Synoptics. In addition, Thomas seems especially interested in downplaying the role of Israel's scriptures in Jesus's teaching.[114] Its tendency to distance Jesus from this Jewish backdrop raises questions about its value for understanding his message within his original context.

Nevertheless, here we must be reminded that caution is necessary regarding tradition history. Redaction criticism cannot be equated with tradition history. In places where Matthew has tweaked Mark's account, one might conclude the evangelist is the source of such divergence. This, however, cannot always be assumed.

The *Ipsissima Verba Jesu* vs. the Gist of Jesus's Teaching

The older preoccupation with recovering the *ipsissima verba Jesu* ("the exact words of Jesus") has waned in Jesus studies.[115] A cursory look at our sources indicates that concern to preserve the precise phrases used by Jesus was not a priority. In some instances, the parallel reports of Jesus's words involve marked *differences* in meaning. For example, in Mark, Jesus sends the twelve out in pairs by telling them that they must "take nothing for their journey *except a staff*" (Mark 6:8: *mēden airōsin eis hodon ei mē rabdon monon*). In Matthew and Luke, however, Jesus explicitly tells the disciples *not* to take a staff (Matt 10:9–10//Luke 9:3). Augustine's explanation for this discrepancy is that the term for staff means different things in the two sayings,[116] yet this is far from clear from our texts. What all three Synoptics affirm, however, should not be overlooked; they all agree that Jesus sent the twelve out after giving them specific instructions about what they should (or should not) take. Which version preserves the earliest account will probably depend upon more than one's preferred solution to the Synoptic problem. Among other things, it will also likely include other considerations such as views about the kinds of aims Jesus had. One must also recognize that the earliest literary expression of the tradition may not represent the earliest memory of it. The issue is further complicated if Jesus originally spoke in Aramaic, as many have supposed.

An even more fundamental issue should be raised: it is difficult to believe that the gospel writers even felt it necessary to relate the *ipsissima verba Jesu*. It is generally recognized that, though literary genres are

---

[114] See, e.g., Goodacre, *Thomas and the Gospels*, 144, 187–191.
[115] See Pitre, *Jesus and the Last Supper*, 46–50.
[116] Augustine, *De Consensu Euangelistarum*, 2.30.74.

always marked by some fluidity,[117] the gospels were likely read as some form of ancient Greco-Roman biography.[118] Writers of such works had a wide degree of latitude in relating the details of their subject's speeches.[119] For all of these reasons, our focus will therefore be on larger questions such as: Did Jesus reject the legitimacy of the temple and its rites? In each instance, the place where I will begin is recurrent attestation.

It is necessary to clarify that I am not specifically appealing to "multiple attestation," which, although similar, is not the same tool as "recurrent attestation." The initial step of our investigation does not hinge upon whether reports of specific traditions are literarily dependent or independent (a key feature of "multiple attestation"). We will simply ask whether, in broad strokes, a particular feature of the Jesus tradition is broadly attested. In addition, our starting point will not involve weighing the results of recurrent attestation against other indices; recurrent attestation, then, serves as a kind of "first hurdle." I feel I must clarify this because many have attempted to conflate recurrent attestation with multiple attestation to argue that the conventional criteria are inescapable. This ignores the differences between the two, at least as explained by Allison. Recurrent attestation is simply a point of departure for the discussion of each topic; it does not, of itself, settle discussion about whether a particular feature of the tradition reflects some aspect of Jesus's public ministry. The appeal to recurrent attestation should not be understood as a historical proof; it is not an expression of a naïve appeal to "gist" memory as if it were itself definitive evidence. As in Allison's work, recurrent attestation is the place where our investigation will begin, not where it finishes. To render historical judgments, as explained earlier, we will need further analysis. We will also ask: Is this broadly attested idea coherent within a first-century Jewish setting and does it make sense given the effects of Jesus?

Finally, the attempt to identify the "very words" of Jesus rests on dubious assumptions. It presupposes, as in Jefferson's approach, that the overall narrative contexts of the gospels amount to little more than

---

[117] See the helpful discussion in Daniel Lynwood Smith and Zachary Lundin Kostopoulos, "Biography, History and the Genre of Luke-Acts," *NTS* 62 (2017): 390–410.

[118] See, e.g., Helen Bond, *The First Biography of Jesus: Genre and Meaning in Mark's Gospel* (Grand Rapids: Eerdmans, 2020); Richard Burridge, *What Are the Gospels? A Comparison with Graeco-Roman Biography*, 2nd ed. (Cambridge: Cambridge University Press, 1995).

[119] Bond, *First Biography of Jesus*, 66–71; Craig S. Keener, *Christobiography: Memory, History, and the Reliability of the Gospels* (Grand Rapids: Eerdmans, 2019), 158–160.

literary "dunghills." This should be viewed with suspicion. There is no reason to insist that material consistent with a particular evangelist's agenda is necessarily unhelpful to reconstructing the message of the historical Jesus. Part of the historical task should include the fascinating question: Why did the evangelists portray Jesus in *this* way – for example, as accepting or rejecting the temple's validity?

At the outset of this chapter, I spotlighted a quotation from Morna Hooker, who writes, "If we concentrate on the whole rather than the details ... we shall find that we know quite a lot about Jesus."[120] My goal is to show that Matthew's interpretation of Jesus should not be cut out of the historical equation. Matthew's Jewish perspective can be valuable for thinking through the kinds of concerns that would have shaped Jesus's own teaching. As Amy-Jill Levine explains, "It is likely that Jesus and the early church ... were substantially continuous rather than distinct."[121] I will argue that this continuity is especially exhibited in Matthew's presentation of Jesus's teachings about the temple's holiness. This leads us to the discussion in our next chapter: Jesus's attitude toward the Jerusalem sanctuary.

---

[120] Hooker, "Foreword: Forty Years On," in *Jesus, Criteria, and the Demise of Authenticity*, ed. Keith and Le Donne, xv.

[121] Levine, "Introduction," in *Jesus in Context: Princeton Readings in Religion*, ed. Levine, Allison, Jr., and Crossan, 10.

3

Jesus and the Jerusalem Temple

If Jesus had indeed acted and taught against the Temple service, then his
immediate followers completely missed his point.
– Paula Fredriksen[1]

If Jesus actually explicitly opposed one of the main institutions of Judaism
[i.e., the temple], he kept it secret from his disciples.
– E. P. Sanders[2]

The notion that Jesus denied the validity of the temple's cult has long had
its advocates. It is not difficult to account for this. As mentioned in the
Introduction, biblical scholarship has a history of antipathy toward sacrificial worship. More recent work, however, is moving away from such
biases. Studies on the Jewish temple and Israel's ritual worship are now
being published at a steady rate. One especially significant recent volume
that dispels the notion that Jesus's early followers were necessarily hostile
to the Jerusalem temple is *The Temple and Early Christianity* by Eyal
Regev.[3] Regev makes some careful distinctions that will be important for
our investigation.

In his study, Regev notes four types of texts that describe Jesus and/or
his early followers' relationship to the temple:

---

[1] Paula Fredriksen, *Jesus of Nazareth, King of the Jews: A Jewish Life and the Emergence
of Christianity* (New York: Vintage, 1999), 209.
[2] Sanders, *Jesus and Judaism*, 67. See also Joachim Jeremias, *New Testament Theology:
The Proclamation of Jesus*, trans. John Bowden (New York: Scribner's, 1971), 207.
[3] Eyal Regev, *The Temple in Early Christianity: Experiencing the Sacred*, AYBRL (New
Haven: Yale University Press, 2019).

43

1. *Participation*: Jesus and/or his followers are depicted as in the temple and taking part in its cultic life.
2. *Analogy*: ideas and/or practices are interpreted using symbolism from the temple and its cult.
3. *Criticism*: abuses related to temple worship are identified.
4. *Rejection*: the earthly temple is replaced with something else.[4]

Regev allows some overlap in these categories. For example, a text may use a temple metaphor in the service of advancing the view that the Jerusalem sanctuary has been replaced. Yet – and this is a crucially important distinction – the fact that a text uses a temple metaphor does not *necessarily* signal the nullification of sacrificial worship. For example, the book of Sirach speaks of almsgiving as a thanksgiving sacrifice and explains that forsaking unrighteousness effects atonement (Sir 35:2–5). Nevertheless, as the following verses make clear, the author also believes in the efficacious power of the temple's rites (Sir 35:8–10). The use of temple imagery to explain an idea or practice, therefore, does not automatically involve a repudiation of the sanctuary.

In this chapter, we will analyze the question of Jesus's general attitude toward the temple and its ritual worship. The discussion will begin with an analysis of the overall impression we get from the source texts, which seem to depict him endorsing the temple's rites. We will also ask whether this portrait of him fits with what we know of Jesus's Jewish context and his effects. After this we shall then turn to Matthew's narrative, making mention of traditions that might undermine the view that Jesus recognized the holiness of the temple.

Finally, we shall ask: Does Matthew's unique portrait have value to the quest? Following traditional historical Jesus methodology, researchers have often fallen into the trap of imagining only two ways of approaching this question. On the one hand, some dismiss Matthew's special material as irrelevant because it fails the tests of multiple attestation and dissimilarity. For example, in the Sermon on the Mount, Jesus delivers a teaching about how to offer sacrifices (Matt 5:23–24). Yet this saying is often viewed as having little value to the historian. The logion appears in a section, the so-called "six antitheses" (Matt 5:21–48), that cohere with the evangelist's emphasis on Jesus's relationship to the law.[5] It is therefore ruled out as irrelevant for understanding the historical Jesus. On the other hand, arguments have been made for accepting the "authenticity"

---

[4] Regev, *The Temple in Early Christianity*, 16.
[5] Meier, *A Marginal Jew*, 4:42.

of this saying.[6] For example, the saying may be viewed as historically plausible because it is consistent with a Jewish perspective on sacrifice (cf. t. B. Qam. 10:18).[7] Bultmann affirmed the saying's likely origin in Jesus's teaching, pointing out: "Polemic against the temple cult is completely absent from the words of Jesus."[8] Here, then, we have a prime example of how the "criteria" can be weighed in very different ways.

However, as we have detailed in Chapter 1, a binary approach to Jesus research that simply seeks to arrive at "authentic" and "inauthentic" judgments rests on questionable assumptions. As Allison has argued, even traditions viewed as "inauthentic" may tell us something important about the historical Jesus. This is not to rule out the possibility that Matthew's special material preserves historical memory. Nevertheless, as we shall show, the overall portrait of Jesus's stance toward the temple in Matthew, regardless of the historicity of specific details, should be seen as having important implications for Jesus research.

THE HISTORICAL JESUS AND THE TEMPLE

Recurrent Attestation

As mentioned earlier, there are traditions in which Jesus announces the sanctuary's coming ruin. These will be treated in further detail in the next chapter. What nonetheless strikes us about our sources is the sheer number of passages that depict Jesus as favorably inclined to the Jerusalem temple's sacrificial worship. As the following list reveals, these are broadly attested in the Synoptic Gospels and occur in the Fourth Gospel as well:

Traditions Indicating Jesus's Endorsement of the Temple Cult
1. Jesus Speaks of Coming Judgment Due to Actions That Include Shedding Blood in the Sanctuary
   (Matt 23:34–36//Luke 11:49–51 [Q?])
2. Jesus Sends the Cleansed Leper to the Priest and to Offer Sacrifice
   (Matt 8:1–5//Mark 1:40–45//Luke 5:12–16)

---

[6] See, e.g., Luz, *Matthew*, 1:234

[7] See Craig A. Evans, "The Misplaced Jesus: Interpreting Jesus in a Judaic Context," in The Missing Jesus: Rabbinic Judaism and the New Testament, *ed. Bruce David Chilton, Craig A. Evans, and Jacob Neusner* (Leiden: Brill, 2002), 34.

[8] See Rudolph Bultmann, *Theology of the New Testament*, 2 vols., trans. Kendrick Grobel (Waco: Baylor University Press, 2007), 17. See also his comments in Rudolf Bultmann, *History of the Synoptic Tradition*, rev. ed., trans. John Marsh (Peabody: Hendrickson, 1963), 146–147, 149.

3. Jesus Quotes Isaiah 56's Prophecy of an Eschatological Temple
   (Matt 21:13//Mark 11:17//Luke 19:46)
4. Jesus Commends the Widow Who Gives to the Temple Treasury
   (Mark 12:41–44//Luke 21:1–4)
5. A Future Desolating Sacrilege in the Holy Place Is Linked to Divine Judgment
   (Matt 24:15//Mark 13:14; cf. Luke 21:20)
6. Jesus Directs the Apostles to Prepare the Passover Lamb at the Jerusalem Temple
   (Matt 26:17–19//Mark 14:12–16//Luke 22:7–13; cf. Luke 22:15).[9]
7. Jesus Was in the Temple Teaching Daily
   (Matt 26:55//Mark 14:49//Luke 22:53; Luke 19:47; Luke 21:37–38; cf. Matt 21:14; Matt 21:23; Matt 26:55; Mark 12:35; Luke 20:1; John 8:20, 59; 18:20)
8. Jesus Teaches on How to Rightly Offer Sacrifice
   (Matt 5:23–24)
9. Jesus Affirms the Holiness of the Temple and Its Sacrifices
   (Matt 23:16–21)
10. Jesus's Parents Presented Him as a Child in the Temple and Offered the Purification Sacrifice
    (Luke 2:22–25)
11. Jesus's Family Went Up to the Temple to Keep Passover Annually
    (Luke 2:41)
12. The Child Jesus Identifies the Temple as "My Father's House"
    (Luke 2:49)
13. Jesus Sends Ten Lepers to Be Declared Clean by Priests after Healing Them (Luke 17:12–19)
14. Jesus Describes a Tax Collector and a Pharisee Praying at the Temple
    (Luke 18:10–14)
15. Jesus Visits the Temple at Passover Time
    (John 2:14; cf. 2:23)
16. Jesus Goes into the Temple and Encounters a Man He Healed
    (John 5:14)
17. Jesus Goes to the Temple for the Feast of Tabernacles
    (John 7:10, 14; cf. John 7:37)
18. Jesus Attends the Temple at the Feast of Dedication
    (John 10:22)

[9] See the discussion of this passage later in this chapter.

19. Jesus's "Triumphal Entry" Is Connected with Crowds Going to Jerusalem to Keep Passover
    (John 12:12–13)
20. Jesus Meets Greeks Going Up to Worship at the Temple at Passover
    (John 12:20–21)
21. Jesus's Final Meal Is Connected to the Liturgical Feast of Passover in Jerusalem
    (John 13:1–2)

Here we have *numerous* texts indicating Jesus's favorable stance toward the temple. In fact, other texts could also be mentioned that we have not included here. For instance, Luke's mention that it was Jesus's "custom [*ethos*]" to go to the Mount of Olives would seem to betray an awareness of a tradition that Jesus made multiple trips to Jerusalem (Luke 22:39).[10] The preceding list aims to be conservative. A few caveats, however, are necessary.

First, the point in compiling the preceding catalogue is *not* that any of these traditions are, of themselves, historical "proofs." Rather, it merely shows that *our sources repeatedly depict Jesus as going to the temple and/or as instructing others to participate in its rituals.* Though he appeals to "multiple attestation" and not recurrent attestation, John P. Meier makes a similar point: "Even if we do not think that all of these narratives and sayings are authentic – the sayings in John are especially problematic – we still have widespread multiple attestation of both sources and forms for Jesus's acceptance of the Jerusalem temple of his day."[11] It seems safe to say that Jesus's involvement in temple worship meets the bar of "recurrent attestation."

Second, just because all of these traditions cannot be authenticated, we should not conclude that they are all of equally dubious value. Some are widely viewed as reflecting history. For example, in all four canonical gospels, Jesus's passion takes place in and around Passover time. Whatever one makes of the precise chronology of his last days, that Jesus went up for Passover prior to his death is hard to contest. The setting makes sense. Paula Fredriksen observes, "The only time Jesus could have encountered Roman forces – the prefect and his soldiers – was when he went up to Jerusalem, to celebrate one of these holidays."[12] It seems likely, then, that

---

[10] Francis J. Moloney, S.B.D., "Revisiting the Temple: Mark 11:15–16 and 13:2," in *The Figure of Jesus in History and Theology: Essays in Honor of John Meier*, ed. Vincent T. M. Skemp and Kelley Coblentz Bautch, CBQI 1 (Washington, DC: CBA, 2020), 66.

[11] Meier, *A Marginal Jew*, 3:500.

[12] Paula Fredriksen, *When Christians Were Jews: The First Generation* (New Haven: Yale University Press, 2018), 19.

Jesus participated in the temple rites – for example, eating a lamb ritually slaughtered in the temple – as part of this.

Third, what does not appear in the preceding catalogue are the traditions that may be seen as challenging the temple's validity. For example, Jesus's statement that the "house" is "desolate [*erēmos*]" (Matt 23:38; cf. Luke 13:35) would seem to imply that, at some point in his public ministry, Jesus denied that God dwelt in the sanctuary. As we work through Matthew in the next section of this chapter, we will discuss many of these texts. We will complete our treatment of them in the next chapter. Here, however, it is necessary to say a few words about the Fourth Gospel.

The Gospel of John contains a number of passages that have been read as portraying Jesus's negative attitude toward the temple. The scene of Jesus's temple action in John 2 is perhaps the most discussed. The statement "Destroy this temple and in three days I will raise it up" (John 2:19) has led many to believe that John depicts Jesus as renouncing the temple's legitimacy. Ernst Haenchen writes of the scene: "Jesus rejects ... the delusion that man can buy God's favor with sacrifices."[13] Other passages in the Gospel would seem to confirm John's anti-cultic bent.

For example, John 4 has Jesus tell the Samaritan woman that true worship will take place "in spirit and truth," occurring neither at Jerusalem nor at the place reverenced by Samaritans at Gerizim (John 4:23). Andreas Köstenberg claims that this means, "no longer must worshippers come to God by sacrificing in the temple; they can simply approach God through prayer in Jesus's name."[14] Others hold that John presents Jesus as celebrating Passover in accord with the Essene calendar, thereby rejecting the Jerusalem cult.[15] These readings, however, are not convincing.

Jesus's statement equating the temple with his body in John 2 is explicitly interpreted by the narrator as referring to his own resurrection (John 2:21–22). According to the evangelist, the saying is *not* about the destruction of the Jerusalem sanctuary. More significantly, nowhere in the account does Jesus explicitly renounce the temple's validity. On the contrary, his approval of the temple is implied; Jesus refers to it as "my Father's house [*ton oikon tou patros mou*]" (John 2:16). His disciples

---

[13] Ernst Haenchen, *John*, Hermeneia, 2 vols., trans. Robert Funk, ed. Robert W. Funk with Ulrich Busse (Minneapolis: Fortress Press, 1984), 184.

[14] Andreas Köstenberger, "The Destruction of the Second Temple and the Composition of the Fourth Gospel," in *Challenging Perspectives on the Gospel of John*, WUNT 2/219, ed. John Lierman (Tübingen: Mohr Siebeck, 2006), 106.

[15] Annie Jaubert, *The Date of the Last Supper*, trans. I. Rafferty (Staten Island: Alba House, 1965 [orig. 1957]).

even attribute his action to his "zeal [*zēlos*]" for the temple (John 2:17). If anything, this suggests that Jesus's action was remembered as expressing his devotion to the sanctuary.[16]

The other supposed anti-cultic passages in John should also be reconsidered. While the statement in John 4 speaks of a coming day involving worship in spirit and in truth, Jesus does not declare that worshipping in Jerusalem is itself wrong or illegitimate. Rather, Jesus explains that, unlike the Samaritans who worship at Gerizim, the Jews do *not* worship in ignorance: "You worship what you do not know. We *worship what we know*, because salvation is from the Jews" (John 4:22). This cannot be used to support the position that Jesus maintains that the Jerusalem cult is invalid.[17]

In short, there is no unambiguous evidence in John that Jesus opposed the worship in the temple or departed from the calendar followed by the priests.[18] Jesus repeatedly goes to Jerusalem to participate in cultic celebrations of the Jewish festivals at the same time the masses do (e.g., John 2:14; 7:10, 14; 10:22). John, therefore, cannot be used to prove that Jesus opposed the temple worship.

Fourth, we should mention one final text that often receives attention in treatments of Jesus's attitude toward the temple. In Mark's account of Jesus's so-called "trial," we read that witnesses came forward and claimed: "We heard him say, 'I will destroy this temple [*naon*] made by hands, and within three days I will build[19] another not made by hands'" (Mark 14:58). In a number of Jewish texts, the phrase "made by hands [*ton cheiropoiēton*]" has idolatrous connotations.[20] Might we find in this text a memory that Jesus actually viewed the temple as an object of idolatry? That conclusion is unwarranted. Philo says that the Jerusalem temple was constructed by human hands without in any way implying its illegitimacy (*Spec.* 1.67). The saying attributed to Jesus can be seen as suggesting that the Herodian temple will be replaced with an eschatological sanctuary, which Jewish texts indicate would be established by God himself (cf.

---

[16] Paul M. Hoskins, *Jesus as the Fulfillment of the Temple in the Gospel of John*, PBM (Carlisle: Paternoster, 2006), 110.

[17] For a critique of the position that Jesus followed the Essene calendar, see Pitre, *Jesus and the Last Supper*, 260–280; Meier, *A Marginal Jew*, 3:391–394.

[18] See Regev, *The Temple in Early Christianity*, 197–221.

[19] The variant (D it) "I will raise [*anastēsō*]" is best seen as secondary. Adela Yarbro Collins, *Mark*, Hermeneia (Minneapolis: Fortress Press, 2007), 696.

[20] See, e.g., LXX Lev 26:1; Isa 2:18; 10:11; 19:1; Dan 5:4, 23; 6:28; Craig A. Evans, *Mark 8:27–16:20*, WBC 34B (Nashville: Thomas Nelson, 2001), 446; Timothy J. Geddert, *Watchwords: Mark 13 in Markan Eschatology*, JSNTSup 26 (Sheffield: JSOT, 1989), 132; Martin Scharlemann, *Stephen: A Singular Saint* (Rome: Biblical Institute, 1968), 106.

especially, Exod 15:17). Nevertheless, as Adela Collins argues, to insist that idolatrous connotations are necessarily intended in the language of the charge is to overread the text.[21]

The general shape of the tradition, then, indicates that Jesus affirmed the divine institution of the temple and even instructed others to worship there. This is usually acknowledged by Jesus scholars. As examples, here are some quotations from James Charlesworth, John Meier, and Amy-Jill Levine:

> there are inchoate traditions in the Gospels that suggest Jesus revered the Temple, considered it the House of the Father (John 2:16) and a House of Prayer for all nations (Mark 11:17). To enter the Temple, Jesus must have obeyed the Temple *halakot* (entering a *mikveh* to be purified and paying the Temple tax). He certainly, and frequently, taught and worshipped in the Temple.[22]

> Whether we accept as historical the one journey of Jesus to the Jerusalem temple presented in Mark or the many journeys to the Jerusalem temple presented in John, it is to Jerusalem, not Qumran, that Jesus goes to celebrate the major Jewish feasts. Be it during the days immediately preceding the feast (so for Passover in the Synoptics) or during the feast itself (so for Tabernacles in John 7–8), Jesus is active in the Jerusalem temple.[23]

> The Gospels and Acts depict Jesus, his family, and his followers worshipping in the Temple and participating in the Temple sacrificial system. Apparently, they didn't get the message that it was a "domination system."[24]

In short, the overwhelming impression one gets from our sources is that Jesus endorsed and even participated in the Jerusalem cult. This leads us to a second consideration: Does this make sense within Jesus's Jewish context? Though the answer may seem to be obviously in the affirmative, nuance is required.

Jesus's First-Century Jewish Context

For many Jesus historians, the simple fact of Jesus's Jewish identity makes it difficult to think that he rejected the temple cult. Bart Ehrman and Helen Bond make precisely this observation:

---

[21] Collins, *Mark*, 702–703. An idolatrous meaning in Acts 7:48 also seems unlikely given the way the Acts highlights the community's ongoing respect for the temple (cf. Acts 2:46; 3:1; 21:17–26).

[22] James H. Charlesworth, "Jesus and the Temple," in *Jesus and Temple: Textual and Archaeological Explorations*, ed. James H. Charlesworth (Minneapolis: Fortress Press, 2014), 179.

[23] Meier, *A Marginal Jew*, 1:392.

[24] Amy-Jill Levine, *A Misunderstood Jew: The Church and the Scandal of the Jewish Jesus* (San Francisco: HarperOne, 2006), 154.

Jesus agreed that one should worship in the Temple and, evidently, perform the proper sacrifices there. That *is* part of the Law given to Moses, and Jesus does, for example, keep the Passover in Jerusalem.[25]

There is no indication that Jesus was *opposed to sacrifice* ... Blood sacrifice ... was the normal expression of religious piety in every ancient culture. It is inconceivable that any first-century Jew could have been "against sacrifice", and if Jesus really held such a view, it is incredible that such an attitude has not shown up elsewhere in his teachings.[26]

Ehrman's point is worth highlighting: the Torah itself requires sacrifices to be made at the temple. To believe Jesus rejected these practices requires dismissing this rather significant datum.

Still, it should be acknowledged that basing conclusions about Jesus's attitude toward the temple cult on his Jewishness alone is insufficient. After all, at least *some* Jews did withdraw from the temple. It is therefore possible to imagine a "Jewish Jesus" who took a similar position. This, however, seems unlikely. We will have more to say about this after analyzing Matthew. For now, however, a more general comment is in order.

The key concern of Jesus research is not determining the *possible* but the *probable*. Whether it is *possible* that Jesus was among Jews like the Essenes who dissented from the Jerusalem cult is not the question. Many things are "possible." It is "possible" that he studied with Gamaliel, frequently traveled to Rome, and learned Latin. Since there is no evidence that he did any of these things, however, they remain *improbable*. Since we are interested in "probability" we must first begin with the data we possess. Because there are numerous traditions that indicate that Jesus respected the temple and instructed others to worship there, we start by asking an obvious question: Does this portrait fit with what we know about Jesus's historical context? Since it does, unless we have some reason to think otherwise, it would seem strange to insist this aspect of tradition was invented out of whole cloth. Are there texts in the Synoptics that might point in another direction? Yes, and we will deal with them later. Yet since the idea that Jesus reverenced the cult is recurrently attested and makes eminent sense in a first-century Jewish context, we are hard-pressed to prefer an alternative scenario. Nevertheless, there remains one significant matter to which we must attend: the tendencies of Jesus's earliest followers.

[25] Bart Ehrman, *Jesus: Apocalyptic Prophet of the New Millennium* (Oxford: Oxford University Press, 1999), 172.

[26] Helen K. Bond, *The Historical Jesus: A Guide for the Perplexed* (London: T&T Clark, 2012), 139, 140.

The Effects of Jesus's Ministry

Does the portrait of a Jesus who embraced the validity of the temple cult fit with what we know about the early Jesus movement? It would seem so. The Gospel of Luke ends with the disciples "continually in the temple blessing God" (Luke 24:53). The book of Acts also indicates that the disciples went up to worship in the temple after the resurrection (e.g., Acts 2:46; 3:1; 5:25). Acts 3 has Peter and John attend the temple at the very hour Jews gathered for the daily Tamid ritual (cf. Luke 1:9–10; cf. Acts 10:3, 30; Dan 9:3–19; Ezra 9:4–5; Jdth 9:1–14).[27]

Acts 21 stands out as especially important for our study. Here the Jerusalem believers inform Paul of a rumor circulating among them. Apparently, some are claiming that he teaches Jews in the Diaspora to abandon the law and Jewish customs (Acts 21:21). How is Paul to dispel the slander that he has renounced the law? The answer: temple worship. Paul is encouraged to join four men who are under a vow and who are about to go to the sanctuary for "the rite of purification" (Acts 21:24). We read:

> Then Paul took along the men, and the next day, having purified himself, he entered into the temple with them to announce the completion of the days of purification, until an offering should be offered for each one of them [*heōs hou prosēnechthē hyper henos hekastou autōn hē prosphora*]. (Acts 21:26)

The precise meaning of the vow is a bit obscure, but most interpreters think it refers to the one sworn by Nazarites.[28] In this case, the "offering" in view would involve an animal sacrifice (Num 6:14, 17; m. Naz. 8–11). Regardless of what one makes of the specifics, Paul himself is depicted as participating in the temple cult.[29]

That the temple was viewed as sacred to Paul is also suggested by the fact that the apostle applies cultic images to Jesus and/or believers in his letters:

---

[27] See Dennis Hamm, S.J., "The Tamid Service in Luke-Acts: The Cultic Background behind Luke's Theology of Worship (Luke 1:5–25; 18:9–14; 24:50–53; Acts 3:1; 10:3, 30)," *CBQ* 25 (2003): 215–231.

[28] See Regev, *The Temple in Early Christianity*, 156; Craig S. Keener, *Acts: An Exegetical Commentary*, 4 vols. (Grand Rapids: Baker Academic, 2012–2015), 3:3135–3139; Joseph A. Fitzmyer, S.J., *Acts of the Apostles*, AB 31 (New Haven: Yale University Press, 1998), 694.

[29] James H. Charlesworth, "The Temple and Jesus's Followers," in *Jesus and Temple: Textual and Archaeological Explorations*, ed. James H. Charlesworth (Minneapolis: Fortress Press, 2014), 193. This was recognized as early as Augustine, who used the passage to show that Paul observed the law (*Letter* 82.2,8). See discussion in Paula Fredriksen, *Augustine and the Jews: A Christian Defense of Jews and Judaism* (New Haven: Yale University Press, 2008), 299.

Pauline Texts Applying Cultic Imagery to Jesus and/or Believers

1. Christ's Blood Is a Covenant Sacrifice (1 Cor 11:24–26)
2. Christ Is a *hilastērion* (Rom 3:25)
3. Cleansing Out the Old Leaven and Christ's Paschal Sacrifice (1 Cor 5:7–8)
4. Believers Offer Themselves as Living Sacrifices (Rom 12:1)
5. Paul's Death Is a Cultic Offering (Phil 2:17)
6. Paul's Ministry Is Priestly (Rom 15:16)
7. Ministers of the Gospel Receive a Living Like Priests Receive Food from the Altar (1 Cor 9:13–14)
8. Believers Are the Aroma of Christ (2 Cor 2:15)
9. Donations to the Poor Are Cultic Sacrifices (Phil 4:18; 2 Cor 9:9–15)
10. Christ Is the "First Fruits" (1 Cor 15:20)
11. The Church Is a Temple (1 Cor 3:9, 16–17; 6:19; 2 Cor 6:16)[30]

Some have argued that by using sacrificial imagery in reference to Jesus's death and by speaking of the community as the temple, Paul must have implied that the Jerusalem sanctuary's holiness had been nullified. Yet Paul never makes an explicit statement to that effect. As Charlesworth says, "Paul takes cultic language out of the cult and moves sacred space from Temple to the individual, *but that does not mean the Temple and the sacred cult ceased to be important for Paul.*"[31]

Regev observes that even if Paul thought that Jesus's death brought about definitive atonement in such a way that atonement was no longer achieved through animal sacrifices, this would not necessarily mean he rejected the temple in toto. Atonement was not the only function of the temple and its offerings. Regev writes: "A Jew who believes in Jesus may nevertheless feel the need to visit the Temple and offer sacrifices to fulfill other aspects of cultic worship."[32] It should also be noted that atonement was not solely associated with the temple; Sirach links it to things such as honoring one's parents and almsgiving (e.g., Sir 3:3, 30; 20:28).[33]

---

[30] For a treatment of the cultic themes in Paul's letters, see Michael P. Barber and John A. Kincaid, "Cultic Theosis in Paul and Second Temple Judaism," *JSPL* 5, 2 (2015): 237–256.

[31] Charlesworth, "The Temple and Jesus's Followers," 192. See also Regev, *The Temple in Early Christianity*, 53–95; emphasis added. See also Jonathan Klawans, "Interpreting the Last Supper: Sacrifice, Spiritualization, and Anti-Sacrifice," *NTS* 48 (2002): 11–15.

[32] Regev, *The Temple in Early Christianity*, 5.

[33] For more on the implications of this for certain positions regarding the ramifications of the destruction of the temple, see Levine, "Concluding Reflections," 460.

To be sure, some have used statements in Paul to argue that he thought the Jewish calendar had been abrogated. For example, in Galatians 4, Paul says those who "carefully observe days and months and seasons and years" are in "bondage" (cf. Gal 4:9–10). Yet if Paul is writing to gentile believers, this may reflect his understanding of their particular relationship to the Torah. It might be significant to note that Acts says Paul did not bring a gentile into the temple (Acts 21:29). In addition, even if Paul believed that obligatory calendar observance had been lifted by the Messiah's coming, it would not necessarily follow that he taught that all of the temple's functions had ceased to be valid. Acts 21 would certainly not lend itself to that idea. Furthermore, since elsewhere we discover that Paul oriented his plans around the Jewish calendar (cf. 1 Cor 16:8; cf. Acts 18:21; 20:6),[34] it is difficult to believe he had renounced it altogether. In fact, whether Galatians 4 is speaking of the *Jewish* calendar is debated.[35] A stronger case for abrogation of the Jewish calendar might be made from Colossians, where the author talks of "questions about food and drink, or with regard to a feast or a new moon or a Sabbath" (Col 2:16). Yet there are difficulties here as well. Paul's authorship of the letter is famously disputed. In addition, it is debated whether the passage is condemning the notion of keeping Jewish observances or whether it is condemning rigorist ascetics who believe Jewish celebrations are inappropriate (cf. Col 2:18).[36] In short, *there is no clear-cut evidence that Paul renounced the temple's holiness.*

Finally, the epistle to the Hebrews unambiguously affirms that Jesus's death entails the abrogation of the Levitical cult. Admittedly, this may seem to represent a weakness for my argument. Nonetheless, had Jesus himself articulated the idea that his death would involve the nullification of the Jerusalem cult, it is difficult to explain the reports of the early community's participation in the temple's worship. What is more, Hebrews never claims to represent the message of the historical Jesus, but, rather, it presents itself as a post-Easter theological reflection on the significance

---

[34] For a discussion, see Brian Louis Allen, "Removing an Arrow from the Supersessionist Quiver: A Post-Supersessionist Reading of Colossians 2:16–17," *JSPL* 8 (2018): 132–136.

[35] See, e.g., Brigitte Kahl, *Galatians Re-Imagined: Reading with the Eyes of the Vanquished* (Minneapolis: Fortress Press, 2010), 225; Mark Nanos, *The Irony of Galatians: Paul's Letter in First-Century Context* (Minneapolis: Fortress Press, 2002), 267–268; Troy W. Martin, "Pagan and Judeo-Christian Time-Keeping Schemes in Gal 4:10 and 2:16," *NTS* 42 (1996): 105–119.

[36] See Allen, "Removing an Arrow," 127–146.

of the Christ event that goes beyond "the elementary message of Christ [*archēs tou Christou*]" (Heb 6:1).[37]

The best explanation of the data is that Jesus likely endorsed and participated in the Jerusalem temple's ritual life. If Jesus was opposed to participation in the temple's cult and condemned it as inherently invalid, it is almost impossible to explain why his early followers were remembered as having continued to worship there in the post-Easter period. Paula Fredriksen and Helen Bond put it well:

On the evidence of Paul's letters, the Gospels, and the Acts of the Apostles, these earliest Christians chose to live in Jerusalem, to worship in the Temple, to keep the festivals, the Sabbath, and the food laws, and to regard Torah as the word of God. If Jesus had indeed acted and taught against the Temple service, then his immediate followers completely missed his point.[38]

If Jesus had been against the Temple *per se*, it is very strange that his followers continued to gather there according to the early chapters of Acts.[39]

In sum, what we know about Jesus's early followers would seem to confirm the broadly attested tradition that he accepted the temple's legitimacy. An alternative reconstruction is not more probable.

THE TEMPLE IN JESUS'S MINISTRY IN MATTHEW

Matthew, as we have seen, reflects a perspective that seems especially focused on addressing Jewish concerns about Jesus. With that in mind, we now turn to the Matthean portrait of Jesus's relationship to the temple. The historical implications of what follows will be discussed in the next section. For now, what we wish to demonstrate is that *Matthew emphasizes Jesus's respect for the temple*. While some have appealed to certain episodes in Matthew as indicators that he rejected the validity of the temple's rites, we shall see such arguments are not convincing. In addition, perhaps even more significant is this: *Matthew's narrative suggests that Jesus believed the eschatological age would itself include a cultic dimension.*

Here we will temporarily set aside one crucial episode: the account of Jesus's "cleansing" of the temple. Since Jesus quotes a passage from Jeremiah 7 which foretells the destruction of the temple, many have

---

[37] Heb 2:3 affirms continuity with Jesus's teaching, but this cannot be said to necessarily involve an affirmation that he taught during his public ministry that the Levitical cult had been rendered obsolete.
[38] Fredriksen, *Jesus of Nazareth*, 209.
[39] Bond, *Historical Jesus*, 140.

grouped this scene with traditions that indicate Jesus anticipated the coming ruin of the Jerusalem sanctuary. We will therefore analyze this story in greater detail in the next chapter. In fact, the scholarly focus on this episode can easily cause it to overshadow other material that might be overlooked.

Jesus's Instructions on Offering Sacrifice (Matt 5:23–24)

In the first of the so-called "antitheses" recorded in Matthew 5, Jesus makes a statement about offering temple sacrifice that is particularly relevant to our discussion:

You have heard that it was said to those of ancient times, "You shall not commit murder," and "Whoever commits murder shall be subject to judgment." But [*de*] I say to you that everyone who is angry at his brother will be subject to judgment; and whoever says to his brother, "Raka!," will be liable to the Sanhedrin; and whoever says, "You fool!," will be liable to the Gehenna of fire. Therefore, *if you are offering your gift on the altar* [*prospherēs to dōron sou epi to thusiastērion*] and there remember that your brother has something against you, *leave your gift there before the altar* [*aphes ekei to dōron sou emprosthen tou thusiastēriou*] and go; first be reconciled with your brother and then come and *offer your gift* [*prosphere to dōron sou*]. Amen, I say to you, you will not come out of there until you have paid back the last penny. (Matthew 5:21–26)

A few comments are in order here.

First, Jesus's teaching seems to expand on his insistence in the preceding verses that his fulfillment of the law requires a "'surpassing' righteousness" (Matt 5:20).[40] For Matthew, then, Jesus's eschatological outlook does not nullify cultic worship. The passage's significance should not be overlooked: *according to Matthew, Jesus's vision of the eschatological age includes cultic worship.*

Second, Jesus appears to make his argument about the relationship between anger and murder by alluding to a famous episode in which the former is seen as precipitating the latter: the story of Cain and Abel.[41] It is impossible to think that Jesus's teaching – which combines "anger," "murder," conflict with a "brother," and sacrifice – would not have been

---

[40] See Donald Hagner, *Matthew*, 2 vols., WBC 33a–b (Dallas: Word, 1993–1995), 1:118; Daniel J. Harrington, S.J., *The Gospel of Matthew*, SP 1 (Collegeville: Liturgical Press, 1991), 91. This interpretation is also attested in Origen (*Frag.* 103) and Chromatius (*Tract. Matt.*, 21.1.1–2).

[41] See Dale C. Allison, Jr., *Studies in Matthew: Interpretation Past and Present* (Grand Rapids: Baker Academic, 2005), 65–78.

connected to the narrative in Genesis 4. The story is a perfect illustration of the way in which anger leads to murder.

Third, the saying coheres well with Jewish sensibilities in general. The basic message is that interpersonal conflicts must be resolved *prior* to bringing a sacrifice.[42] In fact, various Jewish texts indicate that the acceptability of sacrificial offerings is contingent upon the worshipper's interior disposition (cf. 1 Sam 15:22; Isa 1:10–18; Hos 6:6; Mic 6:6–8; Ps 51:16–17, 19; Sir 7:8–9; 34:21–24).

Fourth, Jesus's words in Matthew 5 about offering a "gift" (*dōron*) at the "altar" find a certain parallel in Matthew 23, where the "gift" clearly refers to a sacrificial offering:

Woe to you, blind guides, who say, "Whoever swears by the temple, it is nothing, but whoever swears by the gold of the temple is bound." You blind fools! For which is greater, the gold or the temple that makes the gold holy [*mōroi kai typhloi, tis gar meizōn estin, ho chrysos ē ho naos ho hagiasas ton chryson*]? And, "If anyone swears by the altar, it is nothing, but whoever swears by the gift that is on it is bound." You blind men! For which is greater, the gift or the altar that makes the gift holy [*to thysiastērion to hagiazon to dōron*]? Therefore, whoever swears by the altar, swears by it and by everything that is on it. And whoever swears by the temple, swears by it and by the one who dwells in it. (Matthew 23:16–22)

Jesus here not only affirms the sanctity of the temple, *but he also explicitly teaches that the temple and its altar causes things to be made holy.* It is hard to imagine a more definitive statement regarding the temple's holiness. This passage must be kept in mind as we interpret other temple passages in Matthew. If the evangelist intended to indicate that Jesus rejected the holiness of the temple, it is hard to explain the inclusion of these lines.

Jesus's Instructions to the Leper to Offer Sacrifice (Matt 8:1–4)

The story of Jesus's healing of a leper in Matthew 8, an account which also appears in Mark, offers another important insight into Matthew's perspective on Jesus's stance toward the Jerusalem temple (cf. Matt 8:1–4; Mark 1:40–45). After pronouncing the leper clean, Jesus instructs him to follow the Torah's sacrificial prescriptions, saying, "go show yourself to the priest, and offer the gift that Moses commanded as a testimony to them" (Matt 8:4). Jesus's instruction to the leper to offer a "gift"

---

[42] See, e.g., Davies and Allison, *Matthew*, 1:518.

(*dōron*) once again uses the same term for sacrificial offerings found in the preceding passages we have examined (cf. Matt 5:23; Matt 23:18–19). However, whereas the Sermon on the Mount has Jesus presupposing participation in cultic worship, here Jesus explicitly *commands* it. In instructing the leper to offer sacrifice, Jesus upholds the Torah, which requires lepers to be inspected by the priest and, when cleansed, to offer sacrifice (cf. Lev 14:1–32; 11Q19 48:17–49:4).

Admittedly, the rationale Jesus provides for his instruction to the leper is ambiguous. Jesus says the leper's sacrificial offering will serve as "a testimony to/against them [*eis martyrion autois*]" (Matt 8:4). First, the meaning of "them" is undefined. Jesus could have in mind the people in general. More likely, however, considering the context, it refers to the priests at the temple, one of whom will perform the necessary purification rite.[43] In addition, it is unclear what Jesus means when he says that the sacrifice will serve as a "a testimony [*martyrion*]." Does the offering authenticate the leper's recovery? Perhaps something else is in view.[44] The expression could be taken negatively, that is, as "a testimony *against* them," that is, as a witness against those who do not acknowledge Jesus. Whatever the exact meaning, the story ultimately portrays Jesus as taking a positive stance toward the temple's rite as such – he specifically *instructs* the leper to fulfill the ritual obligations of the Torah.

Crispin Fletcher-Louis argues that Jesus's act of declaring the leper clean is a priestly act.[45] Jesus would here be identifying himself as a priestly figure. Yet if Jesus's intention was to reveal a priestly identity for himself, it would seem odd that he still orders the man to go to the priest to be declared clean.

Finally, it is especially significant that, like the teaching in the Sermon on the Mount, *the pericope suggests that Jesus's eschatological program does not rule out the validity of ritual worship*. While healing was not necessarily viewed as an eschatological activity, Jesus's healings in Matthew are specifically seen as pointing to the dawning of the eschatological age in him (cf. Matt 11:5; cf. also Matt 9:27–31; 12:23; 15:21–28; 20:29–34). According to the story, then, the age to come includes a cultic dimension.

---

[43] Daniel M. Gurtner, *The Torn Veil: Matthew's Exposition of the Death of Jesus*, SNTSMS 139 (Cambridge: Cambridge University Press, 2007), 104; Ernst Lohmeyer, *Lord of the Temple*, trans. Stewart Todd (Richmond: John Knox Press, 1962 [orig. 1942]), 25–26.

[44] See the other possible solutions surveyed by Hendrik van der Loos, *The Miracles of Jesus* (Leiden: Brill, 1965), 487–489.

[45] Crispin Fletcher-Louis, "Jesus as the High Priestly Messiah: Part 2," *JSHJ* 5/1 (2006): 64.

The Healing of the Paralytic (Matt 9:1–8)

The story of the healing of the paralytic has sometimes been regarded as relevant for understanding Jesus's estimation of the cult. Within the Synoptic Gospels, the purpose of the miracle is unmistakable – it demonstrates that Jesus has the authority to forgive sins:

> And behold, they brought to him a paralytic lying on a stretcher. And when Jesus saw their faith, he said to the paralytic, "Take heart, child, your sins are forgiven [*aphientai sou hai hamartiai*]." And behold, some of the scribes said in themselves [*en heautois*], "This man is blaspheming." But Jesus, knowing their thoughts, said, "Why do you think evil in your hearts? For which is easier to say, 'Your sins are forgiven [*Aphientai sou hai hamartiai*],' or to say, 'Rise up and walk'? But in order that you may know that the Son of Man has authority on earth to forgive sins [*exousian echei ho huios tou anthrōpou epi tēs gēs aphienai hamartias*]," he said to the paralytic, "Rise, pick up your stretcher, and go to your home." And he rose up and went to his home. But when the crowds saw this, they were afraid and glorified God, who had given such authority to men. (Matthew 9:2–8)

At the heart of this episode is the controversy over Jesus's claim to pardon sin. Some treatments downplay this feature of the story.[46] The scribes objection that Jesus has blasphemed is frequently glossed over by commentators who marshal evidence from other texts to show that divine agents could announce the forgiveness of sins. Yet such readings ignore a major aspect of the story – Jesus's declaration is received with utter amazement. Furthermore, none of the texts often invoked as precedents offer a precise parallel to what happens with Jesus.[47] Davies and Allison put it well: "Jesus has taken to himself a divine prerogative. He has made himself out to be more than an intermediary. He has acted not as a channel of forgiveness but as its source (cf. Jn 10:33)."[48]

Many, however, have viewed the story as relating an anti-temple polemic.[49] Since the Torah repeatedly associates atonement of sin with

---

[46] For an overview of different treatments, see Beniamin Pascut, *Redescribing Jesus's Divinity Through a Social Science Theory: An Interdisciplinary Analysis of Forgiveness and Divine Identity in Ancient Judaism and Mark 2:1–12*, WUNT 2/438 (Tübingen: Mohr Siebeck, 2017), 3–9.

[47] For an overview of different treatments, see Pascut, *Redescribing Jesus's Divinity Through a Social Science Theory*, 129–153.

[48] Davies and Allison, *Matthew*, 2:91.

[49] See, e.g., James D. G. Dunn, *Jesus Remembered*, vol. 1 of *Christianity in the Making* (Grand Rapids: Eerdmans, 2003), 787; Eric Broadhead, "Christology as Polemic and Apologetic: The Priestly Portrait of Jesus in Mark," *JSNT* 47 (1992): 27; Ernst Lohmeyer, *Das Evangelium nach Markus*, KEK I/2 (Göttingen: Vandenhoeck & Ruprecht, 1937), 53.

the priests' activity in the temple cult,[50] some have interpreted the story as suggesting Jesus's usurpation of priestly authority.[51] The charge of blasphemy is seen as resulting from Jesus's apparent insult to the priests; Jesus assumes their role. Yet this reading overlooks two crucial problems.

First, there is no evidence that announcing the forgiveness of sins was solely a priestly task. The remittance of sins is declared apart from temple worship in other texts. For example, the prophet Nathan pronounces David's sins forgiven apart from a priestly context (2 Sam 12:13). Nowhere does the prophet imply that he must go to the priests or to the temple to ratify this. Other examples could also be given.[52]

Second, to insist that the point of the story is to indicate Jesus's anti-temple attitude ignores its overall thrust. Jesus specifically claims authority as the Son of Man to forgive sins "on earth [*epi tēs gēs*]," suggesting his authority relates to his heavenly identity. As others have shown, Jesus's role as the Son of Man in Matthew should be understood against Jewish apocalyptic traditions in which the figure is portrayed as suprahuman.[53] This is a compelling reading since Matthew elsewhere indicates that Jesus is to be identified with the God of Israel. For example, the double vocative, "Lord, Lord [*kyrie, kyrie*]," is applied to Jesus in the Sermon on the Mount (Matt 7:21). As Jason Staples has shown, this expression always represents an allusion to the Tetragrammaton in the Septuagint.[54] In places where the Hebrew has "Adonai Yʜᴡʜ," the Septuagint has *kyrie, kyrie* (cf., e.g., Deut 3:24; Ps 108:21 LXX [109:21 MT]; Ezek 37:21). That Matthew has this divine meaning in mind is supported by another element attested in the story of the paralytic's healing: Jesus knows his interlocutors' inner thoughts (Matt 9:4). Davies and Allison remark: "So just as Jesus is like God in that he has the power to forgive sins (9:6), so is he like God in that he knows what people think in their hearts (cf. 1 Sam 16:7; Jer 11:20; Ps. Sol. 14:8; etc.)."[55]

---

[50] Lev 4:20, 26, 31, 35; 5:10, 13, 16, 18; 6:7; 19:22; Num 15:25, 28.

[51] See Sanders, *Jesus and Judaism*, 240; Marcus, *Mark*, 1:216; Dunn, *Jesus Remembered*, 787–788; Edwin K. Broadhead, *Naming Jesus: Titular Christology in the Gospel of Mark*, JSNTSup 175 (Sheffield: Sheffield Academic Press, 1999), 69–70.

[52] See Tobias Hägerland, *Jesus and the Forgiveness of Sins: An Aspect of His Prophetic Mission*, SNTSMS 150 (Cambridge: Cambridge University Press, 2011), 133–142; Daniel Johansson, "'Who Can Forgive Sins but God Alone?' Human and Angelic Agents and Divine Forgiveness in Early Judaism," *JSNT* 33, 4 (2011): 351–374.

[53] See, e.g., Hägerland, *Jesus and the Forgiveness of Sins*, 171–177; Leslie W. Walck, *The Son of Man in the Parables of Enoch and in Matthew*, JCT 9 (New York: T&T Clark, 2011).

[54] Jason Staples, "'Lord, Lᴏʀᴅ': Jesus as Yʜᴡʜ in Matthew and Luke," *NTS* 64 (2018): 1–19.

[55] Davies and Allison, *Matthew*, 2:92.

Other features of Matthew's narrative can also be seen as reinforcing the divine identity of Jesus. For example, Joshua Leim analyzes the use of *proskyneō* in the account of the paralytic's healing, looking at, among other things, Matthew's redaction of Mark.[56] Though the word is often used of merely human figures (e.g., 1 Chr 2:13 LXX), Leim points out that it is necessary to read the term within the specific context of Matthew's narrative. As he shows, a conundrum is introduced by the scene in Matthew 4: when the devil asks Jesus to "worship [*proskynēsēs*]" him, Jesus protests by quoting from the Shema: "You shall *worship* the Lord your God [*kyrion ton theon sou proskynēseis*]" (Matt 4:10). Yet Jesus has already been the object of "worship" in the story of the magi (cf. Matt 2:11: *prosekynēsan*). As the story goes on, Jesus continues to be the object of worship in other various contexts.[57] Something more than Jesus's royal role seems to be in view.

A scene in Matthew 14 stands out. In this chapter, Jesus exercises a "unique prerogative of YHWH," namely, walking on the water (cf. Matt 14:25–26; Job 9:8; Ps 77:19; Isa 43:16; Hab 3:15; 4Q169 1+2:1–3).[58] Other aspects of the story also suggest Jesus is being placed in the position usually assumed by YHWH: Jesus is the subject of a cry for salvation (cf. Matt 14:30; 143:7, 9–10), he extends a saving "hand" (cf. Matt 14:31; Exod 7:5; Ps 143:7 LXX), and he stills the storm (Matt 14:32; Ps 89:9; 107:29). Keeping in mind the preceding point that "Lord, Lord [*kyrie, kyrie*]" evokes the divine name in the Septuagint and that it is applied to Jesus in the Sermon on the Mount (Matt 7:21), Peter's use of "Lord [*kyrios*]" in Matthew 14 is not insignificant. Its use here is suggestive of the Greek version of Psalm 69 (Ps 68 LXX), a psalm that many have detected in Matthew's passion narrative (cf. Matt 27:34, 48= Ps 68:22 LXX; Matt 27:44= Ps 68:21 LXX):[59]

Matthew 14:22–33	Psalm 68 LXX (Psalm 69 MT)
Jesus walking on the "*sea*" (*thalassa*) (Matt 14:25)	The psalmist is in the "*sea*" (*thalassa*) (Ps 68:2 LXX)
Jesus/Peter walks on "*waters*" (*hydōr*) (Matt 14:28–29)	The psalmist is in the "*waters*" (*hydōr*) (Ps 68:1 LXX)
Peter "*sinks*" (*kantapontizō*) (Matt 14:30)	The psalmist "*sinks*" (*kantapontizō*) (Ps 68:3 LXX)

[56] Joshua E. Leim, *Matthew's Theological Grammar: The Father and the Son*, WUNT 2/402 (Tübingen: Mohr Siebeck, 2015).

[57] Leim, *Matthew's Theological Grammar*, 4.

[58] Leim, *Matthew's Theological Grammar*, 129.

[59] Davies and Allison, *Matthew*, 3:608–609; Luz, *Matthew*, 3:530.

Peter cries out to Jesus,	The psalmist cries out to YHWH,
"*Lord* [*kyrie*]"	"*Lord, Lord* [*kyrie, kyrie*]"
(Matt 14:30)	(Ps 68:7 LXX)
"*Save me* [*sōson me*]"	"*Save me* [*sōson me*]"
(Matt 14:30)	(Ps 68:2, 15 LXX)

Given the psalm's use in Matthew's Passion Narrative, it is difficult to insist that the evangelist was unaware of these parallels. Moreover, since they place Jesus in the position of the Lord God, it is hard to think that Jesus's expression, "It is I [*egō eimi*]" (Matt 14:27), has no connection to YHWH's use of the expression in the story of the burning bush (Exod 3:14 LXX; cf. Isa 43:10 LXX). With these potential parallels in place, the story's climactic scene is stunning: the disciples "worship [*prosekynēsan*]" Jesus (Matt 14:33). This is especially remarkable against the backdrop of Jesus's words to the devil in Matthew 4, where worship seems reserved for God.[60] This also converges with Jesus's use of "Lord, Lord [*kyrie, kyrie*]" in reference to himself in the Sermon on the Mount (Matt 7:21). Staples concludes that Matthew's use of the phrase amounts "to calling him [=Jesus] God, a figure to be obeyed and worshiped alongside God the father."[61]

The foregoing discussion raises questions about Matthew's view of God and, in particular, Jesus's relationship with the Father. A crucial passage in this regard is found in Matthew 11:

At that time Jesus answered and said, "I thank you, *Father*, Lord of heaven and earth, because you have hidden these things from the wise and understanding, and have revealed [*apekalypsas*] them to infants. Yes, Father, for so it was pleasing before you. All things have been handed over to me by *my Father* [*tou patros mou*], and *no one knows the Son, but the Father; and no one knows the Father, except the Son, and anyone to whom the Son wills to reveal* [*apokalypsai*] *him.*" (Matthew 11:25–27)

Elsewhere in Matthew, Jesus speaks to the disciples of "your Father" (Matt 5:16, 45, 48; 6:1, 4, 6; etc.), instructing them to address God as

---

[60] J. R. Daniel Kirk (*A Man Attested by God: The Human Jesus of the Synoptic Gospels* [Grand Rapids: Eerdmans, 2016], 252) cites 1 Chr 29:20 as an analogue for the imagery in Matthew but ignores the dynamic created by Matt 4:9 as well as other features of Matthew's narrative insisting that Jesus is a human *rather* than divine figure in the Gospel (374–375). This, however, seems to ignore aspects of Matthew's Christology such as Matt 11:25–27 and the application of *kyrios, kyrios* to Jesus in Matt 7:21, which do not have precedent in royal ideology. Likewise, see the treatment on the parallel account of the temptation narrative in Luke in Amy-Jill Levine and Ben Witherington III, *Luke*, NCBC (Cambridge: Cambridge University Press, 2018), 111: "Luke has not told the reader that Jesus *is* God, but all the hints are there."

[61] Staples, "'Lord, LORD'," 19.

"*our* Father [*pater hēmōn*]" (Matt 6:9). In Matt 11:27, however, Jesus uses the language of "my Father." Jesus, therefore, possesses divine sonship in an utterly unique way. John Meier writes:

> One sees in 11:27 the central conception about the Father and the Son from which all of Mt's further statements about "Son of God" and "Son of Man" proceed. There is a mutual knowledge between Father and Son which puts them on a level of equality (cf. 28:19). It therefore belongs to the very nature of Jesus to possess a transcendent, *divine sonship, which infinitely exceeds that adoptive sonship he grants as a grace to his disciples* ... It is precisely to share in his relationship with the Father that Jesus invites his disciples in vv. 28–30.[62]

Meier goes on to see significance in Jesus's instructions on the formula for baptism at the end of the Gospel: "baptizing them in the name of the Father and of the Son and of the Holy Spirit" (Matt 28:19). Meier writes:

> one could hardly imagine a more forceful proclamation of Christ's divinity—and, incidentally, of the Spirit's distinct personality—than this listing together, on a level of equality, of Father, Son, and Spirit. One does not baptize people in the name of a divine person, a holy creature, and an impersonal divine force.[63]

In addition, Leim concludes, "Matthew's *theo*logical grammar is radically reshaped... Matthew's narrative requires us to relearn how to say *theos.*"[64] Amy-Jill Levine similarly concludes that Matthew has "changed the image of the deity," maintaining that for Matthew it involves "something that looks like bitheism."[65] The major take-away is this: divine identity is somehow being *reconfigured* to include Jesus. It is not as if Matthew is trying to fit Jesus into a prefabricated concept of God; his understanding of God seems to be expanded in light of Jesus's revelation.

To be sure, Matthew does not use the later language of ecclesiastical councils. The evangelist never resolves the tension of how Jesus is "Lord" (*kyrios*) and receives worship (*proskynesis*) with the Shema's affirmation of the one Y HWH with a neat dogmatic definition. The matter of how to understand Jesus's relationship with the Father is left mysteriously unexplained. Reductive attempts to resolve it by appealing to terms used to explain Jewish texts – for example, "divine agency" – fail to capture Matthew's message, which seems to be that the divine revelation that comes in Jesus bursts the bounds of what "flesh and blood" perceives (Matt 16:17) and the understanding of the wise (cf. Matt 11:25).

---

[62] John P. Meier, *Matthew*, NTM 3 (Wilmington: Michael Glazier, 1980), 127.
[63] Meier, *Matthew*, 371.
[64] Leim, *Matthew's Theological Grammar*, 14.
[65] Levine, "Concluding Reflections," 452.

The preceding discussion leads to the following conclusion: to attribute the charge of blasphemy in Matthew's account of the healing of the paralytic to the notion that Jesus simply usurped the authority of the priests overlooks the larger message of the Gospel. Jesus is *never* accused of usurping the prerogatives of the priests; that idea is not present in the story of the paralytic's healing at all. Jesus is portrayed as doing something more stupendous, he shares in the prerogatives of the Lord God. It is this that leads to the charge of blasphemy. Attempting to locate here a polemic against the temple reads a controversy into the story that simply is not there. If the crowds thought priests enjoyed the authority Jesus apparently possesses, the end of the story makes little sense: "they glorified God, who had given such authority to men" (Matt 9:8). The blasphemy charge flows from the perception that Jesus claims to do something that is understood in Matthew to be *unprecedented*. Yet what they do not know, the reader does: Jesus reads hearts, and walks on water – he acts as "God with us" (Matt 1:23).

"I Desire Mercy, and Not Sacrifice" (Matt 9:13; 12:7)

In Matthew, Jesus twice affirms a line from the book of Hosea: "But go and learn what this means, 'I desire mercy, and not sacrifice'" (Hos 6:6; cf. Matt 9:13; Matt 12:7). The verse employs a Hebraic idiom that expresses a comparative contrast rather than a strict antithetical negation. The declaration is therefore best understood as indicating: "I desire mercy *more* than sacrifice."[66] Not only is this the likely sense of the original passage,[67] Luz points out that this is how the Targum and other Jewish sources interpret Hosea's words.[68] To suggest that Jesus's quotation of Hosea entails the abrogation of all sacrifice not only disregards the way Jewish audiences would have heard the saying, but such a reading also ignores depictions of Jesus's reverence for the cult elsewhere in the Gospel. The point being made is that God rejects the sacrifices of those who do not show mercy to others; a lesson that ties in with other Matthean texts (Matt 5:23–24; 6:12, 14–15).

---

[66] See, e.g., Luz, *Matthew*, 2:34; Regev, *The Temple in Early Christianity*, 136–137; Gurtner, *Torn Veil*, 105–106.

[67] See, e.g., Francis I. Andersen and David Noel Freedman, *Hosea: A New Translation with Introduction and Commentary*, AYB 24 (New Haven: Yale University Press, 2008), 430; Douglas Stuart, *Hosea-Jonah*, WBC 31 (Dallas: Word, Incorporated, 1987), 110.

[68] Luz, *Matthew*, 2:34.

Jesus's use of Hosea 6 is not attested in Mark and Luke, however, there is a tradition reported in Mark that is worth mentioning here. In Mark 12, Jesus commends a scribe for his statement that loving God and neighbor "is more than all the whole burnt offerings and sacrifices" (Mark 12:33). Again, this should not be taken as implying the wholesale rejection of sacrificial worship. If that were the case, aspects of Mark's narrative, such as Jesus's instructions to the leper to offer sacrifice (Mark 1:40–45), would make no sense. The rabbis likewise affirmed that loving God and neighbor was more important than sacrificial offerings without implying that the temple cult had been nullified.[69]

"Something Greater Than the Temple Is Here" (Matt 12:6)

In Matthew 12, Jesus defends his disciples' act of plucking grain on the Sabbath by appealing to the story of David eating the bread of the presence (1 Samuel 21:1–9). While Matthew's account seems dependent on Mark's Gospel, it does include a statement from Jesus that is not attested in the Markan or Lukan versions: "Or have you not read in the law that on the sabbath the priests in the temple profane the sabbath [*to sabbaton bebēlousin*], and are guiltless [*anaitioi eisin*]?" (Matt 12:5). As commentators regularly note, the logion likely refers to the regulations in Numbers (Num 28:9–10; cf. 11Q19 13:17), which directs the priests to offer sacrifices on the Sabbath.[70] Jesus then makes yet another statement unique to Matthew: "Something greater than the temple is here [*tou hierou meizon estin hōde*]" (Matt 12:6). Do any of these sayings suggest Jesus rejects the temple? The answer is, no.

First, Jesus appeals to the temple cult as a basis for what his disciples are doing. Far from rejecting cultic worship, Jesus's argument presupposes that priestly service is not only acceptable to God, but that it also takes precedence over Sabbath obligations. Second, Jesus's statement that something greater than the temple is present need not imply a repudiation of the sanctuary. For Jesus's saying to have any force whatsoever, the temple's holiness would have to be assumed.[71] Third, to interpret the story as a rejection of the temple's validity would be to read too much into it. Such an interpretation would make little sense of the statements made by Jesus elsewhere in Matthew that endorse the sanctuary's rites

---

[69] See Regev, *The Temple in Early Christianity*, 113.
[70] See, e.g., Davies and Allison, *Matthew*, 2:314.
[71] See, e.g., Regev, *The Temple in Early Christianity*, 138–139; Keener, *Matthew*, 299.

and uphold its holiness (Matt 5:23–24; 23:16–22). Finally, claiming to be greater than the temple is not the same thing as saying that its holiness has been voided.

Jesus and the Temple Tax (Matt 17:24–27)

Another passage of importance in any investigation of Jesus's attitude toward the cult in Matthew is found in Matthew 17:

Now when they came into Capernaum, the ones who collected the double drachma [*hoi ta didrachma lambanontes*] came to Peter, and said, "Does your teacher not pay the double drachma [*didrachma*]?" He said, "Yes." And when he came into the house, Jesus spoke to him first, saying, "What do you think, Simon? From whom do the kings of the earth take tolls or taxes? From their own sons, or from others [*tōn huiōn autōn ē apo tōn allotriōn*]? And when he said, "From others," Jesus said to him, "Then the sons are free [*eleutheroi eisin hoi huioi*]. But in order that we not give offense to them, go out to the sea, and cast a hook, and take up the first fish that comes up, and when you open its mouth, you will find a coin worth four drachmas [*statēra*]: take that, and give it to them for me and for you." (Matthew 17:24–27)

At the center of the story is a question about a tax. Because Jesus goes on to speak of "kings of the earth," some have understood it to involve some sort of civic toll.[72] Yet support for this reading is lacking.[73] The language better matches the description of the half-shekel temple tax.[74] Most scholars, therefore, believe it is this institution that is in view.[75]

---

[72] See R. J. Cassidy, "Matthew 17:24–27: A Word on Civil Taxes," *CBQ* 41 (1979): 572–573; A. N. Sherwin-White, *Roman Society and Roman Law in the New Testament* (Oxford: Clarendon Press, 1963), 126; David Hill, *The Gospel of Matthew*, NCB (London: Oliphants, 1972), 272; Rolf Walker, *Die Heilsgeschichte im ersten Evangelium*, FRLANT 91 (Göttingen: Vandenhoeck & Ruprecht, 1967), 102–103.

[73] See, e.g., Davies and Allison, *Matthew*, 1:738–740; William Horbury, "The Temple Tax," in *Jesus and the Politics of His Day*, ed. Ernst Bammel and C. F. D. Moule (Cambridge: Cambridge University Press, 1984), 271–272; David E. Garland, "Matthew's Understanding of the Temple Tax," in *Treasures New and Old: Contributions to Matthean Studies*, SBLSS 1, ed. David R. Bauer and Mark A. Powell (Atlanta: Scholars Press, 1996), 87–88.

[74] See Josephus, *Ant.* 18.312–313; *J.W.* 6.218; Philo, *Spec. leg.* 1.76–77; *Her.* 186; 4Q159 (4QOrd^a) 1 2:7; m. Šeqal. 1–2; Cicero, *Pro Flacco* 168; Seutonius, *Dom.* 12.2.

[75] See, e.g., Davies and Allison, *Matthew*, 1:740; Mikael Tellbe, "The Temple Tax as Pre-70 C.E. Identity Marker," in *The Formation of the Early Church*, ed. Jostein Ådna, WUNT 183 (Tübingen: Mohr Siebeck, 2005), 26; Steven M. Bryan, *Jesus and Israel's Traditions of Judgement and Restoration*, SNTSMS 117 (Cambridge: Cambridge University Press, 2002), 225–259.

The source-text for the temple tax was located in the Torah (cf. Exod 30:11–16).[76] References to it appear in other Jewish texts as well.[77] The Qumran community apparently opposed the annual payment of this toll, arguing that it should be paid only once in a person's lifetime (4Q159 [4QOrdinances^a]). Josephus and Philo report that there was widespread acceptance of the tax.[78] Josephus even tells us that it was one of the primary sources of the temple's revenue.[79] The Mishnah indicates that objections were raised to it (m. Šeqal 1:2), though whether these accounts are reliable is debated.[80] Either way, its importance was so great that it appears to have become a kind of identity marker for Jewish ethnicity in the ancient world.[81] After the destruction of the temple, the Romans still mandated payment of the tax by the Jewish population of the empire to finance the temple of Jupiter (the *fiscus Iudaicus*), which was built on the Jerusalem temple mount.[82] Yet as Luz observes, given the logic of Jesus's teaching, it is "out of the question" that the story is intended to address this later situation.[83]

The tax was apparently seen as having a cultic value.[84] It was especially associated with the Tamid sacrifice, which involved the burnt offering of a lamb twice a day (Exod 29:38–42; Num 28:3–8; m. Tam. 3:3, 5, etc.). The rite was associated with atonement (Jub. 6:14; 50:11; t. Šeqal. 1:6) and it seems some thought that Jews participated in its atoning effects through the payment of the tax (Philo, *Spec.* 177; *Her.* 186; b. B. Bat. 9a). However, one must be careful to recognize that the temple tax was not exclusively associated with the Tamid.[85]

---

[76] See Philo, *Her.* 186; *Spec.* 1.77; b. Meg. 29b and t. Šeqal. 1.6. See the classic study by Jacob Liver, "The Half-Shekal Offering in Biblical and Post-biblical Literature," *HTR* 3 (1963): 173–198.

[77] 2 Kgs 12:4–16; 2 Chr 24:4–16; Neh 10:32.

[78] Josephus, *Ant.* 18.312–313; Philo, *Spec.* 1.76–77.

[79] Josephus, *Ant.* 14.110.

[80] See E. P. Sanders, *Judaism: Practice and Belief, 63 B.C.E.–66 C.E.* London: SCM Press, 1992, 156, 513n.16; John M. G. Barclay, *Jews in the Mediterranean Diaspora: From Alexander to Trajan (323 B.C.E.–117 C.E.)* (Edinburgh: T&T Clark, 1996), 417–418; E. Mary Smallwood, *The Jews under Roman Rule: From Pompey to Diocletian: A Study in Political Relations*, 2nd ed., SJLA 20 (Leiden: Brill, 1981), 124–125.

[81] For further discussion see Tellbe, "The Temple Tax," 19–44 building on the work of identity-markers in Shaye J. D. Cohen, "'Those Who Say They Are Jews and Are Not': How Do You Know a Jew in Antiquity When You See One?," in *Diasporas in Antiquity*, ed. S. J. D. Cohen and E. S. Frerich, BJS 288 (Atlanta: Scholars Press, 1993), 1–45.

[82] Josephus, *J.W.* 7.218; Dio Cassius 66.7.2; Suetonius, *Dom.* 12.

[83] Luz, *Matthew*, 3:415.

[84] See Jostein Ådna, "Jesus and the Temple," in *Handbook for the Study of the Historical Jesus*, 4 vols., ed. Tom Holmén and Stanley E. Porter (Leiden: Brill, 2010), 3:2670.

[85] See Bryan, *Jesus and Israel's Traditions*, 215.

The pericope about the temple tax in Matthew can be neatly divided into two scenes. The meaning of the first is rather straightforward: Peter is asked if Jesus pays the tax (Matt 17:24–25a). In the second part, Jesus offers a teaching on the tax (Matt 17:25b–27). He begins by addressing Peter with a parable-like question. Jesus uses an analogy – just as the sons of the "kings of the earth" are not obligated to pay taxes to their father, neither does God require taxes of his children.[86] The saying draws on the well-established images of God as King and Father. Some believe Jesus rejected the notion of a temple tax on the grounds that it contradicts the Scriptures: since Israel enjoys the status of divine sonship: "the sons are free" (Matt 17:26).[87] Yet this reading ignores key features of the text.

Steven M. Bryan has made a cogent argument that Jesus's words should be read against the larger eschatological message of Jesus in Matthew.[88] While it is true that God was recognized as King and Father, these concepts were especially associated with the *eschatological age.* God's fatherhood and Israel's divine sonship, which is first and foremost associated with the Exodus (cf. Exod 4:22; Hos 11:1–4), are also tied to hopes for a new exodus (cf. Isa 63:10–12, 16–17; 64:8–12; Jer 31:7–9; Hos 1:10–11).[89] The emphasis on sonship in Matthew 17 would seem to be bound up with such traditions. In addition, it was also believed that God's role as King would only be fully revealed in the age to come (cf. Isa 52:3–7; Dan 2:44; Mic 4:5–8).[90] That such themes are important to Jesus in Matthew is attested, for example, in the Lord's Prayer (cf. Matt 6:9–15).

Context also suggests that we should read Jesus's teaching on the temple tax against an eschatological backdrop. The very next pericope includes a discussion about who will be the greatest "in the kingdom of

---

[86] Here we are in substantial agreement with Bryan's critique (*Jesus and Israel's Traditions,* 227) of Richard Bauckham's position ("The Coin in the Fish's Mouth," in *Gospel Perspectives, vol. 6: The Miracles of Jesus* [Sheffield: JSOT Press, 1986], 219–252).

[87] See, e.g., cf. David L. Turner, *Matthew,* BECNT (Grand Rapids: Baker Academic, 2008), 429; Luz, *Matthew,* 2:417–418; R. T. France, *The Gospel of Matthew,* NICNT (Grand Rapids: Eerdmans, 2007), 669; John Nolland, *The Gospel of Matthew,* NIGTC (Grand Rapids: Eerdmans, 2005), 726; Kim Huat Tan, *The Zion Traditions and the Aims of Jesus,* SNTSMS 91 (Cambridge: Cambridge University Press, 1997), 176; Horbury, "The Temple Tax," 283.

[88] Bryan, *Jesus and Israel's Traditions,* 225–229.

[89] See also Tob 13:1–5; 14:1–7; Tg. Ps 89:26–53; Brant Pitre, *Jesus, the Tribulation, and the End of the Exile: Restoration Eschatology and the Origin of the Atonement,* WUNT 2/204 (Tübingen: Mohr Siebeck, 2005), 138–140.

[90] For other texts and further discussion, see Bryan, *Jesus and Israel's Traditions,* 227; Jeanine K. Brown, *The Disciples in Narrative Perspective* (Leiden: Brill, 2002), 68.

heaven" (cf. Matt 18:1–4). Reading Jesus's teaching on the tax in light of this is encouraged by the observation that both involve concern about giving "offense" (Matt 17:27: *skandalisōmen*; Matt 18:6: *skandalon*). The same terminology reappears throughout Matt 18:6–9 in a context which focuses on eschatological judgment.

Jesus's use of the phrase "the kings of the earth [*hoi basileis tēs gēs*]" (Matt 17:25) is also suggestive of eschatological connections. The language surfaces in places where God's final victory over evil is envisioned.[91] In particular, a number of commentators hold that Jesus's teaching draws from Psalm 2, a passage that links the definitive triumph over the wicked with the elevation of a Davidic king (cf. Ps 2:1).[92] The psalm contains some significant points of contact with Jesus's teaching regarding the temple tax.

Psalm 2 highlights the divine *sonship* of the Davidide, who is identified as the Lord's "anointed" (MT: *mashiah*; LXX: *tou christou*), which of course corresponds to Jesus's emphasis on divine sonship in his teaching on the temple tax. Even more notable, however, is another parallel: in the Septuagint's version of the psalm, we find the precise phrase employed by Jesus – "the kings of the earth [*hoi basileis tēs gēs*]":

> The *kings of the earth* [*hoi basileis tēs gēs*] stood side by side, and the rulers gathered together, *against the Lord and his anointed* [*tou christou*]... The Lord said to me, "*My son you are, today I have begotten you. Ask of me, and I will give you the nations as your heritage, and as your possession the ends of the earth.* (Psalm 2:2a–b, 7–8 LXX; NETS)[93]

The Dead Sea Scrolls indicate that this psalm was interpreted eschatologically (4Q174 [4QFlorilegium] *frag.* 1, *col.* i, 21, 2:18–19).[94] A messianic reading of Psalm 2 is also attested in the Psalms of Solomon, 1 Enoch, 4

---

[91] See the LXX of Ps 2:2; 75:13; 88:28; 101:16; 137:4; 148:11; Isa 24:21; Ezek 27:33.

[92] See William G. Thompson, *Matthew's Advice to a Divided Community: Mt. 17,22–18,35*, AnBib 44 (Rome: Biblical Institute Press, 1970), 56; Hagner, *Matthew*, 2:212; Warren Carter, *Matthew and the Margins: A Socio-Political and Religious Reading* (London: T&T Clark, 2004), 74; Anthony J. Saldarini, *Matthew's Christian-Jewish Community* (Chicago: University of Chicago Press, 1994), 144.

[93] Quoted from Albert Pietersma and Benjamin G. Wright, eds., *A New English Translation of the Septuagint* (Oxford: Oxford University Press, 2007), 548.

[94] See George J. Brooke, *Exegesis at Qumran: 4QFlorilegium in Its Jewish Context* (JSOT-Sup 29; Sheffield: JSOT Press, 1985), 209; D. Goldsmith, "Acts 13:33–37: A Pesher on 2 Samuel 7," *JBL* 87 (1968): 321–324. Likewise, it may also account for the imagery of the begetting of eschatological anointed one described in 1Q28a 2:11. See Craig A. Evans, *Jesus and His Contemporaries: Comparative Studies* (Boston: Leiden, 2001), 97; Craig A. Evans, "Qumran's Messiah: How Important Is He?," in *Religion in the Dead Sea Scrolls*, ed. John J. Collins and Robert A. Kugler (Grand Rapids: Eerdmans, 2000), 146 n. 34.

Ezra, and rabbinic literature,[95] as well as in other New Testament texts.[96] The psalm's imagery fits well with the broader message of Matthew: as the psalm announces the victory of the eschatological Davidic king, the *christos*, Matthew depicts Jesus as the eschatological son of David, the *christos*, who brings about the definitive deliverance of God's people (Matt 1:21). Given the connections with the Davidic imagery in Psalm 2, Jesus would seem to be extending the prerogatives of David to his disciples.[97] Perhaps we are to think of Isaiah's eschatological vision, which describes how the covenant with David will be shared with all the people (cf. Isa 55:3). Either way, the teaching about the temple, therefore, appears related not only to eschatological motifs but also, in keeping with Matthew's general Davidic focus, to Davidic traditions in particular.

Yet, despite claiming an exemption from the tax, Jesus goes on to say that it should be paid in order "not to give offense to them [*mē skandalisōmen autous*]" (Matt 17:27). As others have noted, this suits Matthew's purpose: Jesus wants to avoid the impression that he rejects the validity of the Torah.[98] In this case, that entails concerns about his stance toward the temple. This itself is significant and we will return to it later. For now, let us make a more fundamental observation: Jesus's teaching that he and Peter are exempted from the tax cannot be taken to mean that Jesus condemned the temple's sacrificial worship altogether.[99] As many have posited, Jesus could have easily assumed that financing the temple could be achieved in ways other than a tax; for example, through voluntary offerings.[100]

A potentially relevant background text can be found in Ezekiel. After describing a kind of tithe that is expected only of the princes (cf. Ezek 47:9, 13–16),[101] Ezekiel's vision of the eschatological temple indicates that the eschatological royal leader, who is elsewhere clearly a Davidide (cf. Ezek 34:23–24; 37:24–25), will provide for sacrifices:

And *on the prince* shall be the requirement of the burnt offerings, grain offerings, and drink offerings at the feasts, the new moons, and the sabbaths, all

---

[95] Pss. Sol. 17:23–24 (Ps 2:9); 1 En. 46:5 (Ps 2:10–12); 1 En. 48:10 (Ps 2:2); 4 Ezra 13:35 (Ps 2:6–7); b. Sukkah 52a; Midr. Ps 2:9 [on Ps 2:7]).

[96] See Acts 4:25–26 (Ps 2:1–2); Acts 13:33 (Ps 2:7); Heb 1:5 (Ps 2:7); Rev 12:5 (Ps. 2:9).

[97] France, *Gospel of Matthew*, 669; Tellbe, "The Temple Tax," 28.

[98] See, e.g., Daniel M. Gurtner, "Matthew's Theology of the Temple and the 'Parting of the Ways,'" in *Built upon the Rock: Studies in the Gospel of Matthew*, ed. Daniel M. Gurtner and John Nolland (Grand Rapids: Eerdmans, 2008), 137.

[99] See, e.g., the sources in Gurtner, "Matthew's Theology of the Temple," 137.

[100] See, e.g., Luz, *Matthew*, 3:418; Davies and Allison, *Matthew*, 2:746; Bauckham, "The Coin in the Fish's Mouth," 223.

[101] See Walther Zimmerli, *Ezekiel*, trans. Ronald E. Clements, 2 vols., Hermeneia (Philadelphia: Fortress Press, 1979), 2:475–476.

the assemblies of the house of Israel: *he shall provide the sin offerings, grain offerings, the burnt offerings, and the peace offerings to make atonement for the house of Israel.* (Ezekiel 45:17)

This coheres well with our scene in Matthew 17, where Jesus, the Davidic messiah, takes care of Peter's responsibility for the temple tax. The fact that Matthew draws heavily from Ezekiel's portrait of the eschatological Davidic shepherd-king elsewhere[102] makes it difficult to think the parallel is unintended. The astute reader, noting connections to the book throughout the text, may assume that Jesus as the Davidide will provide the sacrifices of the future age. The conclusion of this story – Jesus's provision for the tax – would certainly reinforce this idea.

Whatever one thinks of the possible connection to Ezekiel, the crucial upshot for our discussion here is that we should not read the temple tax story as suggesting Jesus rejected the temple's worship. It seems that priests and Sadducees did not pay the tax (cf. m. Šeqal. 1:4; b. Menaḥ. 65a).[103] Of course, the historical reliability of these later sources may be questioned. For our purposes, however, their veracity is almost immaterial. The simple fact is, no one would use these traditions as evidence that priests and Sadducees rejected the validity of the cult. The Sadducees are said to have believed that the temple service should be supported through voluntary giving (b. Menaḥ 65a),[104] a position Jesus may have taken. In a Jewish context, then, not paying the tax would not necessarily signal rejection of the sanctuary's legitimacy.

"Behold, Your House Has Been Left to You Desolate" (Matt 23:38)

After issuing a blistering condemnation of the scribes and Pharisees in Matthew 23, Jesus announces, "Behold, your house has been left to you desolate [*idou aphietai hymin ho oikos hymōn erēmos*]" (Matt 23:38). Jostein Ådna refers to this saying as "the most outstanding negative tradition" regarding the temple in the gospels.[105] Likewise, Simon Joseph says, "A 'forsaken' temple is not one in which sacrifices are either efficacious or

---

[102] See, e.g., H. Daniel Zacharias, *Matthew's Presentation of the Son of David* (London: Bloomsbury, T&T Clark, 2017), 96–101; Young S. Chae, *Jesus as the Eschatological Davidic Shepherd*, WUNT 2/216 (Tübingen: Mohr Siebeck, 2006); John Paul Heil, "Ezekiel 34 and the Narrative Strategy of the Shepherd and Sheep Metaphor in Matthew," *CBQ* 55 (1993): 698–708.

[103] Liver, "Half-Shekel Offering," 189.

[104] Liver, "Half-Shekel Offering" 189.

[105] Ådna, "Jesus and the Temple," 3:2672.

capable of reconciling Israel and God."[106] Viewed as a free-floating logion, Joseph's view makes sense. However, when viewed in its Matthean context, this reading is not compelling.

To begin with, as we have seen, Jesus makes a clear statement affirming the holiness of the temple just a few verses earlier in the same chapter (cf. Matt 23:16–22). Is Matthew presenting a hopelessly contradictory Jesus? One might insist that Matthew's portrait is radically incoherent. This, however, is far from likely. Anders Runesson argues that Jesus's condemnation of the temple as "desolate" represents a pivotal point in the narrative; after this, Jesus announces in no uncertain terms that the temple will be destroyed (cf. Matt 24:2).[107]

Jesus's declaration that the temple is "desolate" precedes his own departure from it. In this, he – the one identified as "God with us" (Matt 1:23) – seems to prophetically act out the divine departure from the temple.[108] Daniel Gurtner rightly observes that divine abandonment is typically "a prelude to the city's destruction."[109] Runesson explains:

> Jesus's leaving the temple and walking to the Mount of Olives thus initiates the process of abandonment of the temple. Matthew's story leaves little doubt that the temple, as well as Jerusalem, will be destroyed, and that God leaves the temple before this happens.[110]

Runesson also shows that, after departing from the temple, Jesus moves to the Mount of Olives. In this, we have a parallel with a scene from Ezekiel. After hearing of Jerusalem's coming destruction, the prophet watches as the glory of the Lord leaves the city and takes its stance "on the mountain that is on the east side of the city" (Ezek 11:23).[111] Going on, Runesson is careful to describe Jesus's statement about the temple's desolation as "initiating" the process of divine abandonment. It is not yet a fait accompli. According to Runesson, God's presence quits the sanctuary when the temple veil is torn at the moment of Jesus's death (Matt 27:51).[112] While Runesson's analysis is insightful, certain features

---

[106] Simon J. Joseph, *Jesus and the Temple: Crucifixion in its Jewish Context*, SNTSMS 165 (Cambridge: Cambridge University Press, 2016), 105.

[107] Runesson, *Divine Wrath*, 58.

[108] See, e.g., Runesson, *Divine Wrath*, 127; Gurtner, *Torn Veil*, 119; David D. Kupp, *Matthew's Emmanuel: Divine Presence and God's People in the First Gospel*, SNTSMS 90 (Cambridge: Cambridge University Press, 1996), 93–94.

[109] Gurtner, *Torn Veil*, 118 citing Josephus, *J.W.* 5.9.3. §§412–413; 6.5.3 §§295–300; Tacitus, *Hist.* 5.13; 2 *Bar.* 8:2; 64:6–7; 4 *Bar.* 4:1.

[110] Runesson, *Divine Wrath*, 127.

[111] Runesson, *Divine Wrath*, 127.

[112] Runesson, *Divine Wrath*, 127.

of Matthew's narrative, however, suggest the temple is not yet abandoned by God at the moment of Jesus's death.

For one thing, immediately following the tearing of the temple veil, Matthew goes on to call Jerusalem "the holy city" (Matt 27:53). If Matthew's intention in narrating the torn veil is to highlight the Lord's departure from the temple, it would be excessively odd for him to go on a few verses later to define the city by its *sanctity*. Second, after calling the temple desolate, Jesus warns in the next chapter that those who live in Judea should flee once they see "the abomination of desolation [*to bdelygma tēs erēmōseōs*] spoken about by the prophet Daniel" (Matt 24:15). For Jesus, then, the desolation of the temple is a *future* event. Notably, in Daniel this language is repeatedly connected to the notion of the cessation of sacrifice (cf. Dan 9:26–27; 11:31; 12:11).[113] All of this would suggest that, for Matthew, the desolation of the temple is not simply identified with Jesus's death. It is worth considering that Luke appears to link Jesus's statement about the coming "desolation" of the temple to the days when gentile armies will surround Jerusalem (cf. Luke 21:20).

Another parallel in Luke is worth noting. In Luke 13, Jesus says that the temple has been "forsaken" (Luke 13:35: *aphietai*). Yet this does not appear to signify its delegitimization; even after this statement, Jesus goes on to instruct others to engage in sacrifice there (cf. Luke 17:14; 22:7–13). Furthermore, as we have already observed, the Gospel ends with a report that the disciples were "continually in the temple blessing God" (Luke 24:53). This would be a strange detail to include if Jesus's statement about the temple being forsaken was thought to mean the sanctuary had become invalid. Relevant here also is Acts of the Apostles, which builds on Luke's Gospel. Acts certainly does not take the statement in Luke 13 as indicating a complete rejection of the temple's life. The disciples not only continue to pray there (Acts 2:46; 3:1), they even participate in its cultic activity (Acts 21:17–26).

Jesus's statement in Matthew 23 that the temple is "desolate" and his departure from it, therefore, should not be taken as a rejection of its legitimacy. Rather, Jesus is portrayed as performing a prophetic action like those associated with Jeremiah and Ezekiel. In speaking of the temple as empty and then leaving it, Jesus pronounces and enacts what *will* take place – God's presence will vacate the sanctuary in anticipation of its demise.[114]

---

[113] See Pitre, *Jesus, the Tribulation, and the End of the Exile*, 303–309.
[114] See, e.g., Peter *Walker, Jesus and the Holy City: New Testament Perspectives on Jerusalem* (Grand Rapids: Eerdmans, 1996), 166.

That Jesus uses the present tense in describing the temple as desolate is not difficult to explain. According to Jewish traditions, the future is already seen by God (cf. Jub. 1:4). Prophetic oracles were understood as offering a glimpse into God's vision of history. Morna Hooker explains that the judgment oracles of the prophets reveal a "reality that lies beyond time and place, disclosing not simply events which will one day take place on earth, but the truth as it already exists in heaven."[115] Jesus's saying in Matthew 23 is best read along these lines. In calling the temple "desolate," Jesus uses a "prophetic present." What seals this reading is the fact that Jesus speaks of other future events in the present tense in Matthew. In Matthew 26, before the feast of Passover, he declares: "*the Son of Man is handed over* to be crucified [*ho huios tou anthrōpou paradidotai eis to staurōthēnai*]" (Matt 26:2).[116] Jesus's saying about the house being desolate, then, cannot be used as definitive evidence that he viewed the temple as void of God's presence. This conclusion is cemented by an analysis of a key scene in Matthew 26.

Jesus's Participation in the Passover (Matt 26:17–19)

There is a further detail in Matthew's narrative that makes it impossible to believe that Matthew 23 represents the moment Jesus suddenly repudiates the sanctity of the temple. In Matthew 26, Jesus is portrayed as celebrating a Passover meal. The implication of this for understanding Jesus's view of the temple is often underappreciated. Whatever one wishes to make of the apparent tension between the chronologies of the Synoptics and John,[117] there can be little doubt that, in Matthew, Jesus himself participates in a Passover meal. The evangelist describes how, at Jesus's direction, the disciples "prepared the Passover [*hētoimasan to pascha*]" (Matt 26:19). Though the Greek term *pascha* can be translated as "Passover meal," the noun was also often used to describe the paschal lamb *itself*. When Matthew says that the disciples "prepared the *pascha*" it is very likely that the evangelist means that the disciples were specifically preparing the Passover lamb.[118] Indeed, it would have constituted

[115] Morna D. Hooker, *The Signs of a Prophet: The Prophetic Actions of Jesus* (Harrisburg: Trinity Press International, 1997), 4. See also R. B. Y. Scott, *The Relevance of the Prophets* (New York: Macmillan Company, 1960), 98.

[116] See the discussion in Janice Capel Anderson, *Matthew's Narrative Web: Over, and Over, and Over Again*, JSNTSup 91 (Sheffield: JSOT Press, 1994), 167.

[117] For the most recent comprehensive discussion, see Pitre, *Jesus and the Last Supper*, 251–373.

[118] See the discussion in Pitre, *Jesus and the Last Supper*, 352–356.

a radical break with the Torah for Jesus to celebrate a Passover meal that did not consist of a lamb sacrificed in the temple.[119] Had Matthew intended to communicate that Jesus had done such a thing, he surely would have needed to make more explicit mention of it. The natural reading of Matthew 26, then, is that Jesus directs his disciples to participate in the temple cult.

Mark, Matthew's source, leaves little room for doubt about the meaning of *pascha*, linking the disciples' question about the preparation of it to the sacrificial offerings in the temple. While English translations such as the NRSV render the various appearances of *pascha* differently in their versions of Mark 14:12–16 (e.g., "Passover lamb," "Passover"), it is best to read the section as using the term with one referent throughout, namely, as referring to the Passover lamb itself. Here I provide a translation:

And on the first day of Unleavened Bread, when they killed *the Passover lamb* [*pascha*], his disciples said to him, "Where do you want us to go and *prepare* [*hetoimasōmen*] so that you may eat the *Passover lamb* [*pascha*]?" And he sent two of his disciples, and said to them, "Go into the city and you will meet a man carrying a jar of water; follow him. And where he enters, say to the householder, 'The teacher says, Where is the guest room where I may eat the *Passover lamb* [*pascha*] with my disciples?' And he will show you a large upper room furnished and *prepared* [*hetoimon*]: and there *prepare* [*hetoimasate*] for us." And the disciples went out and came into the city, and found everything just as he had told them, and they *prepared* [*hētoimasan*] the *Passover lamb* [*pascha*]. (Mark 14:12–16)

In its first appearance, the meaning of the term *pascha* is unmistakable – the context involves a reference to the sacrifice of the Passover lamb (*pascha*). To insist that the meaning of *pascha* suddenly changes throughout the passage so that the later appearances of the word do not refer to the Passover lamb is "contextually indefensible."[120] The *pascha* being "prepared" is the lamb. In fact, the work of "preparation" (*hetoimazō*) carried out by the disciples cannot refer to the room in general since Mark tells us that it had already been "prepared [*hetoimon*]" (Mark 14:15). The obvious meaning of the passage, then, is that the *lamb* is prepared in accord with the proper ritual requirements. There is no good reason to think Matthew departs from Mark's meaning and intends a different one in his report of the scene.

---

[119] See, e.g., Craig A. Evans, *Matthew*, NCBC (Cambridge: Cambridge University Press, 2012), 428–429. For the paschal character of the Last Supper in the Synoptics, see the discussion in Pitre, *Jesus and the Last Supper*, 315–324.

[120] See, e.g., Pitre, *Jesus and the Last Supper*, 291 (cf. 290–292).

As Paula Fredriksen notes, therefore, the scene implies that "at least one of Jesus's circle of disciples had been up to the temple to offer the lamb during the afternoon of the day of 14 Nisan. That would have been the only way to secure '*the* Passover', that is, the sacrificial meat at the ceremonial center of the meal."[121] Suffice it to say, Jesus's celebration of a Passover meal makes it untenable to hold that Jesus's saying about the house being desolate (Matt 23:38) involves him revoking his earlier statements endorsing participation in the cult. As in Mark, Jesus is remembered in Matthew as speaking about the temple's coming destruction. *Yet he never calls into question the validity of the temple's sacrificial worship.* As Daniel Gurtner remarks, "Matthew is positive towards the temple in general, affirming the validity of its sacrifices and the presence of God within it."[122]

IMPLICATIONS FOR THE HISTORICAL JESUS

Despite the fact that the general impression we gain from our sources is that Jesus recognized the validity of the cult, some have pointed to certain logia that are viewed as undermining this portrait. Our analysis here, however, has shown that anti-cultic interpretations of these passages are not persuasive. Aside from the traditions indicating that Jesus announced that the temple would be destroyed – which we will examine in greater detail later – *there is no unambiguous evidence that Jesus opposed cultic worship or the Jerusalem temple's sanctity.*

The Holiness of the Cult in Matthew

Matthew especially emphasizes Jesus's reverence for the temple cult. Among other things, Jesus directs others to offer temple sacrifice (Matt 5:23–24; 8:4; 26:17–19), he recognizes the priests' exemption from Sabbath rest (Matt 12:5), and he affirms the holiness of the sanctuary and its sacrifices (Matt 23:16–22). While Jesus foretells the temple's future desolation, the Gospel makes clear that Jesus still participated in its life and expected others to do so as well.

For Matthew, Jesus's endorsement of the temple seems bound up with the larger issue Matthew 5 seeks to address, namely, Jewish concerns about Jesus's relationship to the Torah. This leads to the conclusion that,

---

[121] Fredriksen, *When Christians Were Jews*, 39.
[122] Gurtner, *Torn Veil*, 99.

for the evangelist, *an anti-cultic Jesus would be viewed as an antinomian Jesus*. The same idea is operative in the episode involving the temple tax; Jesus tells Peter to pay the tax because not doing so might give "offense" (Matt 17:27). Jesus's direction to the leper to offer sacrifice may also be related to this theme (Matt 8:4). Others were apparently looking for reasons to accuse Jesus of being hostile to the sanctuary, as the scene of his interrogation before the Sanhedrin confirms (Matt 26:59–61).

Matthew's interest in confirming Jesus's reverence for the temple is significant. After all, we know that there were Jews who, despite being devoted to the Torah, withdrew from the Jerusalem temple. Matthew, however, does not share that perspective. The implications of this should not be overlooked – Matthew appears unconcerned with appealing to Jews who believed the temple was illegitimate. It is not as if those who took such a position were deemed criminals. We have no evidence that Essenes were rounded up and punished for failing to acknowledge the cult's validity. Rejecting the legitimacy of the Herodian sanctuary was a live option for Jews. *Yet Matthew rejects that perspective.*

That Matthew cares little for the position of the Essenes is confirmed by Jesus's endorsement of the Pharisees' teaching authority. While he goes on to excoriate them for hypocrisy, his support for their doctrine is forceful: "The scribes and the Pharisees sit on Moses's seat. Therefore, *do and observe whatever they tell you*" (Matt 23:2–3). In addition, Matthew presents Jesus as suggesting that no one in his hearing would have believed it would be wrong to rescue an animal on the Sabbath: "What man of you, if he has one sheep and it falls into a pit on the sabbath, will not lay hold of it and lift it out?" (Matt 12:11). Yet we know that there were some Jews in the first century who took the precise position that Jesus assumes all in his hearing would oppose. The Damascus Document reads: "No one should help an animal give birth on the sabbath day ... And if it falls into a well or a pit, he should not take it out on the sabbath" (CD-A 11:13–14).[123] Matthew is writing to a Jewish audience, but this audience does not seem to include those associated with the community described in the Qumran documents, a community that rejected the temple's validity.

Perhaps Matthew's audience was unique. Perhaps Essenes joined other communities who accepted Jesus. This scenario should be viewed

---

[123] Unless otherwise noted, translations from the Dead Sea Scrolls are taken from Florentino García Martínez and Eibert J. C. Tigchelaar, *The Dead Sea Scrolls Study Edition* [henceforth *DSSSE*], 2 vols. (Leiden: Brill, 1997, 1998). In this case, the translation is slightly adapted from 1:569.

as *possible* but not *probable*. Why? Because we have no evidence that
Jesus's earliest followers included individuals who rejected the temple's
legitimacy. In Luke and Acts, Jesus's early disciples continue to reverence the temple in the post-Easter period (cf. Luke 24:53; Acts 2:46; 3:1;
21:17–26; etc.). Furthermore, while the New Testament books contain
references to Pharisees and priests who joined the Jesus community (cf.
Phil 3:5; John 3:1; Acts 6:7; 15:5; 23:6; 26:5), we have no evidence that
Essenes joined their ranks. The suggestion made by some that Jesus's
relationship with the Essenes is hinted at by his directions that the disciples look for a man carrying a jar rest on the erroneous assumption
that this necessarily represented women's work (cf. Deut 29:10–11; Josh
9:21–27).[124]

If an un-Jewish Jesus is indeed an unhistorical Jesus, Matthew's overall presentation should be considered significant. If a Jewish believer in
Jesus like the evangelist felt the need to underscore Jesus's view of the
cult's sanctity, how probable is it that Jesus himself rejected it? Some
might insist that such traditions are due to later Jewish believers in Jesus
who felt the need to double-down on the validity of the temple cult, yet
this is based more on speculation rather than evidence. What we know
about Matthew suggests that Jesus appealed to those who embraced the
temple. The evidence from other sources like Luke and Acts offers further
corroboration for this conclusion. Here we can revisit the observations
of Paula Fredriksen and E. P. Sanders quoted at the beginning of this
chapter. Fredriksen points out that if Jesus taught that the temple had
been nullified, "his immediate followers completely missed his point."[125]
Likewise, Sanders insists that if Jesus really did reject the temple, "he
kept it secret from his disciples."[126]

The Temple in Jesus's Eschatological Program in Matthew

The First Gospel also suggests that Jesus's eschatological program itself
entailed a cultic dimension. As we will see in the next chapter, Matthew
alone depicts Jesus bringing his healing ministry *into the temple* (Matt
21:14). For Matthew, this is no minor detail. Jesus's healing ministry
is central to his messianic identity (cf. Matt 11:4–5). Furthermore, in

---

[124] See the fuller evidence discussed in Marcus, *Mark*, 2:945; Davies and Allison, *Matthew*,
       3:457n.15.
[125] Fredriksen, *Jesus of Nazareth*, 209.
[126] Sanders, *Jesus and Judaism*, 67.

Matthew 5, Jesus's teaching that he has come to bring eschatological fulfillment to the law and prophets (Matt 5:17–20) is followed by a lesson on
how to offer acceptable temple sacrifice (cf. Matt 5:23–24). In Matthew
17, Jesus links the temple tax to eschatological themes and seems to tie
his teaching about it to his role as the eschatological Davidide by using
language from Psalm 2 (Matt 17:24–27). In all of this, Matthew seems to
amplify what we find in the other canonical Gospels.

   The other evangelists also view Jesus's miracles as evidence of his
eschatological role (e.g., Luke 7:22; Mark 2:1–12//Luke 5:17–26; John
6:14; 20:30–31; cf. John 7:31) and link them to the temple's life (e.g.,
Mark 1:44//Luke 5:14; Luke 17:14).[127] Likewise, as we will explore in
the following chapter, while Jesus applies the judgment oracle of Jer 7:11
to the Jerusalem sanctuary, he also quotes from Isaiah's description of a
future eschatological temple (Matt 21:13//Mark 11:17//Luke 19:46; Isa
56:7). In this, Jesus seems to affirm a prophecy that envisions cultic worship in the eschatological age.

   That the temple would be restored after being rendered desolate is also
explicitly affirmed in apocalyptic works like Daniel, a work that seems
to have had special influence on Jesus's teaching. In Daniel 8, we read:

> And I heard a holy one speaking, and another holy one said to the one that was
> speaking, "For how long is this vision concerning the regular burnt offering,
> the transgression that makes desolate, and the giving over of the sanctuary and
> host to be trampled?" And he answered him, "For two thousand three hundred
> evenings and mornings. *Then the sanctuary shall be restored to its rightful state.*"
> (Daniel 8:13–14)

Daniel, like Jesus, speaks of the sanctuary being rendered "desolate."
Yet, for the prophet, this would not stand. The age to come would
include a restored temple. If Jesus was inspired by apocalyptic traditions like those found in Daniel, we might expect that he would not only
anticipate the temple becoming "desolate" – which we have seen that
he does in Matthew – but that he would also affirm that the eschaton
would involve temple realities. The evangelist's portrayal would seem to
confirm what we might expect – an apocalyptic Jesus would support the
place of acceptable sacrifice in the temple.

---

[127] Levine and Witherington, *Luke*, 205–206 observe that while nonmessianic figures also
     performed miracles, in Luke 7:22 there is an intertextual connection with Jesus's speech
     at the synagogue at Nazareth where he reads from Isaiah 61, a prophecy understood as
     referring to the messiah.

Yet perhaps the traditions of Jesus announcing the coming demise of the sanctuary should be dismissed as merely reflecting the post-temple situation. Or maybe they should be viewed as revealing that Jesus was, in actuality, anti-temple after all. Another possibility is that Jesus changed his mind about the validity of the temple at some point.[128] The next chapter will consider these matters in depth.

[128] See, e.g., Ådna, "Jesus and the Temple," 3:2674.

4

Jesus and the Destruction of the Temple

The conflict over the temple seems deeply implanted in the tradition, and that there was such a conflict would seem indisputable.

– E. P. Sanders[1]

Matthew is more concerned with the judgment theme than any other New Testament text.

– Anders Runesson[2]

"Exhibit A" in the case for an anti-cultic Jesus could very easily be the traditions that remember him as foretelling the temple's destruction. Should we not simply assume these aspects of the Jesus tradition owe their origin to the attempt to cast Jesus as a prophet aware of the future? If these memories do have some origin in Jesus's own teaching, would this not suggest that he rejected the Jerusalem temple's legitimacy? In this chapter, we will address these questions.

First, we will argue that the traditions indicating Jesus anticipated the temple's demise likely reflect an aspect of his historical ministry. As we shall see, such traditions are broadly attested and difficult to dismiss as the mere invention of the community. That Jesus made a prediction regarding the temple's future ruin makes sense considering his first-century Jewish context and the effects of his ministry, including, among other things, material in Paul.

---

[1] Sanders, *Jesus and Judaism*, 61.
[2] Runesson, *Divine Wrath*, 7.

Second, we will look at the way this particular aspect of the Jesus tradition is handled by Matthew, beginning with an analysis of one of the key episodes involving Jesus's temple activity: the so-called "temple cleansing" episode. This scene must be contextualized within Matthew who, as we shall see, connects Jesus's predictions of coming catastrophe to apocalyptic judgment.

Finally, we will look at some important considerations the First Gospel's portrait raises for Jesus research. Specifically, what our analysis will show is that – contrary to what might be expected – *Jesus's predictions of the temple's destruction need not be seen as implying his rejection of the temple's legitimacy.* Within a Jewish context, these two features of the tradition are not necessarily in tension. In particular, Matthew's emphasis on the apocalyptic element of Jesus's teaching likely broadly reflects Jesus's own emphases. This is significant – apocalyptic traditions frequently recognize that divine judgment will include the loss of the temple. At the same time, they also affirm the holiness of the temple and look forward to its restoration.

JESUS'S PREDICTIONS OF THE TEMPLE'S DESTRUCTION

That Jesus spoke of the coming ruin of the Jerusalem sanctuary is clearly attested in all four canonical gospels and the Gospel of Thomas.[3] Of course, closely associated with these oracles are the sayings in which Jesus speaks of a future devastation of Jerusalem. As is widely recognized, "Jerusalem" and "Mt. Zion" were often used interchangeably with the "temple."[4] The fall of the former would easily have been viewed as implying the demise of the latter (cf., e.g., Jer 50:28). Given the remarkable accuracy of these oracles, would it not seem more likely that these traditions emerged only in the post-70 period? Could they actually reflect some aspect of Jesus's teaching? Following the methodology outlined in the introduction, we will begin by looking at the broad shape of the tradition. We will then consider whether the general impressions made by our sources make sense in light of the Jewish situation of Jesus's day and given what we know about his effective history.

---

[3] Since the Fourth Gospel claims the saying in John 2:19 was meant to refer to Jesus's body, it is not "clearly" about the Jerusalem temple but see John 4:21–23.

[4] See David E. Aune and Eric Stewart, "Restoration in Jewish Apocalyptic Literature," in *Restoration: Old Testament, Jewish, and Christian Perspectives*, ed. James H. Scott, SJSJ 72 (Leiden: Brill, 2001), 163.

Recurrent Attestation

While it may be tempting to dismiss Jesus's predictions of the temple's coming destruction as *ex eventu* prophecies, there are good reasons to resist that conclusion. First, the notion that Jesus anticipated Jerusalem's demise is deeply ingrained in our sources. Consider the following catalogue of traditions.

Traditions Involving Jesus's Predictions of the Fall of the Temple/ Jerusalem

1. Jesus Pronounces Judgment Over Jerusalem
   (Matt 23:37–39//Luke 13:34–35 [Q?])
2. Jesus Appeals to Jeremiah's Oracle of the Temple's Destruction
   (Matt 21:12–13//Mark 11:15–19//Luke 19:45–46)
3. Jesus Predicts the Destruction of the Temple as He Leaves the Temple with the Disciples
   (Matt 24:1–2//Mark 13:1–2//Luke 21:5–6)
4. Jesus Warns Those in Judea Will Have to Flee
   (Matt 24:15–16//Mark 13:14//Luke 21:20–21)
5. Jesus Is Accused of Announcing the Temple's Destruction
   (Matt 26:61//Mark 14:58).
6. Bystanders at the Cross Say Jesus Spoke of the Temple's Destruction
   (Matt 27:40//Mark 15:29)
7. Jesus Weeps over Jerusalem
   (Luke 19:41–44)
8. Jesus Announces Jerusalem Will Be Trampled Under Foot
   (Luke 21:24)
9. Jesus Speaks of the Coming Desolation of Jerusalem on His Way to the Cross
   (Luke 23:28–31)
10. The Crowd is Shocked by Jesus's Words about Temple Destruction
    (John 2:19–20)
11. Jesus Indicates Worship at the Temple in Jerusalem Will Cease
    (John 4:21–23)
12. Jesus Announces He Will Destroy the Temple
    (Gos. Thom. §71)

This list could easily be further expanded. We have not included some material that is widely viewed as pointing forward to the Jewish war such as the Parable of the Marriage Banquet (Matt 22:2–13, esp. Matt 22:7),[5]

---

[5] See, e.g., Runesson, *Divine Wrath*, 127; Davies and Allison, *Matthew*, 3:197.

and the Cursing of the Fig Tree (Matt 21:18–22//Mark 11:12–14, 20–25; cf. Luke 221:29–33).[6] Yet even a minimalist approach produces an impressive array of texts.

To be clear, once again, my argument is not that all of the traditions in the preceding catalogue are "authentic." As explained earlier, establishing the reliability of any particular tradition is difficult. Nevertheless, logia indicating Jesus's perceptions of what was coming can be found throughout our sources, including the Synoptics, John, and Thomas. It seems this was no marginal feature of the early believers' recollection of Jesus's preaching. How can we best account for this?

For many, the most natural explanation of the data is that they reflect an aspect of Jesus's message. Consider some of the following statements from James D. G. Dunn, Tom Holmén, and Marcus Borg, who represent a wide spectrum of perspectives on Jesus:

According to the tradition, the key charge brought against Jesus was that he had threatened to destroy the Temple (Mark 14.58 parr.)... The core of the tradition is clear, as also its diverse elaboration in the different versions: Jesus's talk of destroying (*katalysai*) the temple. The case for recognizing historical memory enshrined here is surprisingly strong.[7]

There are altogether three different independent sources, Q, Mark, and Luke's special source, witnessing to the portent. It is also important to notice that the sources display at least two *different* predictions. The Q passage and Mark 13:1–2 (Luke 19:44) are not variations of one and the same saying but represent two vaticinations each conveying the idea of the future destruction of the Temple in their own way. It is hard to think that *both* types of prediction would have been fabricated without there being *any* point of departure in the teachings of Jesus.[8]

If Jesus did not prophesy about Jerusalem, then who was the insightful prophet in that generation who was responsible both for this concern and this use of the Hebrew Bible? Of course, the rhetorical question does not imply that the oracles contain the *ipsissima verba* Jesus, but it does imply that they reflect the *ipsissima vox* Jesus. Quite probably the Jesus movement and perhaps the evangelist reworked the language of the threats, but without an initial impulse from Jesus, it is difficult to account for their presence in the primitive tradition.[9]

---

[6] See, e.g., Lawrence M. Wills, "The Gospel According to Mark," in *The Jewish Annotated New Testament*, ed. Amy-Jill Levine and Marc Zvi Brettler, 2nd ed. (Oxford: Oxford University Press, 2017), 94; Marcus, *Mark*, 2:790; Davies and Allison, *Matthew*, 3:153–154; Joseph A. Fitzmyer, *The Gospel According to Luke*, 2 vols., AB 28–28A (Garden City: Doubleday, 1981, 1985), 2:1353.

[7] Dunn, *Jesus Remembered*, 631–632.

[8] Tom Holmén, *Jesus and Jewish Covenant Thinking*, BIS 55 (Leiden: Brill, 2001), 300.

[9] Marcus J. Borg, *Conflict, Holiness, and Politics in the Teachings of Jesus* (Harrisburg: Trinity Press International, 1998 [orig. 1984]), 203.

The last quotation from Borg is especially worth highlighting: if Jesus himself was not responsible for initiating this aspect of the tradition, one must posit that it emerged from someone else. Yet can we name a *more probable* source than Jesus for this feature of the tradition? Some have tried.

According to one view, the predictions of the temple's destruction were invented by the author of Mark.[10] The vast majority of scholars, however, have found this unlikely. Consider the charge made at Jesus's trial in Mark: "We heard him say, 'I will destroy this temple [*naon*] *made by hands*, and within three days I will build another *not made by hands*'" (Mark 14:58). Mark's discomfort with attributing this exact saying to Jesus is undeniable. He explicitly tells us that the witnesses "gave false testimony [*epseudomartyroun*]" (Mark 14:57). That being said, because Mark likely thinks the other charges and mocking derisions involved in Jesus's passion – such as the title "king of the Jews" – ironically profess a truth, he probably detects *some* truth in the charge concerning the temple. It is difficult to avoid the conclusion that the evangelist expects the reader to connect the charge about the temple to Jesus's resurrection. Up until this point in Mark's narrative, Jesus has repeatedly used the language of "three days" to refer to his future act of rising from the dead (cf. Mark 8:31; 9:31; 10:34). Indeed, when the Fourth Gospel repeats a similar saying (John 2:19), it emphasizes that *Jesus was talking about his resurrection and not the physical temple building* (John 2:21). Still, John makes it clear that the connection to the resurrection was only made *after* the Easter experience of the community. Likewise, Mark gives no indication that Jesus's original hearers connected the supposed saying of the false witnesses (Mark 14:58) to resurrection imagery. For them, the saying simply concerns the temple. The charge, therefore, indicates that Jesus's earlier prediction of the coming destruction of the temple (Mark 13:2) had become known outside Jesus's circle of disciples. Nevertheless, Mark's handling of their report indicates he is uncomfortable with the way it has been formulated. Perhaps this is because Jesus's earlier statements about the downfall of the sanctuary never involve the claim that he himself would destroy it.

Matthew's handling of this material also suggests it represented a tradition that required explanation. As in Mark, the accusation in Matthew is also best seen as attributed to the false witnesses (Matt 26:60). Like

---

[10] See, e.g., Burton L. Mack, *A Myth of Innocence: Mark and Christian Origins* (Philadelphia: Fortress Press, 1988), 10n.4.

Mark, Matthew probably sees it as reflecting a garbled account of Jesus's prediction that the temple will be torn down (Matt 24:1–2). Matthew, however, omits the claim that Jesus described the temple as "made by hands." Scholars regularly note that Matthew's version of the charge appears to downplay the polemic against the temple attributed to him by the witnesses in Mark; rather than claiming Jesus said he would destroy the temple, the witnesses in Matthew simply accuse of him saying, "I am able to destroy [*dynamai katalȳsai*] the temple of God" (Matt 26:61).[11] Most likely, the evangelist is worried that the charge could give the false impression that Jesus opposed the temple per se. Matthew has the witnesses affirm that Jesus called the sanctuary "the temple of God [*ton naon tou theou*]" (Matt 26:61). Given what we have seen so far, the Jewish impulses of Matthew probably reflect concerns Jesus himself would have had. Indeed, elsewhere we find memories of him that indicate that, motivated by a desire not to be viewed as contrary to the temple, he signaled his reverence for it (cf. Mark 1:44 and parr.; Matt 17:27).

Should the saying reported by the false witnesses be viewed as reflecting something Jesus actually said? As Allison writes, "When the tradition struggles this much with a saying one is prodded to infer that it goes back to something Jesus said."[12] Luke omits the saying altogether, though Acts tells us that Stephen was charged by "false witnesses" with claiming that Jesus would destroy the temple (Acts 6:13–14).[13] Did Mark simply invent this tradition? That seems hard to believe. I would not use the word "embarrassing" to describe this tradition – the logion is certainly not embarrassing to John! *More accurately, our sources suggest Jesus spoke of the temple's future ruin but in ways that were not always comprehended by those around him.*[14]

Another saying that is often highlighted is Jesus's statement that "not one stone will be left here upon another stone [*ou mē aphethē hōde lithos epi lithon*]" (Mark 13:2). Some scholars point out that the saying does not correlate to any specific description of how the temple was destroyed.[15]

---

[11] Gurtner, *Torn Veil*, 121–122.

[12] Allison, *Jesus of Nazareth*, 100.

[13] Loyd Gaston's speculative solution that Stephen is the origin for the tradition that Jesus predicted the destruction of the temple (*No Stone on Another: Studies in the Significance of the Fall of Jerusalem in the Synoptic Gospels*, NovTSup 23 [Leiden: Brill, 1970], 161) is unlikely. See Sanders, *Jesus and Judaism*, 364–65n.5.

[14] See, e.g., Sanders, *Historical Figure of Jesus*, 257–259.

[15] Attempts to reconcile this saying with the fact that the wailing wall was left standing are not convincing. See, e.g., Collins, *Mark*, 601; Marcus, *Mark*, 1:38.

The claim that the inaccuracy simply reflects "emotional rhetoric"[16] begs the question of why one should think emotionally charged rhetoric must be inaccurate. In short, if one wanted to invent a saying that made Jesus look prescient, it is hard to believe one would come up with a saying that looked like this. Because of this, scholars such as Amy-Jill Levine and Bart Ehrman have argued that the prediction is best traced back to Jesus himself.[17] In addition, the position that Jesus's oracle was invented by Mark out of whole cloth rests on speculation rather than evidence. We have no data indicating that some *other* source gave the Jesus tradition this feature.

As we will see later, the more we learn about Jewish first-century figures, the more probable it seems that Jesus would have issued such a prediction. Is it possible that Mark invented the tradition? Of course. Is it the *most probable* explanation of the data? Definitely not. One can come up with any number of scenarios which trace out how such a prophecy *might* have evolved out of other impressions made by Jesus. Conjecture does not constitute *evidence* though. Aside from meeting the bar of recurrent attestation, this aspect of the Jesus tradition fits well with the wider portrait of Jesus as a first-century Jew. As we will explain in further detail later, the temple's end was often a feature of Jewish apocalyptic traditions, the very kinds of Jewish traditions that seem to have informed Jesus's message.

Jesus's First-Century Jewish Context

That Jesus foresaw the coming destruction of Jerusalem is perfectly coherent within a first-century Jewish context. As many have observed, Josephus informs us that another figure also named Jesus made similar predictions:

Four years before the war ... there came to the feast, at which it is the custom of all Jews to erect tabernacles to God, one Jesus, son of Ananias, a rude peasant, who, standing in the temple, suddenly began to cry out, "A voice from the east, a voice from the west, a voice from the four winds; a voice against Jerusalem and the sanctuary, a voice against the bridegroom and the bride, a voice against all the people [Jer 7:34]." ... Some of the leading citizens, incensed at these ill-omened words, arrested the fellow and severely chastised him. But he, without a word on his own behalf or for the private ear of those who struck him, only continued his cries as before. Thereupon, the magistrates ... brought him to the Roman governor; there,

---

[16] Moloney, "Revisiting the Temple," 74.
[17] See, e.g., Levine, *A Misunderstood Jew*, 153; Ehrman, *Apocalyptic Prophet*, 157.

although flayed to the bone with scourges, he neither sued for mercy nor shed a tear but, merely introducing the most mournful of variations into his ejaculation, responded to each stroke with "Woe to Jerusalem!" When Albinus, the governor, asked him who and whence he was and why he uttered these cries, he answered him never a word, but only unceasingly reiterated his dirge over the city until Albinus pronounced him a maniac and let him go... His cries were loudest at the festivals... [W]hile going his round and shouting in piercing tones from the wall, "Woe once more to the city and to the people and to the temple" ... a stone hurled from the *ballista* struck and killed him on the spot. (*Jewish War* 6.300–309)[18]

There are numerous parallels between Josephus' account of Jesus ben Ananias and the depiction of Jesus of Nazareth in the Gospels:

- Both enter "the temple [*to hieron*]" (Mark 11:11, 15, 27; 12:35; 13:1; 14:49 and par.; *J.W.* 6.301)
- Both issue condemnations against the backdrop of Jewish festivals (Mark 14:2; 15:6; and par.; John 2:23; *J.W.* 6.300)
- Both foretell the destruction of the city (Luke 19:41–44; 21:20–24; *J.W.* 6.301) as well as the "temple [*naos*]" (Mark 14:58; *J.W.* 6.301)
- Both cite from Jeremiah 7 (Mark 11:17 and parr.=Jer 7:11; *J.W.* 6.301=Jer 7:34)
- Both are "arrested [*syllambanō*]" by Jewish authorities (Mark 14:48; Luke 22:54; John 18:12; *J.W.* 6.302) and "beaten [*paiō*]" (Matt 26:68; Luke 22:64; *J.W.* 6.302)
- Both are led to the Roman governor (Luke 23:1: *ēgagon auton epi ton Pilaton*; *J.W.* 6.303: *anagousin ... epi ton ... eparchon*), who interrogates them (Mark 15:2–4 and par.; *J.W.* 6.305)
- Both are scourged (Luke 18:33; John 19:1: *mastigoō*; *J.W.* 6.304: *mastix*)
- Pilate has the option to "release [*apoluoō*]" Jesus of Nazareth (Mark 15:9), while Albinus "releases [*apoluō*]" Jesus ben Ananias (*J.W.* 6.305).[19]

It might be argued that the similarities between Josephus' story of Jesus ben Ananias and the gospels' description of Jesus of Nazareth are the result of literary dependence. This is highly unlikely. The verbal overlap between these reports is mostly limited to the legal language that occurs in both places.[20]

Yet is it not more likely than not that Josephus and the gospel writers invented these predictions *ex post facto*? Without a doubt, the story

---

[18] Thackeray, LCL.
[19] Evans, *Jesus and His Contemporaries*, 360–361; Evans, *Mark 8:27–16:20*, 176–177.
[20] Evans, *Jesus and His Contemporaries*, 361n.48.

of Jesus ben Ananias' prediction is self-serving for Josephus. He had turned against his own people during the war. The claim that God himself brought the judgment on the city could prove that Josephus was on the right side of history. Moreover, it is not challenging to see why early believers would make up a tradition that Jesus issued an announcement of what was to come. In fact, given their desire to lead people to believe Jesus was a prophet, would we not *expect* the gospel writers to indicate that Jesus foresaw such a major catastrophe? What makes it not only possible but *probable* that Jesus of Nazareth made such predictions about the temple's demise? Two observations are worth mentioning.

First, Jesus is routinely portrayed in our sources as a prophetic figure. There is no good reason to insist that men claiming to be prophets could not have emerged in the first century. To the contrary, the data from the New Testament and Josephus points in the opposite direction. Indeed, scholars generally agree that Jesus of Nazareth was influenced by prophetic traditions.[21] As Tobias Hägerland puts it, "The characterization of the historical Jesus as a prophet is, in fact, almost unanimously affirmed by scholarship."[22] Our treatment here supports this conclusion. That Jesus was a prophetic figure is recurrently attested (see the preceding list), jives with Jesus's Jewish context (as this section acknowledges), and coheres with the effects of Jesus (e.g., Jesus's followers are said to have exercised the gift of prophecy, cf., e.g., 1 Thess 5:5:20; 1 Cor 11:4–5; 12:10, 28–29; 13:8–9; 14:1, 3–6, 22, 24, 29, 31, 32, 37, 39; Rom 12:6; Acts 19:6; 21:9–10). The idea that Jesus issued warnings of a coming judgment is consistent with all of this. Indeed, if Jesus did *not* make such predictions, it would be hard to figure out why he was specifically remembered as a prophetic figure; teachers and leaders need not be prophets.

It is worth noting that our sources repeatedly connect Jesus's preaching to Danielic motifs and allusions.[23] This comports well with the

---

[21] See Hägerland, *Jesus and the Forgiveness of Sins*, 202n.82 who cites the following texts: Mark 6:15//Luke 9:8; Mark 8:28 parr. Matt 21:11, 46; Luke 7:16; 24:19; John 4:19; 6:14; 7:40; 9:17; Acts 3:22–26; cf. Mark 6:4 parr./John 4:44/GThom 31:1 = POxy 1 30–33; Mark 14:65 and parr.; Luke 13:33; John 7:52.

[22] Hägerland, *Jesus and the Forgiveness of Sins*, 202. See also, e.g., Borg, *Conflict, Holiness, and Politics*, 240–247; Ehrman, *Apocalyptic Prophet*, 21, 125–139, 243–245; Meier, *A Marginal Jew*, 3:623–626; Sanders, *Jesus and Judaism*, 237–239.

[23] See Craig Evans, "Daniel in the New Testament: Visions of God's Kingdom," in *The Book of Daniel: Composition and Reception*, 2 vols., ed. John J. Collins and Peter W. Flint (Leiden: Brill, 2001), 2:490–527.

likelihood not only that Jesus was a prophet but also that he specifically drew upon apocalyptic traditions. It is especially noteworthy, then, that Daniel specifically speaks of the end of the sanctuary – and does so repeatedly:

And I heard a holy one speaking, and another holy one said to the one that was speaking, "For how long is this vision concerning the continual burnt offering, *the transgression that makes desolate,* and *the giving over of the sanctuary and host to be trampled?*" And he answered him, "For two thousand three hundred evenings and mornings. Then the sanctuary shall be restored to its rightful state." (Daniel 8:13–14)

After the sixty-two weeks, an anointed one shall be cut off, and shall have nothing. And the people of the prince that shall come *shall destroy the city and the sanctuary.* And *its end shall come with a flood, and to the end there shall be war.* Desolations are decreed. He shall make a strong covenant with many for one week, and for half of the week *he shall make sacrifice and offering cease*; and in their place shall be *an abomination that desolates.* (Daniel 9:26–27)

Forces sent by him shall occupy and profane the sanctuary stronghold. *They shall abolish the continual burnt offering* and set up *the abomination that makes desolate.* (Daniel 11:31)

Strikingly, all three Synoptic Gospels have Jesus using the language of these prophecies (Matt 24:15; Mark 13:14; Luke 21:20). If Jesus did draw from works like Daniel – a notion that seems especially credible – it would not be at all surprising for him to have announced the coming demise of the temple. Given its prominence in Daniel's visions, it would be surprising if Jesus did *not* express the idea that the sanctuary would be defiled. It also bears noting that, while Josephus never links Jesus ben Ananias to Danielic traditions, Steve Mason nevertheless shows that Josephus' perspective on the catastrophes associated with Jewish War was likely influenced by Danielic traditions.[24]

Second, Jesus of Nazareth is often remembered as rooting his prediction of a coming national disaster in the idea that judgment was coming *due to sin*. The same is true for Jesus ben Ananias, who is described as issuing a cry of "woe." This terminology evokes prophecies of *judgment* found in prophetic and apocalyptic literature. The message in these texts is clear: devastation is coming because evil has been perpetrated. A few examples from Jeremiah and 1 Enoch illustrate this idea:

---

[24] Steve Mason, *Josephus and the New Testament,* 2nd ed. (Grand Rapids: Baker Academic, 2003), 93–94.

Behold, he comes up like clouds,
  and his chariots like the whirlwind;
his horses are swifter than eagles:
  Woe to us, for we are ruined!
Cleanse your heart from evil, O Jerusalem,
  that you may be saved. (Jeremiah 4:13–14)

I have seen your abominations,
  your adulteries and neighings, your shameless prostitutions,
  on the hills in the field.
Woe to you, O Jerusalem!
  How long shall you remain unclean? (Jeremiah 13:27)

Woe to *those who build iniquity and violence,*
  and lay deceit as a foundation;
for quickly they will be overthrown,
and they will have no peace. (1 Enoch 94:6)

Here we can also include 4Q179 (4QApocryphal Lamentations), which, though fragmentary, seems to use "woe" language to foretell coming judgment on Jerusalem and its temple due to sin.

all our sins. And it is not in the power of our hands, because *[we] have not lis-tened* [... at the time of] the visitation, so that all these things will happen to us because of the evil of [...] his covenant ... *Woe to us!* [...] *It has been burned by fire and ravaged* [...] our honour, and in it *there is no pleasing odour; upon the al[tar]* [...] our holy courtyards were ... *Jerusalem,* city [... a la]ir of animals, and there is no [...] And her squares ... Alas! *All her palaces are desolate* [...] and *those who used to come to the festival are not in them.* All the cities of [...] *Our inheritance has been turned into a desert,* land which does not [... the soun]d of j[oy] is not heard in her. And he who is looking for [...] for our incurable wounds. All our debts [...] our [trans]gressions and ... our sins. (4Q179 [4QApocryphal Lamentations], *frag.* 1, *col.* 1)[25]

Although we would like to have greater clarity about this text, it seems clear that it describes the desolation of Jerusalem and the cessation of sacri-fice in connection with "woe" language and judgment due to sin. Jesus ben Ananias' message is therefore consistent not only with prophetic traditions in general but also with the apocalyptic judgment traditions we know influ-enced other Jews of his time. The same is true about Jesus. Of course, as we have seen, the Dead Sea Community's attitudes cannot simply be equated with Jesus of Nazareth's, this dimension of the Scrolls' contents does give us further context for Jesus's warnings of the temple's destruction. If other

---

[25] Quoted and slightly adapted from *DSSSE* 1:369.

Jews were anticipating divine judgment that would render its places "deso-late," there is no reason to insist that either Jesus of Nazareth or Jesus ben Ananias was unlikely to make such pronouncements.

We can add that Jesus of Nazareth's predictions of coming judg-ment are often viewed as resulting from the corruption of the Jerusalem leadership. Other Jews in the first century expressed concerns that the temple authorities had become unfaithful. For example, 1QPesher to Habakkuk (1QpHab) describes the high priest as the "wicked priest" (cf. 1QpHab 8:8–9; 9:9; 11:4), speaking of how he had robbed the destitute (1QpHab 8:12; 9:5; 10:1; 12:10) and defiled the sanctuary (1QpHab 12:8–9). Josephus reports that the chief priests were known to commit violence against lower ranking priests (cf. *Ant.* 20.179–181, 207). The sinfulness of the priests is also recounted in 1 Enoch and other first-century Jewish texts.[26] Such a view would cohere well with the gospels' portrait of Jesus criticizing the Jerusalem authorities. He condemns the teaching of the Sadducees (cf., e.g., Matt 16:11–12; Matt 22:23–33//Mark 12:18–27//Luke 20:27–38). Likewise, the chief priests are presented as evil and as conspiring to act wickedly (cf., e.g., Mark 11:18–19//Luke 19:47–48; Matt 21:43; Matt 21:45–46//Mark 12:12// Luke 20:19; Matt 26:59–61//Mark 14:55–56; Matt 27:3–4; Matt 27:18–20//Mark 15:10–11; Matt 27:41//Mark 15:31; Matt 28:11–15; cf. John 19:15). Moreover, as we will explain later, the report that Jesus referred to the temple as a house of "robbers [*lēstōn*]" (Matt 21:13// Mark 11:17//Luke 19:46) may also underscore the temple authorities' reputation for violence. There is no reason to suppose such portraits only emerged later out of conflicts the early followers of Jesus had with such figures. Literature from the Second Temple period offers ample indication that first-century Jews raised concerns about the Jerusalem leadership's moral turpitude.

The Effects of Jesus's Ministry

Finally, the effects of Jesus's ministry must be considered. For Paula Fredriksen this is precisely where the case for Jesus's predictions of the temple's ruin collapses. She points out that Paul makes no mention of

---

[26] See 4QMMT[C] 4:8–10; CD-A 6:14–17; 1 En. 89:72–73; Test. Levi 14:1–15:1; 17:8–11; Test. Judah 23:1–3; Test. Moses 5:3–6:1. See the exhaustive survey in Evans, *Jesus and His Contemporaries*, 219–344 in which he demonstrates that Sanders' assertion that no evidence of such corruption existed (cf. Sanders, *Jesus and Judaism*, 367n.39) is false.

such a teaching from Jesus.[27] Her argument, of course, is quite literally an argument from silence, which she acknowledges. Nonetheless, for her, that Paul is mum on that matter indicates he had no knowledge that Jesus forecasted the event. The data supporting the gospels' portrait all emerge in the post-70 period. Francis Moloney concurs.[28] I disagree with this assessment.

First, one can think of any number of reasons why Paul might not mention a prediction of Jesus announcing the Herodian temple's destruction. For example, if Pauline scholars have taught us anything, it is that the apostle is writing occasional letters primarily for gentile audiences living in the diaspora for whom the destruction of the Jerusalem temple would not have been – to say the least – a matter of supreme pastoral importance. That Paul says nothing of Jesus's prediction is not entirely inexplicable. Paul certainly does not believe his letters were the only source his readers had for coming to know what Jesus said. The apostle assumes that his communities have already gained some familiarity with the Jesus tradition. For example, when the apostle speaks of the Lord's Supper, he apparently believes that the Corinthians are already are aware of the story (cf. 1 Cor 11:23). If it was not for the precise situation at Corinth, Paul would never have provided us any evidence that he knew of the Last Supper tradition. Indeed, Allison's warnings against operating with a kind of "Pauline fundamentalism" in historical research are apropos here. As Allison observes, Paul makes no mention of Jesus speaking in parables, healing, casting out demons, being the son of "Mary," or his proclamation of the "kingdom of God," yet no one argues that any of these traditions should be discounted because of the apostle's silence on these matters.[29] The relevance of a tradition that Jesus foresaw the future destruction of the sanctuary may not have been seen as significant for his gentile audiences.

Second, and even more significant, while Paul never mentions Jesus's prediction of the destruction of the temple, the idea that the Jerusalem leaders would be judged for rejecting Jesus is specifically affirmed in 1 Thessalonians. In this epistle, widely recognized as one of Paul's earliest,[30]

---

[27] Paula Fredriksen, "Gospel Chronologies, the Scene in the Temple, and the Crucifixion of Jesus," in *Redefining First-Century Jewish and Christian Identities: Essays in Honor of Ed Parish Sanders*, ed. Fabian E. Udoh, Susannah Heschel, Mark Chancey, and Gregory Tatum (Notre Dame, IN: University of Notre Dame Press, 2008), 262.

[28] Moloney, "Revisiting the Temple," 74.

[29] See Allison, *Resurrection of Jesus*, 92.

[30] See, e.g., Abraham J. Malherbe, *The Letters to the Thessalonians*, AYB 32B (New Haven: Yale University Press, 2008), 75.

we read that divine judgment will come upon those in Judea who pre-
vented the preaching of the gospel:

For you, brothers, became imitators of the churches of God that are in *Judaea*
[*Ioudaia*] in Christ Jesus. For you also have suffered the same things from your
own countrymen just as they themselves did also from the *Judeans* [*Ioudaiōn*],
who killed both the Lord Jesus and the prophets [*tōn kai ton kyrion apokteinantōn
Iēsoun kai tous prophētas*], and drove us out [*kai hēmas ekdiōxantōn*], and dis-
please God, and oppose all people [*pasin anthrōpois enantiōn*] by preventing us
from speaking to the peoples [*ethnesin*] that they might be saved, *so they always
fill up their sins* [*eis to anaplērōsai autōn tas hamartias pantote*]. But wrath has
come upon them *to the end* [*eis telos*]. (1 Thessalonians 2:14–16)

Some have called into question this passage's authenticity, arguing that it
is best viewed as an interpolation; this view is far from compelling. The
observations cited in support of this position have received important critiques.[31] For example, a common argument in favor of the interpolation
view centers on the line that God's wrath has "come upon [*ephthasen*]
them at last." This, it is claimed, reflects a post-70 situation. Yet this
is far from certain. In fact, other plausible readings account for it. For
example, the expression could easily be taken as proleptic or prophetic.[32]
Indeed, Paul elsewhere describes how judgment is realized in the present and anticipated in behavior and circumstance (cf. Rom 1:27; Phil
1:27–28). In short, the majority of commentators do not agree with the
interpolation hypothesis since, among other reasons, (1) it lacks any support from the manuscript evidence; and (2) there are reasonable explanations that do not require a post-70 setting.[33] The notion that the Judeans
who were responsible for Jesus's death are under a heavenly indictment
is therefore attested in what may very well be the earliest literary source
from a follower of Jesus.

Where did Paul get the notion that judgment would come upon those
who rejected Jesus in Judea? Scholars have long noted the similarities
between Paul's teaching in 1 Thessalonians and Jesus's rebuke of the
Jerusalem leaders in Matthew and Luke:

Therefore you witness against yourselves that you are the sons of those who
killed the prophets [*tōn phoneusantōn tous prophētas*]. Fill up [*plērōsate*], then,

---

[31] See the comprehensive discussion in Matthew Jensen, "The (In)authenticity of 1 Thessalonians 2.13–16: A Review of the Arguments," *CurBR* 18, 1 (2019): 59–79.

[32] See the sources and discussion cited in Jensen, "(In)authenticity of 1 Thessalonians," 67.

[33] Jensen ("[In]authenticity of 1 Thessalonians," 71) explains that inclusion of these lines is
favored by the "scholarly consensus," who typically do not even engage with the minor-
ity interpolation view.

the measure of your fathers... For this reason, behold, I send to you prophets and wise men and scribes, some of them you will kill [*apokteneite*] and crucify, and some of them you will flog in your synagogues, and *persecute from city to city* [*diōxete apo poleōs eis polin*]. That upon you may come all the righteous blood poured out upon the earth, from the blood of righteous Abel to the blood of Zachariah son of Barachiah, whom you murdered between the temple and the altar. Amen, I say to you, all these things will come upon this generation. (Matthew 23:31–32, 34)

So you are witnesses and you approve of the deeds of your fathers, for they killed them, and you build their sepulchers. For this reason also the wisdom of God said, "I will send to them prophets and apostles, and some of them they will kill [*apoktenousin*] and persecute [*diōxousin*]. That the blood of all the prophets poured out from the foundation of the world may be required of this generation. From the blood of Abel to the blood of Zachariah, who perished between the altar and the house [*tou oikou*]." Yes, I say to you, it will be required of this generation. (Luke 11:48–51)

(For those who accept the existence of Q, this saying is recognized as belonging to that work.) Whatever one makes of the relationship between Matthew and Luke, the parallels between Jesus's teaching in these texts and Paul's in 1 Thessalonians are unmistakable:

- All three envision a coming judgment on those who oppose Jesus (1 Thess 2:16; Matt 23:35; Luke 11:51).
- All three speak of prophets being killed (1 Thess 2:15; Matt 23:34; Luke 11:49).
- Like the Pauline passage, Matthew 23 uses the imagery of "filling up" (1 Thess 2:16; Matt 23:32).

What are we to make of these similarities?

Explanations that Matthew is dependent on 1 Thessalonians[34] or that the text in 1 Thessalonians is an interpolation[35] have failed to convince.[36] While the Lukan version's citation of "the Wisdom of God" has sometimes been viewed as a citation of a now lost Jewish source,[37] the existence of such a work would hardly rule out the possibility that Jesus cited it himself. The safest bet seems to be that Paul, who wrote before 70 CE, bears witness to a tradition that was later used by

---

[34] *Pace* Michael Goulder, *Midrash and Location in Matthew* (London: SPCK, 1974), 165.

[35] See, e.g., the representatives in Allison, *Constructing Jesus*, 399n.55.

[36] See the discussion and sources in Allison, *Constructing Jesus*, 399–401.

[37] See, e.g., Bultmann, *History of the Synoptic Tradition*, 114; Walter Grundman, *Das Evangelium nach Lukas*, THNKT (Berlin: Evangelische Verlagsanstalt, 1966), 249.

Matthew and Luke.[38] Either way, prior to the destruction of the temple by the Romans, we have a source that indicates that Jesus's early followers believed judgment would come upon those Judeans who rejected their Lord.

While Paul does not give us a direct quotation from Jesus about the coming downfall of the temple, the notion of an imminent judgment on Judea is quite specific and goes beyond the apostle's general statements about the final judgment elsewhere. In fact, in Romans, Paul specifically asks for prayers that he be delivered from "those who are disobedient in Judea" (Rom 15:31). The consensus position is that 1 Thessalonians is written long before Romans. The judgment 1 Thessalonians envisions coming upon the Judeans, then, has not yet been realized. Moreover, nothing suggests Paul intends to exclude the temple from being affected by the wrath that will befall Judea.

Second, that Jesus predicted the downfall of the temple is supported by features of the Acts of the Apostles. First, the book reports that Stephen claimed Jesus would destroy the sanctuary. Stephen's accusers make this charge:

This man never ceases speaking words *against the holy place* [*kata tou topou tou hagiou*] and the law. For we have heard him saying that this Jesus the Nazarene *will destroy this place* [*katalysei ton topon touton*] and will change the customs that Moses handed on to us. (Acts 6:13–14)

In this, Acts likely shows knowledge of the tradition attested in Mark that Jesus was known to have spoken about the temple's destruction.[39]

Furthermore, according to Acts, the believers in Jerusalem sold their property and held all things in common (Acts 4:32–37). They were also quick to flee the city once persecution against the community began (Acts 8:1). Acts never indicates that there was any effort to bring the disciples back to take up a permanent residence in Jerusalem. All of this suggests that the disciples of Jesus were not necessarily committed to remaining in the city. We also do not read about members of communities elsewhere selling off their property and pooling their resources in other cities. All of this fits well with the idea that Jesus spoke of Jerusalem's eventual fall. Of course, this is not "proof-positive" that Jesus made such announcements

---

[38] David Luckensmeyer, *The Eschatology of First Thessalonians* (Göttingen: Vandenhoeck & Ruprecht, 2009), 150; Graham Twelftree, *Paul and the Miraculous: A Historical Reconstruction* (Grand Rapids: Baker Academic, 2013), 120–122.

[39] See, e.g., Raymond E. Brown, S.S., *Death of the Messiah*, 2 vols. (Doubleday, 1994), 1:435

about the future. Other explanations of the data are *plausible*. Yet, having weighed all the considerations, this study agrees with those who have concluded that the most probable explanation of the data is that Jesus, in some way, announced the destruction of the temple.

JESUS'S TEMPLE ACTION AND DIVINE JUDGMENT IN MATTHEW

In Matthew's narrative, when Jesus arrives in Jerusalem, he performs an action in the temple.

> And Jesus went into the temple of God and cast out all those who sold and bought in the temple, and overturned the tables of the moneychangers, and the seats of those who sold doves. And said to them, "It is written, 'My house shall be called a house of prayer; but you are making have it a den of thieves.'" And the blind and the lame came to him in the temple, and he healed them. But when the chief priests and scribes saw the astonishing things that he did, and the children crying out in the temple, and saying, "Hosanna to the son of David!," they were indignant. And they said to him, "Do you hear what these children are saying?" But Jesus said to them, "Yes. Have you never read, 'Out of the mouths of infants and nursing babies you have prepared praise?'" (Matthew 21:12–16)

Does this scene signal Jesus's rejection of the worship in the Jerusalem temple? Some believe that it does. Commenting on the parallel account in Mark, Herman Waetjen argues that by his action Jesus indicates the "abolition of the temple institution itself" and the "negation of the temple institution."[40] This interpretation, however, does not bear up under careful scrutiny. As we shall see, in Matthew's account, Jesus's temple action is bound up with a motif that runs throughout the evangelist's narrative: judgment.

Historians often detach what Jesus is reported to have done from the account of his words. Yet to interpret the scene in *Matthew* properly, we can do no such thing. We will therefore first look at the meaning of Jesus's quotations from Isaiah and Jeremiah. After this, we will look at the actions he performs in connection with those quotations. We will then consider more broadly the meaning of the episode within Matthew's narrative. Only after we have fully understood how the evangelist handles the data can we then turn back to the historical question of

---

[40] Herman C. Waetjen, *A Reordering of Power: A Socio-Political Reading of Mark's Gospel* (Minneapolis: Fortress Press, 1989), 179, 182. See also Ådna, "Jesus and the Temple," 2670 who views Jesus's action as signaling that the "old atonement cult" has become "obsolete."

what Matthew's overall portrait can contribute to our understanding of Jesus's attitude toward the temple.

The Quotations in Jesus's Temple Action

The first passage Jesus alludes to is found in Isaiah. Although lengthy, it is necessary to read this oracle within its original context. Certain aspects of it will loom large in our discussion:

> Thus says the LORD: "Maintain justice, and do righteousness, for soon *my salvation will come, and my righteousness will be revealed.* Blessed is the man who does this, and the son of man who holds it fast, who keeps the sabbath, not profaning it, and keeps his hand from doing any evil." *Let not the foreigner who has joined himself to the LORD say, "The LORD will surely separate me from his people"*; and let not the eunuch say, "Behold, I am a dry tree." For thus says the LORD: "To the eunuchs who keep my sabbaths, who choose the things that please me and hold fast my covenant, I will give in my house and within my walls a monument and a name better than sons and daughters; I will give them an everlasting name which shall not be cut off. And *the foreigners who join themselves to the LORD, to minister to him, to love the name of the LORD, and to be his servants,* everyone who keeps the sabbath, and does not profane it, and holds fast my covenant—*these I will bring to my holy mountain, and make them joyful in my house of prayer.* Their burnt offerings and their sacrifices will be accepted on my altar, *for my house shall be called a house of prayer for all peoples.* Thus says the Lord GOD, *who gathers the outcasts of Israel, I will gather others to them besides those already gathered."* (Isaiah 56:1–8)

The passage cited by Jesus involves an eschatological vision that looks forward to the future regathering of Israel. This restoration involves a *liturgical* dimension – God's people are brought together *within a temple.* This is hardly surprising. Numerous ancient Jewish texts connect the restoration of Israel from exile to hopes for an eschatological sanctuary.[41]

The other half of Jesus's statement comes from Jeremiah's condemnation of the temple of his day:

> Has this house, which is called by my name, *become a den of robbers* in your eyes? Behold, I also have seen it, says the LORD. Go now to my place that was in Shiloh, where I made my name dwell at first, and *see what I did to it for the wickedness of my people Israel.* And now, because you have done all these things,

---

[41] See, e.g., Isa 2:2–3; 60:3–7; 62:6–12; 66:18–23; Jer 33:11; Ezek 37:21–27; Amos 9:11–15; Neh 1:9; Tob 14:5–7 (cf. Deut 12:10–11); Sir 36:11–14; 2 Macc 1:27–29; 4Q448 (*Apocryphal Psalm and Prayer*) A, 8–10; 1 En. 91:13; Jub. 1:15–17; 2 Bar. 68:4–7; T. Ben. 9:2–3; Tg. on Isa. 53:15; Tg. on Zech 6:12; Gen. Rab. 2.5; 56.2; 56:2; Exod. Rab. 31.10.

says the LORD, and when I spoke to you persistently you did not listen, and when I called you, you did not answer, therefore *I will do to the house which is called by my name, and in which you trust, and to the place which I gave to you and to your fathers, as I did to Shiloh.* (Jeremiah 7:11–14)

Jesus is presented as alluding to a prophecy from Jeremiah that fore-tells the destruction of the Jerusalem temple in the sixth century BCE. As William Holladay writes in his Jeremiah commentary, here the prophet "speaks of the destruction of the temple and surrounding area."[42] The most natural explanation of Jesus's use of this passage is that he intends to indicate that the Jerusalem temple of his own day will be destroyed. Various features of Matthew's narrative would seem to confirm this reading.

First, in the next scene Jesus curses a fig tree, which withers and dies (Matt 21:18–22). His action is almost certainly presented as a prophetic sign of the coming judgment on Jerusalem.[43] The image of the withered fig tree functions as metaphor for judgment in the prophetic literature.[44] In fact, the image of a fruitless fig tree appears in Jeremiah within *the very same context* as the "den of robbers" prophecy cited by Jesus (cf. Jer 8:13). This does not appear to be a mere coincidence.[45] Second, Jesus's cursing of the fig tree is joined to a saying involving a "mountain [*oros*]" being cast into the sea (cf. Matt 21:18–22; cf. Mark 11:20–23). Morna Hooker has shown that the most natural explanation of the imagery is that it points to God's coming judgment on Mount Zion.[46] Third, judg-ment is a major theme that runs throughout the Gospel of Matthew.[47] It is hard to believe the story of Jesus's temple "cleansing" is not meant to be connected with this motif given its prominence in the Gospel.

---

[42] See, e.g., William Holladay, *Jeremiah*, ed. Paul D. Hanson, 2 vols., Hermeneia (Philadel-phia: Fortress Press, 1986), 1:249.

[43] For fuller discussions, see, e.g., Scot McKnight, "Jesus and Prophetic Actions," *BBR* 10, 2 (2000): 197–232 (esp. 224); Hooker, *Signs of a Prophet*, 44; David E. Aune, *Prophecy in Early Christianity and the Ancient Mediterranean World* (Grand Rapids: Eerdmans, 1983), 153–170 (esp. 162).

[44] See Isa 34:4; Jer 8:13; 24:1–10; Hos 2:12; 9:10–17; Mic 7:1. See, e.g., Nolland, *Mat-thew*, 852.

[45] See Craig A. Evans, "Jesus and Zechariah's Messianic Hope," in *Authenticating the Activities of Jesus*, ed. Chilton and Evans, 373.

[46] Morna D. Hooker, "Traditions about the Temple in the Sayings of Jesus," *BJRL* 70 (1988): 8.

[47] Runesson, *Divine Wrath*, 10; Daniel Marguerat, *Le Jugement dans l'Évangile de Mat-thieu*, 2nd ed. (Geneva: Labor et Fides, 1995), 3: "Un thème théologique de première importance pour l'évangéliste Matthieu."

Nevertheless, the use of Jeremiah 7 should not be construed as indicating that Jesus rejects the validity of temple worship per se. For one thing, as we have seen, Jesus will go on to affirm the holiness of the temple and its sacrifices a few chapters later:

> which is greater, the gift or *the altar that makes the gift holy*? Therefore, whoever swears by the altar, swears by it and by everything that is on it. And whoever swears by the temple swears by it and by *the one who dwells in it.* (Matthew 23:19–21)

In light of this passage, it is highly implausible that Matthew intends to portray Jesus's use of Jeremiah as indicating that the temple's holiness has been annulled. The same is true for Mark since, as we have seen, he has Jesus go on to have the disciples sacrifice there (Mark 14:12–16).

Moreover, the Jeremiah passage, while consistent with the message of coming devastation, would be an odd source to use to signal the abrogation of all sacrifice. After announcing the temple's demise, the prophet Jeremiah went on to insist that if the people turned from their sin the temple cult would continue (Jer 17:26). In the very oracle foretelling its future downfall, the Lord, speaking through Jeremiah, continues to refer to the sanctuary as the place "called by my name" (Jer 7:14). The temple is understood to be "the house of the LORD" (Jer 26:7), which should be void of evil (Jer 23:11). In all of this, its holy status continues to be assumed. Later, Jeremiah expressly seeks to prevent the temple's vessels from being carried off to Babylon (Jer 27:16). He also desires to see the return of the sanctuary's liturgical vessels plundered by the Babylonians (Jer 28:6).

Jeremiah also maintains that the temple will play a vital role in the eschatological restoration of Israel. In the future day of the ingathering, the Israelites will come "bringing burnt offerings and sacrifices, grain offerings and frankincense, and *bringing thank offerings* [tôdâ] *to the house of the LORD*" (Jer 17: 26). Likewise, in Jeremiah 33, we hear of how the returnees will *"bring thank offerings* [tôdâ] *to the house of the LORD"* (Jer 33:11). So, while the prophet announces that the temple will be destroyed, this does not mean, however, that he rejects its validity.

Matthew has Jesus predict the temple's downfall. Yet this does not mean that the evangelist believes Jesus rejected the sanctuary's validity per se. By having Jesus quote from Isaiah 56, the evangelist implies that Jesus, like Jeremiah, endorses an eschatological outlook that anticipates a role for the temple. Jesus, then, brings together two passages which, though sharing affinities with one another, describe two different realities: one involves an oracle about a future eschatological temple, the other involves judgment. Jesus makes it clear which text he believes the temple of his day more closely resembles – the Herodian sanctuary is not the eschatological temple. In effect, by means of these quotations, Jesus says, "Isaiah foretold an eschatological temple, but this one is not it. It shall be destroyed like the one of Jeremiah's day."

The Meaning of Jesus's Actions in the Temple

Having looked at the scriptural quotations used by Jesus in Matthew's account, we can now consider his corresponding deeds. Set alongside his quotations from the prophetic texts of Isaiah and Jeremiah, Jesus's actions are best viewed as "prophetic signs." Indeed, Israel's prophets were known to have performed such symbolic acts.[48] Above all, the connection between prophecy and the performance of signs is associated with the biblical prophet par excellence: Moses (cf. Deut 34:10–12), a figure whose special importance for Matthew's narrative is well documented.[49] Jesus's use of a prophecy from Jeremiah strongly reinforces the likelihood that the scene in the temple should be interpreted as involving a prophetic message since Jeremiah was especially remembered for carrying out deeds with symbolic significance.[50] Strikingly, like Jesus, Jeremiah performed similar such acts *within the temple* (Jer 27:1–28:17).

But what is Jesus's precise aim? Many have gone beyond the texts in the gospels to explain the episode. Bruce Chilton thinks the story should be interpreted against the backdrop of rabbinic disputes regarding sacrificial protocols (cf. t. Ḥag. 2:11; y. Ḥag. 2:3; y. Beṣah. 2:4; b. Beṣah. 20a–b; Philo, *Spec.* 1.198). He also appeals to Simeon b. Gamaliel's protest of the exorbitant cost of sacrificial birds (cf. m. Ker. 1:7).[51] In addition, Chilton follows Victor Eppstein's suggestion that Jesus's action could be seen as a response to a decision made by Caiaphas to allow merchants within the temple courts, a change in policy that enabled these vendors to compete with Sadducean shops on the Mount of Olives.[52] Others have suggested that Jesus was principally concerned with the

---

[48] See, e.g., McKnight, "Jesus and Prophetic Actions," 197–232.

[49] See, e.g., Dale C. Allison, Jr., *The New Moses: A Matthean Typology* (Minneapolis: Fortress Press, 1993).

[50] See Kelvin G. Friebel, *Jeremiah's and Ezekiel's Sign Acts: Rhetorical Nonverbal Communication*, JSOTSup 283 (Sheffield: Sheffield Academic Press, 1999), 14.

[51] Bruce D. Chilton, *The Temple of Jesus: His Sacrificial Program within a Cultural History of Sacrifice* (University Park: Pennsylvania University Press, 1992), 100–111.

[52] Bruce D. Chilton, "Caiaphas," ABD 1:805–806; Victor Eppstein, "The Historicity of the Gospel Account of the Cleansing of the Temple," ZNW 55 (1964): 42–58.

use of Tyrian coins in the temple.[53] These explanations, however, have failed to persuade most scholars. One of the key problems is that they detach Jesus's deeds from the eschatological context established by his quotation from Isaiah's vision of the age to come. That Jesus is presented as being motivated by eschatological hopes seems especially likely.[54] Moreover, the suggestion that Jesus opposed Caiaphas' decision to move the traders rests on a questionable reading of a rather late Jewish text.[55] Furthermore, that Jesus is especially worried about the kinds of shekels in use is unsupported. Nothing in Matthew (or any of the gospels!) suggests this. On the contrary, Jesus targets *the commerce itself*, not merely the currency used.

Citing a Mishnaic tradition, some have argued that Jesus's action is directed against stations that were set up for the collection of the temple tax at Passover time.[56] Yet money-changing tables were not exclusively devoted to handling the tax. Pilgrims would also have needed to purchase sacrificial animals for the week-long celebration of Passover and Unleavened Bread. The demand for lambs alone would have been exceptionally high. For these transactions, Tyrian coins were apparently necessary (cf. t. Ketub. 13:3), accounting for the money-changing tables. Since we are told that Jesus targets those selling "doves" (Matt 21:12; cf. Mark 11:15//John 2:16), which are sold for the poor to offer (cf. Lev 5:7, 11; 12:6, 8; 14:22; 15:14, 29; Luke 2:24), it seems unlikely that Jesus has the temple tax in his sights.

Instead, by interrupting activity in the temple associated with its everyday operation, Jesus appears to symbolically enact its coming end.[57] This would be true even if Jesus's actions are more limited in scope than

---

[53] Peter Richardson, "Why Turn the Tables? Jesus's Protest in the Temple Precincts," in *Society of Biblical Literature Seminary Papers 1992* (Atlanta: Scholars Press, 1992), 507–523.

[54] See Bryan, *Jesus and Israel's Traditions*, 208; Evans, *Jesus and His Contemporaries*, 354–365.

[55] See Regev, *The Temple in Early Christianity*, 26.

[56] See m. Šeqal. 1:3; Jostein Ådna, "Jesus's Symbolic Act in the Temple (Mark 11:15–17): The Replacement of the Sacrificial Cult by His Atoning Death," in *Gemeinde ohne Tempel = Community without Temple: Zur Substituierung und Transformation des Jerusalemer Tempels und seines Kults im Alten Testament, antiken Judentum und frühen Christentum*, ed. B. Ego, A. Lange, and P. Pilhofer (Tübingen: Mohr Siebeck, 1999), 461–475; Jacob Neusner, "Money Changers in the Temple: The Mishna's Explanation," *NTS* 35 (1989): 287–290; Richard Bauckham, "Jesus's Demonstration in the Temple," in *Law and Religion: Essays on the Place of the Law in Israel and Early Christianity*, ed. B. Lindars (Cambridge: James Clark & Co., 1988), 72–89.

[57] See, e.g., Davies and Allison, *Matthew*, 3:136–137.

suggested by Matthew; a possibility that should not be dismissed.[58] The Jeremiah quotation – present in all three of the Synoptic accounts – further indicates that Jesus's action symbolizes coming judgment. With this in mind, it seems significant that Matthew, following Mark, uses the Greek term *katastrephō* for Jesus's action of "overturning" the tables (Matt 21:12; Mark 11:15). The word is frequently linked with calamitous punishment and destruction in the Septuagint (e.g., Gen 19:25 LXX; Deut 29:22 LXX; Isa 13:19 LXX), notably, including in Jeremiah (Jer 20:16; 27:40 LXX).[59]

Jesus's use of Jeremiah's phrase "den of robbers [*spēlaion lēstōn*]" adds an especially stinging flavor to his indictment. The term "robber" (*lēstēs*) "means more than 'swindler' … the word connotes force."[60] John's Gospel uses it to describe Barabbas (John 18:40), a figure Mark identifies as a "revolutionary" (*stasiastēs*) responsible for murder (Mark 15:7). Josephus uses the cognate (*lēsteia*) to describe the violent rebels of the Jewish War (*J.W.* 4.134).[61]

Jesus's language of "robbers" (*lestēs*) may be explained in context. Within Matthew's narrative, the "chief priests" send a crowd to arrest Jesus that carries *swords* and *clubs* (Matt 26:47).[62] The Parable of the Wicked Tenants, a story which is described as targeting the chief priests (cf. Matt 21:45), may also confirm this reading. In the story, the tenants (who represent the temple leaders) act *violently*, attacking and killing those sent to them. Ezekiel's oracle against the shepherds, which scholars detect in the backdrop of various Matthean texts,[63] speaks of the shepherds of Israel not only neglecting the sheep but condemns them because "you slaughter the fatlings" (Ezek 34:3). Matthew, therefore, likely means to tap into the tradition that the religious leaders acted violently against others (cf. Matt 23:29–36). In fact, Josephus reports that priests had been known for brutalizing others, including lower ranking

---

[58] See, e.g., Sanders, *Jesus and Judaism*, 69–70.

[59] See Emilio G. Chávez, *The Theological Significance of Jesus's Temple Action in Mark's Gospel*, TST 87 (Lewiston: Edwin Mellen Press, 2002), 139.

[60] Davies and Allison, *Matthew*, 3:140. See also Fredriksen, *When Christians Were Jews*, 46.

[61] On this basis, some have found in Jesus's words a condemnation of revolutionary nationalistic agendas, yet this is without support. See Sanders, *Jesus and Judaism*, 68; Paula Fredriksen, "Arms and the Man: A Response to Dale Martin's 'Jesus in Jerusalem: Armed and Not Dangerous,'" *JSNT* 37, 3 (2015): 312–325.

[62] Evans also points out that "only a little later Jesus will tell a parable in which the ruling priests are depicted as violent murderers (Mark 12:1–12)" (*Mark 8:27–16:20*, 175).

[63] See, e.g., Zacharias, *Matthew's Presentation*, 96–101; Chae, *Jesus as the Eschatological Davidic Shepherd*; Heil, "Ezekiel 34 and the Narrative Strategy," 698–708.

colleagues.[64] Although it serves his agenda, there is no reason to insist that this aspect of Josephus' account of the priests' reputation is wholly invented. In context, then, "robbers" might refer to the same chief priests who will later have Jesus crucified.

Finally, there is good reason to think that the story of Jesus's action in the temple in Matthew alludes in some way to the eschatological vision of Zechariah. In driving out the merchants, Jesus evokes the prophet's oracle of the future eschatological sanctuary:

And there shall no longer be *a trader*[65] in *the house of the* LORD *of hosts* on that day. (Zechariah 14:21)

Although the passage is not explicitly quoted, there are good reasons to think it is in the background. First, by citing Isaiah's oracle, Jesus's act is linked to eschatological hopes. Second, and even more compelling, a reference to Zechariah would seem probable given the way echoes from Zechariah frequently appear in the accounts of Jesus's final week in Jerusalem, especially in Matthew.[66] This makes it difficult to dismiss the similarity between Jesus's action and the climactic vision of Zechariah as a fluke. That Zechariah is in view is especially likely given that Jesus's temple action follows closely upon his entry into Jerusalem – an event which is closely tied to the oracle in Zechariah 9 (cf. Matt 21:4–5; Zech 9:9).

The Leaders' Failure to Recognize Jesus's Messianic Role in the Temple

Finally, unlike the other Synoptic accounts, Matthew's report of Jesus's temple action immediately gives way to another scene: "the blind [*typhloi*] and the lame [*chōloi*] came to him in the temple, and he healed them"

---

[64] Josephus, *Ant.* 20.179–181, 207.

[65] It is clear that the Hebrew term was understood not simply as referring to a "Canaanite" but to "merchants." For further discussion, see Henk Jan de Jonge, "The Cleansing of the Temple in Mark 11.15 and Zechariah 14.21," in *The Book of Zechariah and its Influence: Papers of the Oxford-Leiden Conference* (Aldershot: Ashgate, 2003), 90; Craig A. Evans, "Zechariah in the Markan Passion Narrative," in *Biblical Interpretation in Early Christian Gospels: The Gospel of Mark*, ed. Thomas R. Hatina, LNTS 304 (London: T&T Clark, 2004), 71; Collins, *Mark*, 529–530.

[66] For an exhaustive catalogue, see Evans, "Jesus and Zechariah's Messianic Hope," 386; Evans, "Zechariah in the Markan Passion Narrative," 64–80. For Matthew's special emphasis on Zechariah themes, see Clay Alan Ham, *The Coming King and the Rejected Shepherd: Matthew's Reading of Zechariah's Messianic Hope*, NTM 4 (Sheffield: Sheffield Phoenix Press, 2005).

(Matt 21:14). The chief priests and scribes are "indignant" at this. The scene is of critical importance for Matthew's overall narrative.

First, in healing the blind and lame in the temple, Jesus's identity as the Davidic messiah – a major motif in Matthew (cf., e.g., Matt 1:1) – is reinforced. There apparently was a tradition that the blind and the lame were to be excluded from the sacred precincts due to an episode from David's life. According to 2 Samuel, when David was on his way to conquer Jerusalem, the inhabitants of the city mocked him, saying, "the blind and the lame will turn you back" (2 Sam 5:6). After David prevailed, he is said to have announced that he "hates" the blind and the lame (2 Sam 5:8). The narrator then adds: "Therefore it is said, '*The blind* [*typhloi*] and *the lame* [*chōloi*] shall not come into the *house* [LXX: *oikon*]'" (2 Sam 5:8). Jesus's healing of these people in the temple – which he later calls a "house [*oikos*]" (Matt 21:13) – represents a kind of eschatological reversal; the son of David lifts the barring of them from the temple that was due to what had happened to David.[67] Like the crowds in the preceding scene of Jesus's arrival at the city, the children recognize Jesus's Davidic role in all of this, crying out: "Hosanna to *the son of David!*" (Matt 21:15), drawing on language from Psalm 118.

Second, the leaders fail to perceive what the crowds have understood. Jesus's appeal to Psalm 8:2 highlights this: "Out of the mouths of *infants* [*nēpiōn*] and nursing babies you have prepared praise" (Matt 21:16). The language here is reminiscent of an earlier saying. In Matthew 11, Jesus condemns Chorazin, Bethsaida, and Capernaum, announcing that judgment will come upon them for rejecting him:

Woe to you, Chorazin! Woe to you, Bethsaida! For if the mighty works done in you had been done in Tyre and Sidon, they would have repented long ago in sackcloth and ashes. But I say to you, it will be more bearable for Tyre and Sidon on the day of judgment than for you. And you, Capernaum, shall you be exalted to heaven? You will be brought down to Hades. For if the mighty deeds done in you had been done in Sodom, it would have remained until today. But I say to you, it will be more bearable for the land of Sodom at the day of judgment than for you. (Matthew 11:21–24)

Jesus then prays to the Father:

you have hidden these things from the wise and the understanding and have revealed them to *infants* [*nēpiois*]. (Matthew 11:25)

---

[67] See, e.g., Konradt, *Matthew*, 312–313; France, *Gospel of Matthew*, 788; Eduard Schweizer, *Das Evangelium nach Matthäus*, DNT 2, 3rd ed. (Göttingen: Vandenhoeck & Ruprecht, 1981), 266.

In Matthew 21, then, it is no surprise that the chief priests and scribes are incensed by the cries of the children – what has been made known to the little ones is unknown to the leaders. When Jesus quotes the psalmist's words about the infants in the temple, his words from Matthew 11 are confirmed – the elite have failed to grasp what the "infants" know.

Within Matthew's narrative, the scene in the temple suggests that the Jerusalem leadership has made themselves liable to judgment. Jesus warned the cities of Chorizin, Bethsaida, and Capernaum that judgment would come upon them "because they did not repent" (Matt 11:20). For Matthew, repentance is a constituent aspect of Jesus's message (Matt 4:17), a theme foreshadowed in John the Baptist's preaching (Matt 3:2, 8, 11). As in Matthew 11, then, those who do not embrace Jesus are under divine indictment.

To be sure, as we have noted, Matthew's judgment theme is not rooted in some sort of anti-Jewish polemic. The emphasis on the leadership's failure is important here. The contrast between their reception of Jesus and that of the crowds is stressed in the earlier depiction of Jesus's "triumphal" entry into Jerusalem. When Jesus enters the city riding on a donkey – evoking the figure of Solomon, who similarly rode into Jerusalem on a beast of burden amid a gleeful throng (cf. 1 Kgs 1:38–40) – the crowds are portrayed as recognizing Jesus's Davidic role, shouting, "Hosanna to the son of David!" (Matt 21:9).[68] People also spread garments on the ground before him (Matt 21:8), greeting him in the manner of a newly crowned king (2 Kgs 9:13).

It is perhaps relevant that Matthew insinuates that the people who hail Jesus are non-Jerusalemites. The shouts of "Hosanna!" from Psalm 118 are attributed to "the crowds *that went before him* [*hoi proagontes auton*] and *the ones that followed* [*hoi akolouthountes*]" (Matt 21:9). The evangelist informs us that "the city" needed these people to explain to them who Jesus was: "And when he came into Jerusalem all the city was shaken, saying, 'Who is this?' And the crowds said, 'This is Jesus the prophet of Nazareth of Galilee'" (Matt 21:10–11). As Matthew's narrative goes on, the point is further clarified: the rejection of Jesus is not so much the fault of the crowds as it is that of the leaders, who conspire against him. The scene of Jesus's temple action in Matthew, therefore, plays up this dynamic – what the crowds and the children recognize, namely, that Jesus is the Davidic messiah, the leaders do not.

---

[68] The crowd's action of spreading garments on the ground before Jesus (Matt 21:8) also mirrors the way the people greet the newly crowned king in 2 Kgs 9:13.

Judgment, Desolation, and Innocent Blood

That the future desolation of the temple is ultimately due to divine judgment is indisputable in Matthew 23. Jesus's warning that the "house" is "desolate," which we examined in the previous chapter, appears after he pronounces a seventh and climactic "woe" against the scribes and Pharisees. It is important to look at this saying in the larger setting of the chapter:

Woe to you, scribes and Pharisees, hypocrites! For you build the tombs of the prophets and decorate the graves of the righteous. And you say: "If we had lived in the days of our fathers, we would not have been *sharers in the blood of the prophets [koinōnoi en tō haimati tōn prophētōn].*" Therefore, you witness against yourselves that you are the sons of those who murdered the prophets. *Fill up [plērosate],* then, the measure of your fathers. You serpents, you brood of vipers, how will you escape the judgment of Gehenna? For this reason, behold, I send to you prophets, and wise men, and scribes: and some of them you will kill and crucify, and some of them will flog in your synagogues, and pursue from city to city: in order that upon you may come all *the righteous blood poured out on the earth [pan haima dikaion ekchynnomenon],* from *the blood of righteous Abel [tou haimatos Abel tou dikaiou]* to *the blood of Zechariah* son of Barachiah, whom you murdered between the temple and the altar. Amen, I say to you, all these things shall come upon this generation. O Jerusalem, Jerusalem, who kills the prophets, and stones those who are sent to her! How often I wanted to gather your children together, as a hen gathers her young under her wings, and you were not willing! Behold, your house is left to you desolate. For I say to you, you will not see me from now on, until you say, "Blessed is he who comes in the name of the Lord [Ps 118:26]." (Matthew 23:29–36)

The leaders of Jesus's day are seen as participating in the crimes of previous generations. Because of their actions, the fate of the city is sealed. Of course, in context, Jesus's death is interpreted as the culmination of the history of wickedness. Notably, the crescendo is reached with an account of a murder that took place *in the sanctuary.* Jesus is here clearly concerned with the temple's holiness.

Anders Runesson suggests Jesus's words in Matthew 23 indicates that the temple has now become incapable of rendering atonement and that this is why Jesus must suffer:

Contrary to common Christian theology, in Matthew, the temple is not destroyed as a punishment for the death of Jesus. The logic goes in the opposite direction: Jesus has to die precisely because the temple has already been defiled and will, as a consequence, inevitably be destroyed.[69]

---

[69] Runesson, *Divine Wrath*, 128.

Yet Runesson's analysis has two problems. First, as we have seen, there is evidence that even after Matt 23:38 Jesus acknowledges the validity of the cult (cf. Matt 26:17–19). Second, as Jonathan Klawans and Amy-Jill Levine notice, we must be careful not to assume that Jews would have thought atonement was only available through the cult. Atonement, for example, was understood to be available through almsgiving (cf. Sir 3:3, 30; 20:28; 35:5). Strikingly, Josephus, 4 Ezra, and 2 Baruch – all written in the aftermath of the sanctuary's destruction – offer no indication that Jews were concerned about lacking a means of atonement in the temple's absence.[70] In fact, other considerations lead us to believe that Matthew sees the future devastation coming on the city not as a result of a lack of a valid means of atonement, but because of Jesus's death.

Catherine Sider Hamilton brings attention to the way in which Matthew especially stresses the connection between the shedding of righteous blood and coming judgment in Matt 23:35.[71] She shows that the logic of Jesus's speech in this section mirrors what is found in other Jewish literature where the shedding of righteous blood results in divine punishment (cf. Gen 4:10; 2 Chr 24:25). Even more, Hamilton shows that the spilling of righteous blood is also seen as unleashing cosmic and apocalyptic catastrophe (e.g., 1 En. 9:1–3),[72] which fits well with the allusion to Jesus's *parousia* at the end of the speech in Matthew 23: "You will not see me from now on, until you say, 'Blessed is he who comes in the name of the Lord'" (Matt 23:39). The theme of the spilling of righteous blood is picked up again later in the narrative, where it is indisputably linked to the killing of Jesus. It first reappears in the story of Judas' attempt to reverse his betrayal of Jesus. Judas tells the priests, "I have sinned by handing over *innocent blood [haima athōon]*" (Matt 27:4). The chief priests then refuse to put the money he returns into the temple treasury "because it is the price of blood" and as a result use it to buy the place called "the Field of Blood" (Matt 27:6–8). The story highlights the priests' complicity in Jesus's death.

The motif of innocent blood returns again in the story of Pilate, whose wife instructs her husband to "have nothing to do with that *righteous*

---

[70] Jonathan Klawans, "Imagining Judaism after 70 C.E.," in *Companion to Ancient Jews and Judaism: Third Century BCE to Seventh Century CE*, ed. Naomi Koltun-Fromm and Gwynn Kessler (Hoboken: Wiley Blackwell, 2020), 208; Jonathan Klawans, "Josephus, the Rabbis, and Responses to Catastrophes Ancient and Modern," *JQR* 100 (2010): 305; Levine, "Concluding Reflections," 459-60.

[71] Catherine Sider Hamilton, *The Death of Jesus in Matthew: Innocent Blood and the End of the Exile*, SNTSMS 167 (Cambridge: Cambridge University Press, 2017).

[72] Hamilton, *Death of Jesus in Matthew*, 47–70.

man [to dikaiō]" (Matt 27:19). Pilate, however, shamefully relents and gives in to the crowd's demands, handing Jesus over to be crucified. Matthew is emphatic, however, that the crowd's demand was due to the chief priests and elders, who instigated the crowds to ask for Barabbas' release and have Jesus killed instead: "Now the chief priests and the elders persuaded the people to ask for Barabbas and destroy Jesus" (Matt 27:20). Once again, the imagery of "innocent blood" is prominent:

> When Pilate saw that he was accomplishing nothing, but that a riot was developing instead, he took water, and washed his hands before the crowd, saying, "I am *innocent* [*athōos*] of *the blood of this one* [*tou haimatos toutou*]: see to it yourselves." Then answered all the people, and said, "*His blood* [*haima*] be on us, and on our children." (Matthew 27:24–25)

The unfortunate use of this scene to justify antisemitism is well known and must be condemned in the strongest possible terms. As Hamilton shows, the cry of the crowd is best read as pointing to the destruction of Jerusalem.[73] According to Matthew, Jerusalem's demise at the hands of the Romans is the result of the fact that the innocent blood of Jesus was spilled there. The fact that Matthew later ties Jesus's death to the rending of the temple veil (Matt 27:51) likely indicates that the two events are to be viewed as interrelated. As many have recognized, the symbolism is best interpreted as prefiguring the sanctuary's coming dissolution.[74]

None of what we have seen so far supports the idea that Jesus taught that the temple cult was *invalid*. At no point have we found a passage that portrays Jesus as condemning cultic worship per se. Rather, Matthew's overall point is that the spilling of Jesus's righteous blood triggers judgment. Jesus predicts the end of the temple of his day like Jeremiah foretold the coming destruction of Solomon's. In addition, his pronouncement against the city in Matthew 23 is anchored in *concern* for the sanctuary's holiness – an act of murder there stands at the climax of a long line of wickedness that triggers divine judgment. Finally, it is worth mentioning that Jesus's quotation of Psalm 118 at the end of Matthew 23 ties the whole scene back to the "triumphal entry" and the "cleansing" of the temple – the scribes and the Pharisees are liable to judgment because, like the

---

[73] Hamilton, *Death of Jesus in Matthew*, 184–185.
[74] See the comprehensive discussion in Gurtner, *Torn Veil*, especially, 137, 190–191. The event could signify *more* than the sanctuary's end, but, at the very least, it includes that meaning. See also the relevant treatment on the Markan parallel in Dale C. Allison, Jr., *The End of the Ages Has Come: An Early Interpretation of the Passion and Resurrection of Jesus* (Minneapolis: Fortress Press, 1985), 30–33.

chief priests and elders in the temple earlier, they are unable to recognize Jesus's identity. We will have more to say about this in the next chapter.

This brings us to a crucial observation about Matthew's narrative: *Jesus's prediction of the temple's end in the Gospel's overall narrative is not the result of a rejection of cultic worship.* Judgment will befall Jerusalem first and foremost because of acts of wickedness committed by its leadership. The rejection of Jesus is part of this, and it is bound up with the failure of the leaders to recognize his messianic identity – the priests fail to grasp this in the temple (Matt 21:15) and the Pharisees do not recognize him as the figure from Psalm 118 who "comes in the name of the Lord" (Matt 23:39). As in other works like Jeremiah and Daniel, the temple will not be spared in the coming cataclysm. Nevertheless, Jesus does not suggest that the sanctuary or its sacrifices are illegitimate. On the contrary, Jesus forcefully affirms their holiness.

IMPLICATIONS FOR THE HISTORICAL JESUS

At the outset of our study, we quoted Ulrich Luz's suggestion that, since Matthew writes from a Jewish perspective similar to Jesus's, the evangelist's "'systematizations' of Jesus" might be "close to Jesus himself."[75] We can now apply that observation to the question of Jesus's sayings about the temple's future ruin. As we will explain later, rather than seeking to bypass Matthew's narrative framework, there are good reasons to think that it can help us better understand the way in which aspects of Jesus's teaching that appear to be in tension can sit alongside one another. At the same time, as we will also later explain, Matthew also leaves us asking a question about the historical Jesus: If he believed the Herodian temple would be destroyed, how did he envision Israel's liturgical life would continue in the age to come? Would there be a future temple as prophets like Isaiah had announced?

Jesus, the Temple's Demise, and Apocalyptic Judgment

Steven Bryan affirms: "it is widely agreed that Jesus predicted the destruction of the temple."[76] The analysis of the data in this chapter supports this conclusion. As E. P. Sanders recognizes, the notion that Jesus was

---

[75] Luz, "Matthew's Interpretive 'Tendencies' and the 'Historical' Jesus," 597.

[76] Steven M. Bryan, "Jesus and Israel's Eschatological Constitution," in *Handbook for the Study of the Historical Jesus*, ed. Holmén and Porter, 3:2850.

involved in some sort of controversy over the temple is "deeply implanted in the tradition."[77] Yet this memory is not only widely attested, it also fits well within a first-century Jewish context and is consistent with Jesus's effects.

In particular, that Jesus would have made such predictions fits well with the idea that his message was informed by apocalyptic imagery. As we have explained, the apocalyptic visions found in Daniel – one of the preeminent apocalyptic works – are repeatedly associated with the sanctuary's end (cf. Dan 8:13–14; 9:26–27; 11:31). That our sources all have Jesus explicitly speaking of the destruction of the temple with *Danielic* language (Matt 24:15//Mark 13:14//Luke 21:20) is not surprising. Indeed, the entirety of Jesus's apocalyptic discourse is shot through with Danielic imagery, including: "tribulation [*thlipsis*]" (Matt 24:[9,] 21, 29//Mark 13:19, 24; Dan 12:1 LXX), nations in conflict that "rise up" (Matt 24:7//Mark 13:8//Luke 21:10: *egeirō*; cf. Dan 7:3 LXX: *anabainō*), the "handing over [*paradidōmi*]" of God's people to the persecution of rulers (Mark 13:9; Dan 7:25 LXX), the falling of the stars (Mark 13:25; Dan 8:10), and the coming of the "Son of Man" figure (Mark 13:26; Dan 7:13). There are good reasons to believe that these kinds of traditions reflect impressions made by Jesus himself.[78] If Jesus was inspired by apocalyptic traditions such as those found in Daniel, it would not only be strange if he did not announce some sort of coming judgment, it would also be surprising if that judgment did not involve a kind of cessation of the temple's activity.

Whatever one thinks about the reliability of specific aspects of the First Gospel's portrait, the evangelist's *overall presentation* reinforces the idea that Jesus connected the temple's future ruin to the failure of the leaders to receive his message. That Jesus announced a coming cataclysm also makes sense in light of another widely attested feature of the tradition: Jesus's message of a coming judgment is often remembered as being bound up with a call to repentance. Though Sanders famously doubted the latter's origin in Jesus's ministry,[79] as Helen Bond writes, "this is perhaps the aspect of Sanders's work which has been most criticized by other scholars."[80] James Crossley notes that the overall message of repentance occurs throughout our sources: "the *theme* of repentance is found across the

---

[77] Sanders, *Jesus and Judaism*, 61.
[78] For a comprehensive argument in favor of the historicity of traditions here and its relationship to Jewish apocalyptic, see Pitre, *Jesus, the Tribulation, and the End of the Exile*, 219–379.
[79] Sanders, *Jesus and Judaism*, 115.
[80] Bond, *Historical Jesus*, 129.

Synoptic tradition, even if the precise words are not."[81] Once again, we can offer a list:

Repentance and Judgment in Jesus's Teaching

1. Woe Upon Chorazin and Bethsaida For Not Repenting
   (Matt 11:22//Luke 10:13 [Q?])
2. Failure to Repent Like Nineveh Leads to Judgment
   (Matt 12:41//Luke 11:32 [Q?])
3. Repentance Is Needed Because "the Kingdom of God Is at Hand"
   (Matt 4:17//Mark 1:15)
4. Whoever Rejects Jesus's Disciples' Message Faces Judgment
   (Mark 6:11)
5. Jesus Sends the Disciples Out to Proclaim Repentance
   (Mark 6:12)
6. Unless One Turns and Becomes Child-like, One Will Not Enter the Kingdom
   (Matt 18:3–4)
7. Jesus Has Come to Call Sinners to Repentance
   (Luke 5:32)
8. "Unless You Repent, You Will All Likewise Perish"
   (Luke 13:3, 5)
9. "There Will Be More Joy in Heaven over One Sinner Who Repents Than Over Ninety-Nine Righteous Persons"
   (Luke 15:7)
10. "There Is Joy before the Angels of God Over One Sinner Who Repents"
    (Luke 15:10)
11. The Rich Man Pleads to Be Allowed to Warn His Brothers to Repent
    (Luke 16:30)
12. "Pay Attention … If Your Brother Repents, Forgive Him"
    (Luke 17:3–4)
13. The Christ Had to Suffer "That Repentance for the Forgiveness of Sins Should Be Proclaimed in His Name to All the Nations"
    (Luke 24:47)
14. "Whoever Hears My Word and Believes … Has Eternal Life" and "Does Not Come under Judgment"
    (John 5:24)

---

[81] Crossley, *Jesus and the Chaos of History*, 109.

15. "For Judgment I Came into This World, That Those Who Do Not See May See, and Those Who See May Become Blind" (John 9:39)
16. "Whoever Hears My Words and Does Not Keep Them ... the Word That I Have Spoken Will Be His Judge" (John 12:47–48)
17. "They Would Not Have Sin, But Now They Have Seen and Hated Both Me and My Father" (John 15:24)

This recurrently attested tradition fits well with Jesus's first-century Jewish culture; Davies and Allison explain that turning from sin is "a central concept" in Jewish works, citing various sources.[82] Finally, we also have evidence that the early Jesus movement attached the message of judgment to repentance (e.g., 1 Thess 1:9–10; 2 Cor 7:9–10; 7:9–10; Rom 2:5). It seems safe to conclude with other scholars that this aspect of the tradition likely reflects a feature of Jesus's own preaching.[83]

Matthew refracts memories of Jesus through the lens Jesus likely used – a Jewish apocalyptic outlook. Anders Runesson may well be right when he asserts, "Matthew is more concerned with the judgment theme than any other New Testament text."[84] Yet this does not mean that Matthew's redactional interests are out of step with Jesus's concerns. The opposite is likely the case; Matthew's emphasis is probably rooted in impressions Jesus himself made. Jesus probably preached the need to repent in order to escape judgment. Indeed, in Matthew, saving his people from "sin" is Jesus's core mission (Matt 1:21), an idea inseparably linked to the message of repentance. For the evangelist, the siege of Jerusalem was the flipside of this feature of Jesus's teaching. Regardless of the authenticity of any particular logion, the overall portrait seems to reflect the general message of Jesus – and reveals that *such predictions were not the result of a repudiation of the cult.*

---

[82] Davies and Allison, *Matthew*, 1:306 citing, among other things, CD-A 4:2; 6:4–5; 8:16; 19:16; 20:17; 1QS 10:20; 1QH^a 2:9; 14:24; 4Q171 3:1–3. See also the texts and discussion in Crossley, *Jesus and the Chaos of History*, 106–108.
[83] Bond, *Historical Jesus*, 95. Pace Sanders, *Jesus and Judaism*, 117. See the critique of Sanders in Bond, *Historical Jesus*, 129; Crossley, *Jesus and the Chaos of History*, 109–111; Craig S. Keener, *The Historical Jesus of the Gospels: Jesus in Historical Context* (Grand Rapids: Eerdmans, 2009), 44–45.
[84] Runesson, *Divine Wrath*, 7.

The Question of the Temple Cult in the Age to Come

There is no reason to believe that, at some point in his ministry, Jesus changed his mind about the temple's legitimacy. We simply do not possess any material that suggests Jesus rejected the sanctuary's holiness. Nevertheless, we are still left with a puzzle: if Jesus did announce the temple's destruction, did he envision another one being established in Israel's future? The Synoptic reports of Jesus's temple action especially raises the question. In their accounts, Jesus quotes from a prophecy in Isaiah that explicitly describes an eschatological sanctuary. How did Jesus envision the cultic dimension of Israel's life continuing in the future age if the temple of his day would be destroyed? To answer that question, I suggest we look more carefully at Matthew's portrait of Jesus.

To begin with, let us note one key feature of Matthew's portrayal of Jesus's temple action: it involves the recognition – and (simultaneously) the rejection – of his *Davidic* identity. For Matthew, Jesus's relationship to the temple is ultimately related to the question of his Davidic role. Is this aspect of the Matthean portrait merely due to the evangelist's creativity or might it reflect some impressions made by Jesus himself? We will consider this in our next chapter.

5

Jesus, David, and the Temple

[T]here are excellent reasons for thinking that Jesus imagined himself as the
messiah, in a very specific and particular sense.
– Bart Ehrman[1]

[I]n a sense, Jesus triggered his own tragedy—at least partly by public actions
that implied a claim to royal authority over Jerusalem and its temple.
– John P. Meier[2]

Any discussion of the Jerusalem temple in the first-century Jewish context of Jesus must inevitably reckon with its connection to David. In
the historical books, it was David's desire to build a temple that elicited
the divine promise of an everlasting kingdom (cf. 2 Sam 7:1–17; 1 Chr
17:1–15). According to the scriptures, not only had David conquered the
city (cf. 2 Sam 5:6–10), he also personally chose and secured the area
next to the palace as the future temple site (cf. 1 Kgs 6–7; 2 Chr 3–4).[3]
Architecturally, then, the "house of David" would quite literally sit at the
"right hand" of the Lord who dwelt in the temple (cf. Ps 110:1).

It is little wonder, then, that David was understood as a kind of
co-founder of Israel's worship with Moses.[4] In several ways, David's

---

[1] Bart Ehrman, *How Jesus Became God: The Exaltation of a Jewish Preacher from Galilee*
(New York: HarperCollins, 2014), 118.
[2] John P. Meier, "Dividing Lines in Jesus Research Today: Through Dialectical Negation
to a Positive Sketch," *Int* 50, 4 (1996): 365.
[3] Tomoo Ishida, *The Royal Dynasties in Ancient Israel: A Study on the Formation and
Development of Royal-Dynastic Ideology* (New York: Walter de Gruyter, 1977), 144.
[4] See Simon J. De Vries, "Moses and David as Cult Founders in Chronicles," *JBL* 107,
4 (1988): 619–639; William M. Schniedewind, *Society and the Promise to David:*

institution of the liturgical worship at Jerusalem is described in terms of his being a "new Moses":[5]

- He assigns the duties of the priests and Levites (cf. 1 Chr 15–16; 23–27; cf. e.g., Exod 29–30).[6]
- He prepares the materials used in the construction of the sanctuary (cf. 1 Chr 22:14–16; 29:1–5; cf. Exod 25–31; 35–40).
- He receives a "pattern" for the sanctuary (cf. 1 Chr 28:19; cf. Exod 25:9, 40; 26:30).
- He offers a sacrifice which is consumed by fire from heaven (cf. 1 Chr 21:26; cf. Lev 9:24).

The Chronicler expressly identifies David's authoritative part in organizing the Jerusalem temple's priestly practices (cf. 2 Chr 8:13–14; 23:18; 35:4). In addition, a number of sources attribute the instruments used in the temple to David (cf. 2 Chr 7:6; 23:18; 29:25–27; Neh 12:36). Many of the very songs (i.e., psalms) sung in the temple were thought to have been composed by him (cf. 2 Chr 29:30; 11Q5 [11Psalms^a] 27:2–9; cf. Josephus, *Ant.* 7.305). David's role as founder of the Jerusalem temple's worship and composer of its liturgical music is also picked up in the book of Sirach (cf. Sir 47:9–10). The Chronicler even goes so far as to suggest that David's empire was known as "the kingdom of the Lord" precisely because the liturgy of the temple was associated with the house of David (cf. 2 Chr 13:8–12).

In addition, it was Solomon, the son of David, who elevated Zadok – father of the famed Zadokite priestly line – to the high priesthood (1 Kgs 2:35). From the perspective of Jewish eschatological hopes, this was highly significant. In numerous sources, the Zadokites are expected to serve as the priests in the temple of the age to come (cf. Ezek 40:46; 1QS 5:2, 9; 9:14; 1Q28b 1:22–28; CD-A 4:1–3; 4Q174 *frag. 1, col. i*, 21, 2:17; 4Q266 [4QDamascus Document^a] *frag. 5, i b, 16*). Here, then, we see yet another way the kingdom under David and Solomon served as a blueprint for restoration hopes.

What is more, the Davidic king is even described as having unique *priestly* prerogatives. Although he was not a Levite, David himself wears the ephod, the priestly garment (2 Sam 6:14; 1 Chr 15:27; cf. Exod

[5] William Johnstone, *1 and 2 Chronicles*, 2 vols. (Sheffield: Sheffield Academic Press, 1997), 190.
[6] Steven Schweitzer, *Reading Utopia in Chronicles*, LBS (London: T&T Clark, 2007), 142.

28:4), erects the tabernacle for the ark (2 Sam 6:17; cf. 1 Chr 15:1; 16:1; Num 1:51; 4:1–33), offers sacrifices (2 Sam 6:17; cf. 1 Chr 16:2; cf. Num 3:6–8, 14–38; 4:47; 6:16–17; 8:14–26), and blesses the people (2 Sam 6:18; cf. Num 6:22–27). Stunningly, David's sons are explicitly said to be "priests" (*kōhănîm*; 2 Sam 8:18). Adonijah, David's son, is described as enjoying cultic privileges without reprisal.[7] Especially remarkable is Psalm 110, which calls the Davidide, "a priest forever according to the order of Melchizedek" (Ps 110:4).

Our study of Jesus's relationship to the sanctuary, therefore, brings us to the question raised by the crowds in the Gospel of Matthew: "Can this be the son of David?" (Matt 12:23). The gospels repeatedly affirm the idea that Jesus was regarded as a Davidic figure. Moreover, as we have seen, Matthew in particular emphasizes the way this aspect of Jesus's identity relates to his activity in the temple – there he is hailed as "the son of David" (Matt 21:15). Does the connection between Jesus's temple activity and Davidic traditions reflect history or is it merely the result of later imagination? Here we will consider the matter. First, we will consider whether the community's messianic beliefs were likely anchored in perceptions Jesus himself made during his public ministry. Second, we will look at various ways Matthew ties Jesus's messianic role to temple traditions. Finally, we will ask whether the link Matthew established between Jesus's Davidic identity and his temple concerns is likely the due to impressions made by Jesus himself.

JESUS AND MESSIANIC TRADITIONS

Whether Jesus viewed himself in messianic terms is hotly contested. This is not surprising. There are few places where Jesus is said to have explicitly identified himself as the messiah. Dale Allison can pinpoint only a handful of unambiguous texts that indicate Jesus spoke of himself as such a figure (Mark 9:41; Matt 23:10; Luke 24:26, 46; John 4:25–26; 17:3) and, as Allison admits, these are widely seen as "late and secondary."[8] Nevertheless, the claim that the disciples only came to think of Jesus as the messiah after his death also faces difficulties. Here we will attempt to

---

[7] For further discussion, see A. A. Anderson, *2 Samuel*, WBC 11 (Dallas: Word Books, 1989), 137–138; C. E. Armerding, "Were David's Sons Really Priests?," in *Current Issues in Biblical and Patristic Interpretation*, ed. Gerald F. Hawthorne (Grand Rapids: Eerdmans, 1975), 84.

[8] Allison, *Constructing Jesus*, 282.

steer a middle way through the discussion. Since this is a heavily debated topic, the argument here involves several steps. It is important to understand how this section is organized. A brief overview is necessary.

First, following our stated method, we will begin by examining the general shape of the Jesus tradition. Since a messianic figure need not be a *Davidic* figure, we will first consider data that suggest Jesus saw himself as an eschatological royal figure and only then consider the data that point to his use of *Davidic* traditions. Second, after considering the overall outline of our sources' portrait of Jesus on these matters, we must pause and turn to an individual episode that has often stood at the center of discussion about Jesus's self-understanding, namely, his so-called "triumphal entry" into Jerusalem. Although we do not want to rest our case on a particular tradition, given the fact that so many scholars see this one episode as especially decisive, our treatment would be incomplete without it. Next, we consider the shape of the tradition within Jesus's first-century Jewish context. Finally, we will look at the question of Jesus's messianic role given the effects of his ministry. As we shall see, while Jesus likely did not explicitly go around identifying himself as the Davidic king, the most probable explanation of the early belief in his Davidic identity is that it emerged out of Jesus's own intimations during his public ministry.

Jesus's Royal Identity and the Broad Shape of the Tradition

Once again, let us begin our discussion with observations about the broad shape of the gospel tradition. I consider Dale Allison's work on Jesus's self-understanding to be especially insightful.[9] To begin with, he offers a long list of logia, mostly but not solely derived from the Synoptics (and Q?) that indicate that Jesus believed he would play "a starring role in the eschatological drama."[10] These include but are not limited to passages in which Jesus talks about the future coming of the Son of Man, a figure the evangelists identify as Jesus. The following catalogue is my own, but builds on Allison's treatment.

---

[9] While discussion of Allison's landmark book *Constructing Jesus* has often focused on his discussion of method, it should be recognized that his treatment of that matter is primarily found in the first chapter alone. The book also includes a comprehensive study of other matters. In particular, the careful analysis on Jesus's self-understanding in Chapter 2 ("More Than a Prophet: The Christology of Jesus," pp. 221–304) merits more substantive responses from scholars than it has heretofore received.

[10] Allison, *Constructing Jesus*, 226, 231.

Traditions Affirming Jesus's Central Role in His Message

1. Jesus Identifies Himself as Lord and Says Those Who Fail to Do His Words Will Suffer Downfall
   (Matt 7:21–23//Luke 6:47–49 [Q?])

2. Jesus Equates Himself with the One Who Is to Come
   (Matt 11:2–4//Luke 7:18–23 [Q?])

3. Those Who Receive Jesus's Disciples, Receive Him and Avoid Judgment
   (Matt 10:15//Luke 10:12; Matt 10:40//Luke 10:16 [Q?])

4. Those Who Fail to Respond to Jesus Will Face Judgment
   (Matt 11:21–24//Luke 10:13–15 [Q?])

5. Jesus Is a Moses-Like Figure Who Casts Out Demons by "The Finger of God"
   (Matt 12:28// Luke 11:20 [Q?])

6. The Son of Man Will Not Acknowledge Those Who Fail to Acknowledge Him (Matt 10:32–33//Luke 12:8–9 [Q?]; cf. Mark 8:38)

7. The Son of Man Will Come Like a Thief in the Night
   (Matt 24:43–44//Luke 12:39–40 [Q?])

8. Jesus Fulfills Micah's Prophecy of the Eschatological Tribulation
   (Matt 10:34–36//Luke 12:51–53 [Q?])

9. Jesus Is the One Who "Comes in the Name of the Lord"
   (*Matt 23:37–39*//Luke 13:34–35 [Q?])

10. The Son of Man's Coming Will Be Like Lightning in the Sky
    (Matt 24:27//Luke 17:24)

11. The Day of the Son of Man Will Be Like the Days of Noah
    (Matt 24:37–39//Luke 17:26–30 [Q?])

12. The Twelve Appointed by Jesus will Judge the Twelve Tribes of Israel
    (Matt 19:28//Luke 22:28–30 [Q?])

13. Peter Confesses Jesus Is the Messiah
    (Matt 16:15//Mark 8:29//Luke 9:20)

14. Jesus Responds to a Question about His Identity by Using Royal Language from Psalm 110 and Son of Man Imagery from Daniel 7 in Reference to Himself
    (Matt 26:64//Mark 14:62//Luke 22:69)

15. Jesus Avoids Answering Whether He Is "King of the Jews"
    (Matt 27:11–14//Mark 15:2–5//Luke 22:1–3)

16. The Sons of Zebedee Imply That Jesus Will Grant Thrones in the Kingdom
    (Matt 20:20–23//Mark 10:35–40)

17. Jesus Is Identified as Son of David by the Blind Seeking Healing
    (Matt 20:29–34//Mark 10:46–52)
18. Jesus Is Identified as the Son of David at His Triumphal Entry
    (Matt 21:9//Mark 11:9–10)
19. The Son of Man Will Come on the Clouds and Send the Angels to
    Gather the Elect
    (Matt 24:30–31//Mark 13:26–27)
20. Jesus Is Mocked by Romans Soldiers as "King of the Jews"
    (Matt 27:27–31//Mark 15:16–20)
21. False Witnesses Claim Jesus Said He Would Destroy and Rebuild
    the Temple
    (Matt 26:61//Mark 14:58)
22. Bystanders at Calvary Claim Jesus Said He Would Destroy and
    Rebuild the Temple
    (Matt 27:39//Mark 15:29)
23. "You Will Not Have Gone Through all the Towns of Israel before
    the Son of Man Comes"
    (Matt 10:23)
24. The Son of Man will Gather the Wicked Out of the Kingdom
    (Matt 13:41)
25. Jesus Is Identified as the Son of David in the Temple
    (Matt 21:15)
26. The Parable of the Ten Virgins and the Coming of the Bridegroom
    (Matt 25:1–13)
27. The Son of Man Will Sit on a Glorious Throne as King and Judge
    the Nations
    (Matt 25:31–36)
28. Jesus Begins His Ministry by Announcing His Fulfillment of the
    Coming of the Anointed Prophet of Isaiah 61
    (Luke 4:16–19)
29. "Be Like Those Who Are Waiting for Their Master's Return"
    (Luke 12:35–38)
30. "I Have Come to Cast Fire on the Earth"
    (Luke 12:49–50; cf. *Gos. Thom.* §§10, 16, 82)
31. "When the Son of Man Comes, Will He Find Faith on the Earth?"
    (Luke 18:8)
32. Jesus Is Identified as a "King" at His Arrival at Jerusalem
    (Luke 19:38)
33. Jesus is Mocked by Herod's Soldiers as a Royal Figure
    (Luke 23:11)

Allison complains that scholars have become so accustomed to dividing up these statements into various categories (e.g., "Son of Man" passages; "Messianic" sayings) that they have essentially missed the forest for the trees. These passages, Allison says, "constitute a family of traditions that requires explanation... [W]hen they look into the future, they see Jesus, and indeed Jesus front and center."[11] Along similar lines, Simon Joseph observes that though Q is typically viewed as "non-messianic," many of its characterizations of Jesus nonetheless seem to "cry out for a messianic interpretation."[12]

Here we do not have the space to enter into a detailed analysis of Jesus's use of apocalyptic Son of Man traditions. That Jesus is some-times remembered as referring to the Son of Man in the third person has caused some to dispute that Jesus identified himself with this figure. Of course, the evangelists view the term as referring to Jesus (e.g., Matt 8:20//Luke 9:58; Matt 9:6//Mark 2:10//Luke 5:24; Matt 11:19; Matt 12:40//Luke 11:30; Matt 16:13; Matt 17:22–23//Mark 9:31//Luke 9:44). Nevertheless, in a detailed treatment, Allison shows that even if Jesus spoke of the Son of Man in the third person, it would not negate the general impression that Jesus envisioned himself as "the center of his own eschatological scenario."[13] Among other things, we should mention that we have good evidence that speaking of oneself in the third person – "illeism" – was a known practice in antiquity (cf., e.g., 2 Cor 12:1–4).[14]

In addition, for Allison two features of the preceding list are especially significant. First, Jesus's appointment of a group of twelve disciples. This dimension of our sources' portrait of Jesus is widely believed to reflect historical memory.[15] It is attested as early as the letters of Paul, who seems to assume that their existence is well-known (cf. 1 Cor 15:5). It is very difficult to imagine that the notion of the twelve emerged only later.[16] That Jesus had a group of twelve disciples is widely accepted

---

[11] Allison, *Constructing Jesus*, 231.

[12] Simon J. Joseph, *The Nonviolent Messiah: Jesus, Q, and the Enochic Tradition* (Minneapolis: Fortress Press, 2014), 112.

[13] Allison, *Constructing Jesus*, 303 (cf. 293–303).

[14] See also the extensive analysis of illeism in ancient literature in Roderick Elledge, *Use of the Third Person for Self-Reference by Jesus and YHWH: A Study of Illeism in the Bible and Ancient Near Eastern Texts and Its Implications for Christology*, LNTS 575 (London: T&T Clark, 2017), 25–117.

[15] See, e.g., Meier, *A Marginal Jew*, 138; Ehrman, *Apocalyptic Prophet*, 186; Richard Horsely, *Jesus and the Spiral of Violence: Popular Jewish Resistance in Roman Palestine* (Minneapolis: Fortress Press, 1993), 206–207.

[16] See the extensive treatment in Meier, *A Marginal Jew*, 3:125–197.

by scholars and is typically seen as expressive of his expectation of the eschatological ingathering of the twelve tribes (cf. Matt 19:28//Luke 22:30).[17] How does the existence of the twelve relate to the question of Jesus's self-understanding? Allison draws on Étienne Trocmé's important observation that Jesus does not appear to be counted among this unit but is, rather, the one who appoints them and leads them. The arrangement suggests his leadership of eschatological Israel.[18]

Second, Allison highlights the tradition that Jesus was mocked and crucified as "the King of the Jews" (Matt 27:11//Mark 15:2//Luke 23:3// John 18:33; Mark 15:9, 12//John 18:39; Matt 27:29//Mark 15:18//John 19:3; Luke 23:3; Matt 27:37//Mark 15:26//Luke 23:38//John 19:19; John 19:20–21) appealing to John Collins' argument that this feature of the community's memory indicates that Jesus "was viewed as a messianic pretender."[19] The sentence of crucifixion, Allison observes, was typically reserved for "theft, murder, and insurrectionists."[20] There is no reason to think Jesus was ever accused of the first two crimes. The most likely explanation of Jesus's death on a cross, therefore, is that Jesus was perceived as some sort of political threat – precisely as the titulus suggests. What lends further probability to this tradition is the titulus' term for Jesus, "King of the Jews." The phrase is hard to attribute to the theological convictions of the community. Joseph Fitzmyer is correct that had the titulus tradition originated with Jesus's followers, "they would have used *christos*, for early Christians would scarcely have called their Lord 'the king of the Jews.'"[21] "King of the Jews" has a distinctly non-Jewish ring to it; Jews preferred, "king of Israel" (cf. Matt 27:42; cf. also 1 Sam 24:14; Prov. 1:1; John 1:49).[22] Even more, the ironic title coheres well with the parodic character of crucifixion.[23]

---

[17] See, e.g., Bond, *Historical Jesus*, 96–97; John P. Meier, "Jesus, the Twelve and Restoration," in *Restoration*, ed. Scott, 365–404; Sanders, *Jesus and Judaism*, 98–106.

[18] Allison, *Constructing Jesus*, 233, citing Étienne Trocmé, *The Childhood of Christianity*, trans. John Bowden (London: SCM Press, 1977), 10.

[19] John J. Collins, *The Apocalyptic Imagination: An Introduction to Jewish Apocalyptic Literature*, 2nd ed. (Grand Rapids: Eerdmans, 1998), 257.

[20] Allison, *Constructing Jesus*, 236

[21] Fitzmyer, *Luke*, 1:773.

[22] See Allison, *Constructing Jesus*, 235, citing Jorg Frey, "Der historische Jesus und der Christus der Evangelien," in *Der historische Jesus: Tendenzen und Perspektiven der gegenwärtigen Forschung*, ed. Jens Schröter and Ralph Brucken, BZNW 114 (Berlin: Walter de Gruyter, 2002), 305. See also Jack Finegan, *Die Überlieferung der Leidens- und Auferstehungsgeschichte Jesu* (Giessen: Töpelmann, 1934), 78.

[23] Allison, *Constructing Jesus*, 234–235, drawing on Nils Alstrup Dahl, "The Crucified Messiah," in *Jesus the Christ: The Historical Origins of Christology Doctrine*, ed.

For these reasons, the titulus tradition is widely thought to be extremely significant for historical reconstructions of Jesus. Consider the following from Paula Fredriksen and E. P. Sanders:

> Whether at any time in his ministry Jesus claimed for himself the title *messiah* – the evidence on this point is extremely ambiguous – he certainly died as if he had.[24]

> We should begin our study with two firm facts before us: Jesus was executed by the Romans as would-be "king of the Jews," and his disciples subsequently formed a messianic movement which was not based on the hope of military victory.[25]

The titulus is therefore a significant historical datum that makes it difficult to think Jesus was not perceived as making some sort of *political* claim.

Finally, Allison highlights another consideration that virtually all Jesus scholars accept, namely, that the kingdom of God was likely "the major theme of Jesus's preaching."[26] For example, James Dunn says that "one of the least disputable, or disputed, facts about Jesus" is that his message centered on the "kingdom of God."[27] Sanders writes, "It is beyond doubt that Jesus proclaimed the kingdom. We know this not from analyzing any one saying or group of sayings, but from noting the ubiquity of the theme 'kingdom.'"[28] Not only is this recollection of Jesus's teaching deeply embedded in our sources,[29] it is easily situated within Jesus's Jewish setting[30] – especially Danielic hopes, which Jesus likely invoked[31] – and figured, albeit with less frequency, in the proclamation of the early followers of Jesus (e.g., 1 Thess 2:12; Gal 5:21; 1 Cor 4:20; 6:9–10; 15:24, 50; Rom 14:17).[32] Given the recurrence of this theme in

---

Donald H. Juel (Minneapolis: Fortress Press, 1991), 36–37. On the historical probability of this tradition, see also Meier, *A Marginal Jew*, 3:24; Evans, *Jesus and His Contemporaries*, 301–318.

[24] Fredriksen, *From Jesus to Christ*, 123.

[25] Sanders, *Jesus and Judaism*, 294. See also Gerd Theissen, "From the Historical Jesus to the Kerygmatic Son of God: How Role Analysis Contributes to the Understanding of New Testament Christology," in *Jesus Research*, ed. Charlesworth, 249.

[26] Allison, *Constructing Jesus*, 244.

[27] Dunn, *Jesus Remembered*, 383.

[28] Sanders, *Jesus and Judaism*, 139. See, similarly, Meier, *A Marginal Jew*, 1:174–175.

[29] See the overview of texts in Allison, *Constructing Jesus*, 164–168; Dunn, *Jesus Remembered*, 383–487.

[30] See the classic study in Bruce D. Chilton, *God in Strength: Jesus's Announcement of the Kingdom*, SNTSU 1 (Freistadt: Plöchl, 1979).

[31] See Evans, "Daniel in the New Testament," 2:490–527, who argues that Jesus's kingdom proclamation bore a particularly Danielic stamp.

[32] For fuller treatments, see Keener, *Historical Jesus*, 196–197.

our sources, it is remarkable that God's identity as king appears only rarely in Jesus's teaching. As Allison remarks, this makes especially good sense if Jesus saw *himself* as the one who would reign on the throne.[33] Therefore, not only is the position that Jesus viewed himself in royal terms consistent with the recurrently attested idea that he would play a pivotal role in the age to come, it also fits well with other features of the tradition that are considered particularly weighty.

Jesus and Davidic Messianism

There are also good reasons to think that the specific association of Jesus with Davidic hopes was made during his lifetime. John P. Meier shows the conviction that Jesus was the son of David "reaches back in many forms to the earliest days of the church and continues to be referred to throughout the first and second Christian generations."[34] Meier submits that Jesus's Davidic pedigree is attested in the genealogies of Matthew and Luke (which he attributes to independent sources), in Paul (Rom 1:3–4), the Fourth Gospel (John 7:42), Mark's source (Mark 10:47–48; 11:1–10; 12:35–37), and other New Testament works (Heb 1:5; 7:14; Rev 3:7; 5:5; 22:16). All of this is surprising since "no New Testament author makes Davidic descent the main focus of his redactional Christology."[35]

Meier's attempt to downplay Davidic forms of messianism in the New Testament, however, is not convincing.[36] Since he penned the preceding words, a flood of works has been published that detail the numerous ways the different evangelists accentuate Davidic traditions in their accounts of Jesus's life, ministry, and teaching.[37] Nonetheless, this is not

---

[33] Allison, *Constructing Jesus*, 251.

[34] John P. Meier, "From Elijah-Like Prophet to Royal Davidic Messiah," in *Jesus: A Colloquium in the Holy Land*, ed. Doris Donnelly (New York: Continuum, 2001), 61.

[35] Meier, "From Elijah-Like Prophet," 61.

[36] On the need to avoid homogenizing the diverse forms of messianic expectations articulated in different ancient sources, see the careful study in Matthew V. Novenson, *The Grammar of Messianism: An Ancient Political Idiom and Its Users* (Oxford: Oxford University, 2017).

[37] On the New Testament in general, see Joshua W. Jipp, *The Messianic Theology of the New Testament* (Grand Rapids: Eerdmans, 2020). On Matthew: Nicholas G. Piotrowski, *Matthew's New David at the End of Exile: A Socio-Rhetorical Study of Scriptural Quotations*, NovTSup 170 (Leiden: Brill, 2016); Joel Willitts, *Matthew's Messianic Shepherd-King: In Search of the "The Lost Sheep of the House of Israel,"* BNZW 127 (Berlin: Walter de Gruyter, 2007); Chae, *Jesus as the Eschatological Davidic Shepherd*; Lidija Novakovic, *Messiah, the Healer of the Sick: A Study of Jesus as the Son of David in the Gospel of Matthew*, WUNT 2/170 (Tübingen: Mohr Siebeck, 2003). On Mark: Max Botner, *Jesus*

a problem for our study as it is for Meier's. We have already made the case that "dissimilarity from Christianity" is a questionable criterion. There is no reason to insist a priori that the evangelists' priorities were opposed to Jesus's. A powerful argument in this regard has been offered by Anthony Le Donne.

Le Donne shows that Jesus's healing and exorcistic ministry is remembered in specifically Jewish terms in Matthew. In contrast to Mark, Matthew anchors Jesus's powers over demonic forces in long-standing Jewish traditions about Solomon, who was remembered as a healer and exorcist.[38] Whereas Mark's depiction of Jesus healing by his spit (Mark 8:22–26) is reminiscent of non-Jewish therapeutic methods, Jesus's therapeutic activity in Matthew is especially tied to Davidic imagery. Though Le Donne plays it down, Jesus's Davidic identity does surface in Mark's story of the healing of Bartimaeus (Mark 10:46–52). Nevertheless, as Le Donne demonstrates, Matthew reinforces the Davidic character of Jesus's therapeutic ministry, particularly in regard to his exorcisms (cf., e.g., Matt 12:12–23; 15:22). Le Donne concludes that in localizing commemoration of Jesus within this larger interpretive framework, Matthew "reflects the apologetic of an insider, and in this way is probably closer to how Jesus would have wanted to be perceived. Although the statement might seem counterintuitive, Matthew's refraction of the tradition might provide a better historical portrait of Jesus than the memories against which this refraction reacted."[39]

Christ as the Son of David in the Gospel of Mark, SNTSMS 174 (Cambridge: Cambridge University Press, 2019); Bernardo Cho, *Royal Messianism and the Jerusalem Priesthood in the Gospel of Mark*, LNTS 607 (London: T&T Clark, 2019); Stephen P. Ahearne-Kroll, *The Psalms of Lament in Mark's Passion: Jesus's Davidic Suffering*, SNTSMS 142 (Cambridge: Cambridge University Press, 2007). On Luke: Sarah Harris, *The Davidic Shepherd King in the Lukan Narrative*, LNTS 558 (London: T&T Clark, 2016); Yuzuru Miura, *David in Luke-Acts*, WUNT 2/232 (Tübingen: Mohr Siebeck, 2005); Mark L. Strauss, *The Davidic Messiah in Luke-Acts: The Promise and Its Fulfillment in Lukan Christology*, JSNTSup 110 (Sheffield: Sheffield Academic Press, 1995). On John: Jipp, *Messianic Theology*, 117–147; Joel Willitts, "David's Sublation of Moses: A Davidic Explanation for the Mosaic Christology of the Fourth Gospel," in *Reading the Gospel of John's Christology as Jewish Messianism*, ed. Benjamin E. Reynolds and Gabriele Boccaccini, Ancient Judaism and Early Christianity 106 (Leiden: Brill, 2018), 203–225. Though published a year before Meier's piece, see also Margaret Daly-Denton, *David in the Fourth Gospel: The Johannine Reception of the Psalms* (Leiden: Brill, 2000).

[38] See the more recent monograph-length treatment in Jiří Dvořáček, *The Son of David in Matthew's Gospel in the Light of Solomon as Exorcist Tradition*, WUNT 2/415 (Tübingen: Mohr Siebeck, 2016).

[39] Le Donne, *Historiographical Jesus*, 181.

Meier himself writes that Mark's account of the healing of Bartimaeus likely signals that Jesus's contemporaries believed he intended to evoke Davidic traditions:

The isolated allusion to the Son of David as a Solomonic miracle-worker in the Bartimaeus story is most probably not a product of Christian theology but a relic of how some Palestinian Jews with infirmities actually looked upon this particular Jewish miracle-worker and teacher of wisdom, who was believed to be of Davidic descent. [T]his extremely primitive "Jewish Christology" ... most probably goes back to the time of Jesus himself.[40]

The redactional tendency of Matthew, therefore, which amplifies Jesus's Davidic role, need not be seen as antithetical to historical memory.[41]

As Meier explains, the claim that Jesus's crucifixion as "king of the Jews" would on its own necessarily lead to the conclusion that he was a Davidic figure is also improbable. Jews knew of non-Davidic monarchs such as the Hasmoneans. Notably, Herod decided the best way to legitimate his power was to attach himself to *these* traditions. There is little evidence that he styled himself as a Davidide.[42]

What should we make of the fact, then, that the gospels indicate that Jesus was hesitant to identify himself as the messiah and instructed others to keep quiet about it? In his influential 1901 monograph, William Wrede famously identified the "messianic secret" as a critical piece of Mark's narrative.[43] It was Rudolf Bultmann, however, who first insisted that this was a Markan invention, a position Wrede himself later rejected.[44] Yet, given that Jesus was likely crucified as "king of the Jews," another possibility also exists: Jesus hesitated to go around referring to himself as the Davidic messiah because he understood the potential consequences of making royal claims. Jesus would have been especially cautious if he understood himself to be a different *kind* of Davidic king as his early followers apparently believed he was.[45]

---

[40] Meier, *A Marginal Jew*, 2:690.

[41] See also Rodríguez, *Structuring Early Christian Memory*, 192–195.

[42] Meier, "From Elijah-Like Prophet," 62.

[43] William Wrede, *Das Messiasgeheimnis in den Evangelien* (Göttingen: Vandenhoeck & Ruprecht, 1901).

[44] For an overview, see Hans Rollmann and Werner Zager, "Unveröffentlichte Briefe William Wredes zur Problematisierung des messianischen Selbstverständnisses Jesu," *Zeitschrift für neuere Theologiegeschichte* 8 (2001): 274–317.

[45] Some have insisted that Jesus could not have understood himself in terms of eschatological Davidic traditions due to the way he is remembered as resisting violence. Since David was a warrior and military leader, it is said to be improbable that he would have evoked the figure of one of Israel's greatest warriors. This objection, however, is not ultimately

Moreover, if Jesus was preaching an eschatological message, he would have probably viewed his kingship as a *future* reality. Bart Erhman writes:

I think there are excellent reasons for thinking that Jesus imagined himself as the messiah, in a very specific and particular sense. The messiah was thought to be the future ruler of the people of Israel. But as an apocalypticist, Jesus did not think that the future kingdom was going to be won by a political struggle. It was going to be brought by the Son of Man ... Then the kingdom would arrive. And I think Jesus believed he himself would be the king in that kingdom.[46]

This is essentially where Allison leans:

I would, if forced, place my bet on this last option, Jesus as *messias designatus*: he saw kingship as a hope or a destiny, not an accomplishment.[47]

This seems to have been precisely the way believers such as Paul understood Jesus's rule, as we explain later. To sum up, we can say the following: it seems credible that Jesus really was crucified as "king of the Jews."

While Jewish eschatological hopes took different forms, the dominant form took a Davidic shape. In light of this, one might conclude that if Jesus evoked expectations for a future kingdom, it seems more likely than not that this would have triggered Davidic associations. Indeed, given that Davidic hopes prevailed among the people, by drawing on eschatological traditions, Jesus likely also caused people to ask: Who then will be the Davidic king? It would have been natural for them to wonder if it was Jesus himself. As we have seen, Jesus's healing activity certainly would have to fit a Davidic profile. Other aspects of the tradition largely viewed as reflecting Jesus's ministry also would have brought Davidic traditions to mind:

- *Jesus's Selection of Twelve (e.g., Matt 19:28//Luke 22:30).* Jesus's selection of the twelve – a feature of the Jesus tradition often viewed as reflecting historical memory[48] – seems to have been rooted in expectations regarding the restoration of the twelve tribes. Yet such beliefs were closely connected with Davidic hopes (cf., e.g., Isa 11:1–16;

---

convincing. Jesus's followers applied martial passages such as Psalm 110 to Jesus, recognizing that he had transformed Davidic kingship. As Allison points out, if Jesus's followers could reimagine a Davidic reign, there is no reason to insist Jesus could not have. See Allison, *Constructing Jesus*, 286. Furthermore, the therapeutic son of David tradition reveals that Davidic traditions were multifaceted.

[46] Ehrman, *How Jesus Became God*, 118.
[47] Allison, *Constructing Jesus*, 289–290.
[48] See the sources in n. 17.

Jer 30:1–9; Ezek 37:15–28).[49] Notably, Solomon himself appointed
twelve officers (cf. 1 Kgs 4:7).[50]

* ***Jesus as Teacher of Parables (e.g., Matt 21:33–43//Mark 12:1–11//
  Luke 20:9–18).*** That Jesus taught by means of parables is repeatedly
  attested and is largely viewed as, in some way, reflecting impressions
  he made.[51] This would fit well with Davidic traditions; Solomon, the
  son of David, was remembered as the wisdom teacher par excellence
  (Prov 1:1; 1 Kgs 4:29–34; Sir 47:17; Wis 7:7–22; Josephus, *Ant.* 8.42–
  44, 49). Notably, he was remembered for teaching in "parables" (cf.
  parabolē in 3 Kgdms 5:12 LXX; Prov 1:6 LXX).
* ***Jesus as a Prophet (Matt 21:12–13//Mark 11:15–19//Luke 19:45–46).***
  As we saw in the temple "cleansing" story, Jesus appears to act in
  ways that evoke the prophets. Many believe he in fact did act as a
  prophetic figure, performing prophetic signs.[52] Perhaps he saw himself
  acting in imitation of Moses.[53] Yet Jesus's role as prophet may also
  be viewed as consistent with Davidic traditions since David himself
  was recognized as a prophetic figure (11QPs^a 27; *L.A.B.* 59; Josephus,
  Ant. 6.166; cf. also Targum on 2 Sam 22:1; 23:1).[54]

It seems unlikely that these sorts of potential Davidic connections would
have gone unnoticed by those already primed to look for a coming eschatological son of David.

Given all the data, it is hard to imagine that Jesus's proclamation of the
"kingdom of God," the historicity of which is strongly supported, would not
have in some way been related to David's kingdom. The Chronicler expressly
identifies the Davidic kingdom as the "kingdom of the LORD" (1 Chr 28:5;
cf. 2 Chr 13:8). It would seem that a myopic focus on the terminology of
"messiah" or "son of David" has caused scholars to overlook the broader
typological allusions to Davidic and Solomonic traditions in our sources.[55]

---

[49] Isa 9:1–9; 11:1, 11–13; Jer 23:5–6; 30:1–11; Ezek 34:23–31; 37:15–19; *Pss. of Sol.*
17:31.

[50] See Benedict Viviano, O.P., "A Woman's Quest for Wisdom and the Adoration of the
Magi as Part of Matthew's Program of Solomonic Sapiential Messianism," in *The Gospel of Matthew at the Crossroads*, ed. Senior, 686.

[51] See, e.g., Meier, *A Marginal Jew*, 5:370–71; Bond, *Historical Jesus*, 97–99; Ehrman,
Apocalyptic Prophet, 179–180.

[52] See, e.g., Aune, *Prophecy in Early Christianity*, 161

[53] See, e.g., Allison, *Constructing Jesus*, 270–274.

[54] For further discussion, see Miura, *David in Luke-Acts*, 128–132.

[55] See Martin Hengel, "Jesus, the Messiah of Israel: The Debate about the 'Messianic
Mission' of Jesus," in *Authenticating the Activities of Jesus*, ed. Chilton and Evans, 335.

To write off all of the preceding indicators as unrelated to impressions made by Jesus himself seems like a failure to come to terms with the data. Of course, historical investigation must deal with *probabilities* and is unable to attain certainty. In this case, however, the probability seems high that Jesus said and did things that he knew would elicit Davidic hopes from his audience.

Jesus's "Triumphal Entry"

While we have attempted to keep our discussions of the historical Jesus focused on broadly attested themes, there is, however, one incident reported in the gospels that has an especially important place in the quest: Jesus's "triumphal" entry into Jerusalem. All four canonical gospels report the story (Matt 21:1–11//Mark 11:1–10//Luke 19:29–38//John 12:12–15).[56] The scene bears a striking resemblance to the story of Solomon's coronation (1 Kgs 1:33, 38). It also calls to mind Zechariah's eschatological prophecy: "Behold, your king comes to you ... humble and riding on a donkey" (Zech 9:9).[57] That Davidic allusions were made with the story is suggested by the fact that all of the Synoptics have the crowd uttering something relating to Davidic or kingship themes.[58] *All three* Synoptic accounts report the crowd's action of spreading garments on the ground before Jesus (Matt 21:8//Mark 11:8//Luke 19:36), a detail that suggests he is being perceived as a king (2 Kings 9:13). Mark, in keeping with his subtle style, makes no explicit mention of the connection with Zechariah. Matthew, however, puts a spotlight on it (cf. Matt 21:4–5).

Of course, the key question for Jesus studies is whether the accounts of the episode preserve a memory of an event from Jesus's ministry. Some are skeptical. Sanders makes the case that had Jesus engaged in such behavior, the Romans would have acted more swiftly.[59] Although

---

[56] See, e.g., Dunn, *Jesus Remembered*, 641–642; Ben F. Meyer, *The Aims of Jesus* (London: SCM, 1979), 199; Sanders, *Jesus and Judaism*, 306–307; Brent Kinman, *Jesus's Entry into Jerusalem in the Context of Lukan Theology and the Politics of His Day* (Leiden: Brill, 1995), 159–172.

[57] It seems clear that the imagery in Zech 9:9 was linked with Davidic traditions. See, e.g., Le Donne, *Historiographical Jesus*, 200–204.

[58] See, e.g., Kinman, *Jesus's Entry into Jerusalem*, 79–80; Meier, *A Marginal Jew*, 3:496; Sanders, *Jesus and Judaism*, 306–307; Ben Witherington, III, *Christology of Jesus* (Minneapolis: Fortress Press, 1990), 113–115. See, e.g., France, *Gospel of Matthew*, 779.

[59] Sanders, *Jesus and Judaism*, 306.

Bultmann writes that the episode was derived from a "grain of remembrance," he nonetheless dismisses the possibility that Jesus intended the crowds to deduce his messianic identity from his actions and finds it hard to believe the onlookers would have made the association with Zechariah 9.[60] Yet these objections are far from insurmountable.

Paula Fredriksen observes that had Jesus brought his healing and teaching ministry to Jerusalem in the past, the Roman authorities may have already decided he was harmless.[61] The Fourth Gospel has Jesus going up to Jerusalem for the various festivals (John 2:13; 4:45; 5:1; 7:14; 10:22–23; 12:12), which is very plausible. Francis Moloney also helpfully observes that Luke seems to be aware that Jesus frequently went up to the city; the gospel indicates that it was Jesus's "custom [*ethos*]" to go to the Mount of Olives (Luke 22:39).[62] Whatever one makes of this detail, however, the fact remains: according to the Synoptics and John, Jesus's arrest and death occurred not long after he entered the city. In their retellings, then, Jesus did not, therefore, "get away" with the provocation caused by his "triumphal entry" for long. Moreover, even if the Zechariah connection was not originally perceived, the essential core of the story could be historical. Mark never even mentions Zechariah's prophecy. Moreover, although the Fourth Gospel connects the scene to the messianic oracle, it also states: "His disciples did not understand these things at first, but when Jesus was glorified, then they remembered that these things had been written about him and these things had been done to him" (John 12:16). Not even Matthew claims the fulfillment of Zechariah's vision was perceived by the crowds.

In addition, details of the story point away from an origin in mere imagination. First, the specific use of *hosanna* by the crowds has long baffled commentators. The Synoptics link it to Psalm 118, yet the Septuagint never transliterates the term as Mark does. Instead, it consistently renders the Hebrew grammatically with *sōson*, "save." As Le Donne shows, it is less likely that Mark invented this feature of the story to align it with the scriptures of Israel than that he received it and preserved it. This is not hard to believe. The crowd's use of the psalm – which is attested in all four canonical gospels – makes good historical sense. It seems to have been chanted in the temple at Passover (m. Pesaḥ 5:7). The Mishnah

---

[60] Bultmann, *History of the Synoptic Tradition*, 261–262.
[61] See Fredriksen, *Jesus of Nazareth*, 243.
[62] Moloney, "Revisiting the Temple," 66.

also says it was sung by pilgrims headed to Jerusalem (m. Sukkah 4:5).[63] While we do not have sources reporting that it was sung by pilgrims as they arrived at Jerusalem for Passover, given its apparent festal use, it is difficult to insist it could not have been. The psalm itself seems to depict a procession to the temple (cf. Ps 118:26–27) and thus lent itself to such contexts. Its appearance, then, is eminently credible.[64]

Second, Jesus's act of sitting on a donkey would have been noteworthy. Pilgrims normally came on foot, as the rest of Jesus's entourage does in the gospel accounts. Nowhere else in any of our sources' depiction of his travels do they ever suggest he used a donkey. In addition, that Jesus would have performed an action meant to evoke the traditions of Israel meshes not only with stories like the temple "cleansing" but also with what we know about other first-century prophetic figures.[65]

Third, the crowds' words and deeds indicate they caught the royal allusions. That others would have perceived Jesus in messianic terms is quite plausible. Messianic hopes were rampant and expectations of a deliverance through an eschatological Davidic figure seem to have been particularly widespread. The Passover backdrop would have reinforced such longings. Political tensions with Rome ran high and Josephus indicates that Jewish eschatological beliefs helped fuel the rebellion that led to the Jewish War.[66] Furthermore, if Jesus did ride into Jerusalem, there likely would have been some present who would have known that features of Jesus's teaching – for example, his proclamation of the kingdom – were consistent with an eschatological message. For them, an act like riding into Jerusalem on a donkey would naturally have been seen as evoking messianic hopes.

Many scholars, therefore, believe that the basic outline of the "triumphal entry" story reflects a historical event.[67] John Meier and John Collins even suggest that the basic outline of the Jesus story is incoherent without it.[68] According to Meier, if we reject it:

---

[63] For a fuller study of the use of Psalm 118 in Jewish texts, see Andrew C. Brunson, *Psalm 118 in the Gospel of John: An Intertextual Study of the New Exodus Pattern in the Theology of John*, WUNT 2/158 (Tübingen: Mohr Siebeck, 2003), 22–101.

[64] See Le Donne, *Historiographical Jesus*, 219.

[65] John J. Collins, *The Scepter and the Star*, ABRL (New York: Doubleday, 1995), 206.

[66] Josephus' account of figures such as Theudas (*Ant.* 20.97–99) and the Egyptian (*Ant.* 20.167–168) indicates that they attracted followers by evoking New Exodus hopes. See Allison, *New Moses*, 23–28.

[67] See, e.g., Dunn, *Jesus Remembered*, 640–642.

[68] Collins, *Scepter and the Star*, 206; Meier, "Dividing Lines in Jesus Research Today," 365; Joel B. Green, "The Death of Jesus," in *Handbook for the Study of the Historical Jesus*, ed. Holmén and Porter, 3:2400.

we are hard pressed to explain why Jesus's execution happened exactly when it did and for the precise reason it did ("King of the Jews"). After all, as John's Gospel indicates, Jesus regularly went up to Jerusalem for the great feasts. Why was he arrested and executed *this* time, at *this* particular feast? The answer may sound strange; but in a sense, Jesus triggered his own tragedy – at least partly by public actions that implied a claim to royal authority over Jerusalem and its temple.[69]

Had Jesus simply predicted the temple's destruction, he probably would not have been crucified. Jesus ben Ananias, while killed, was not *crucified*. However, if Jesus had also done something – something like what is described in the "triumphal" entry episode – it is easier to see why he would have ultimately been perceived as a political threat.

Paula Fredriksen's take is also worth mentioning. She believes Jesus "lost control of his audience."[70] In her view, Jesus unintentionally triggered messianic hopes by entering Jerusalem as he did. Yet to think Jesus was haplessly unaware of the associations the people around him would make is far-fetched. Furthermore, the broad spread of the tradition indicates Jesus acted in other ways that triggered Davidic associations.

In the end, the account of Jesus's regal arrival at Jerusalem makes sense of the shape of the Jesus tradition as we have received it. Jesus was hesitant to publicly identify himself in royal terms because he knew it would bring the authorities down on him. According to our sources, this is precisely what happened not long after Jesus did such a thing. That Jesus waited to perform an act that made explicit what he had previously only hinted at is highly probable. As Meier and others rightly observe, it is harder to explain Jesus's crucifixion without an episode like this one. Why we should prefer an account of the Jesus story that omits this episode is hard to fathom. The most probable explanation of the data is that here the community's memory is rooted in history.

Nevertheless, the argument here is not dependent on this one particular episode. For us, it forms another piece of the larger puzzle. It can be added to the other traditions that indicate Jesus likely triggered Davidic expectations in the minds of his hearers. Given that Jesus's association with Davidic imagery is well supported, we now turn to consider the portrait of Jesus as a Davidic figure within his Jewish context and in light of the effects of his ministry.

---

[69] Meier, "Dividing Lines in Jesus Research Today," 365.
[70] See, e.g., Fredriksen, *Jesus of Nazareth*, 247.

Jesus's First-Century Jewish Context

To hold that Jesus drew upon Davidic imagery is to situate his ministry squarely within the first-century Jewish world. While visions of Israel's future restoration did not necessarily always involve a Davidic element, Collins shows that our best evidence suggests Davidic messianism was a "dominant notion."[71] Such hopes were anchored in the belief that God had promised to give David a kingdom that would last "forever" (2 Sam 7:13–16; 1 Chr 17:11–14; Ps 89:3–4, 35–37). The period of the United Kingdom of David and Solomon also provided the ideal model for visions of the future reconstitution of the twelve tribes (cf., e.g., Isa 11:1–16; Jer 30:1–9; Ezek 37:15–28).[72] The Dead Sea Scrolls, therefore, frequently merge historical texts about David with eschatological hopes.[73] That Jesus drew upon such traditions places him securely among his contemporaries.

The Effects of Jesus's Ministry

Jesus's early followers believed he was the Davidic messiah. In his letter to the Romans, Paul writes that Jesus "was descended from David according to the flesh and was designated son of God in power according to the spirit of holiness by his resurrection from the dead" (Rom 1:3–4). Certain literary features of these verses, including the use of non-Pauline language, has led to "a fairly wide consensus"[74] that Paul is here drawing on traditional material.[75] This makes sense given the circumstances of the letter. Unlike his other epistles, Romans is written to a community Paul has yet to meet (cf. Rom 1:10; 15:20–24). Because of this, he likely begins his correspondence by signaling a commitment to a shared

---

[71] Collins, *Scepter and the Star*, 209. See CD-A 7:16–21; 4Q174 (4QFlorilegium) *frag.* 1, col. i, 21, 2:10–13; 4Q252 (4QCommentary on Genesis A) 5:1–5; 4Q285 (4QSefer ha-Milhamah) 5:2–3; Pss. Sol. 17:4–10, 21; 4 Ezra 12:31–32.

[72] See also Shemaryahu Talmon, "'Exile' and 'Restoration' in the Conceptual World of Ancient Judaism," in *Restoration*, ed. Scott, 119; Antti Laato, *A Star is Rising: The Historical Development of the Old Testament Royal Ideology and the Rise of the Jewish Messianic Expectations* (Atlanta: Scholars Press, 1997), 104.

[73] See, e.g., 4Q174 (4QFlorilegium) *frag.* 1, col. i, 21, 2; 4Q457b (4QEschatological Hymn); 4Q504 (4QDibHamᵃ) 1–2; 4Q522 (4QProphecy of Joshua) 9.

[74] Robert Jewett, *Romans*, Hermeneia (Minneapolis: Fortress Press, 2007), 104.

[75] For further discussion and sources, see Allison, *Resurrection of Jesus*, 32–33, 38–39; Jerry L. Sumney, *Steward of God's Mysteries: Paul and Early Church Tradition* (Grand Rapids: Eerdmans, 2017), 52–56.

kerygma.[76] Paul returns to Davidic imagery again at the end of the letter, referring to Jesus as "the root of Jesse [*hē riza tou Iessai*]" (Rom 15:12). The expression is taken from the oracle of a future Davidide in Isaiah 11, a prophecy that is interpreted in other ancient Jewish works as a messianic text.[77]

Paul's teaching in Romans is also important because it reveals how early believers conceived of Jesus's messianic rule. Paul says that Jesus was "designated [*horisthentos*]" as the messianic son of God *at his resurrection* (Rom 1:4).[78] The language agrees with numerous other texts in the New Testament which indicate that Jesus's messianic enthronement was realized *after* his death.[79] What explains these beliefs?

The argument that Jesus's messianic identity was invented to explain his death and resurrection is not convincing. There is no evidence that Jews in Jesus's day expected a messiah to die and to be raised from the dead ahead of the resurrection at the eschaton. Furthermore, resurrection did not necessarily equal divine enthronement.[80] In addition, since there is little reason to suspect Jesus styled himself as a military leader, one might have expected Jesus to be cast in a non-Davidic messianic role. The best way to account for the early belief in Jesus's Davidic identity is to accept that it originated out of perceptions he himself initiated. Martin Hengel explains:

Because Jewish hopes about the future nowhere include the enthronement in messianic-eschatological honour through resurrection from the dead, the origin of christology appears unthinkable without the messianic claim of Jesus.[81]

---

[76] See, e.g., Sumney, *Steward*, 55; Jewett, *Romans*, 107–108; James D. G. Dunn, *Romans 1–8*, WBC 38A (Dallas: Word Books, 1988), 122–123.

[77] See Ps. Sol. 18:6–8; 4Q285 5:2; 4Q161 (4QIsaiah Pesher^a) 8–10 iii 18–19; cf. also b. Sanh. 39b. See also the discussion in Collins, *Scepter and the Star*, 49–73.

[78] For further discussion, see Brant Pitre, Michael P. Barber, and John A. Kincaid, *Paul, A New Covenant Jew: Rethinking Pauline Theology* (Grand Rapids: Eerdmans, 2019), 98–101.

[79] Allison, *Constructing Jesus*, 247 n. 94, who cites, Mark 14:62; Ps.-Mark 16:19; Acts 2:30–35; 5:31; 7:55–56; Rom 8:34; Eph 1:20; 4:10; Phil 2:9–11; Col 3:1; 1 Tim 6:15; Heb 1:3; 8:1; 10:12; 12:2; 1 Pet 3:22; Rev 3:21; 7:17; 12:5; 22:1, 3; 1 Clem. 36:5; Apoc. Pet. 6:1; Barn. 12:10; Pol. *Phil.* 2:1; Ep. Apost. 3; Mart. Ascen. Isa. 10:14; 11:32–33; Sib. Or. 2:243.

[80] Allison, *Constructing Jesus*, 248–249; Timo Eskola, *Messiah and the Throne: Jewish Merkabah Mysticism and Early Christian Exaltation Discourse*, WUNT 2/142 (Tübingen: Mohr Siebeck, 2015), 248.

[81] Martin Hengel, "Sit at My Right Hand," in *Studies in Early Christology*, trans. Rollin Kearns (Edinburgh: T&T Clark, 1995), 217.

Likewise, Bart Ehrman writes:

> Jesus's followers must have considered him to be the messiah in some sense before his death, because nothing about his death or resurrection would have made them come up with the idea afterward.[82]

The reasoning here is sound. This, however, raises an important issue: How did the Jesus movement come to a general consensus so early about Jesus's Davidic identity?

If Jesus repudiated the role as the Davidic messiah outright, it is next to impossible to see how the idea that he was such a figure ever gained traction. Davies and Allison are correct: "If Jesus so clearly rejected the title 'Messiah', it is incomprehensible how it came to be so widely employed in the early church and indeed embedded in primitive formulas of faith."[83] The best accounting for our data would seem to be that while he did not go around introducing himself as the messiah, he nonetheless said and did things that caused those who were paying attention to conclude that he believed he was fulfilling messianic hopes. This would have been extremely risky, and one would expect that had he totally rejected being the messiah, he would have been eager to shut down misperceptions about it. Instead, he seems to have done things that would have only encouraged such perceptions. In sum, the evidence suggests that, as Allison puts it, he saw himself not as the currently reigning king, but as *messias designatus*.[84]

JESUS'S DAVIDIC TEMPLE AUTHORITY IN MATTHEW

While all of the canonical gospels portray Jesus as the eschatological son of David, it is widely known that Matthew gives special emphasis to this feature of the tradition.[85] What is especially pertinent for our study is this: in Matthew, *the Davidic aspect of Jesus's identity is frequently juxtaposed with temple traditions.* My argument here is not that Matthew always gives us "authentic" material. As we saw in the last chapter, Matthew's value to the quest should not simply be reduced to the particulars of his message. Matthew's penchant for tying Jesus's Davidic identity to the temple is, as we shall see, significant. The connection is not altogether difficult to explain. Davidic traditions and the temple had long

---

[82] Erhman, *How Jesus Became God*, 118.
[83] Davies and Allison, *Matthew*, 2:654.
[84] Allison, *Constructing Jesus*, 290.
[85] See, e.g., Davies and Allison, *Matthew*, 2:334.

been paired in Jewish thought. Matthew, it would seem, plays this up. After examining this dimension of Matthew's portrait, we shall then consider its implications for Jesus research.

Davidic Traditions and Eschatological Temple Hopes

Given David's connection to the temple, it was natural that hopes regarding an eschatological Davidic figure would be combined with the re-establishment of a temple and the renewal of the cult. In Jeremiah 33, the preservation of the Levitical cult is expressly said to be bound up with God's covenant with David (cf. Jer 33:14–26). Surprisingly, in some places a Davidic messiah is explicitly said to perform a liturgical role. In the book of Jeremiah, we read:

> Their prince shall be one of their own, their ruler shall come out from their midst; I will make him *draw near* and he shall *approach me*, for who would dare of himself to approach me? says the LORD. (Jeremiah 30:21)

The Hebrew term translated here "draw near [*qāreb*]" frequently appears in cultic settings (cf. Exod 29:4, 8; 40:12, 14; Lev 7:35; 8:6, 13, 24; Num 8:9, 10; 16:5, 9, 10), as is the word for "he shall approach me" (*nāgaš*; cf. Exod 28:43; 30:20; Lev 21:23; Ezek 44:13).[86] Likewise, in Ezekiel 37, the coming of a Davidic shepherd-king is interrelated with the establishment of God's sanctuary. As we have seen, in Ezekiel 45 the eschatological royal figure also has a prominent role in the future temple's cult, providing it with sacrifices (cf. Ezek 45:17). In addition, the Davidic figure Zerubbabel is tasked with rebuilding the temple in Haggai and Zechariah (Hag 2:2–9; Zech 4:9; 6:11–14). The description of the Davidic messiah in Psalms of Solomon also seems to suggest he has cultic responsibilities (esp. Pss. Sol. 17:30–31).[87]

A Davidic messiah was also associated with the hope for an eschatological temple at Qumran. A key prophecy for the Dead Sea Community was Amos 9:11: "In that day I will raise up the *booth* [*sukkat*] of David that is fallen and repair its breaches." In 4Q174, the "booth" of David

---

[86] See Hans-Joachim Kraus, *Psalmen*, rev. ed., 2 vols., BKAT (Neukirchen-Vluyn: Neukirchener, 1978), 1:317; Laato, *A Star is Rising*, 177.

[87] See Jostein Ådna, *Jesu Stellung zum Tempel: Die Templaktion und das Tempelwort als Ausdruck seiner messianischen Sendung*, WUNT 2/119 (Tübingen: Mohr Siebeck, 2000), 65–70; G. L. Davenport, "The 'Anointed of the Lord,' in Psalms of Solomon 17," in *Ideal Figures in Ancient Judaism: Profiles and Paradigms*, ed. John J. Collins and George W. E. Nickelsburg, SBLSCS 12 (Chico: Scholars Press, 1980), 75, 91n.28; Paul N. Franklyn, "The Cultic and Pious Climax of Eschatology in the Psalms of Solomon," *JSJ* 18 (1987): 1–17.

is linked with 2 Samuel 7 and seems to be used to describe a coming eschatological sanctuary (cf. 4Q174 *frag.* 1, *col.* i, 21, 2).[88] In addition, in 4Q522 (4QProphecy of Joshua) *frag.* 9, 2:3–9 we read:

3 of the times. For, behold, a son is born to Jesse, son of Perez, son of Ju[dah ...]
4 the Rock of Zion, and he will drive out from there / all / the Amorites, from [...]
5 *to build the house for* YHWH, God of Israel. Gold and silver [...]
6 he will bring cedar and cypress [from] Lebanon for its construction; but his son, the younger, [...]
7 he will officiate there first [...] ... [...] and to him [...]
8 [in al]l the [re]sidence from the heaven[s, because] the beloved of YHW[H] will dwell in safety [...]
9 [the] days, [and] his people will dwell forever. But now, the Amorites (are) there, and the Canaan[ites ...][89]

The fragment is badly damaged, but line 9 suggests that it involves an eschatological vision. In that case, it seems probable that the future Davidide is described as the builder of the future sanctuary. This reading gains support from the fact that the vision draws from Jeremiah 23:5–6, using the exact same language in its description of Israel under the rule of the Davidic messiah (*yiškōn lābeṭaḥ*; cf. 4Q522 [4QProphecy of Joshua] *frag.* 9, 2:2–9 and Jer 23:6). Likewise, line 3 ("a son is born") seems to draw on Isa 9:6 ("For to us a child is born, a son is given"), a passage which is elsewhere understood as an eschatological prophecy (cf. 1QH[a] [1QHodayot[a]] 11:10).[90] For what it is worth, later rabbinic tradition also attached the rebuilding of the temple to the coming of a messianic figure, frequently employing Davidic traditions.[91] All of this provides a helpful backdrop for thinking about Matthew's portrait of Jesus.

Davidic Themes in Matthew and the Temple

The First Gospel stresses the theme of Jesus's Davidic messiahship in multiple ways. In addition, certain motifs that are widely viewed as characteristic of Matthew, such as the "kingdom," would have been difficult

---

[88] See Bryan, *Jesus and Israel's Traditions*, 199; Donald Juel, *Messiah and Temple*, SBLDS 31 (Missoula: Scholars Press, 1977), 172–179.

[89] *DSSSE*, 2:1049.

[90] See Miura, *David in Luke-Acts*, 74–75; Collins, *Apocalyptic Imagination*, 123–126.

[91] See Num. Rab. 18:21; Lev. Rab. 9:6; Num. Rab. 13:2; Song Rab. 4:16. See Juel, *Messiah and Temple*, 196–197; Craig A. Evans, "'House of Prayer' to 'Cave of Robers': Jesus's Prophetic Criticism of the Temple Establishment," in *The Quest for Context and Meaning: Studies in Biblical Intertextuality in Honor of James A. Sanders*, ed. Craig A. Evans and Shemaryahu Talmon (Leiden: Brill, 1997), 430–431.

to see as unrelated to Davidic imagery. Here we offer a brief overview of some of the ways Davidic traditions seem to inform the Gospel's narrative. To be clear, by pointing these out I am not claiming that any of the following are necessarily "authentic," though some have a good claim on reflecting impressions made by Jesus (e.g., his so-called "triumphal entry" at Jerusalem). We simply list them to show how frequently Matthew reiterates Jesus's *Davidic* connections.

1. *"The Son of David."* The evangelist opens the book by tying Jesus's status as the messiah (*christos*) to his identity as the son of David (Matt 1:1). This gives way to a genealogy that, as we mentioned before, concentrates on Jesus's Davidic pedigree.

2. *Born in the City of David.* Jesus is born at Bethlehem, the city that is both David's hometown (e.g., 1 Sam 16:1; John 7:42) and the place where, according to Matthew, the Davidic messiah was to be born (cf. Matt 2:4).

3. *The Anointing of the "Son of God" in a River.* The narrative of Jesus's baptism in Matthew also appears to be colored with Davidic and Solomonic traditions. When Samuel anointed David, the spirit of the Lord comes on him (1 Sam 16:13). Furthermore, Solomon was taken down to a river on the day of his anointing (1 Kgs 1:38–40). Both events seem to be in the background of Jesus's baptism in Matthew. The spirit descends on Jesus when he is baptized in a river (cf. Matt 3:16). God then speaks from heaven and calls Jesus "my beloved son" (Matt 3:17) – a notion frequently associated with the son of David (cf., e.g., 2 Sam 7:14; 1 Chr 17:13; cf. 2 Sam 12:25: "Jedidiah"="beloved of Yhwh").

4. *Jesus's Davidic Exorcistic and Healing Powers.* As we have already discussed, Jesus's Davidic identity seems connected to his role as healer and exorcist.[92] Those who approach him seeking healing specifically address him as "son of David [*huios David*]" (cf. Matt 9:27; 20:3). His role as an exorcist is also tied to this title (cf. Matt 15:22).

5. *The Son of David Enters the City.* Matthew's account of Jesus's arrival at Jerusalem recalls the scene of Solomon's coronation (1 Kgs 1:33, 38). It is also linked to Zechariah's oracle of an eschatological king (Zech 9:9), a passage modeled on Solomonic

---

[92] Wayne S. Baxter, "Healing and the 'Son of David': Matthew's Warrant," *NovT* 48, 1 (2006): 36–50.

traditions.[93] The crowd's acclamation underscores the imagery present: "Hosanna to the son of David!" (Matt 21:9).

6. **The Passion of the Davidic King.** Matthew's passion narrative is replete with echoes of Davidic traditions. Aside from the fact that Jesus suffers as "the King of the Jews" (Matt 27:29, 37), Caiaphas explicitly links Jesus's supposed identity as the "Christ" to the notion of divine sonship (cf. Matt 26:63). Those at the foot of the cross also apparently connect Jesus's messianic role with his reputation as the son of God (Matt 27:42–43). As pointed out earlier, the combination of the title "anointed one" with divine sonship coheres especially well with Davidic traditions. Given this, it can hardly be a mere coincidence that Jesus's suffering is repeatedly described with allusions to Davidic psalms (e.g., Matt 27:46=Ps 22:1; Matt 27:43=Ps 22:8).[94] There are also many parallels between David's sufferings and Jesus's: (1) like Jesus, David was himself betrayed by a confidant (2 Sam 15:31); (2) David went up to the Mount of Olives when his life was being sought, the same place Jesus ends up after the Last Supper (2 Sam 15:30; Matt 26:30); and (3) like Judas, David's betrayer also hanged himself (2 Sam 17:23; Matt 27:5).

7. **Jesus as the Davidic Shepherd King.** Scholarship has emphasized Matthew's penchant for depicting Jesus as a Davidic shepherd-king.[95] Among other things, the evangelist repeatedly draws from prophets such as Micah (cf. Matt 2:6=Mic 5:2; cf. Mic 3:5–12) and Ezekiel (cf. Matt 9:35–36=Ezek 34:16, 23–24) to show that Jesus is the eschatological figure long-awaited to shepherd God's people.

Donald Verseput correctly recognizes that, for Matthew, Jesus's Davidic role is "at the heart of his presentation," having such "central importance" that it "determines the dynamic of the gospel's plot."[96] The question here is whether this connection also informs Matthew's portrait of Jesus's relationship to the temple. There is good evidence that it does.

---

[93] See, e.g., Le Donne, *Historiographical Jesus*, 200–204.

[94] For a fuller discussion, see Ahearne-Kroll, *Psalms of Lament*.

[95] See, e.g., Zacharias, *Matthew's Presentation of the Son of David*; Chae, *Jesus as the Eschatological Davidic Shepherd*; Heil, "Ezekiel 34 and the Narrative Strategy," 698–708.

[96] Donald J. Verseput, *The Rejection of the Humble Messianic King: A Study of the Composition of Matthew 11–12* (New York: Peter Lang, 1986), 35.

Revisiting the Disciples in the Fields and
the Teaching on the Temple Tax

In Matthew 12, Jesus defends his disciples' actions in the grainfields by referring to the way David enjoyed unique cultic prerogatives, namely, how he ate the bread of the presence, which was lawful "only for the priests" (Matt 12:4). Some have argued that Jesus's teaching here should simply be understood as acknowledging that feeding the hungry trumps the obligations of Sabbath rest.[97] However, there is no indication here that the disciples are in danger of starving to death. Nicholas Perrin rightly notes, "It is awkward to say the least to hold that both Matthew and Luke would have their readers emulate a Jesus who came to the brink of starvation out of devotion to the word of God, only later to brush holy writ aside because he and his friends were peckish."[98] The story cannot simply be a tale about weighing priorities. As Adela Collins shows, the fact that in all three Synoptics the story climaxes with a Christological claim reveals that it reflects something more than concern about Sabbath priorities.[99] The typology highlights the sacerdotal role of Jesus and the disciples, a point Matthew accentuates.

The Temple Action of the Son of David

Recall that Matthew adds a detail to his account of the "cleansing" of the temple not found in Mark or Luke: Jesus's act of healing the blind and the lame in the temple (Matt 21:14). As we have seen, this likely draws attention to traditions about David's relationship to the blind and the lame from 2 Samuel. In fact, Matthew adds a further detail – the children in the temple, recognize the significance of Jesus's actions, proclaiming: "Hosanna *to the son of David*!" (Matt 21:15). As we saw earlier, in this, God is shown to make known to the little ones what the wise and understanding fail to perceive (cf. Matt 11:25). The temple authorities actually, then, are the blind ones (cf. Matt 15:14; 23:16).[100] All of this focuses the reader on Jesus's Davidic identity. Le Donne writes, "'Son of David'

---

[97] See the various positions outlined by Lutz Doering, *Schabbat: Sabbathalacha und -praxis im antiken Judentum und Urchristentum*, TSAJ 78 (Tübingen: Mohr Siebeck, 1999), 199–200.

[98] Nicholas Perrin, *Jesus the Priest* (London: SPCK, 2018), 193–194. See the larger discussion where Perrin discusses why other readings are also unsatisfactory.

[99] Collins, *Mark*, 205.

[100] See Le Donne, *Historiographical Jesus*, 173.

connects Jesus to Solomon in that Jesus is portrayed in terms of therapy and in terms of temple authority."[101]

The Davidic imagery in the scene has not emerged out of nowhere. Matthew primes the reader to catch these echoes by the stories he tells leading up to it. The temple scene immediately follows the account of Jesus's Solomonic-like arrival at Jerusalem. Mark inserts material between the two events, but in Matthew there is nothing separating the two episodes – Jesus rides into Jerusalem and immediately performs his action in the temple. Matthew neatly ties the two scenes together by having the children in the temple repeat the words heard in the "triumphal entry": "Hosanna to the *son of David!*" (Matt 21:9, 15). Working further backward, we can also see how the Davidic imagery has been set up by what happens in the previous chapter: Jesus heals two blind men who petition him as "son of David" (Matt 20:29–34), using the same title the children who witness his temple action will use (Matt 21:15).

Jesus's Authority in the Temple and Psalm 110

The Davidic nature of Jesus's authority in the temple is also suggested by what happens after Jesus's healings there. It is important to follow the details of the narrative closely. The next time Jesus returns to the sanctuary, the chief priests and elders approach him and ask, "By what authority are you doing these things, and who gave you this authority?" (Matt 21:23). In context, the question likely has his temple act in view. In response to them, Jesus asks the leaders whether John's baptism was from God or whether it was simply of human origin (Matt 21:24–25). When they refuse to answer, Jesus explains that he will not provide an answer to their query about his authority (Matt 21:26–27). He then begins to speak to them in parables (Matt 21:28–22:14), a teaching method which he earlier attributed to his desire to conceal his message (cf. Matt 13:13). Because his parables do not provide sufficient ammunition for their purposes, the leaders then begin to ask Jesus pointed questions, which he deftly answers (Matt 22:15–40). In all of this, there are echoes of Solomon, who was similarly tested with hard questions by the queen of Sheba (1 Kgs 10:1), an episode Jesus refers to earlier in the Gospel (Matt 12:42):[102]

---

[101] Le Donne, *Historiographical Jesus*, 174.
[102] See, e.g., Viviano, "A Woman's Quest," 683–700; Dunn, *Jesus Remembered*, 697; Davies and Allison, *Matthew*, 2:359.

Jesus then asks a question of his own. Here let us consider the scene:

While the Pharisees were gathered together, Jesus asked them, saying, "What do you think about the Christ? Whose son is he?" They said to him, "David's." He said to them, "How then does David by the Spirit call him Lord, saying, 'The Lord said to my Lord, Sit at my right hand, until I put your enemies under your feet'? If then David calls him Lord, how is he his son?" And no one was able to answer him a word, nor did anyone dare from that day on to ask him any more questions. (Matthew 22:41–45; Mark 12:45–47//Luke 20:41–44)

It is sometimes argued that in this scene Jesus denies that the messiah would be a Davidic figure.[103] Three observations are in order here. First, nowhere in the account does Jesus ever deny that the messiah is the son of David. Rather than rejecting that supposition, Jesus seems to be making another point, namely, that the messiah is *superior* to David (i.e., his "Lord").[104] To believe Jesus is here expressly portrayed as denying a link between the "Christ" and David's line is to read something into the text that is not there. Second, as Fitzmyer states, Davidic messianic hopes were so prevalent by the first century CE it seems "inconceivable" that the evangelists would present Jesus as rejecting it.[105] Finally, it must be acknowledged that the very inclusion of this teaching in the Synoptics weighs strongly *against* reading it as a denial of the messiah's Davidic descent. Throughout their narratives the Synoptic writers all show that Jesus truly is the son of David and the messiah.[106] Only a tortured reading of the scene can lead to the conclusion that the evangelists understood it as ruling out Jesus's Davidic role.

Once again, then, Jesus's temple activity seems to lead to Davidic associations. Yet Jesus's question also provides us with an answer to the question that was posed earlier in the narrative, a question that emerged as a result of his temple action: "By what authority are you doing these things, and who gave you this authority?" (Matt 21:23). Given the cultic

---

[103] See, e.g., T. W. Manson, *The Teaching of Jesus* (Cambridge: Cambridge University Press, 1963), 266n.2. For a fuller discussion, see Le Donne, *Historiographical Jesus*, 221–257.

[104] See, e.g., Davies and Allison, *Matthew*, 3:254; Novakovic, *Messiah, Healer of the Sick*, 50–63; Meier, *A Marginal Jew*, 1:240; Raymond E. Brown, S.S., *The Virginal Conception and Bodily Resurrection of Jesus* (New York: Paulist Press, 1973), 55n.87.

[105] Fitzmyer, *Luke*, 2:1312.

[106] See, e.g., Timothy C. Gray, *Temple in the Gospel of Mark: A Study in Its Narrative Role*, WUNT 2/242 (Tübingen: Mohr Siebeck, 2008), 79–80; Raymond E. Brown, S.S., *Birth of the Messiah: A Commentary on the Infancy Narratives in the Gospels of Matthew and Luke*, rev. ed., ABRL (New Haven: Yale University Press, 1993), 509.

themes in play, it is probably relevant that Psalm 110 goes on to highlight the *priestly* prerogatives of the royal figure it speaks of: "*You are a priest forever* according to the order of Melchizedek" (Ps 110:4). While interpreters have often seen this line as unimportant for understanding Jesus's use of the psalm here, I believe this position overlooks some key pieces of data.

First, some background. The priestly role of Melchizedek is attested in Genesis 14, where we read that he was both "priest of God Most High" and "king of Salem" (Gen 14:18). The psalmist's application of Melchizedekian imagery to the Davidic king was fitting. Salem was identified with Jerusalem (cf. Ps 76:2). The Davidide ruled Jerusalem as Melchizedek once did. The connection was also natural given the cultic role attributed to David and his sons; like Melchizedek, as we have seen, in the scriptures of Israel, David and his sons exercise a priestly function.

Melchizedek's cultic significance was not forgotten or unimportant to Jews in the first century. Josephus identifies Melchizedek as the first temple-builder:

[Jerusalem's] original founder was a Canaanite chief, called in the native tongue "Righteous King"; for such indeed he was. In virtue thereof he was the first to officiate as priest of God and, *being the first to build the temple*, gave the city, previously called Solyma, the name of Jerusalem. (*Jewish War* 6.438)[107]

Josephus' use of "Righteous King" is a translation of "Melchizedek."[108] The figure of Melchizedek, then, according to Josephus, was connected to the temple.

There are other indications that Psalm 110 had an important role in validating cultic practices in the Second Temple period. The Hasmoneans saw in Melchizedek an important precedent for their role as priestly rulers. In 1 Maccabees, Simon Maccabeus is specifically described as "high priest forever [*archierea eis ton aiōna*]" (1 Macc 14:41), a title taken from the very psalm at the heart of Jesus's question to the Pharisees, Psalm 110 (cf. Ps 110:4).[109] In addition, as Daniel Schwartz shows, the title, "priest of God Most High" – language taken from Genesis 14's depiction of Melchizedek – is frequently applied to the Hasmonean kings (cf.

---

[107] Thackeray, LCL.
[108] See, e.g., Eric Mason, '*You Are A Priest Forever*': Second Temple Jewish Messianism and the Priestly Christology of the Epistle to the Hebrews, STDJ 74 (Leiden: Brill, 2008), 157.
[109] Gray, *Temple in the Gospel of Mark*, 87.

Josephus, *Ant.*, 16.163; T. Mos. 6.1; b. Roš Haš. 18b).[110] The use of the expression in other texts like Jubilees and the Testament of Levi is probably also shaped by Hasmonean ideology (T. Levi 8:3; Jub 36:16).[111] To insist that the cultic resonances of Psalm 110 are unimportant for Matthew's narrative is to ignore the way it was cited in defense of the priestly authorities. It should not be dismissed as mere coincidence, then, that after having been questioned about his authority to perform actions in the temple – actions which are closely tied to his messianic entry into the city – Jesus goes on to quote the one psalm that explicitly identifies the Davidide as having a priestly role.

There is yet still another reason to think that Psalm 110's cultic echoes are intended to be heard in Jesus's question: Jesus asks the question about it *while teaching in the temple.* To hold that the priestly reference in the psalm is immaterial simply because the line is not explicitly quoted by him ignores this context. It strains credulity to think that this feature of the passage is irrelevant; Jesus quotes the psalm amid controversy about his action in the temple. In addition, it also fails to account for the way in which ancient Jews cited psalms. The Mishnah indicates that the first line of the psalms served as their title (cf. e.g., m. Tam. 7:4). There is no good reason to doubt Matthew's awareness of this convention. Jesus does not need to quote the entire psalm; quoting its first line would have been sufficient to evoke the whole context.

Finally, it should be pointed out that Jesus once again alludes to this psalm when he is questioned by Caiaphas. The scene – especially in Matthew – has strong thematic links with the episode we are discussing here. In both contexts, Jesus is confronted with claims about his activity in the temple, which leads to questions revolving around messianic issues (cf. Matt 26:61–64). Davies and Allison perceptively note that the convergence of messianic and temple themes coheres not only with Nathan's oracle to David (2 Sam 7:13–14) but also with what is found in Zechariah:

> Thus says the LORD of hosts:
> Behold, a man whose name is Branch;
> And he shall branch out from his place,
> And *he shall build the temple of the LORD.*
>
> (Zechariah 6:12)[112]

---

[110] See Daniel Schwartz, *Studies in the Jewish Background of Christianity,* WUNT 60 (Tübingen: Mohr Siebeck, 1992), 47: "This title points clearly to Melchizedek (Genesis 14:18)." Likewise, see David M. Hay, *Glory at the Right Hand: Psalm 110 in Early Christianity* (Nashville: Abingdon Press, 1973), 24–25.

[111] See Hay, *Glory,* 24–25.

[112] Davies and Allison, *Matthew,* 3:528.

An allusion to this prophecy is possible, yet we need not go beyond Jesus's quotation of Psalm 110 to explain the logic of the scene. As he does earlier in the temple with the Pharisees, Jesus turns to the *one text* in which the Davidic messiah's priestly identity could be viewed as most explicitly defined. To write the connections off as coincidence appears to be special pleading. Moreover, if the belief that Melchizedek was the first temple builder was well known, Jesus's quotation from Psalm 110 within a context of an accusation regarding *rebuilding the temple* fits astonishingly well.

While teaching in the temple, then, Jesus is challenged about his authority to do things there. The narrative leads him to ask a pointed question about the Messiah in which he quotes from Psalm 110, a Davidic psalm. Jesus uses the psalm to highlight the superiority of the messiah to David. Yet it cannot be without significance that in a context charged with cultic themes, Jesus targets a psalm that explicitly highlights a royal figure's priestly privileges.

IMPLICATIONS FOR THE HISTORICAL JESUS

We have just argued that Jesus likely intended his audience to connect his teaching and activity to Davidic traditions. Did this inform his relationship to the temple? Matthew's overall narrative suggests that it did. In Matthew, Jesus's Davidic identity is especially entwined with his activity in the temple. Is this merely the result of Matthean redaction or might this feature of the evangelist's portrait tell us something about the kinds of impressions Jesus himself made?

Whatever one makes of "authenticity" debates about specific details of Matthew's narrative, I would argue that writing off the Davidic-temple connection in the First Gospel as irrelevant to the quest is a mistake. The connection between Jesus's Davidic identity and the temple is attested throughout our sources. Here we will first survey the data, arguing that it has good claim to historical memory. It obviously fits well within a Jewish setting; no further explanation of that is needed here. Yet this feature of the gospels' portrait also makes sense in light of Jesus's effects. One *could* make the case that it was only later Jewish believers who tied Jesus's relationship to the temple to Davidic hopes. Yet, once again, we are interested in *probability* not simply in other *possible* options. As I will argue here, Matthew's emphasis on the Davidic shape of Jesus's relationship to the temple most likely reflects impressions Jesus himself made.

Jesus's Davidic Identity and the Temple in the Gospel Tradition

It is not believable that Matthew himself simply invented the connection between Jesus's Davidic identity and his concern for the temple. A brief survey reveals that the connection is made throughout our sources. The following represents an overview of such traditions. The argument here is *not* that any of the following traditions are necessarily "authentic." A stronger case for an origin in Jesus's ministry can be made for some of the following (e.g., Jesus's "triumphal entry") than for others (such as the unique Johannine material). Here I simply wish to indicate that the connection between Jesus's Davidic role and temple contexts frequently occurs.

1. *David's Ability to Eat the Bread of the Presence (Matt 12:1–8//Mark 2:23–28//Luke 6:1–5)*. Like Matthew, both Mark and Luke record Jesus's reference to David's unique cultic prerogative of eating the bread of the presence, which is used to justify his disciples' activity.

2. *The Combination of the "Triumphal Entry" and Temple Action (Matt 21:1–17//Mark 11:1–11, 15–19//Luke 19:28–40, 45–48)*. Like Matthew, Mark and Luke closely connect Jesus's "triumphal entry" at Jerusalem with Jesus's temple concerns. Mark explicitly colors Jesus's arrival at Jerusalem with Davidic hues (cf. Mark 11:10: "Blessed is the coming kingdom of our father David!"). He then has Jesus visit the temple immediately afterwards (Mark 11:11). Therefore, though the temple action takes place the next day in his narrative, Jesus's Davidic identity and cultic concerns are interlaced in Mark. Likewise, Luke also has Jesus head straight into the temple after arriving in the city (Luke 19:45), giving the impression that the temple action occurred on the same day. In all three Synoptics, then, it is noteworthy that the episode that most loudly proclaims Jesus's fulfillment of Davidic hopes (Jesus's Solomon-like arrival at Jerusalem) and the scene that is arguably most emphatic about his cultic concerns (the temple "cleansing") are woven together.

3. *Jesus as Solomon in the Temple (Matt 22:15–40//Mark 12:13–34//Luke 20:19–40)*. Like Matthew, Mark and Luke record that Jesus was challenged with hard questions, which he answers in ways that astonished or silenced others. As we mentioned earlier, this is evocative of Solomon's encounter with the queen of Sheba (1 Kgs 10:1–13). Like Matthew, Luke specifically contains a reference to that scriptural story (Luke 11:31 [Q?]). Moreover, as in Matthew, Mark and Luke record that the testing of Jesus with questions occurred *in the temple* (Matt 21:23//

Mark 11:27//Luke 20:1). Jesus would therefore display his identity as the wise son of David *while in the temple*.

4. *Jesus Turns to Psalm 110 after Being Questioned about His Authority in the Temple (Matt 22:41–46//Mark 12:35–37//Luke 20:41–44)*. Like Matthew, Mark and Luke both have Jesus quoting from Psalm 110 in the temple after being questioned about his authority there. As we have seen, the use of this psalm is fitting given Jesus's Davidic identity.

5. *Jesus's Messianic Identity and the Accusation about Rebuilding the Temple at His So-Called "Trial" in Mark (Mark 14:48–61)*. When Jesus is questioned before the council in Mark, he is ultimately accused not only of identifying himself as "the Christ" but also of threatening to destroy and rebuild the temple. Mark tells us "false witnesses" claim Jesus said: "I will destroy this temple made by hands, and within three days I will build another not made by hands" (Mark 14:58). After relating that their testimony was in disagreement, the high priest turns to Jesus and asks him point-blank whether or not he is the messiah: "Are you the Christ, the son of the Blessed?" (Mark 14:61). This second question seems unrelated to the first. What connection is there between the temple and messianic identity? Yet the follow-up question makes sense if the reader understands that Jesus is the Davidic messiah and is aware that Jewish tradition tied the Davidide to the temple. The question about him being the "son of God" seems to cement a connection to this Davidic matrix. As we shall see in the next chapter, the Davidide's role as "son of God" is often linked to his role as temple-builder. Here we have another instance where "temple" and Davidic connections go hand-in-hand.

6. *The Mockery of Jesus as the Messiah and as Temple-Destroyer at the Cross (Mark 15:29–31)*. The scene at Golgotha in Mark also picks up on the temple-messiah connection. Standing at the foot of the cross, Jesus is mocked by those who say, "You who would *destroy the temple* and *build it* in three days, save yourself, and come down from the cross!" (Mark 15:29–30). Once again, Jesus is charged with claiming to not only destroy the temple, but also rebuild it. The bystanders then add, "He saved others; he cannot save himself. *Let the Christ, the king of Israel*, come down now from the cross, that we may see and believe" (Mark 15:32). As before, the claim that Jesus is the "Christ" – specifically, "the King of Israel" – is preceded by the supposition that Jesus spoke of taking responsibility for the temple. The appearance of the two charges side by

side may appear odd – unless there is an awareness that Jesus's messianic role involves *Davidic* traditions.

7. *Jesus's Davidic Role in the Temple-Cleansing Episode in John (John 2:13–22).* The Davidic-temple association is not merely found in the Synoptics. Johannine scholarship has increasingly recognized the importance of the temple in the Fourth Gospel.[113] There the temple theme is frequently linked to Davidic imagery.[114] For example, in the Gospel's account of Jesus's action in the temple, he is portrayed as calling the sanctuary, "My Father's house" (John 2:16). This statement is probably, at least in part, indebted to Davidic traditions. Earlier in the narrative, Nathanael declares: "Rabbi, you are *the son of God!* You are *the king of Israel!*" (John 1:49). Jesus's divine sonship is therefore bound up with his royal identity, an assumption that makes sense within a Davidic matrix. The Davidic connotation of Jesus's saying is reinforced by another detail in John's account – Jesus's action in the temple is said to have reminded his disciples of the words of the psalmist: "Zeal for your house will consume me" (John 2:17; Ps 69:9). This psalm's superscription attributes it to David. Pseudo-Philo even uses it for biographical data about David (LAB 59:4=Ps 69:8).

8. *Jesus, Temple Imagery, and the Question of His Davidic Identity (John 7:37–43).* Another relevant passage is found in John 7, where Jesus is said to have gone up to Jerusalem for the Feast of Sukkoth or "Tabernacles" (cf. John 7:2–10). Later in the chapter, we learn the following:

Now on the last day of the feast, the great day, Jesus stood and cried out, saying, "If anyone is thirsty, let him come to me, and drink. The one who believes in me, as the scripture has said, 'Out of his belly will flow rivers of living water.'" (John 7:37–39).

Jesus then goes on during the same festival to declare, "I am the light of the world" (John 8:12). Commentators widely believe that these sayings allude to temple symbolism associated with the feast.[115] The

---

[113] See, e.g., Hoskins, *Jesus as the Fulfillment*; Stephen T. Um, *The Theme of Temple Christology in John's Gospel*, LNTS 312 (Sheffield: Sheffield Academic, 2006); Alan Kerr, *The Temple of Jesus's Body: The Temple Theme in the Gospel of John*, JSNT-Sup 220 (Sheffield: Sheffield Academic, 2002); Mary L. Coloe, *God Dwells with Us: Temple Symbolism in the Fourth Gospel* (Collegeville: Liturgical Press, 2001); Johannes Frühwald-König, *Tempel und Kult: Ein Beitrag zur Christologie es Johannesevangeliums*, BU 27 (Regensburg: Friedrich Pustet, 1998).

[114] See, especially, Jipp, *Messianic Theology*, 132–137.

[115] See, e.g., Hoskins, *Jesus as the Fulfillment*, 160–170; Craig Koester, *Symbolism in the Fourth Gospel: Meaning, Mystery, Community*, 2nd ed. (Minneapolis: Fortress Press, 2003), 194–195; Coloe, *God Dwells*, 119–122.

Mishnah reports that during the feast water was poured out at the altar (m. Sukkah 4:9) in order to evoke the vision of the eschatological temple in Ezekiel (Ezek 47:1–17). In addition, the Mishnah indicates that the feast involved a particularly memorable custom of lighting of menorahs in the sanctuary (m. Sukkah 5:3). There is good reason to think that this practice was intended to evoke traditions that coupled hopes for an eschatological Zion/temple with light imagery (cf. Isa 60:1–4; Zech 14:6–9; Tob 13:10–11; 1 En. 14:8–23; 71:2–47; Sib. Or. 4.191; 5.420).[116] Jesus's reference to "rivers of living water" (John 7:38) and his saying about being "the light of the world" (John 8:12; cf. John 9:5) ties in nicely then with the temple imagery of the festival. In all of this, Jesus seems to apply temple-related traditions to himself and/or his disciples.

What is remarkable for our purposes is this: the saying of Jesus evoking temple imagery is immediately followed by a discussion of Jesus's messianic identity and the question of Davidic descent:

> Then some of the crowd, when they heard these words, began to say, "This man is truly the prophet." Others said, "This one is the Christ." But others were saying, "Surely the Christ does not come from Galilee, does he? Has not the scripture said that the Christ comes from the seed of David and from the village of Bethlehem, where David lived?" So there was a division in the crowd because of him. (John 7:40–43)

The impression seems to be that by evoking temple imagery, Jesus unavoidably caused his hearers to wonder about his Davidic identity.

9. *Jesus Questioned about Being the Messiah in Solomon's Portico (John 10:22–30).* In John 10, Jesus goes up to Jerusalem for the Feast of Dedication, a festival that commemorates the reconsecration of the temple under the Maccabees (cf. 1 Macc 4:36–49). Walking in "the portico of Solomon" (John 10:23), Jesus is asked if he is the messiah. That Jesus is questioned about his messianic identity not only in the temple but also in *Solomon's portico* ties together the Davidic and temple themes we have been exploring. Going on, Jesus responds to the question about his identity by speaking of his sheep (John 10:27). Earlier in the chapter, Jesus has already spoken of himself as the "good shepherd" (cf. John 10:11–16). He also refers to God as "my Father" (John 10:29). As Mary Coloe explains, the combination of "messiah," "divine sonship," and "shepherding" signals Davidic traditions.[117] Not only was David himself

---

[116] See, e.g., Perrin, *Jesus the Priest*, 115; Hoskins, *Jesus as the Fulfillment*, 168–170.
[117] See, e.g., Coloe, *God Dwells*, 150.

a shepherd, but, as we have seen, the eschatological Davidide is also frequently depicted as a shepherd (cf. Ezek 34:23; Mic 5:4; Ps. Sol. 17:40;
4 Ezra 2:34). Once again, then, Jesus is portrayed as alluding to Davidic
traditions within the context of his activity in the temple.

   10. *Jesus's Promise to Prepare a Place for Disciples (John 14:1–2).*
Temple traditions also seem to shape Jesus's teaching in John 14, where
Jesus speaks of how he will "prepare a place [*topos*]" for the disciples
in "*my Father's house* [*tē oikia tou patros mou*]" (John 14:1–2). The
expression, "my Father's house," is applied to the temple earlier in the
Gospel (John 2:16). Other considerations further support a connection with the sanctuary, including (but not limited to) the repeated use
of "place [*topos*]" in John 14. The language is frequently used in the
scriptures of Israel to refer to the sanctuary (*topos* or *māqōm*; cf., e.g.,
Deut 12:5, 11–14; 1 Kgs 8:6–7, 21, 28–30; Isa 60:13; Jer 7:12, 20; Ezek
37:27).[118] In fact, the term appears in the Fourth Gospel elsewhere in
connection with the temple (cf. John 4:20; 11:48).[119] Furthermore, Coloe
observes that Jesus's words about going to "prepare a place [*etoimas-
sai topon*]" reminds the reader of David. The Chronicler recounts how
David established the ark in a tent in Jerusalem using the same language:

> [David] *prepared a place* [LXX: *hētoimasen ton topon*] for the ark of God and
> pitched a tent for it... And David assembled all Israel at Jerusalem to bring up
> the ark of the LORD to its *place, which he had prepared for it* [*ton topon hon
> ētoimasen autē*]... Then David summoned the priests Zadok and Abiathar, and
> the Levites ... and said to them ... "Consecrate yourselves, you and your brothers,
> so that you may bring up the ark of the LORD, the God of Israel, to the place that
> *I have prepared it* [*hou hētoimasa autē*]." (1 Chronicles 15:1, 3, 11, 12)

Even if an allusion to this particular story is not intended, it is difficult
to deny that Jesus's speech seems evocative of traditions that connected
Davidic imagery to the temple.

The Effects of Jesus and the Davidic-Temple Matrix

The combination of Davidic and temple imagery may also be found in
the letters of Paul. In 1 Corinthians 3, Paul describes the community as
a temple:

---

[118] See, e.g., Kerr, *Temple of Jesus's Body*, 303–306
[119] See, e.g., Coloe, *God Dwells*, 164–167; Raymond E. Brown, S.S., *The Gospel According to John*, 2 vols., AB 29–29A (New York: Doubleday, 1966), 2:439.

Do you not know that you are the temple of God and that the Spirit of God dwells in you? If anyone destroys the temple of God, God will destroy him. For the temple of God is holy, and you are that temple. (1 Corinthians 3:16–17)

Just prior to this, Paul speaks of his own community-founding work by portraying himself as a *"wise master builder [sophos architektōn]"* who laid a "foundation" (1 Cor 3:10). He explains that "if anyone builds on the foundation with gold, silver, precious stones, wood, hay, straw – the work of each one will become manifest for the day will reveal it" (1 Cor 3:12–13). What can be easily overlooked, however, is the way the language throughout this section seems to be influenced by Israel's cultic traditions.[120] The reference to the community as temple does not appear *ex nihilo*; the apostle has prepared the reader for it.

For one thing, Paul's self-description reminds us of what is said of Bezalel, who is tasked with building the sanctuary in the book of Exodus:

Exodus' Description of the Sanctuary Builders	*Paul's Self-Description as the Builder of the Temple-Community*
[The LORD] filled him with a divine spirit of *wisdom [sophias]* ... to be *a master builder [architektonein]* according to all the works of *a master builder [architektonias]*.	like a *wise master builder [sophos architektōn]*.
(Exodus 35:31–32a LXX)	(1 Corinthians 3:10)
to work with gold [*chrysion*] and silver [*argyrion*] ... and works in stone [*lithon*].	if anyone builds on the foundation with gold [*chryson*], silver [*argyron*], precious stones [*lithous timious*].
(Exodus 35:32b, c)	(1 Corinthians 3:12)

The imagery of a foundation being laid and gold, silver, and precious stones being built onto it calls to mind the construction of Solomon's temple (cf. 1 Kgs 5:17; 6:20–21; 1 Chr 29:1–7). As Gordon Fee writes, "Paul does not have some 'fabulous building' in view, but the OT description of Solomon's temple, thus anticipating the imagery of vv. 16–17."[121] A parallel can also be found in David's words concerning his work regarding the temple:

---

[120] For the following, see G. K. Beale, *The Temple and the Church's Mission: A Biblical Theology of the Dwelling Place of God*, NSBT 17 (Downers Grove: InterVarsity Press, 2004), 247.

[121] Gordon D. Fee, *The First Epistle to the Corinthians*, NICNT (Grand Rapids: Eerdmans, 1987), 140–141; *pace* Hans Conzelmann, *1 Corinthians*, trans. James W. Leitch, Hermeneia (Philadelphia: Fortress Press, 1975 [1969]), 76.

David's Description of His Temple-Building Work	Paul's Description of His Work Building the Temple-Community

I have prepared, for a divine house, gold [*chrysion*], silver [*argyrion*] … wood [*xylon*] … and precious stones [*lithous polyteleis*].
    (1 Chronicles 29:2 LXX)
	if anyone builds on the foundation with gold [*chryson*], silver [*argyron*], precious stones [*lithous timious*], wood [*xula*].
	    (1 Corinthians 3:12)

As we have seen, elsewhere Paul is quite unambiguous that Jesus is the Davidic Messiah (Rom 1:3–4; 15:12). If he is building a temple, it is surely to be seen as that belonging to the son of David. Yet there are further reasons to think Davidic imagery is in play in 1 Corinthians 3.

Paul seems to have been priming the reader to hear the temple imagery in 1 Corinthians 3 earlier in his letter. Commentators have detected echoes of Zechariah's oracle concerning the temple-building work of the Davidic figure Zerubbabel in 1 Corinthians 2. Allusions to it are then picked up again in 1 Corinthians 3. To recognize the echoes involved it is worth looking at the Zecharian prophecy once more, this time quoting from the Septuagint:

> And [the angel] answered … "This is the word of the Lord to Zerubbabel, saying, *Not in great power nor in strength, but in my spirit,* says the Lord Almighty. Who are you, you great mountain, to prosper before Zerubbabel? And you will bring forth *the stone of inheritance,* equality of *grace, grace* for it." And a *word* of the Lord came to me, saying, "The hands of Zerubbabel *laid the foundation* of this house; his hands shall also complete it. And you will know that the Lord Almighty has *sent* [*exapestalken*] me to you." (Zechariah 4:5, 6–9 LXX)[122]

According to the angel, Zerubbabel's temple-building project will succeed not because of "power" but because of God's spirit. With this in the background, let us revisit the train of thought in 1 Corinthians 2–3.

First, Paul explains in 1 Corinthians 2 how he established what he later identifies explicitly as a "temple-community," drawing on Zechariah's oracle. As commentators have shown, there are numerous points of contact between the prophecy concerning Zerubbabel and Paul's teaching in 1 Corinthians 2.[123]

---

[122] NETS, slightly adapted.
[123] See, e.g., H. H. Drake Williams, III, *The Wisdom of the Wise: The Presence and Function of Scripture within 1 Cor. 1:18–3:23,* AGJU 49 (Leiden: Brill, 2001), 137; see also 152.

Zechariah 4:6	1 Corinthians 2:4-5
This is *the word* [LXX: *ho logos*] of the Lord to Zerubbabel: *Not in* great *power* [LXX: *ouk en dynamei megalē*], nor in strength *but in* [*all' ē en*] my *spirit* [*pneumati*], says the Lord Almighty.	[A]nd *my word* [*ho logos mou*] and my preaching were *not in* the plausibility of wisdom *but in* [*all' en*] a demonstration of the *spirit* [*pneumatos*] and *power* [*dynameōs*] in order that your faith would not be in the wisdom of men *but in the power* [*all' en dynamei*] of God.

Paul's explanation that his "word [*logos*]" is not related to human power but (*all'*) is demonstrated by the "spirit [*pneumatos*]" and "power [*dynameōs*]" *of God* evokes what is said about Zerubbabel's temple-building work – it is not through "power [*dynamei*] but (*all'*) through the "spirit [*pneumati*]" of the Lord. The allusion to the oracle makes sense: Paul explains *how* he laid the foundation of the community by his preaching before going on to explicitly describe his work as temple-building.

Remarkably, when Paul explains that he laid the "foundation [*themelion*]" of the temple-community (1 Cor 3:10), he once again uses imagery evocative of Zechariah's oracle; Zerubbabel is said to have "laid the foundation" of the temple (Zech 4:9 LXX: *ethemeliōsan*). In addition, Paul says he did this, "According to the *grace of God* [*charin tou theou*]" (1 Cor 3:10). This is reminiscent of the work of the Davidic Zerubbabel, who is said to bring the top stone of the sanctuary amid shouts of "*grace, grace*" (Zech 4:7 LXX: *charitos, charita*). Paul therefore seems to recall his community-founding work in Corinth not only in terms of temple-building, but also in ways that are evocative of the Davidide Zerubbabel.[124] Finally, one cannot help but notice that the Greek version of Zechariah 4:9 uses a form of the word for being "sent," *exapostellō*, that evokes Paul's repeated self-description of his role as an "apostle [*apostolos*]" (1 Cor 1:1; 9:1-2; 15:9), a term that becomes central to his discussion in 1 Corinthians 4. The allusion to Zechariah, therefore, seems to unite Paul's imagery.

In 2 Corinthians, we find another text that links the community-as-temple motif to Davidic traditions. After Paul writes, "For we are the temple of the living God" (2 Cor 6:16), he goes on to give a catena of

---

[124] Paul's language about faith moving mountains in 1 Cor 13:2 may also be an allusion to Zech 4:6-7. See Maureen W. Yeung, *Faith in Jesus and Paul: A Comparison with Special Reference to "Faith that Can Remove Mountains" and "Your Faith Has Healed/Saved You,"* WUNT 2/147 (Tübingen: Mohr Siebeck, 2002), 25-26.

quotations that ends, "and I will be a father to you, and you shall be my sons and daughters," a line that is recognized as a reworking of Nathan's oracle to David (2 Sam 7:14). This is the place where God rewards David's desire to build a temple with an everlasting kingdom.[125] Some have argued that these lines in 2 Corinthians represent a later interpolation, yet this view has been heavily critiqued.[126] Either way, the passage is a very early text. What is significant here is that it shows how the role of the *Davidic* king could be expanded to believers. Of course, this also fits with 1 Corinthians 3, where Paul identifies himself as the builder of the temple-community. This dynamic should not take us by surprise since Paul repeatedly emphasizes that believers are "in Christ" (e.g., 1 Cor 1:2, 4, 30; 3:1; 4:10, 15 [2x], 17; 15:18, 19, 22, 31; 16:24; 2 Cor 1:21; 2:14, 17; 5:17; 12:2, 19).

That Jesus's role as the Davidic messiah includes a cultic dimension is also evident in the Apocalypse. In the letter to the Philadelphians, Jesus begins by identifying himself as the one who holds "the key of David, who opens and no one will shut, who shuts and no one opens" (Rev 3:7). Jesus then goes on to say: "The one who conquers, I will make him a pillar in the temple of my God" (Rev 3:12). Here Jesus's Davidic role is linked to his ability to make promises involving the heavenly sanctuary.

Learning from Matthew's Jewish Arrangement of the Pieces

We have seen that it seems probable that Jesus said and did things that evoked Davidic hopes. Bart Ehrman is likely correct when he says that "[t]here are excellent reasons for thinking that Jesus imagined himself as the messiah, in a very specific and particular sense."[127] At the same time, it also appears likely that Jesus expressed concerns about the temple. In a first-century Jewish context, it strains credulity to think these facets of his ministry would be viewed as unrelated. In fact, we have shown that indications of Jesus's use of the Davidic-temple connection can be found throughout our sources. That he did so fits well into a first-century

---

[125] See, e.g., Victor Paul Furnish, *II Corinthians*, AB 32A (New York: Doubleday, 2008), 364; Murray J. Harris, *The Second Epistle to the Corinthians*, NIGTC (Grand Rapids: Eerdmans, 2005), 509–510; C. K. Barrett, *The Second Epistle to the Corinthians*, BNTC (London: Continuum, 1973), 201.

[126] For an overview see, Larry Kreitzer, *2 Corinthians*, NTG (Sheffield: Sheffield Academic Press, 1996), 30–35.

[127] Ehrman, *How Jesus Became God*, 118.

Jewish environment. As John Meier notes in a quotation which was spot-lighted at the beginning of this chapter, "in a sense, Jesus triggered his own tragedy—at least partly by public actions that implied a claim to royal authority over Jerusalem and its temple."[128] Within Jesus's Jewish context, the temple was closely bound up with royal associations. That Jesus evoked Davidic temple associations also explains his effects: Paul and the author of the Apocalypse specifically draw together Davidic and temple themes.

While Matthew especially plays up the relationship between Jesus's Davidic identity and his relationship to the temple, this should not be viewed as the result of pure imagination. Rather, it seems that Matthew provides us with a window into the way in which Jesus's teachings struck his first-century Jewish audiences. The combination of Davidic and temple imagery would have been natural.

It was certainly possible for ancient Jews to think about the cult without making recourse to Davidic imagery. In addition, Jews could envision the cult in the eschatological age without appealing to Davidic traditions. Nevertheless, Davidic messianism was a particularly popular form of Jewish eschatological hopes and, as we have seen, some sources specifically link the future Davidide to the renewal/restoration of the cult. It would therefore seem prima facie possible that the cultic aspect of Jesus's eschatological vision would have involved a Davidic element.

Yet, once again, let us be reminded that the *possible* is not what the Jesus historian is after. The real question is whether it is *more probable than not* that Jesus's vision of the cult in the eschatological age was influenced by Davidic traditions. Matthew is helpful here but not because he necessarily contains a greater quantity of "authentic" material than the other gospels do. What is especially interesting about the First Gospel is that it shows us how hard it was within a Jewish interpretive matrix to see Jesus's Davidic identity and his temple concerns as unrelated.

An instructive parallel can be found in Matthew's tendency to connect Jesus's healing ministry to son of David traditions. While it is already suggested in Mark's story of the healing of Bartimaeus (Mark 10:46–52), Matthew emphasizes Jesus's role as the Therapeutic Son of David (cf., e.g., Matt 12:22–23; 15:22). As Le Donne shows, in this Matthew likely provides us with a better window into how Jesus was perceived in his original Jewish setting – to perform exorcisms in connection with

---

[128] Meier, "Dividing Lines in Jesus Research Today," 365.

a kingdom message was irresistibly Davidic. Given the kinds of things Jesus said and did, it would have been hard for his Jewish contemporary *not* to assume he was evoking Davidic traditions. The same would seem to apply to Matthew's propensity to interpret Jesus's relationship to the temple through a Davidic lens. Because he breathes the same Jewish air as Jesus and his hearers, the evangelist's framing of this material cannot be written off as irrelevant to the historian.

In short, the Davidic and the cultic aspects of the Jesus story were crying out to be read as one piece. To imagine Jesus was the source of both of these features of the early community's memory of him but that he himself did not see them as interrelated is a stretch. That he expected his audience to connect these features of his ministry would seem the best way to account for the evidence.

Yet there is more: as we shall see, for Matthew, Jesus's role as the son of David not only has implications for the temple, but also is connected to the community. Paul, the earliest New Testament writer, explicitly identifies believers as a "temple" (1 Cor 3:16; 6:19; cf. 2 Cor 6:16). Is this merely the result of Pauline creativity or might this bear some resemblance to Jesus's own teaching? In the next chapter, we will look at how Matthew portrays the community in temple terms. Not surprisingly, the imagery is soaked in Davidic traditions. Does this aspect of Matthew's narrative preserve a historical memory of Jesus's own teaching? This question will be addressed in our remaining chapters.

6

The Son of David and the Temple-Community

For Matthew, to have an ecclesiology that was not totally dependent on
Christology would be unthinkable.

    – John Meier[1]

Jesus is confessed as both Christ and Son of God; he builds a new church
or temple... These are all Davidic motifs.

    – W. D. Davies and Dale C. Allison, Jr.[2]

We have seen that while Jesus announces the coming destruction of the
temple in Matthew, he also endorses the Jerusalem temple's sacrificial
rites. In addition, for Matthew, Jesus's teaching about the age to come
seems to entail the existence of some sort of eschatological sanctuary.
Among other things, Jesus quotes from Isaiah's oracle announcing an
eschatological temple (Matt 21:13). With that in mind, it is significant
to note that Matthew portrays Jesus as drawing on temple traditions in
other ways. In this chapter, we will look at the way in which Jesus uses
temple imagery to describe the community of his disciples in Matthew.
First, we will analyze the presence of such imagery in Jesus's exchange
with Peter, which takes place in the region of Caesarea Philippi (Matt
16:13–19). We will then move on to see that this is hardly an isolated
occurrence; Jesus applies temple and priestly metaphors to the disciples
elsewhere in the gospel. Finally, our discussion will conclude with an
analysis of the historical value of Jesus's exchange with Peter in Matthew

[1] John P. Meier, *The Vision of Matthew: Christ, Church, and Morality in the First Gospel*
(New York: Paulist Press, 1979), 97.
[2] Davies and Allison, *Matthew*, 2:603.

16. Is it probable that Matthew conveys historical information by relating what happened in the district of Caesarea Philippi?

JESUS AS THE DAVIDIC MESSIAH
AND THE *EKKLĒSIA* AS TEMPLE

A good case can be made that Peter's confession of faith in Matthew 16 marks a pivotal moment in Matthew's narrative. After this episode, like Mark, the evangelist tells us that Jesus began to tell his disciples that he would go to Jerusalem and suffer. Following the scene, Matthew uses the phrase, "From that time on Jesus began [*apo tote ērxato ho Iēsous*]" (Matt 16:21). With that phrase, the evangelist repeats the same narrative pointer that introduces the beginning of Jesus's public ministry in the Gospel (cf. Matt 4:17). While one should be cautious about exaggerating the function of this one story,[3] it is hard to deny its significance: for the first time, one of Jesus's disciples affirms what the reader has known from the first verse of the Gospel – Jesus is the "Christ." Once this has occurred, Jesus begins his movement to his passion at Jerusalem (Matt 16:21). Yet the cultic implications of this pivotal episode are often overlooked. Temple and priestly imagery unite the various elements of the pericope.

Jesus as the Davidic Temple-Builder

Peter unambiguously announces who Jesus is: "You are the Christ, the son of the living God" (Matt 16:16). For Matthew, Jesus's identity as the "Christ" is inseparable from Davidic traditions. This is clear from the first verse of the Gospel where he is identified as "Jesus Christ, the son of David" (Matt 1:1). Peter's declaration of Jesus's divine sonship serves, therefore, to reinforce this Davidic typology.[4] As we have mentioned, divine sonship was frequently associated with the son of David. What frequently goes unnoticed, however, is the way the Davidic imagery of Peter's confession is then further developed in Jesus's response, in which he promises to "build" (*oikodomeō*) his *ekklēsia* (Matt 16:18).

---

[3] See Frans Neirynck, "APO TOTE ERKXATO and the Structure of Matthew," in *Evangelica II 1982–1991: Collected Essays by Frans Neirynck*, ed. F. Van Segbroeck (Leuven: University Press, 1991), 141–182.

[4] Michael Patrick Barber, "Jesus as the Davidic Temple Builder and Peter's Priestly Role in Matthew 16:17–19," *JBL* 132, 4 (2013): 935–953.

In addition to being known as the "son of God," the son of David was also remembered as the temple-builder extraordinaire. The connection between the two ideas appears in both biblical descriptions of Nathan's oracle, the crucial prophecy that serves as the basis of Davidic hopes.

When your days are fulfilled and you lie down with your fathers, I will raise up your offspring after you, who shall come forth from your body, and I will establish his kingdom. *He shall build a house for my name*, and I will establish the throne of his kingdom forever. I will be his father, and *he shall be my son*. (2 Samuel 7:12–13; cf. 1 Chr 17:11–13)

David said to Solomon, "My son, I had it in my heart *to build a house* to the name of the LORD my God. But the word of the LORD came to me, saying, 'You have shed much blood and have waged great wars; you shall not *build a house* to my name … Behold, a son shall be born to you. He shall be a man of peace. I will give him peace from all his enemies round about. For his name shall be Solomon, and I will give peace and quiet to Israel in his days. *He shall build a house for my name. He shall be my son, and I will be his father*, and I will establish his royal throne in Israel forever.'" (1 Chronicles 22:7–10)

One of the Dead Sea Scroll fragments, 4Q174, also combines Nathan's prophecy with texts that refer to the eschatological temple.[5] Given Peter's use of imagery elsewhere associated with the Davidide – for example, his declaration that Jesus is the "son of God" and the "Christ" – Jesus's self-description as a "builder" is a natural follow-up to what the apostle says. By it, Jesus extends the Davidic allusions introduced by Peter's confession; the Davidic divine son would build a temple.

That Jesus explains that he will build his church on a "rock" further reinforces the impression that his reply to Peter involves an allusion to temple-building. In Jewish tradition, temples and other cultic sites were typically linked with "stone" imagery (cf. Gen 28:10–22; Isa 8:14–15; 28:16; Zech 4:7–9).[6] Jewish tradition specifically linked the construction of the temple by the son of David with the stone motif. Most prominently, in Zechariah 4, we find an oracle that speaks of the Davidide Zerubbabel's role in rebuilding the temple:

---

[5] See, e.g., Cho, *Royal Messianism*, 29; Meyer, *Aims of Jesus*, 179–180; Otto Betz, "*Die Frage* nach dem messianischen Bewusstsein Jesu," *NovT* 6 (1963): 20–48.

[6] See, e.g., Davies and Allison, *Matthew*, 2:626–668; 2; Meyer, *Aims of Jesus*, 185–202; Peter Schäfer, "Tempel und Schöpfung. Zur Interpretation einiger Heiligtumstraditionen in der rabbinischen Literatur," in *Studien zur Geschichte und Theologie des rabbinischen Judentums*, AGJU 15 (Leiden: Brill, 1978), 122–133. Later Jewish texts would also link cultic sites to "stone" imagery (cf. m. Yoma 5.2; b. Yoma 54a–b; Lev. Rab. 20.4; Num. Rab. 12.4; Bet ha-Midr. 5.63; cf. also T. Sol. 23:6–8; 4 Ezra 13:36).

Who are you, O great mountain? Before Zerubbabel you shall become a plain; and he shall bring forward *the top stone* amid shouts of "Grace, grace to it!" And the word of the LORD came to me, saying, "The hands of Zerubbabel have *laid the foundation of this house*; his hands shall also complete it. And you will know that the LORD of hosts has sent me to you." (Zechariah 4:7–8)

Because Zerubbabel is tied to the reestablishment of the temple, a motif that was otherwise associated in prophetic literature with the age to come, this passage likely had eschatological undertones for its readers. In fact, Zerubbabel is tied to messianic-like prophecies elsewhere (cf. Hag 2:21–23; Zech 6:9–15).[7]

It is also worth considering that Jesus's promise to "build" (*oikodomeō*) parallels the saying attributed to him at his trial and at the cross, namely, that he would "build" (*oikodomeō*) the temple (cf. Matt 16:18; 26:61; 27:40).[8] Here, then, Jesus's Davidic role has a necessary implication: *he will establish a sanctuary*. For Matthew, however, this is understood in terms of the *ekklēsia*. As Davies and Allison put it, "Jesus is the Son promised in 2 Sam 7:4–16, the king who builds the eschatological temple."[9] John Meier is correct: "For Matthew, to have an ecclesiology that was not totally dependent on Christology would be unthinkable."[10]

The identification of the community as a temple certainly fits well within first-century Jewish sectarianism. We have already mentioned that it finds a close parallel with the Qumran documents, where the community is understood as the temple:

the Community council shall be founded on truth, to be an everlasting plantation, *a holy house for Israel* and *the foundation of the holy of holies* for Aaron, true witnesses for the judgment and chosen by the will (of God) to atone for the land and to render the wicked their retribution. This (the Community) is the tested rampart, *the precious cornerstone*. (Community Rule [1QS] 8:5–10)

Significantly, this fragment goes on to call the community "the most holy dwelling for Aaron" and "a house of perfection and truth in Israel" (1QS 8:8–9). Here not only is the community described as a temple, but also its leadership is depicted as the *foundation* of this community temple.

---

[7] See Frederick Carlson Holmgren, *Israel Alive Again* (Grand Rapids: Eerdmans, 1987), 24; Laato, *A Star is Rising*, 178, 186–207; Talmon, "'Exile' and 'Restoration,'" 133–141, 154.

[8] See Hans Kvalbein, "The Authorization of Peter in Matthew 16:17–19: A Reconsideration of the Power to Bind and Loose," in *The Formation of the Early Church*, ed. Jostein Ådna, WUNT 183 (Tübingen: Mohr Siebeck, 2005), 155.

[9] Davies and Allison, *Matthew*, 2:642.

[10] Meier, *Vision of Matthew*, 97.

That it talks about a "cornerstone" reinforces the cultic resonances since such terminology is associated with temple architecture elsewhere (Ps 118:22; cf. Isa 28:16). The similarity with Matthew 16 is remarkable. There not only does the *ekklēsia* serve as the temple, but Jesus also goes on to explain that he will build the community *on* Peter (Matt 16:18). George Beasley-Murray writes, "This is not to suggest that Matt 16:18 is in any way dependent on the Qumran passage; it does show, however, that the ideas in the former passage were abroad."[11]

Those who have interacted with the argument that Matthew 16 evokes Davidic temple-building traditions have usually agreed with it.[12] Some, however, have demurred. Herman Waetjen argues that Jesus deliberately uses *ekklēsia* to distinguish his movement from the synagogue. Jesus's words to Peter, he argues, alludes to the Greek version of Isaiah 51, where Abraham and Sarah are said to be the "rock [*petran*]" out of which the restored Israel has been "hewn" (Isa 51:1–2 LXX).[13] Aside from Waetjen's dubious assumption that *ekklēsia* is necessarily used in opposition to "synagogue" – something that seems unlikely given the fact that *ekklēsia* was employed for synagogue gatherings[14] – the imagery from Isaiah 51 does not match Matthew's context. Rather than building *upon* a rock, Isaiah speaks of Israel being carved "out" of the rock of Abraham. Even more problematic is the way this interpretation ignores the obvious Davidic motifs in play.

Eyal Regev opines that the intertextual allusions to Davidic traditions discussed above are too subtle to be intentional.[15] I simply respond by pointing out that Matthew – though often less subtle than Mark (e.g., cf. Matt 17:13 with Mark 9:11–13) – is recognized as making indirect allusions elsewhere,[16] such as echoing the story of Cain and Abel in the Sermon on the Mount (Matt 5:23–24). To think that the description

---

[11] George R. Beasley-Murray, *Jesus and the Kingdom of God* (Grand Rapids: Eerdmans, 1986), 184.

[12] See, e.g., Jipp, *Messianic Theology*, 56n.102; Mothy Varkey, *Salvation in Continuity: Reconsidering Matthew's Soteriology*, Emerging Scholars (Minneapolis: Fortress Press, 2017), 205–206; Joseph, *Jesus and the Temple*, 221; Zacharias, *Matthew's Presentation*, 112.

[13] Herman Waetjen, *Matthew's Theology of Fulfillment, Its Universality and Its Ethnicity: God's New Israel as the Pioneer of God's New Humanity* (London: Bloomsbury, T&T Clark, 2017), 184–185

[14] See the sources in n.55 of Chapter 1.

[15] Regev, *The Temple in Early Christianity*, 140.

[16] See Richard Hays' treatment on intertextuality in Matthew in *Echoes of Scripture in the Gospels* (Waco: Baylor University Press, 2016), 105–190.

of Jesus as the "son of God" who "builds" would not have evoked
Solomonic traditions when such traditions are already foregrounded elsewhere in the Gospel is unconvincing. That Jesus is portrayed as the son of
David who builds the temple is therefore recognized by many commentators.[17] To quote Davies and Allison, in Matthew:

> Jesus is "the Christ, the Son of the living God"... He is *the realization of the mes-
> sianic hopes of Judaism, the fulfiller of the Davidic promises... He also builds the
> church, which is the eschatological temple.*[18]

Or, as we quoted these same two scholars at the beginning of the chapter: "Jesus is confessed as both Christ and Son of God; he builds a new
church or temple... These are all Davidic motifs."[19]

The Community as Temple Elsewhere in Matthew

Commentators have noticed other places where Jesus appears to apply
temple imagery to his disciples in Matthew. Here we look at three
instances: (1) the comparison of disciples to a "city set on a hill" in the
Sermon on the Mount (Matt 5:14); (2) the description of the disciple as a
"wise man" who "builds" a "house," also in the Sermon on the Mount
(Matt 7:24); and (3) Jesus's words about his presence within the community (Matt 18:15–20).

1. *Jesus's Disciples as a City on a Hill (Matt 5:14).* In the Sermon
on the Mount, Jesus compares the disciples to "salt," a "city upon a
hill," and a "light" (*phōs*) / "lamp" (*lychnos*, Matt 5:13–16). Are these
three images somehow interrelated? Following Hans Dieter Betz, we can
observe that the imagery of a "city on a hill" would have immediately
reminded Jews of Zion.[20] That such a reading is intended is further supported by the pairing of "city" with "light." As we have already mentioned, the eschatological Zion and future temple were associated with
the latter (cf. Isa 60:1–4; Zech 14:6–9; Tob 13:10–11; 1 En. 14:8–23;
71:2–47; Sib. Or. 4.191; 5.420). Combined with the imagery of salt,
which, was easily associated with cultic traditions (cf. Lev 2:13; Ezek

---

[17] See, e.g., Nolland, *Matthew*, 672; Meier, *Matthew*, 182; Ben F. Meyer, *Christus Faber: The
Master-Builder and the House of God* (Allison Park: Pickwick Publications, 1992), 259.

[18] Davies and Allison, *Matthew*, 2:641.

[19] Davies and Allison, *Matthew*, 2:603.

[20] Hans Dieter Betz, *The Sermon on the Mount: A Commentary on the Sermon on the
Mount, Including the Sermon on the Plain (Matthew 5:3–7:27 and Luke 6:20–49)*, ed.
Adela Yarbro Collins (Minneapolis: Fortress Press, 1995), 161.

43:24), the three metaphors in Matt 5:13–16 seem to be tied together by a cultic thread. The city on a hill is thus most likely an allusion to Zion, which unavoidably called to mind the temple. Perrin writes:

> This cannot simply be any city on any hill, or any light. Rather, given the fluidity between the concepts of "Zion" and "temple" in Second-Temple Judaism, Matthew's point also seems to be that those who are faithful to the messiah Jesus ... will likewise shine forth as the true Jerusalem and the true temple.[21]

Perrin's language of "true Jerusalem" and "true temple" might be taken to indicate that Jesus's use of cultic metaphors represents a wholesale rejection of the holiness of the Jerusalem or temple of his day. That would be a mistake. Matthew, as we have seen, calls Jerusalem, "the holy city" (Matt 4:5; 27:53). Nonetheless, that Jesus applies Zion imagery to the disciples here makes tremendous sense. Indeed, in the Dead Sea Scrolls, the community is not only compared to the temple, but is also likened to the eschatological *Zion* (cf. 11Q13 2:23–24; 4Q164 1–7), a comparison that makes sense given the way Zion and temple were used interchangeably. Matthew seems to contain a similar idea here. However, whereas the Scrolls' identification of the community with the temple is due to a rejection of the holiness of the Jerusalem sanctuary, that is not the case in Matthew.

2. *The Disciple as the Wise House-Builder (Matt 7:24).* Later in the Sermon on the Mount, Jesus compares the one who hears his words to "a *wise* [*phronimō*] man who built [*ōkodomēsen*] his *house* [*oikian*] upon a rock" (Matt 7:24). It is hard to believe that a description of a man of *wisdom* building *a house* would not evoke Solomon. The king was known both for his *wisdom* (e.g., 3 Kgdms 3:12: *phronimos*; 3 Kgdms 3:28; 5:9: *phronēsis*) and for *building* (3 Kgdms 6:2: *oikodomeō*) the temple (cf. also Sir 47:12–13). The themes come together neatly in the account of Hiram of Tyre's exchange with Solomon. After the Davidide announces his plans to "build [*oikodomēsai*] a *house* [*oikon*] for the name of the Lord" (3 Kgdms 5:17), Hiram declares: "Blessed be God today, who gave to David a *wise* [*phronimon*] son over this numerous people" (3 Kgdms 5:21 [NETS adapted]).

The likelihood of a Solomonic reference in Jesus's saying about the wise man's building efforts is further reinforced by the fact that Solomonic allusions frequently pop up in Matthew, starting with the programmatic opening chapter (Matt 1:6, 7). Jesus explicitly talks about Solomon earlier

---

[21] Perrin, *Jesus the Priest*, 115.

in the same sermon (Matt 6:29). In addition, Matthew later records that Jesus compared himself with Solomon, saying, "something greater than Solomon is here" (Matt 12:42). We have also seen that Matthew uses Solomonic typology in recounting Jesus's entry into Jerusalem and in portraying Jesus as a wisdom teacher, healer, and exorcist. All of this strengthens the likelihood that Jesus's saying about the wise man has a Solomonic connection. Jesus would thus seem to describe the life of discipleship in terms of Solomonic temple-building.

3. *Jesus's Presence and the Cultic Activity of the Disciples (Matt 18:20)*. In Matthew 18, Jesus explains how to deal with a conflict within the community. Within this context, he says:

> Again, amen, I say to you, if two of you agree on earth about anything that they ask, it shall be done for them by my Father who is in heaven. For where two or three are gathered in my name, *there I am in the midst of them*. (Matthew 18:19–20)

In speaking of being present to believers, Jesus is once again presented as Immanuel / "God with us" (cf. Matt 1:23). Commentators often speculate that his teaching might be related to a tradition found in the Mishnah:

> But if two sit together and words of the Law [are spoken] between them, the Divine Presence rests between them. (m. Abot 3:2)[22]

Whether this tradition informs the logion in Matthew 18 is unclear. It should be pointed out, however, that – at least in Matthew – God's presence is *especially* linked not with study but *with the temple*. Jesus proclaims that it is there that God "dwells" (cf. Matt 23:21). Moreover, Jesus's saying takes place within a cultic context, namely, of communal prayer. Later, Matthew will report that, quoting from Isaiah, Jesus spoke of the temple as "a house of prayer" (Matt 21:13; Isa 56:7).

As we have seen, the motif of God's presence in the temple is important for interpreting Jesus's saying about the sanctuary being "desolate" in Matthew 23. In departing from the temple, Jesus pre-enacts as Immanuel the departure of the divine presence from the sanctuary. Within the larger context of the gospel, therefore, Jesus's promise about being present to the disciples in Matthew 18 indicates that the divine presence he later connects to the temple will be found in the community.[23]

[22] Herbert Danby, trans., *The Mishnah: Translated from the Hebrew with Introduction and Brief Explanatory Notes* (Oxford: Oxford University Press, 1933), 450. See, e.g., Davies and Allison, Matthew, 2:789–790.
[23] See Runesson, *Divine Wrath*, 127.

Finally, we might also point out that Jesus's use of "name [*onoma*]" ties in neatly with temple traditions. The sanctuary was often identified as the place where God's "name [*onoma*]" dwells (cf., e.g., Deut 12:11; 14:23; 16:2 LXX) or as the house "called by [God's] name [*onoma*]" (cf., e.g., 3 Kgdms 8:43 LXX; 2 Chr 6:33 LXX; 1 Macc 7:37 LXX). The *ekklēsia*, in effect, becomes the locus of the divine presence in a way analogous to what is found in the temple, which, in Matthew, Jesus calls "the house of prayer" (Matt 21:13; Isa 56:7). Davies and Allison write, "With the old house of prayer gone, it was appropriate to give instruction on prayer in the new temple, the Christian community."[24]

THE PRIESTHOOD OF THE DISCIPLES IN MATTHEW

For ancient Jews, the temple was inexorably united to the priesthood; there could be no temple liturgy without priests. If Matthew has Jesus speak of the community as a temple, it would only be natural for the evangelist to have Jesus describe his disciples in priestly terms. Here I will argue that this is precisely what we find in Matthew. Once again, our analysis will begin with Matthew 16. We will then explore other passages in Matthew where Jesus appears to use priestly imagery.

Peter as a Priestly Figure in Matthew 16

We saw earlier that Matthew 16 depicts the community as a temple. With that in mind, it makes sense that Matthew would have Jesus speak of its leaders not only as teachers and missionaries, but also as having some sort of priestly role. Indeed, this logic seems to be present in Jesus's words to Peter. To recognize this, however, we must pay close attention to the way the scene uses scriptural traditions.

As many scholars have noted, Jesus's words concerning the "keys" given to Peter most probably draws upon an oracle found in Isaiah 22.[25] It is important to read this passage in its original context:

Thus says the Lord GOD of hosts, "Come, go to this steward, to Shebna, who is over the house, and say to him... And it will happen on that day that I will call my servant Eliakim the son of Hilkiah, and I will clothe him with your

---

[24] Davies and Allison, *Matthew*, 3:154.
[25] See, e.g., H. Benedict Green, *Matthew, Poet of the Beatitudes* (Sheffield: Sheffield Academic Press, 2001), 135; Davies and Allison, *Matthew*, 2:640; J. A. Emerton, "Binding and Loosing—Forgiving and Retaining," *JTS* 13 (1962): 325–331.

robe, and will bind your sash on him, and will bind your authority to his hand. And he shall be like a father to the inhabitants of Jerusalem and to the house of Judah. And I will place on his shoulder *the key* of the house of David. *He shall open, and none shall shut; and he shall shut, and none shall open.* And I will drive him in like a peg in a sure place, and he will become like a throne of honor to his father's house. And they will hang on him all of the weight of his father's house, the offspring and issue, every small vessel, from the cups to all the flagons." (Isaiah 22:15, 20–24)

Aside from the obvious parallel with the key imagery, Jesus's words to Peter in Matthew 16 mirror Isaiah 22 in a number of ways:

- Both texts relate the giving of authority, using idiomatic language (cf. "opening and shutting" in Isa 22:22; "binding and loosing" in Matt 16:19).
- Both texts use Davidic motifs – Isa 22:22 has "the keys of the house of David," while in Matthew 16 we find numerous links to Davidic traditions (e.g., Jesus's identity as "son of God," "anointed one," and temple-builder).
- As the *ekklēsia* is built on Peter in Matthew 16, the "weight of his father's house" is on Eliakim in Isaiah (cf. Isa 22:24).

Moreover, some have discerned a linguistic connection between the Aramaic words for "open" and "shut" in Isa 22:22 and the Greek words for "bind" and "loose" in Matthew 16.[26] It is no wonder, then, that scholars regularly identify Isaiah 22 as the quarry for Jesus's response to Peter.

More frequently neglected, however, is the way Isaiah 22 was seen to evoke temple traditions. Later Jewish interpreters were explicit in their priestly reading of the passage. The oracle appears in the backdrop of the judgment of the wicked priests in 2 Baruch:

You, priests, *take the keys of the sanctuary* and cast them to the highest heaven, and give them to the Lord and say, "Guard your house yourself, because, behold, *we have been found to be false stewards.*" (2 Baruch 10:18)[27]

The pairing of wicked "stewards" with "keys" is often attributed to the influence of Isaiah 22 where Shebna is said to be a "steward" (Isa 22:15) and the "key" of the "house" (Isa 22:22) is removed from him.[28] In fact, the scene in 2 Baruch is widely attested in Jewish literature (cf., e.g., 4

---

[26] See Emmerton, "Binding and Loosing," 325–331; Davies and Allison, *Matthew*, 2:640.
[27] Cited from *OTP* 1:624.
[28] See, e.g., J. Andrew Overman, *The Church and Community in Crisis: The Gospel According to Matthew* (London: Bloomsbury, 1996), 241.

Bar 4:4–5).²⁹ Likewise, in the Targum on Isaiah 22, Eliakim is said to receive "the key of *the sanctuary*" (v. 22).³⁰ In addition, the Midrash Rabbah specifically calls Shebna, the man whose office Eliakim takes, the "high priest" (cf. Lev. Rab. 5.5).³¹ Why do so many Jewish sources tie the priesthood to Isaiah 22? It is not difficult to explain such readings. They result from the imagery used in the original Hebrew of the passage.

In Isaiah 22, Eliakim is portrayed as wearing the *kuttōnet* ("tunic") and *abnēt* ("sash," Isa 22:21), garments typically linked to the high priest.³² While the mere appearance of one of these garments may not be enough to establish a sacerdotal reference, the combination of the two makes it difficult to insist that they are non-priestly in character. The high priest is repeatedly said to wear these garments together (cf. Exod 28:4, 39–40; 29:5–9; 39:27–29; Lev 8:7; 16:4; cf. Wis 18:24). Josephus says the two garments are worn by the high priest (cf. *Ant.* 3:153–154).

Other considerations also suggest Eliakim has a priestly role. In the LXX, Eliakim receives a "crown" (*stephanon*, Isa 22:21 LXX), which suggests a sacerdotal office. We learn from other Jewish sources that the high priest wore a "crown" (*stephanos*, Sir 50:12; Zech 6:11; 1 Macc 10:20; Josephus, *Ant.* 3.172). Eliakim's responsibility in the sanctuary may also be drawn out of Isa 22:24, where he is given authority over "every small vessel, from the cups to all the flagons." Such food vessels appear elsewhere in contexts describing the temple's sacred objects, especially in connection with the table of the bread of the presence.³³ While Isaiah says the house Eliakim is given charge over belongs to David, a cultic reading is certainly encouraged by the appearance of the priestly garments. Furthermore, as we have seen, it would have been natural to think of the temple as a house constructed by the Davidide. Either way, while the original author probably did not have the temple in mind, ancient Jewish readers clearly found cultic symbolism in the passage.

---

²⁹ See also b. Ta'an. 29a; y. Shek. 6:3; A'bot R. Nat. A. 4:5; Lev. Rab. 19.6; Pesiq. Rab. 26:6; Tg. II on Esther 1:3.

³⁰ See Bruce Chilton, *The Isaiah Targum*, ArBib 11 (Collegeville: Liturgical Press, 1987), 44.

³¹ For further discussion on the priestly role of Eliakim, see Beale, *The Temple and the Church's Mission*, 187–188; Bruce Chilton, "Shebna, Eliakim and the Promise to Peter," in *Jesus in Context: Temple, Purity, Restoration*, ed. B. Chilton and C. A. Evans (Leiden: Brill, 1997), 319–352; Bruce Chilton, "Temple Restored, Temple in Heaven: Isaiah and the Prophets in the Targumim," in *Restoration*, ed. Scott, 343–349.

³² The *kuttōnet*: Exod 28:4, 39–40; 29:5, 8; 39:27; 40:14; Lev 8:7, 13; 10:5; etc.; the *abnēt*: Exod 28:4, 39, 40; 29:9; 39:29; Lev 8:7, 13; 16:4.

³³ See, for example, Exod 37:16; Num 4:7–15; 1 Kgs 7:50; 1 Chr 28:13, 16–17; Jer 52:19; 1 Macc 4:48–51.

Having noted the likelihood that priestly associations were made with Eliakim in Isaiah 22, it is also relevant that "keys" had sacerdotal significance in Jewish texts. In 1 Chronicles, the priests are said to open the temple each day, having charge over the key (*maptēaḥ*) of the sanctuary (1 Chr 9:27). Josephus also makes special mention of the priests' use of keys. They apparently played a prominent role in the ceremonial handing over of priestly duties when the outgoing division of priests transferred authority to the incoming group. Josephus writes:

> For, although there are four priestly tribes, each comprising upwards of five thousand members, these officiate by rotation for a fixed period of days; when the term of one party ends, others come to offer the sacrifices in their place, and assembling at mid-day in the temple, *take over from the outgoing ministers the keys of the building* and all its vessels, duly numbered. (*Against Apion* 2.108 [LCL Thackery])

The priestly responsibility over the keys of the temple is also attested in the Mishnah, which tells us that within the temple "the eldest of the father's house used to sleep with the keys of the Temple Court in their hand."[34] The passage goes on to detail the routine of the priests who would unlock the sanctuary doors each day (m. Mid. 1:9).[35] Keys are also referenced in the account of the priestly treasurers' duties in the Tosefta (t. Šeq. 2:25). The priestly duty of locking up the temple with the keys belonged to their role as guardians of the sanctuary (cf., e.g., Num 3:5–10; 8:26; 18:7).

Since Isaiah 22 describes Eliakim as wearing garments otherwise associated with the high priest and given the fact that priestly responsibilities were symbolized with keys, it is not surprising that the Targum on Isaiah 22 identifies the key given to Eliakim as "the key of the sanctuary." Matthew 16 draws out the cultic implications of Isaiah 22 that were later picked up by other Jewish sources. Recall that Matthew is himself best seen as a *Jewish* writer in his own right. Matthew, therefore, simply anticipates what later Jewish writers would also do with the text of Isaiah.

The preceding discussion explains Jesus's use of Isaiah 22 in context. *If the community is a temple, Peter, who is identified as having a leadership role, is naturally presented as a priestly figure.*

The Twelve's Task of Judging Israel as a Priestly Task (Matt 19:28)

Jesus applies priestly imagery to the disciples elsewhere in Matthew. We have already looked at one instance of this, namely, Jesus's appeal to the

---

[34] Taken from Danby, *Mishnah*, 591.
[35] Danby, *Mishnah*, 591.

priests' exemption from Sabbath rest as precedent for the apostles' act of plucking grain (Matt 12:5). In the episode, Jesus also likens the disciples to David's men who ate the bread of the presence which is "only for the priests" (Matt 12:4). Yet other examples can also be found.

In Matthew 19, Jesus tells the twelve that they will "sit [*kathēsesthe*] on twelve thrones, *judging* [*krinontes*] the twelve tribes of Israel" (Matt 19:28). As we saw earlier, this logion likely evokes restoration hopes. The language of "thrones" is unmistakably royal in character.[36] Yet we should not imagine that royal and priestly roles were hermetically sealed categories. As we have seen, the Davidide could be spoken of as a priest (cf. Ps 110:4; cf. 2 Sam 8:18) and perform priestly duties (cf. 2 Sam 6:17–18). Likewise, during the Hasmonean period, the high priest was treated as a royal figure.[37] With that in mind, we ought to recognize that Jewish sources specifically view judging the twelve tribes as a *priestly* duty. This is particularly true in eschatological visions.

While lay people could exercise juridical authority, this responsibility was prominently linked to the priesthood (cf. Deut 17:9; cf. also 2 Chr 19:8–11). By the Second Temple period, judicial power became acutely sacerdotal. As E. P. Sanders points out, Josephus assigns the task of judging *solely* to the priests (cf. *Ag. Ap.* 2.165; 4.304), omitting the Torah's references to lay judges.[38] Likewise, Daniel Grossberg explains: "In Hellenistic times the high priest replaced the king as the principal judge (cf. 2 Chron 19:8)."[39] The high priest's special function as a juridical figure is rooted in the Torah and is tied to his use of the mysterious Urim and Thummim. Regardless of how they should be understood, there can be little doubt that these objects were associated with judgment (cf. Exod 28:30; Num 27:21; Sir 45:10; cf. Lev 8:8; Ezra 2:63; Neh 7:65). It was therefore fitting that the high priest served as president of

---

[36] See, e.g., S. Légasse, "Aproche de l'épisode préévangélique des Fils de Zébédée (Marc X.35–40 par.)," *NTS* 20 (1974): 161–177; Meier, *A Marginal Jew*, 3:218.

[37] See, e.g., Kenneth Atkinson, *A History of the Hasmonean State: Josephus and Beyond* (London: Bloomsbury T&T Clark, 2016), 32, who shows that this is the case as early as Simon's reign. Because it was apparently considered inappropriate by some for a figure to be both high priest and ruler, Simon is not officially called "king." Nonetheless, the high priest's authority "was essentially that of a Hellenistic monarch."

[38] See Sanders, *Judaism: Practice and Belief*, 171.

[39] Daniel Grossberg, "Judges," in *Eerdmans Dictionary of the Bible*, ed. David N. Freedman, Allen C. Myers, and Astrid B. Beck (Grand Rapids: Eerdmans, 2000), 752. See also Sanders, *Judaism: Practice and Belief*, 171.

the Sanhedrin (cf. 1 Macc 14:44; Acts 5:17; Josephus, *Ag. Ap.* 2.194; *Ant.* 20.200, 251).⁴⁰

In the gospel traditions the priestly leaders have a conspicuously promi-nent part in the juridical condemnation of Jesus (cf. Matt 26:57–65; Mark 14:43, 53–64; Luke 22:54, 66; John 18:13, 24). Among other things, Jesus is said to be brought before "*the chief priests and the whole council*" (Matt 26:59; Mark 14:55). In the Synoptics and John, it is the *high priest* who is the last authority to question Jesus. In the Fourth Gospel, Jesus is also brought before the high priest, Annas (John 18:13, 19–24).

The priests' juridical role is emphasized in texts describing the escha-tological age. In Ezekiel's vision, it is solely priests who are identified as judges in the age to come:

No priest shall drink wine when they come into the inner court. They shall not marry a widow or a divorced woman, but only a virgin of the offspring of the house of Israel, or a widow who is the widow of a priest. They shall teach my people the difference between the holy and the common, and show them how to distinguish between the unclean and the clean. In a dispute, they shall act as judges, and *they shall judge it according to my judgments.* (Ezekiel 44:21–24)

Significantly, no lay eschatological judges are mentioned by Ezekiel.

The prominent role of priestly leaders in the eschaton is also attested in the Dead Sea Scrolls. The Damascus Document refers to "the priest who governs [ov]er the Many" (cf. 4Q266 *frag.* 11:8; cf. 4Q267 *frag.* 9, 10; 4Q270 *frag.* 7, 1:16; 4Q289 1:4). Likewise, though the Davidic mes-siah is not subordinate to the priests in the Scrolls,⁴¹ it seems that even he will defer to them in legal matters:

according to what they teach him, he will judge, and upon their authority [...] with him will go out one of the priests of renown, holding in his hand clothes. (4QpIsaiah Pesherᵃ [4QpIsaᵃ] *frags.* 8–10, 24–25)

In short, if Jesus is presented as envisioning the disciples as judges in the eschaton it would be natural to assume that he sees them as having some sort of sacerdotal identity.

The context of Jesus's saying about the apostles' juridical role in Matthew 19 would seem to confirm that that a priestly meaning is intended. In the very next line, Jesus promises: "And everyone who has

---

⁴⁰ See Graham H. Twelftree, "Sanhedrin," in *Dictionary of Jesus and the Gospels*, ed. Joel B. Green, Scot McKnight, and I. Howard Marshall (Downers Grove: InterVarsity Press, 1992), 730.
⁴¹ See the discussion in Cho, *Royal Messianism*, 25–51.

left houses or *brothers or sisters or father or mother or children or lands*, for my name's sake, will receive a hundredfold, and *inherit eternal life*" (Matt 19:29). Here Jesus is referring to the commitment made by the twelve. With that in mind, it is especially significant that Jesus's language is evocative of passages that recall how the Levites received the priesthood after slaying the idolators in the wilderness, indeed, their own brother and sister Israelites:

Today you have ordained yourselves for the service of the Lord, each one *at the cost of his son and of his brother*, that he may bestow a blessing upon you this day. (Exodus 32:29)

The one saying to his *father and his mother* "I have not seen you" and *his brother* he did not acknowledge and his *children* he disowned. (Deuteronomy 33:9 LXX)

Jesus's assurance that the twelve will *"inherit* eternal life" due to their renunciation of "lands [*agrous*]" (Matt 19:29) further strengthens the likelihood that priestly traditions are in view. As Allison observes, Jesus's statement is reminiscent of what is said concerning the Levites. Instead of receiving *land* of their own, Moses explains that the Levites' *inheritance* would be the Lord (cf. Num 18:20, 23; Deut 10:9).[42] Like the Levites, then, the disciples have renounced "brothers," "father," "mother," and "lands" in order to receive a special "inheritance."

That the evangelist portrays Jesus as assigning a priestly role to the twelve is not hard to explain. As we have detailed earlier, Jesus has already been depicted as borrowing on temple imagery to describe the *ekklēsia* as the temple that he, the son of David, will "build" (Matt 16:18). Yet there is further evidence for the disciples' priestly role in Matthew we have yet to consider: Jesus's Parable of the Wicked Tenants.

THE PARABLE OF THE WICKED TENANTS AND TEMPLE IMAGERY

Like Mark and Luke, Matthew includes an account of Jesus's Parable of the Wicked Tenants (Matt 21:33–46; cf. Mark 12:1–12//Luke 20:9–18). That the parable is directed at the Jewish leaders is explicitly stated in both Matthew and Luke (cf. Matt 21:45; Luke 20:19). This is also implicit in

---

[42] See Dale C. Allison, Jr., *The Intertextual Jesus: Scripture in Q* (Harrisburg: Trinity Press International, 2000), 63–64. See also Crispin H. T. Fletcher-Louis, "Jesus Inspects His Priestly War Party (Luke 14:25–33)," in *The Old Testament in the New Testament. Essays in Honour of J.L. North*, ed. S. Moyise, JSNTSup 189 (Sheffield: Sheffield Academic Press, 2000), 126–143.

Mark. There we read that the Jerusalem leaders wanted to arrest Jesus because of the parable (cf. Mark 12:12). As we have seen, in the wider context, these leaders approach Jesus in order to "test" him with questions and challenge his authority in the wake of his temple action.[43] Many commentators have noted that, properly understood, the message of the story involves Jesus's condemnation of the Jerusalem leadership. Yet it is important to recognize that Matthew – like the other Synoptic evangelists – pairs the parable with a logion involving a quotation from Psalm 118 that unavoidably triggers temple traditions. As we shall see, the parable and the allusion to Jesus as the "stone rejected by the builders" has important implications for our study of cultic imagery in Jesus's teaching.

The Meaning of the Parable

It is important to look at the full account of the Matthean version of the Parable of the Wicked Tenants:

Hear another parable: There was a man, a master of a house, who planted a vineyard, and put a hedge around it, and dug in it a winepress, and built a tower. Then he leased it to tenant farmers and went on a journey. And when the time of the fruit drew near, he sent his servants to the farmers, to receive his fruits. And the farmers took his servants, they beat one, killed another, and stoned another. Again, he sent other servants more than the first, and they treated them likewise. So last of all he sent to them his son, saying, "They will respect my son." But when the farmers saw the son, they said to themselves, "This is the heir; come, let us kill him, and have his inheritance." And they took him, and cast him out of the vineyard, and killed him. Now when the lord of the vineyard comes, what will he do to those farmers? They said to him, "He will completely destroy those wicked men, and will lease out the vineyard to other farmers, who will render to him the fruits in their seasons." Jesus said to them, "Have you never read in the scriptures, 'The stone which the builders rejected has become the head of the corner: this came about from the Lord, and it is marvelous in our eyes'? Therefore, I tell you, the kingdom of God will be taken away from you and given to a people producing the fruits of it." (Matthew 21:33–43)[44]

Scholars largely agree about the meaning of the basic elements of the story. The owner represents God, the "tenant farmers" are a cipher for the

---

[43] See, e.g., Nolland, *Matthew*, 867–868.

[44] There has been much recent debate about the authenticity of Matt 21:44. Gregory R. Lanier ("A Case for the Assimilation of Matthew 21:44 to the Lukan 'Crushing Stone' [20:18], with Special Reference to $\mathfrak{P}^{104}$," *TC: A Journal of Biblical Textual Criticism* 21 [2016]: 1–21) makes a compelling case against it, appealing to $\mathfrak{P}^{104}$. Because of the controversy, it is best to leave the matter aside.

Jerusalem leaders, the servants sent by the owner are the prophets (cf. 2 Chr 36:15–16), and the owner's son who is murdered is Jesus.

It is also necessary to say a word about the conclusion of the parable: "the kingdom of God will be taken away from you and given to a *people* [*ethnei*] producing the fruits of it" (Matt 21:43). For many, this line is proof that the evangelist believes that God has rejected Israel in favor of the gentiles.[45] The story has therefore been said to be "[p]erhaps the most dramatic text"[46] suggesting anti-Judaism in the Gospel. This reading, however, should be challenged. First, the parable is specifically said to target the chief priests and the Pharisees (Matt 21:45); it is not directed to the Jewish people as a whole. Notably, then, according to the story, it is not the vineyard that is replaced but the tenants. As Amy-Jill Levine writes, "the only element that changes is the leadership."[47] Second, that the parable means *all Jews* have been rejected is further undermined by the fact that Jesus's own disciples in the Gospel are Jewish. Because of this, it is hard to believe the story implies *all Israel* has been replaced by the gentiles. Third, the word "people [*ethnos*]" does not necessarily refer to a "nation," but can refer more generally to a group of people.[48] In short, to hold up this parable as evidence that Matthew believes Israel as a whole has been replaced by gentiles is unconvincing.

The parable also draws on scriptural traditions. In particular, commentators usually recognize the story's dependence on Isaiah 5.[49] In the latter passage, Israel is described as a vineyard built by the Lord (cf. Isa 5:1–2, 7). The account of the owner's construction of the vineyard in Matthew has numerous similarities to the Isaianic passage:

[45] See, e.g., Wolfgang Trilling, *Das Wahre Israel: Studien zur Theologie des Matthäusevangeliums*, 3rd ed. (Munich: Kösel, 1964), 60–61; Douglas R. Hare, *The Theme of Jewish Persecution of Christians in the Gospel According to St. Matthew* (Cambridge: Cambridge University Press, 1967), 153.

[46] Donald Hagner, "Matthew: Christian Judaism or Jewish Christianity," in *The Face of New Testament Studies: A Survey of Recent Research*, ed. Scot McKnight and Grant R. Osborne (Grand Rapids: Baker Academic, 2004), 275.

[47] Amy-Jill Levine, *The Social and Ethnic Dimensions of Matthean Social History* (Lewiston: Edwin Mellen, 1988), 210.

[48] For a fuller discussion, see Konradt, *Israel, Church, and the Gentiles*, 178–185; Saldarini, *Matthew's Christian-Jewish Community*, 58–61, 78–81.

[49] See, e.g., Bryan, *Jesus and Israel's Traditions*, 54n.18; W. J. C. Weren, "The Use of Isaiah 5, 1–7 in the Parable of the Tenants (Mark 12,1–12; Matthew 21,33–46)," *Bib* 79 (1998): 1–26; Morna D. Hooker, *Mark*, BNTC (London: A & C Black, 1991), 274 and, on Luke, the sources in Joel B. Green, *The Gospel of Luke*, New International Commentary on the New Testament (Grand Rapids: Eerdmans, 1997), 704n.21.

Jesus's Parable of the Wicked Tenants (Matthew 21)	Isaiah's Song of the Vineyard (Isaiah 5 LXX)
"he put a hedge around it [*phragmon auto periethēken*]." (Matt 21:33)	"I put a hedge around it [*phragmon periethēka*]." (Isa 5:2 LXX)
"he dug a winepress [*ōryxen en autō lēnon*]." (Matt 21:33)	"and I dug out a wine vat in it [*prolēnion ōryxen en autō lēnon*]." (Isa 5:2 LXX)
"he built a tower [*ōkodomēsen pyrgon*]." (Matt 21:33)	"I built a tower [*ōkodomēsen pyrgom*]." (Isa 5:2 LXX)

Dunn writes, "it would be surprising if a Jewish audience did not hear an allusion to Israel as God's vineyard."[50]

The biblical quotation that follows the parable must also be explained. After indicating that the tenants will receive retribution from the owner for their actions, Jesus cites Psalm 118: "Have you never read in the scriptures, 'The stone which the builders rejected [*apedokimasan*] has become the cornerstone [LXX: *kephalēn gōnias*]'" (Matt 21:42; cf. Ps 118:22).[51] There is no debate about its symbolism: the saying refers to Jesus's passion (="rejected") and vindication (="has become the cornerstone").[52] Notably, the term "rejected [*apodokimazō*]" appears in Jesus's passion predictions in Mark and Luke (cf. Mark 8:31; Luke 9:22; 17:25; cf. also Heb 12:17; 1 Pet 2:4, 7).[53] Moreover, since the word "builders" is applied to the Jewish leaders in other sources (cf. 1QIsa^a 54:13; CD-A 4:19; 8:12, 18),[54] it seems to have the same meaning here.[55] This meaning is confirmed by the evangelist, who tells us that the chief priests and the Pharisees "perceived that he was speaking about them" (Matt 21:45). For our purposes, however, let us focus on the cultic resonances scholars have detected in the parable itself and in the concluding quotation of Psalm 118.

---

[50] Dunn, *Jesus Remembered*, 722. See also Bryan, *Jesus and Israel's Traditions*, 54n.18.

[51] I use the traditional translation of "cornerstone" here though there is some debate about the stone's precise nature. Its exact function does not change the overall message; what matters most is that the rejected stone becomes the most important one. See, e.g., Davies and Allison, *Matthew*, 3:185n.62; Keener, *Matthew*, 515.

[52] See, e.g., Nolland, *Matthew*, 878.

[53] See Robert D. Row, *God's Kingdom and God's Son: The Background to Mark's Christology from Concepts of Kingship in the Psalms* (Leiden: Brill, 2002), 263.

[54] See also later sources, e.g., b. Šabb. 114a; b. Ber. 64a; Song Rab. 1.5.3.

[55] Klyne R. Snodgrass, *Stories with Intent: A Comprehensive Guide to the Parables of Jesus*, 2nd ed. (Grand Rapids: Eerdmans, 2018), 290.

Temple Allusions in the Parable and the Cornerstone Saying

The appearance of the "stone" saying immediately after the story has been attributed to the well-established play on the Hebrew words for "stone" (*'eben*) and "son" (*ben*) (cf. e.g., Exod 28:9).[56] The pun appears in John the Baptist's preaching earlier in the Gospel (Matt 3:9). This explains the seemingly natural way Jesus couples the story of a rejected "son" with Psalm 118's "stone."

Yet the sudden turn to Psalm 118 also seems related to cultic symbolism embedded in the parable. This needs to be explained. First, the "cornerstone" from Psalm 118 is most likely an allusion to the temple's architecture. Shortly after referring to the placement of the cornerstone, the psalmist says: "We bless you from the *house of the* LORD" (Ps 118:26). That the Mishnah and later Jewish literature associated the psalm with the temple's worship, therefore, is not surprising (cf. m. Pesaḥ 5:5–7, 10:6–7; m. Sukkah 3:9; 4:5; t. Pesaḥ. 4:10–11; b. Pesaḥ 95b). The text of the psalm also appears in the temple-building scene of Ezra 3 (cf. Ezra 3:11; cf. Ps 118:29). Furthermore, it bears mentioning that there is good evidence that the psalm was associated with the feast of Tabernacles (m. Sukkah 4:5), a feast especially tied to hopes for an eschatological temple (cf. Zech 14:16–21; Hag 2:1–9).[57]

Other considerations also suggest the stone-saying involves a cultic connection. For one, "stone" imagery frequently occurs in sources describing temples and sacred sites (e.g., Gen 28:10–22; Isa 8:14–15; 28:16; Zech 4:7–9; m. Yoma. 5:2; b. Yoma 54a–b; Lev. Rab. 20.4; Bet ha–Midr. 5.63; Num. Rab. 12.4). Psalm 118 is also used in concert with temple motifs in 1 Peter 2. In fact, referring to the temple's destruction, Jesus will go on to speak of how "one *stone* [*lithos*] will not be left here upon another *stone* [*lithon*]" (Matt 24:2). Along these lines, a relevant passage is Testament of Solomon 23:2–4, which applies the "cornerstone" of Psalm 118 to the building of a new temple. If this text is influenced by Jesus traditions, it can be cited with 1 Peter as evidence

---

[56] Other examples could also be cited (e.g., Exod 28:9–10; Lam 4:1–2; Zech 9:16; Tg. on Psalm 118:22; Lam. Rab. 4:1; Exod. Rab. 20.9; 46.2; Esth. Rab. 7.10). For further discussion, see George Brooke, "4Q500 1 and the Use of Scripture in the Parable of the Vineyard," *DSD* 2 (1995): 287–288 n. 59; Hagner, *Matthew*, 2:622; Klyne Snodgrass, *Parable of the Wicked Servants: An Inquiry into Parable Interpretation*, WUNT 27 (Tübingen: Mohr Siebeck, 1983), 115–116.

[57] For further discussion on the background of the psalm, see Gray, *Temple in the Gospel of Mark*, 72–77.

that Jesus's early followers thought the psalm's cornerstone language was meant to call to mind the sanctuary. If not, which seems less likely, it can be included with other Jewish works that use "stone" terminology in reference to temple symbolism.[58]

Could something in the text explain the abrupt shift from a story about a vineyard to language referring to the temple's architecture? It seems so. Klyne Snodgrass points out, "Evidence from Jewish sources shows that Isaiah 5 was traditionally associated with the Temple" (cf. 4Q500; 1 En. 89:56, 66–67, 73; t. Meʿil. 1:16; t. Sukkah 3:15).[59] Given the fact that Isaiah 5 was itself apparently linked to the sanctuary, closing a parable based on its imagery with a temple saying makes perfect sense. The temple-vineyard connection may have also been encouraged by the décor of the Jerusalem temple itself; Josephus reports that a giant golden vine was prominently displayed above the main entrance of the temple (*Ant.* 15.395).

What Joel Marcus says about Mark's report of Jesus's parable and quotation from Psalm 118 is applicable to Matthew's account:

It is not necessary … to go as far afield as rabbinic literature, Qumran or even 1 Peter in order to establish the link between the stone imagery of Mark 12:10 and the themes of the Temple. Mark himself confirms this linkage. The setting for our passage is the Temple itself (11:27), and the Temple theme is prominent in the proceeding chapter of Mark (11:9–11, 15–18, 27–33). In the very next chapter, moreover, the eschatological discourse is introduced by a short passage in which stone imagery and the Temple theme are interwoven in a manner strikingly reminiscent of our passage… These links suggest that the Old Testament context of the psalm quotation, with its references to the Temple liturgy, is in view.[60]

Jesus's saying regarding the stone rejected by the "builders" therefore likely involves an allusion to the project of temple-building.[61] The final upshot of the saying's meaning is indisputable: *Jesus* is identified with the sanctuary that is being erected.

---

[58] On the possibility that this work once existed as a Jewish text, see, e.g., Daniel Gurtner, *Introducing the Pseudepigrapha of Second Temple Judaism: Message, Content, and Significance* (Grand Rapids: Baker Academic, 2020), 204–208; Ian K. Smith, *Heavenly Perspective: A Study of the Apostle Paul's Response to a Jewish Mystical Movement at Colossae* (London: T&T Clark, 2006), 83.

[59] Snodgrass, *Stories*, 288.

[60] Joel Marcus, *The Way of the Lord: Christological Exegesis of the Old Testament in the Gospel of Mark* (Louisville: Westminster/John Knox Press, 1992), 120–121.

[61] See Gray, *Temple in the Gospel of Mark*, 70; Michael F. Bird, *Jesus and the Origins of the Gentile Mission*, LHJS 331 (New York: T&T Clark, 2007), 158–159.

The Cornerstone and a Temple-Community

Another implication of Jesus's saying at the end of the parable must also be considered: as its "cornerstone," Jesus is only a *part* of the sanctuary under construction. This raises an important question: of what does the rest of this temple consist? Many have concluded that the community is in view.[62] As Davies and Allison explain, this idea

is particularly appropriate at this juncture because Jesus has just indicated, in vv. 12–22, that judgment hangs over the temple in Jerusalem; and our parable has just foretold the destruction of Jerusalem, including its temple. Thus *the end of the old temple coincides with the establishing of a new temple.*[63]

The stone saying, therefore, answers the conundrum introduced by Jesus's quotations in the temple action – the Jerusalem temple will be torn down, but hopes for a future temple are not completely lost. God will dwell with the community as he dwells in the temple.

Commentators have long recognized a similar logic in Matthew's source, Mark. For instance, M. Eugene Boring writes:

"The builders" was probably a current description of the temple leadership. They had set aside ... the one who would constitute the new temple that would replace the destroyed one. The Christian community is the new "building" that replaces the destroyed temple. A person is the "cornerstone," as the building itself is composed of persons, the new eschatological temple of the Christian community.[64]

Similarly, Arland Hultgren writes, "The risen Jesus is designated the foundation of the new temple (the people of God; cf. Eph 2:20; 1 Pet 2:4–10)."[65] Likewise, Morna Hooker says, "the vineyard which is handed over to new tenants signifies the fact that true worship of God is now centred on the risen Christ, not in the Jerusalem temple."[66]

It would seem, then, that in the Parable of the Wicked Tenants and the accompanying stone saying we find an answer to the question raised by Jesus's temple action: if Jesus is presented as endorsing Isaiah's vision of a future temple while also indicating that the Jerusalem sanctuary will fall, how does Matthew think Jesus sees the Isaianic passage being fulfilled?

---

[62] See, e.g., Davies and Allison, *Matthew*, 3:185–186; Zahn, *Das Evangelium des Matthäus*, 634. See also Collins, *Mark*, 41 on the parallel in Mark 12:10.

[63] Davies and Allison, *Matthew*, 3:186

[64] M. Eugene Boring, *Mark*, NTL (Louisville: Westminster John Knox Press, 2006), 332.

[65] Arland J. Hultgren, *The Parables of Jesus: A Commentary* (Grand Rapids: Eerdmans, 2000), 369.

[66] Hooker, *Mark*, 277.

The appeal to Psalm 118 provides an answer: the temple will be destroyed but the construction of a new "building" is underway. Ironically, the Jerusalem leadership – known as "the builders" – rejects the cornerstone, Jesus himself.

Nevertheless, by identifying the community with temple language, Jesus need not be seen as rejecting the holiness of the temple that stands. What does seem to be the case, however, is that the community's role as temple serves as an appropriate and consoling teaching given the declaration that the present one is passing away. The parable and the stone saying must be understood against the oracles indicating the coming demise of the sanctuary.

What finally seals the likelihood of the reading we are proposing is that Jesus has already used temple imagery for the community in Matthew 16. It would require an impressive feat of exegetical gymnastics to argue that the temple-building imagery in Matthew 21 should be seen as unrelated to Jesus's words to Peter. Furthermore, it is striking that *both* passages are bound up with messianic associations. We have already discussed the Davidic messianism of Matthew 16 earlier. It has also been noted that Psalm 118's description of a figure who has been attacked by the nations (cf. Ps 118:10–12) and who, after gaining victory over them, leads a procession to the gates of the temple (Ps 118:13–27), best fits the description of a royal figure.[67] Given the psalm's general association with David, it would be difficult not to connect that figure to a Davidic ruler. Notably, later Jewish works made that precise inference (e.g., Tg. Psalm 118:28; Exod. Rab. 37.1; Midr. Ps. 118:5; b. Pesaḥ 119a).[68] The Davidic interpretation of the psalm did not arise *ex nihilo*. That later Jewish works explicitly associate the psalm with Davidic traditions simply results from the imagery of the psalm itself. There is good reason, then, to think Matthew viewed the psalm itself as having messianic echoes.

It also bears mentioning that there seems to be an earlier allusion to Ps 118:26 ("Blessed is the one who comes [*ho erchomenos*] in the name of the LORD!") in John the Baptist's question in Matthew 11: "Are you the one who comes [*ho erchomenos*] or should we look for another?" (Matt 11:3).[69] Matthew seems to have John use the language of the psalm in reference to Jesus's messianic identity. This anticipates what

[67] See Brunson, *Psalm 118*, 36n.71.
[68] See Brunson, *Psalm 118*, 36–45.
[69] See Brunson, *Psalm 118*, 112, 121.

will come in the narrative. While the saying in Matthew 11 does not connect Jesus specifically to David, within the larger narrative of the Gospel, his identity as the Davidic messiah is indisputable. That Jesus's answer to John highlights his healing ministry cements the impression that the scene is related to his role as the Davidide. The appearance of Psalm 118, then, is not unexpected and fits with other messianic passages in Matthew.

The Parable and the Appointment of New Priestly Figures

The Parable of the Wicked Tenants does not teach that Jesus has rejected Israel. As many scholars recognize, since the parable is said to be directed at the Jerusalem leaders, the wicked tenants are best seen as a reference to them.[70] It is the tenants – the leadership – which changes; God does not abandon Israel itself.[71] This interpretation also works well with the appearance of the term "builders" in the Psalm 118 quotation. Numerous sources identify Jewish leaders with the terminology of "builders."[72] Of course, as we have seen, Matthew has already shown how the temple officials rejected Christ. This is especially on display in the temple "cleansing" scene. Like the wicked tenants who reject the son of the vineyard's owner, then, the chief priests and ruling elite have rejected Jesus.

Nevertheless, what does it mean for the vineyard to be given to others? It seems that the parable's message is not simply that God will judge the leaders *but that he is also going to appoint new ones.* Consider the following comments from Morna Hooker, Adela Yarbro Collins, and Craig Evans:[73]

The others to whom the vineyard is to be given ought logically – at least in the setting Mark gives the parable – to be *new leaders*, since it is said to be directed against the Jewish authorities.[74]

Here the focus is ... on the removal from power of the leaders who oppose Jesus... Giving the vineyard to others implies that *a new leadership* will emerge among those who accept Jesus as the messiah.[75]

---

[70] See, e.g., Snodgrass, *Parable of the Wicked Tenants*, 77; Evans, *Mark 8:27–16:20*, 239.
[71] See, e.g., Evans, *Mark 8:27–16:20*, 223; Levine, *Social and Ethnic Dimensions of Matthean Social History*, 210.
[72] See 1QIsaᵃ 54:13; CD-A 4:19; 8:12; b. Šabb. 114a; b. Ber. 64a; Song Rab. 1.5 §3; Exod. Rab. 33.10; Tg. Ps. 118:22–28; cf. also Acts 4:11.
[73] See Hooker, *Mark*, 276; Hultgren, *Parables of Jesus*, 360; Evans, *Mark 8:27–16:20*, 237.
[74] Hooker, *Mark*, 276; emphasis added.
[75] Collins, *Mark*, 547; emphasis added.

[Jesus's statement] also conveys a specific threat against the ruling priests, who in v 12 rightly perceive that Jesus had told the parable against them. Their place of power and prestige will soon come to an end. Their positions will be given to others. Giving the vineyard to others means only that *Israel will be governed by people other than the ruling priests.* What others Jesus had in mind is not difficult to determine. The request of James and John and the ensuing squabble among the disciples in Mark 10:35–45 make it clear that Jesus expected God to appoint righteous persons, probably from among his disciples … to govern Israel.[76]

Not only does Jesus seem to speak of new leaders being appointed, given the cultic nuances of the parable and the stone saying, what is in view seems to be new *temple officials*, that is, *priests*.[77] This reading dovetails nicely with the idea that Matthew 16 describes Peter as resembling Eliakim in Isaiah 22; as Shebna was replaced, so too would the leadership of Jesus's day. It also fits neatly with the idea that the twelve would somehow "judge" the twelve tribes in the eschatological age (Matt 19:28) since, as we saw, Jewish texts typically link that task to priests.

IMPLICATIONS FOR THE HISTORICAL JESUS

The use of temple imagery for the community in Matthew 16 is consistent with other aspects of Matthew's presentation. Scholars have been quick to dismiss the passage's historical value on the grounds that it is simply too consistent with the beliefs of the early community and Matthew's redactional interests. Furthermore, Jesus's response to Peter has been deemed secondary since it is not found in either Mark or our other gospel narratives. To be clear, the argument of this book does not at all depend on the "authenticity" of the scene. We have already argued in the previous chapter that Jesus's ministry likely drew upon Davidic traditions. In the next chapter, we will also make the case that Jesus's application of cultic metaphors is found in numerous other logia. Nevertheless, there are good reasons to question the raging skepticism over the historiographical value of Matthew's report of Jesus's exchange with Peter.

The Question of Jesus's Identity and Peter's Response

Many have held that the scene of Jesus's question to the disciples is implausible. For Bultmann, the mere fact that Jesus takes the initiative in asking

[76] Evans, *Mark 8:27–16:20*, 237; emphasis added.
[77] See, e.g., Konradt, *Matthew*, 155, 324.

the disciples questions points away from historicity since the rabbinic custom was for students to ask questions to teachers, not the other way around.[78] He further regarded it as unlikely that Jesus would have had to ask about popular opinion regarding his identity. From these observations, he concludes that the scene does not likely have roots in history.[79]

Others such as David Catchpole have argued that the preoccupation with Jesus's identity points to an origin in the early church, repeating the common refrain that Jesus was concerned with the *kingdom* rather than his own role in it.[80] Catchpole also notes that the disciples' response to Jesus's inquiry about popular opinion regarding his identity has parallels with the story of Herod's reaction to reports about Jesus (cf. Mark 6:14–16). Catchpole argues that the disciples' response to Jesus's inquiry about his identity (Mark 8:28=Matt 16:14) is therefore a reworking of the material in Mark 6.[81]

Peter's confession of Jesus as the "messiah" and "son of God" has also been seen as more likely reflecting the post-Easter period and Matthean redaction than the beliefs of the disciples during Jesus's ministry.[82] In addition, Jesus's command to secrecy, which closes the episode in all three Synoptics, has been dismissed as historical fiction.[83] The story of Peter's confession could easily be seen as an invention meant to solidify his place in the community. These objections, however, are anchored in questionable premises.

First, Bultmann's assumption that Jesus's particular teaching style followed the custom of the later rabbis is doubtful. Not only should we be critical of assuming their teaching style corresponded to Jesus's, Bultmann also dismisses with a wave of the hand the fact that Jesus is frequently presented as one who initiated conversations.[84] The supposition that Jesus would not have needed to learn from the disciples' what others were saying about him ignores the possibility that Jesus's real intent was

---

[78] Bultmann, *History of the Synoptic Tradition*, 257.

[79] Bultmann, *History of the Synoptic Tradition*, 257.

[80] David R. Catchpole, "The 'Triumphal' Entry," in *Jesus and the Politics of His Day*, ed. E. Bammel and C. F. D. Moule (Cambridge: Cambridge University Press, 1984), 327.

[81] Catchpole, "'Triumphal' Entry," 327.

[82] See, e.g., Rudolf Bultmann, "Die Frage nach dem messianischen Bewusstsein Jesu und das Petrus-Bekenntnis," ZNW 19 (1919–1920): 165–174.

[83] See, e.g., Erich Dinkler, "Peter's Confession and the 'Satan' Saying: The Problem of Jesus's Messiahship," in *The Future of Our Religious Past: Essays in Honor of Rudolf Bultmann*, ed. James M. Robinson, trans. Charles E. Carlston and Robert P. Scharlemann (London: SCM, 1971 [1964]), 184.

[84] See, e.g., Mark 3:4; 4:13; 6:38; 7:18–19; 8:17–21; 9:33; 12:24, 35–37.

not simply to satisfy his idle curiosity regarding his reputation but also to use the situation as a teaching moment.

No more convincing is Catchpole's approach. His claim that the exchange between Jesus and his disciples in Mark 8 is based on the story about Herod in Mark 6 should be questioned. The arguments are reversible. In fact, some have taken the opposite view.[85] Furthermore, as we have already seen, there is no reason to think that Jesus's teaching did not include the impression that he himself would play a central role in the age to come. To insist that he and his disciples likely had no discussion about this is virtually inconceivable. Jesus's command to secrecy about his messianic identity is also completely explicable on historical grounds; it would have been deemed politically dangerous, as the Jesus story demonstrates, to confirm a confession like Peter's publicly.

Elements that weigh in the scene's favor are often ignored. That the people recognized Jesus as Elijah is entirely plausible. As we have seen, Jesus couched his message in eschatological terms and Elijah was linked with eschatological expectations in first-century Jewish sources (cf. Mal 4:5; Sir 48:10). Likewise, for the people to believe Jesus was a figure raised from the dead is continuous with the eschatological themes evoked by his ministry. Nothing therefore in the disciples' report about popular opinion concerning Jesus is inconsistent with the broad features of the Jesus tradition, first-century Jewish attitudes, or necessitates a view that it originated in the early community.

With respect to Peter's confession itself, the assumptions upon which it is usually discounted, that is, that Jesus's messianic role and identity as "son of God" point to a Christian setting, are hardly compelling. As we have seen, there is good reason to believe Jesus evoked Davidic traditions. Furthermore, that Peter would be the one to speak up for the disciples coheres with the broad impression of the gospels that he served as a kind of spokesperson for them (e.g., Mark 1:36; 8:29; 9:5; 10:28; 14:29, 37; Matt 15:15; 17:24; 18:21; Luke 12:41; John 6:68).[86] Peter is always listed as the first among the twelve.[87] That he was a significant figure during Jesus's ministry would explain his prominence in the early community, which is attested widely and early.

---

[85] See Bultmann, *History of the Synoptic Tradition*, 302. Another option may also be mentioned: literary independence of the two passages. See Rudolf Pesch, *Das Markusevangelium*, HTKNT 2, 2 vols. (Freiburg: Herder, 1977), 2:31.

[86] Meier, *A Marginal Jew*, 3:222; Dunn, *Jesus Remembered*, 644–645.

[87] Meier, *A Marginal Jew*, 3:221.

The idea that the story was invented by the community to justify Peter's prominence is also difficult to believe. In both Matthew and Mark, the story of Peter's confession is immediately followed by the description of Peter resisting a passion prediction. This earns Peter one of the sharpest rebukes attributed to Jesus in the Gospels – Jesus calls him "Satan" (Matt 16:23//Mark 8:33). As Craig Evans writes, if the account of Peter's confession was included to explain Peter's unique role, "why debunk Peter with a story about his opposition to Jesus's passion prediction? Whatever ground has been gained by the confession has been given up by this opposition."[88]

Jesus's Response to Peter

Scholars are frequently even more skeptical that Jesus's response to Peter in Matthew reflects impressions he himself made. For one thing, it is claimed that it is too continuous with the early community's beliefs. In particular, the appearance of the term "my *ekklēsia*" has especially raised suspicion about the historicity of the episode given its unique Matthean stamp (cf. Matt 18:17).[89] In addition, Jesus uses the future tense to describe Peter's role in Matthew 16, which is said to signal a post-Easter perspective. Many, therefore, believe that the scene reflects a tradition in which the risen Lord appeared to and commissioned Peter (cf. 1 Cor 15:5; John 21:15–22).[90]

Nevertheless, even if Jesus did not use the precise word *ekklēisia* and even if the scene bears other various Matthean elements (e.g., the special beatitude to Peter; cf. Matt 5:3–10), we should question the insistence that the entire statement has no anchor in impressions made by Jesus himself. Without using *ekklēsia*, Jesus could have spoken of Peter's role in the community. In fact, some rather prominent writers, including Ben Meyer, Stanley Porter, and Davies and Allison, have made the case that historical memories are preserved here.[91]

---

[88] Evans, *Mark 8:27–16:20*, 10. See also Dinkler, "Peter's Confession," 169–202; Hooker, "Christology and Methodology," 486; Fitzmyer, *Luke*, 1:772.

[89] See Meier, *A Marginal Jew*, 2:231–233.

[90] See e.g., Bultmann, "Die Frage," 165–174; Walter Grundmann, *Das Evangelium nach Matthäus*, 3rd ed., THKNT I (Berlin: Evangelische Verlagsanstalt, 1972), 277; Catchpole, "'Triumphal' Entry," 328.

[91] See Davies and Allison, *Matthew*, 2:602–618; Meyer, *Aims of Jesus*, 189–193; Porter, *Criteria for Authenticity*, 159–161; Keener, *Historical Jesus*, 247–249; Aquila H. I. Lee, *From Messiah to Preexistent Son: Jesus's Self-Consciousness and Early Christian Exegesis of Messianic Psalms*, WUNT 2/192 (Tübingen: Mohr Siebeck, 2005), 147–149.

The argument that the shorter version of the episode at Caesarea Philippi in Mark is more coherent with what we know about Jesus than Matthew's report is not compelling. It is true that Jesus is often presented as reticent to explicitly call himself the "messiah" – which he does not even explicitly do in Matthew 16. Nevertheless, our preceding treatment shows that he likely saw himself as, in some way, the Davidic king designate: one who *would* reign. This would make sense of the use of the future tense employed in Jesus's response to Peter.

Scholars also too frequently overlook the fact that Mark would have had good reason for omitting Jesus's reply. A response praising Peter's insight would undercut overarching themes in Mark's Gospel; the evangelist regularly stresses the disciples' lack of faith and their failure to understand Jesus.[92] The omission of Jesus's reply to Peter in Mark is not deafening; it should probably be expected. While it fits well with Matthew's respect for Peter, that Jesus said something like what Matthew reports would help explain why Peter was so prominent in the tradition.

Furthermore, some scholars have pointed out that several striking parallels between Galatians and Matthew 16 suggest that the account of Peter's confession is rooted in a very early tradition. Consider the following:

Galatians 1–2	*Matthew 16:13–20*
Jesus as "*Christ*" (*christos*) (Gal 1:12)	Jesus as "*Christ*" (*christos*) (Matt 16:16)
Jesus as "his [=God's] Son [*ton huion autou*]" (Gal 1:16)	Jesus as "son of the living God [*ho huios tou theou zōntos*]" (Matt 16:16)
God's Son has been "*revealed*" (*apocalyptō*) (Gal 1:16)	Jesus's identity as Son of God has been "*revealed*" (*apocalyptō*) (Matt 16:16)
Paul explains that he did not confer with "*flesh and blood*" (*sarx kai haima*) (Gal 1:16)	Jesus tells Peter his knowledge does not come from "*flesh and blood*" (*sarx kai haima*) (Matt 16:17)

---

[92] See Joel F. Williams, *Other Followers of Jesus: Minor Characters as Major Characters in Mark's Gospel*, JSNTSup 102 (Sheffield: JSOT Press, 1994), 89–150; Robert C. Tannehill, "The Disciples in Mark: The Function of a Narrative Role," *JR* 51 (1977): 386–405.

"Peter" (*Petros*) (Gal 2:7)	"Peter" (*Petros*) (Matt 16:16)
Some sought to bring the Galatians into "bondage" (*katadouloō*) (Gal 2:4)	Peter is given authority to "bind" (*deō*) and "loose" (*luō*) (Matt 16:19)
Peter is one of the "pillars" (*stylos*) of the community (Gal 2:9)	The church is built upon Peter the rock (Matt 16:16)[93]

While some have maintained that Jesus's statement about Peter's author-ity is a response to an anti-Petrine polemic in Galatians,[94] this is extraor-dinarily unlikely. Nothing in Jesus's exchange with Peter suggests that the specter of Paul looms in the background of Matthew 16. There is also no sign that polemics are driving the narrative; Jesus does not say, "To you *alone* I give the keys of the kingdom." Moreover, if the passage was meant to justify Peter's unique role, why would Matthew follow the scene up with the story of Jesus calling Peter "Satan"? Such a line would have provided even more ammunition to Peter's detractors.

Still, it is hard to dismiss the similarities of the two passages as the product of mere coincidence. Given the Petrine focus present in Galatians 1–2, does it not seem more likely that the influence is coming from the other direction? While Paul never appears in Matthew 16, Peter definitely appears in Galatians. Moreover, in Galatians, the polemics are strong. In addition, this is also the *only* time Paul speaks of God "revealing" his "son" to him. More strikingly, it is the *sole* instance in which Paul uses the name "Peter" rather than "Cephas," his usual name for the fisherman (1 Cor 1:12; 3:22; 9:5; 15:5; Gal 1:18; 2:9, 11, 14). It is also noteworthy that here we have the *only attestation* of a special commissioning of Peter in the Pauline literature (cf. Gal 2:7–8). If Paul knew that Peter had received such a commission, there is scarcely a tradition more likely to be in view than that found in Matthew 16.[95] As Davies and Allison suggest, the substantial similarities between the two texts strongly suggests that Paul was aware of some version of the tradition preserved in Matthew.[96]

---

[93] For further discussion see David Wenham, "Paul's Use of the Jesus Tradition: Three Samples," in *Gospel Perspectives: The Jesus Tradition Outside the Gospels*, vol. 5 (Shef-field: JSOT Press, 1984), 24–28.

[94] David C. Sim, *The Gospel of Matthew and Christian Judaism* (Edinburgh: T&T Clark, 1998), 201–202.

[95] See Wenham, "Paul's Use of the Jesus Tradition," 25.

[96] Davies and Allison, *Matthew*, 2:610: Likewise, see Bernard P. Robinson, "Peter and His Successors: Tradition and Redaction in Matthew 16:17—19," *JSNT* 21 (1984), 89; Wenham, "Paul's Use of the Jesus Tradition," 27; Ben Witherington, III, *Jesus, Paul, and the End of the World* (Downers Grove: InterVarsity, 1992), 87.

That Peter is specifically spoken of as one of the "pillars" (*styloi*) in Galatians is also worth pausing to consider. The imagery mirrors the way in which Jesus is portrayed as referring to Peter in architectural terms in Matthew 16 – namely, as the "rock" upon which the edifice of the church is built. Yet it is significant to note that many have viewed it also as evoking *temple* symbolism.[97] Of course, the term need not always refer to cultic buildings. Various considerations, however, weigh in favor of such an allusion. James Dunn shows that the Greek term used here (*stylos*) occurs "most frequently in the LXX in reference to the supports of the tabernacle and pillars of the temple."[98] That Christ's followers used the term this way is also evident in the Apocalypse: "I will make him a *pillar* [*stylon*] in the temple [*naō*] of my God" (Rev 3:12). In particular, given Paul's description of the community as temple elsewhere (1 Cor 3:16; 6:19; 2 Cor 6:16) and the other strong parallels with Jesus's words in Matthew 16, where temple imagery is in view, the likelihood that the pillars have a temple meaning in Galatians seems strong. The possible relation with Matthew 16 is reinforced by a further observation: *nowhere else in the undisputed Pauline letters does the apostle use such architectural imagery for the apostles in relation to the community.*

More specifically, that Jesus identified Peter with Isaiah's oracle concerning Eliakim may also be attested in a scene found in Luke. After Peter asks Jesus a question, Jesus responds to him by saying:

Who then is the faithful and wise *steward* [*oikonomos*], whom the master will set over his servants, *to give them their portion of food* at the right time? Blessed is that servant whom his master will find doing so when he comes. Amen, I say to you, *he will put him in charge of all his possessions.* (Luke 12:42–44)

The image of Peter as the faithful "steward" (*oikonomos*) who is put over other servants and placed in charge over the food evokes Isaiah 22, where the "stewardship" (Isa 22:21 LXX: *oikonomia*) is given to Eliakim, who is in turn placed over the house, including "every small vessel," "cups," and "flagons" (cf. Isa 22:24).

Notwithstanding concerns about how Jesus's reply to Peter has been used in papal apologetics, it should be acknowledged that Peter's prominence among the twelve is *regularly* attested.[99] Peter is always named *first*

---

[97] See, e.g., J. Louis Martyn, *Galatians*, AB 33A (New York: Doubleday, 1997), 205.
[98] James D. G. Dunn, *Galatians*, BNTC (London: A&C Black, 1993), 109–110.
[99] See, e.g., Hagner, *Matthew*, 2:466.

in the lists of the twelve (cf. Matt 10:2//Mark 3:16//Luke 6:14//Acts 1:13; Matt 4:18). Peter is also usually depicted as the spokesperson for the disciples (e.g., Matt 19:27//Mark 10:28//Luke 18:28; Matt 17:4// Mark 9:5// Luke 9:33). Peter is also always included as the first among those in Jesus's inner circle (cf. Mark 5:37//Luke 8:51; Matt 17:1//Mark 9:2// Luke 9:28; Matt 26:37//Mark 14:33). It should also be noted that among the evangelists Matthew does not exclusively relate stories in which Peter is prominent. In Luke 22:31, Jesus tells Peter at the Last Supper that he has prayed specifically for Peter in order that the apostle might strengthen the rest of the disciples. Paul also identifies Peter as the one sent to the circumcised in explaining how he has been given a special commission to take the gospel to the gentiles (cf. Gal 2:7). Here he affirms that the same Christ who "worked through Peter," works "through me" (Gal 2:8).

It is important to reiterate that the argument of this book is not dependent upon demonstrating the "authenticity" of the episode related in Matthew 16. It seems to be more probable than not that Jesus had some kind of conversation like the one that reportedly took place in the district of Caesarea Philippi. Though Matthew's report of Jesus's exchange with Peter seems to reflect Matthean shaping, the argument that it has no connection to the life of the historical Jesus should be questioned. The essential features of the story fit well with what we know about Jesus from other texts: Jesus likely saw himself as a Davidic figure and Peter's prominence among the disciples likely did not arise *ex nihilo* in the post-Easter period. It likely had some anchor in Jesus's public ministry.

For our purposes, what matters most is the broader portrait that emerges: the Jewish evangelist, who unflinchingly identifies Jerusalem as the "holy city" (Matt 4:5; 27:53) and emphasizes Jesus's affirmation of the sanctuary's holiness (Matt 23:16–22), has no difficulty affirming that Jesus employed cultic imagery in describing the disciples. In fact, in Matt 16:13–20 the association flows naturally out of Jesus's Davidic identity – the Davidic king builds a temple, identified with the community. The overall message is clear: the temple would be destroyed, but all would not be lost. One temple would be left in ruin, but one was also under construction – even if the Jewish leaders, the "builders," could not recognize it. Though the physical building would pass away, Jesus and the community would somehow serve as a temple.

Why does Matthew remember Jesus this way? Is it simply the result of a post-70 reflection? Such a view is not at all compelling. Paul speaks of believers as a temple in his Corinthians correspondence (e.g., 1 Cor 3:16; 6:19), letters that long predate the Jewish war. It is *not* therefore probable that the notion of the community as a sanctuary simply emerged after Jerusalem fell to the Romans. Jewish believers in Christ like Paul were apparently making the connection long before that had occurred. Obviously, this does not necessarily point to an origin for this view in Jesus's teaching itself. Some might prefer to argue that the idea emerged after Jesus's death from within the circle of his Jewish believers. How likely is it that Jesus himself initiated the idea that the community would be a temple? We look at that question in our final chapter.

7

Jesus, Sacrifice, and Priesthood

The Last Supper traditions ... fit well within the context of ancient Jewish applications of temple significance to non-temple rituals.

– Jonathan Klawans[1]

[In narrating the Last Supper,] Mark does not portray Jesus as being anti-sacrificial. It is even possible that the description is historical and that Jesus uses a sacrificial metaphor while eating the Paschal lamb.

– Eyal Regev[2]

In the previous chapter, we examined Jesus's application of temple-related imagery to himself and his disciples in Matthew. If this dynamic was peculiar to the Matthean portrait, we might suspect that it was merely due to the evangelist's creativity. We have already seen, however, that this is not the case. For example, Matthew's depiction of Jesus as the "cornerstone" of a temple-building project is derived from Mark. Yet can we trace the use of temple metaphors back further? Can it be seen as reflecting Jesus's own teaching?

This chapter begins by explaining that similar use of Israel's temple and priestly traditions can be found in reports of Jesus's teaching throughout our sources – and not simply in the gospels. An even earlier source, Paul, contains such reminiscences. Yet because the use of such temple imagery is often overlooked and underappreciated, we will need to offer a more in-depth treatment of some of the traditions than we have provided so far.

---

[1] Klawans, *Purity, Sacrifice, and the Temple*, 244.
[2] Regev, *The Temple in Early Christianity*, 52.

Catalogues of traditions will be unpersuasive if one does not recognize the relevant data involved.

We will begin by looking at the accounts of the Last Supper in 1 Corinthians and the Synoptic Gospels. As we will show, Jesus is remembered in all four reports as drawing heavily from imagery taken from Israel's cultic life. We will argue that there are strong reasons for believing this tradition reflects impressions made by Jesus himself. Second, we will analyze other features of the Synoptics and John that reinforce the impression that Jesus drew upon symbolism of Israel's temple and priesthood. Many of these are also often viewed as having their anchor in Jesus's own ministry.

Having established that Jesus's use of temple metaphors can meet the bar of recurrent attestation, we will then move on to consider these data in light of Jesus's Jewish context and what we know about his effects. In the end, we will argue that there are in fact good reasons to believe that Jesus himself likely used temple symbolism in reference to himself and to the community of his followers.

THE LAST SUPPER AND TEMPLE TRADITIONS

In his letters, Paul seems mostly uninterested in discussing episodes from Jesus's public ministry. He did not apparently see his letters as the place for recounting such traditions.[3] There is only one major exception to this rule: in 1 Corinthians, he talks about Jesus's Last Supper (1 Cor 11:23–26). Though Paul says the account of it came to him "from the Lord [*apo tou kyriou*]," scholars routinely point out that he uses technical terms for the transmission of traditional material in describing how he "received" and "handed on" the story (1 Cor 11:23: *paralambanō, paradidōmi*; cf. 1 Cor 11:2; 15:3). The apostle is not, therefore, claiming to have learned of it through private revelation. Instead, as E. P. Sanders says, Paul means "that he is passing on material that he believes goes back to Jesus."[4]

Paul's report of Jesus's final meal mirrors what we find in the Synoptic Gospels. While there are some differences, the extent to which our sources agree is remarkable. They all affirm the following details:

---

[3] For a fuller discussion, see Dale C. Allison, Jr., "The Pauline Epistles and the Synoptic Gospels: The Pattern of the Parallels," *NTS* 28 (1982): 22–23.

[4] E. P. Sanders, *Paul: The Apostle's Life, Letters, and Thought* (Minneapolis: Fortress Press, 2015), 210; See also Joseph A. Fitzmyer, S.J., *First Corinthians*, AYB 32 (New Haven: Yale University Press, 2008), 436; Fee, *First Epistle to the Corinthians*, 548.

- Jesus identifies the bread with his body, breaks it, and gives it to those with him (Matt 26:26//Mark 14:22//Luke 22:19//1 Cor 11:24).
- Jesus takes the cup and identifies it with his blood (cf. Matt 26:27// Mark 14:23//Luke 22:20//1 Cor 11:25).
- Jesus uses covenant imagery in his words over the cup (cf. Matt 26:27// Mark 14:23//Luke 22:20//1 Cor 11:25).
- Jesus gives thanks (cf. Matt 26:27//Mark 14:23; Luke 22:19//1 Cor 11:24).

Paula Fredriksen writes, "the coincidence of our two earliest witnesses, Paul and Mark, demonstrates at the very minimum that ... the practice of this communal meal was very early on regarded by these communities as a teaching of Jesus himself."[5]

What interests us here is that, as Jonathan Klawans shows, this extremely early and influential tradition involves numerous allusions to Israel's cultic life. Even if many of the sacrificial metaphors are deemed "inauthentic," it seems difficult to insist that they are all later innovations.[6] In the following sections we will consider these carefully. First, however, let us examine another matter that raises historical questions: the depiction of Jesus anticipating his own death.

Jesus's Anticipation of His Death

For the moment, let us bypass Jesus's words and actions over the bread, which are somewhat more ambiguous than those associated with the cup.[7] In *all four* sources, Jesus identifies the latter with his "blood" and then gives it to the disciples to drink. Many have thought this is especially improbable on the grounds that it would offend Jewish sensibilities.[8] Yet, as others point out, this ignores a crucial fact: the report apparently did not present an obstacle to the earliest Jewish believers.[9] Paul and Matthew – who write from a markedly Jewish perspective – apparently have no trouble including it. In other words, *the claim that the imagery would necessarily be unacceptable to Jews is not only probably wrong, but it is also demonstrably false.* This objection should be retired.

---

[5] Fredriksen, *Jesus of Nazareth*, 119.
[6] Klawans, "Interpreting the Last Supper," 16.
[7] See Tan, *Zion Traditions and the Aims of Jesus*, 200–201.
[8] See, e.g., Gerd Lüdemann, *Jesus After 2000 Years*, trans. John Bowden (London: SCM; Amherst: Prometheus Books, 2001), 96–97.
[9] Pitre, *Jesus and the Last Supper*, 429–430.

At its most basic level, the symbolism involved with the cup points to Jesus's coming death. Since "blood" and "life" were closely related in Jewish thought (cf. Lev 17:11–13; 11Q19 53:6), it is virtually impossible to imagine that in *giving* the cup away, Jesus is presented as symbolizing something other than giving his life away.[10] Other considerations reinforce the impression that Jesus's death is in view:

1. *"Do this in remembrance of me" (1 Cor 11:24–25; Luke 22:19).* In 1 Corinthians and Luke, Jesus says his followers are to repeat what he has done in "remembrance" of him, words which suggest his imminent departure.

2. *Jesus's blood will be poured out (Matt 26:28//Mark 14:24//Luke 22:20).* The expression Jesus uses in connection with his blood ("poured out [*ekchynnomenon*]") in the Synoptics is associated with violent death.[11]

3. *The motif of the "cup" as a reference to Jesus's death (cf. Matt 20:20–28//Mark 10:35–45; Matt 26:39, 42//Mark 14:36//Luke 22:42).* The Synoptic tradition links Jesus's death to cup-drinking in other contexts.

4. *Not drinking until the kingdom (Matt 26:29//Mark 14:25//Luke 22:18).* In the Synoptics, while at table, Jesus speaks of not drinking again until the kingdom arrives (Matt 26:29//Mark 14:25// Luke 22:18) and announces his coming fate (Luke 22:21–22).

There is no reason to dismiss the idea that Jesus foresaw his death as a later invention. In fact, the insistence that Jesus could not have anticipated his own death rests on questionable presuppositions and is contradicted by the best evidence.[12]

If Jesus, like other first-century Jews, looked forward to the restoration of Israel, he may very well have thought suffering would be part of that equation.[13] For one thing, various Jewish sources link the death of Jewish martyrs to hopes for Israel's deliverance. Consider the following:[14]

---

[10] See, e.g., Carter, *Matthew and the Margins*, 506.

[11] See LXX Gen 9:6; Judg 9:25; Isa 59:7; Ezek 18:10; 22:13; 4Q201 4:7; 4Q219 2:18.

[12] See Michael Patrick Barber, "Did Jesus Anticipate Suffering a Violent Death? The Implications of Memory Research and Dale C. Allison's Methodology," *JSHJ* 18, 3 (2020): 191–219.

[13] See Allison, *End of the Ages*, 115–141; Allison, *Jesus of Nazareth*, 145–147.

[14] See, e.g., Scot McKnight, *Jesus and His Death: Historiography, the Historical Jesus, and Atonement Theory* (Waco: Baylor University Press, 2005), 88, 168–170; Kwon, *Historical Jesus's Death*, 191–196.

For we are suffering because of our own sins. And if our living Lord is angry for a little while, to rebuke and discipline us, *he will again be reconciled with his own servants.* (2 Maccabees 7:32–33 [ca. 135–104 BCE])

[The martyrs] became *responsible for the downfall of the tyranny* which beset our nation, overcoming the tyrant by their fortitude so that *through them their own land was purified.* (4 Maccabees 1:11 [ca. 18–55 C.E.])

Through the blood of these righteous ones and through the propitiation [*hilastēriou*] of their death the divine providence rescued Israel. (4 Maccabees 17:22).

It is worth noting that the last passage from 4 Maccabees 17 interprets the death of the martyrs as a propitiation (*hilastērion*), a term derived from Israel's cultic atonement rituals (*hilastērion*; cf., e.g., Exod 25:16; Ezek 43:14, 17, 20).[15] The same term appears in Romans 3:25 where Paul describes Christ's death as a propitiatory sacrifice.[16] Pauline scholars recognize that the apostle was likely influenced by these martyrological traditions.[17] Yet, if early Jewish followers of Jesus interpreted his death against such a backdrop, why not also see it as relevant for reconstructing Jesus's views?

Moreover, *in many Jewish sources the inauguration of the eschatological age is preceded by a period involving the persecution and suffering of the righteous.* Consider the following:

> [The Fourth Beast] shall speak words against the Most High,
> and *shall wear out the saints of the Most High* …
> and *they shall be given into his hand*
> for a time, two times, and half a time …
> And the kingdom and the dominion …
> shall be given to the people of the saints of the Most High;
> their kingdom shall be an everlasting kingdom.
> (Daniel 7:25, 27a, c–d)

It will be *a time of suffering fo[r al]l the nation redeemed by God. Of all their sufferings, none will be like this,* hastening till eternal redemption is fulfilled. (1QWar Scroll [1Q33] 1:11–12)

---

[15] For a discussion, see Stephen Finlan, *The Background and Content of Paul's Cultic Atonement Metaphors* (Atlanta: Society of Biblical Literature, 2004), 29–44; McKnight, *Jesus and His Death*, 169–170.

[16] See, e.g., Kwon, *Historical Jesus's Death*, 196–197.

[17] Douglas A. Campbell, *The Deliverance of God: An Apocalyptic Rereading of Justification in Paul* (Grand Rapids: Eerdmans, 2009), 648–651; Jarvis Williams, *Maccabean Martyr Traditions in Paul's Theology of Atonement: Did Martyr Theology Shape Paul's Conception of Jesus's Death* (Eugene: Wipf and Stock, 2010).

Its [Ps 37.11] interpretation concerns the congregation of the poor who will take upon themselves *the period of affliction* and will be rescued from all the snares of Belial. Afterwards, all who shall po[sse]ss the land will enjoy and grow fat with everything enjoy[able to] the flesh. (4QPsalms Pesher[a] [4Q171] 2:9–12)

Numerous similar texts could also be cited here.[18] As we have seen, Jesus most probably entertained eschatological hopes. It therefore would hardly be surprising for him to have anticipated coming to a violent end. In fact, one feature of Jesus's passion predictions may suggest that he did – they frequently use "Son of Man" language (Mark 8:31; 9:31; 10:45; Matt 26:24//Mark 14:21//Luke 22:22; John 3:14; 12:23).[19] Many have dismissed these sayings as manufactured memories. Yet this overlooks some important data. Building on the insightful but neglected work of T. W. Manson,[20] a number of recent scholars – including Dale Allison, Thomas Kazen, and Scot McKnight – show that such sayings are best viewed as references to the eschatological tribulation described in Daniel 7.[21] In Daniel's original vision, the "son of man" figure serves as a representative of the saints who suffer at the hands of the Fourth Beast during the latter days (cf. Dan 7.18). In sum, if Jesus's project was characterized by eschatology, and our sources are right about his envisioning coming to a violent end, there is good reason to think that Jesus's "son of man" passion predictions reflect impressions he himself made.

Notably, while also holding such an eschatological outlook, Paul himself anticipated suffering: "we told you beforehand that we were to suffer affliction" (1 Thess 3:4). In Philippians he speaks about being "poured out as a libation," cultic language that scholars have widely seen as a martyrological reference (Phil 2:17).[22] The best explanation of this

---

[18] Dan 12:1–3; Zech 13:8–9; 4Q174 *frag.* 1, *col.* i, 21, 2:18–19 and *col.* ii, 3, 24, 5:1–7; 1 En. 46:8–47:2; 56:5–57:3; 91:5–74; 93:1–10; 103.15; Jub. 23:11–31; Sib. Or. 3:182–195; Pss. Sol. 17:11–32; *T. Mos.* 9.1–7.

[19] That the logion in John 3:14 relates to Jesus's crucifixion is widely accepted among scholars. See, e.g., Rudolf Bultmann, *The Gospel of John: A Commentary*, trans. George R. Beasley-Murray et al. (Philadelphia: Westminster Press, 1971 [1964]), 152–153; Brown, *John*, 1:146.

[20] Thomas W. Manson, "The Son of Man in Daniel, Enoch, and the Gospels," *BJRL* 32 (1950): 171–195; Manson, *The Teaching of Jesus*, 229–231.

[21] See, e.g., Allison, *Resurrection of Jesus*, 199; Allison, *End of the Ages*, 136–140; Allison, *Jesus of Nazareth*, 65–66, especially n.242; Thomas Kazen, "The Coming of the Son of Man Revisited," *JSHJ* 5, 2 (2007): 155–174; McKnight, *Jesus and His Death*, 234–239.

[22] Peter Thomas O'Brien, *The Epistle to the Philippians: A Commentary on the Greek Text*, NIGTC (Grand Rapids: Eerdmans, 1991), 304, writes that, although the specific dynamics of Paul's cultic terminology are not entirely clear, "most agree that the apostle is clearly alluding to his martyrdom, the sacrifice of his own life."

dimension of Paul's message would seem to be that the apostle's outlook was shaped by memories of Jesus, whom the community remembered as announcing the coming eschaton and who viewed his own fate against such traditions.[23]

That Jesus anticipated his own demise is broadly attested, but this is not the sole reason for thinking that this aspect of our sources' portrait of Jesus preserves historical memory. There are converging indicators that are difficult to explain away. Not only does this aspect of the tradition fit well with what we seem to know about Jesus, namely, that he was likely motivated by eschatological hopes, but it also makes sense within Jesus's first-century context and his effects. Moreover, that Jesus viewed his death in sacrificial terms would not be all that strange. As we saw earlier, the death of the martyrs could be described with sacrificial imagery, imagery Paul also applies to his own affliction. Indeed, there are further indications that Jesus interpreted his death in precisely such terms. For one thing, as we will explain later, Jesus's words at the Last Supper specifically portray his death in sacrificial terms.

Jesus and Covenant Sacrifice

For our purposes, it is necessary to recognize that the cup-saying involves more than just a prediction of Jesus's passion. The presence of covenant language – which is attested in all four accounts – likely portrays Jesus as understanding his death in sacrificial terms. To this matter we now turn.

In all four reports of the Last Supper, Jesus uses the word "covenant" in connection with his "blood." This is highly significant. In Israel's traditions, covenants were sealed by sacrifice. The psalmist, for example, assumes this when he has God declare: "Gather to me my faithful ones, who *made a covenant with me by sacrifice!*" (Ps 50:5).[24] By pairing his blood to covenant terminology, Jesus seems to be presented as describing his death as a sacrificial offering. This is confirmed by an important intertextual echo.

The parade example of the sacrificial dimension of covenant-making in the scriptures of Israel is found in Exodus 24. In this chapter, we read

---

[23] See Allison, *End of the Ages*, 62–69, for a treatment of eschatological tribulation traditions in Paul. In addition, see Allison, *Constructing Jesus*, 63; Allison, *Resurrection of Jesus*, 185–190.
[24] For further discussions see Dennis J. McCarthy, *Treaty and Covenant* (Rome: Biblical Institute Press, 1981), 91–92.

about how Moses seals the covenant between God and Israel in a ritual ceremony (cf. Exod 24:3–8). As virtually every major commentator recognizes, Jesus's words over the cup in Matthew and Mark allude to Moses' words at this scene:[25]

The Covenant Ceremony at Sinai	Jesus's Words over the Cup
"Behold, the blood of the covenant [*to haima tēs diathēkēs*]." (Exodus 24:8 LXX)	"This is *my blood of the covenant* [*to haima mou tēs diathēkēs*] which is poured out for many." (Mark 14:24; cf. Matthew 26:28)

In the Markan and Matthean accounts, then, Jesus interprets his death as a kind of cultic sacrifice.[26]

Contrary to some claims, Exodus 24 should also be seen as shaping the cup-saying in 1 Corinthians and Luke.[27] While Jesus's words in these accounts refer to a "new covenant" (*kaine diathēkē*), an expression that evokes the prophecy of Jeremiah 31, this allusion on its own cannot be seen as ruling out the influence of Exodus 24. Jeremiah 31 itself recalls the covenant made in Exodus 24.[28] If the former is in the background, the resonances of Exodus 24 are therefore amplified, not muted. Furthermore, the use of Jeremiah 31 alone fails to explain why "blood" and "covenant" imagery are combined in Jesus's saying; *nowhere does Jeremiah link covenant to blood.*

The appearance of "blood" alongside "covenant" is also not the only parallel between Exodus 24 and the Lukan and Pauline accounts. Significantly, Jesus's announcement that his "blood" will be "poured out" mirrors the Exodus story in which the "blood of the covenant" is said to be "poured out":

---

[25] See, e.g., Luz, *Matthew*, 3:380; Davies and Allison, *Matthew*, 3:472; Collins, *Mark*, 496; Hooker, *Mark*, 342.

[26] Although the phrase "blood of the covenant" is also found in Zech 9:11, the language of Matthew/Mark is closer to the LXX of Exod 24:8. For further reasons why the Exodus allusion is more likely, see Allison, *Constructing Jesus*, 272n.208.

[27] Against George Beasley-Murray's attempt to pit an allusion to Exodus 24 in Matthew and Mark against a reference to Jeremiah 31 in Luke and Paul (*Jesus and the Kingdom of God*, 264–265), see the discussion in Tan, *Zion Traditions and the Aims of Jesus*, 204–205; Michael Wolter, *The Gospel according to Luke*, trans. Wayne Coppins and Christoph Heilig, BMSSEC, 2 vols. (Waco: Baylor University Press, 2016), 2:463; Fitzmyer, *First Corinthians*, 443.

[28] See, e.g., A. van der Wal, "Themes from Exodus in Jeremiah 30–31," in *Studies in the Book of Exodus: Redaction, Reception, Interpretation*, ed. Marc Vervenne, BETL 126 (Louven: Leuven University Press, 1996), 559–567.

The Covenant Ceremony at Sinai	Jesus's Cup-Saying in Luke
And Moses, taking the *blood* [*haimatos*] *poured it out* [*enecheen*] into bowls, and half of the *blood* [*haimatos*] he *poured out* [*prosecheen*] towards the altar... Then Moses ... said, "Behold, *the blood of the covenant* that the Lord covenanted with you concerning all of these words." (Exodus 24:6, 8 LXX)	"This cup that is *poured out* [*ekchynnomenon*] for you is the new *covenant* in my *blood* [*haimati*]." (Luke 22:20)

In addition, that Paul and Luke have Jesus speak both of his "blood" and "covenant" while celebrating a *meal* mirrors not only Moses' words concerning the "blood of the covenant" but also the fact that Exodus 24 culminates in a sacred *feast* (cf. Exod 24:8–11). Likewise, just as the covenant in Exodus is established with the *twelve tribes*, the *twelve apostles* are prominent in Luke's Last Supper narrative (cf. Luke 22:14, 30). Taken together, these points of contact are too strong and numerous to be written off as mere coincidence. Therefore, we conclude with others that, like Matthew and Mark, the Last Supper reports in Paul and Luke are shaped by Exodus 24. When Jesus speaks of his blood and a "new covenant," the notion of sacrifice is "inescapable."[29]

Cultic Atonement Imagery

There are additional reasons to believe Jesus's words at the Last Supper in Paul and the Synoptics have sacrificial undertones. In 1 Corinthians, Jesus says his body is "for you [*hyper hymōn*]" (1 Cor 11:24). Later in the same letter, Paul will use similar language, affirming that Christ died, "for our sins" (*hyper tōn harmartiōn*) (1 Cor 15:3). In other places, Paul uses sacrificial analogies in discussing Jesus's suffering. Before reciting the Last Supper story in 1 Corinthians, Paul writes, "Christ our paschal lamb has been sacrificed" (1 Cor 5:7). Elsewhere, the apostle calls Jesus a "sin offering [*peri hamartias*]" (cf. Rom 8:3; cf., e.g., Lev 5:8; 14:31; 2 Cor 5:21) and interprets his bloody death in terms of "atonement" (Rom 3:25: *hilastērion*; cf. Exod 25:21, 22 LXX).[30] It is difficult to maintain

---

[29] I here use the expression employed by I. Howard Marshall, *Last Supper and Lord's Supper* (Exeter: Paternoster, 1980), 91. See also Nolland, *Matthew*, 1079.

[30] See the fuller treatment in Pitre, Barber, and Kincaid, *Paul, A New Covenant Jew*, 149–152.

that his retelling of Jesus's saying over the bread is unrelated to these teachings. For Paul, Jesus's words, "This is my body that is *for you*," undoubtedly indicates the soteriological significance of the cross. Since we know that he understood this through the lens of Israel's cult, it is difficult to insist such a meaning is not in view here.

In the Synoptics, Jesus explains that his blood is "poured out for many [*ekchynnomenon hyper pollōn*]" (Mark 14:24). Given what we have seen, it is likely no coincidence that this terminology is associated with atoning sacrifices (e.g., Lev 4:7, 18, 25, 30, 34; 4Q220 1:3; 11Q19 52:11).[31] As Eyal Regev puts it, "This language is unavoidably sacrificial and signifies atonement."[32] The version of the saying in Matthew spells this meaning out more fully. There Jesus says that his blood will be "poured out for many *for the forgiveness of sins [peri pollōn ekchynnomenon eis aphesin harmartiōn]*" (Matt 26:28). Luke, similar to Paul, has Jesus declare that his body is "given for you [*hyper hymōn didomenon*]" (Luke 22:19). Furthermore, like Matthew, Luke's Gospel also has Jesus speaking of his blood being "poured out [*ekchynnomenon*]" (Luke 22:20), thus evoking sacrificial symbolism.[33]

It should be added that there is nothing un-Jewish about any of this. Other Jewish sources apply sacrificial and atonement terminology to the suffering of the righteous (Isa 53:11–12; Dan 9:24; Wis 3:6; 1QS 8:3–4; 4Q171 2:9–12; 4 Macc 17:21–22). In particular, there are good reasons to think Jesus's words over the bread and the cup are shaped by Isaiah's Suffering Servant passage.

Jesus as the Sacrificial and Priestly Servant

As we have seen, both Luke and Paul report that Jesus said that his body is "for you [*hyper hymōn*]" (Luke 22:20; 1 Cor 11:24). This expression has long been taken as reflecting Isaiah's description of the Suffering Servant, who is said to suffer for others (Isa 53:10–12).[34] As Jesus is "handed

---

[31] The majority of interpreters recognize this connotation. See, e.g., Adela Yarbro Collins, "Finding Meaning in the Death of Jesus," *JR* 78, 2 (1998): 174; Fitzmyer, *Luke*, 2:1391, 1402–1403; Green, *Luke*, 763.

[32] Regev, *Temple in Early Christianity*, 74.

[33] See, e.g., John T. Carroll, *Luke: A Commentary*, NTL (Louisville: Westminster John Knox Press, 2012), 436; John Nolland, *Luke*, 3 vols., WBC 35A–C (Dallas: Word, 1989, 1993), 3:1057.

[34] See, e.g., Ben Meyer, "The Expiation Motif in the Eucharistic Words," in *One Loaf, One Cup: Ecumenical Studies of 1 Cor 11 and other Eucharistic Texts: The Cambridge*

over [*paredideto*]" in Paul's account (1 Cor 11:23), so too is the Servant: "the Lord gave him up [*paraedōken*] for our sins ... he *was handed over* [*paredothē*]" (Isa 53:6, 12 LXX).[35] The same verbal connections can be found in the Lukan formulation of Jesus's bread-saying (cf. Luke 22:19). That Luke intends the reader to think of the Servant is further confirmed in that, while still at table, he has Jesus go on to explicitly quote Isaiah 53 in reference to himself (Luke 22:37; cf. Isa 53:12). That Jesus's blood is shed "for *many* [*hyper pollōn*]" in Mark 14:24 is also often believed to be shaped by Isaiah 53 since the Servant's affliction is said to benefit the "*many* [*pollous*]" (Isa 53:12 LXX).[36] As many have recognized, Matthew's construction (Matt 26:28: *peri pollōn*) is even closer to the Greek version's description of the Servant (Isa 53:53:12), and is likely influenced by it.[37] Since Matthew quotes it earlier in the narrative and applies it to Jesus (Matt 8:17), it is hard to believe a connection is not to be found here. All four accounts of the Last Supper, therefore, appear to identify Jesus with a passage – the Suffering Servant poem – in which suffering is compared to sacrifice.

It bears mentioning that the Isaianic Servant is not only a sacrificial victim but also a priestly figure since he makes a sacrifice of himself for the sins of others (Isa 53:10, 12). Moreover, as R. B. Jamieson suggests, by serving as "sin-bearer" the Servant is like the Levitical priests, who are also said to "bear" sin (cf. Lev 10:17; Num 18:1).[38] By describing Jesus as the Servant, then, the gospels may also be seen as implying that he has a priestly role.

That Luke seems to portray Jesus as a priestly figure is suggested by the scene in which he last appears. Prior to ascending to heaven, the evangelist tells us: "And he led them out as far as to Bethany, and, *lifting up his hands, he blessed them* [*eparas tas cheiras autou*

Conference on the Eucharist August 1988, ed. B. F. Meyer, NGS 6 (Macon: Mercer, 1993), 19; Fee, *First Epistle to the Corinthians*, 551. Many also find an echo of this Isaianic passage in Romans 3:24–26 and 4:25. See James B. Prothro, *Both Judge and Justifier*, WUNT 2/461 (Tübingen: Mohr Siebeck, 2018), 174.

[35] Richard B. Hays, *First Corinthians*, Interpretation (Louisville: John Knox Press, 1997), 198. See also Otfried Hofius, "The Fourth Servant Song in the New Testament Letters," in *The Suffering Servant: Isaiah 53 in Jewish and Christian Sources*, ed. Bernd Janowski and Peter Stuhlmacher (Grand Rapids: Eerdmans, 2004), 176n.54.

[36] See, e.g., Marcus, *Mark*, 2:966–967; Boring, *Mark*, 391; Collins, "Finding Meaning," 176–177.

[37] See, e.g., Konradt, *Matthew*, 306; Davies and Allison, *Matthew*, 3:474.

[38] R. B. Jamieson, *Jesus's Death and Heavenly Offering in Hebrews*, SNTSMS 172 (Cambridge: Cambridge University Press, 2018), 193.

eulogēsen autous]" (Luke 24:50). That Jesus raises up his hands while imparting a blessing matches accounts of the high priest. The Torah reports: "Aaron *lifted up his hands* toward the people and blessed them [*exaras Aarōn tas cheiras epi ton laon eulogeēsen*]" (Lev 9:22). Likewise, Sirach has a similar account of the high priest Simon, who is said to have, "*lifted up* his hands over the whole congregation [*epēren cheiras autou epi pasan ekklēsian*]" to "give the *blessing* [*dounai eulogian*]" (Sir 50:20). Many have recognized that Luke's Gospel climaxes, therefore, with a depiction of Jesus as high priest.[39] Given the way Luke concludes his Gospel, it is difficult to think that the cultic imagery in passages like the Last Supper narrative are inconsequential to his overall portrait.

To be clear, my point in discussing these passages is not that we are necessarily dealing with "authentic" material. I am simply detailing the many ways Jesus is portrayed as using cultic traditions. Whether the broad tradition of Jesus's use of temple and priestly metaphors can be traced back to his own historical teaching awaits a fuller discussion. The notable thing for us to highlight here is that, at least for Luke, priestly themes are surely in play. The account of the ascension simply reinforces the likelihood that cultic imagery is intended in his account of the Last Supper.

"Do This in Remembrance of Me"

It is important to recognize that Jesus does not simply speak of his death as a sacrifice. The directive to repeat Jesus's actions implies that the community's meal *itself* is a cultic event. This is most evident in 1 Corinthians and Luke where Jesus instructs the apostles to repeat what he has done: "Do this in *remembrance* [*anamnēsin*] of me" (Luke 22:19b; cf. 1 Cor

---

[39] See, e.g., Carroll, *Luke*, 495–496; K. M. Kapic, "Receiving Christ's Priestly Benediction: A Biblical, Historical, and Theological Exploration of Luke 24:50–53," *WTJ* 67 (2005): 247–260; Nolland, *Luke*, 3:1227; Josef Ernst, *Das Evangelium nach Lukas*, RNT (Regensburg: Pustet, 1977), 672. Levine and Witherington (*Luke*, 670) point out that non-priests such as fathers of families and figures like Moses are said to lift their hands to offer blessings. Yet Moses is explicitly identified as a priest with Aaron in Ps 99:6 and the specific act of stretching hands *over* another to bless (rather than laying hands upon another) seems to evoke priestly rather than non-priestly blessing scenes. This is particularly the case given other features of Luke's portrait of Jesus we have mentioned, namely, the association of him with Psalm 110.

11:24, 25). The language of "remembrance" or "memorial" (*anamnēsis*) was used in reference to Israel's cult in the Septuagint:[40]

And in the days of your gladness and at your feasts and at your new moons, you shall trumpet with the trumpets over the whole burnt offerings and over your sacrifices of deliverance, and it shall be for you a *remembrance* [*anamnēsis*] before your God. I am the Lord your God. (Numbers 10:10 LXX; NETS adapted)

You shall put on the pile pure frankincense and salt, and they shall be as loaves for *remembrance* [LXX: *anamnēsin*], set before the Lord. (Leviticus 24:7 LXX; NETS)

The liturgical connotation of Jesus's command to "remember" is reinforced by his direction to "do [*poieite*]" what he has done, terminology that scholars also recognize as closely associated with Israel's ritual worship (cf., e.g., Exod 29:35 LXX; Num 15:11–13 LXX).[41] As I. Howard Marshall says, the verb employed, *poieō*, "is used of repeating rites."[42] Similarly, Xavier Léon-Dufour observes that the use of the verb in context "signifies directly a *cultic* action."[43] Again, on their own the terms "remembrance" and "do" need not be cultic; in context – with all of the other sacrificial motifs in play – and used together, the ritual inference is hard to avoid.

Do Jesus's words evoke any specific temple rites? Before exploring that question, it is important to point out that sacrificial categories should not be seen as hermetically sealed. An allusion to one type of offering does not necessarily rule out the likelihood that another is also intended. Jewish sources frequently correlate various rites. For example, Philo links the unleavened bread of Passover to the bread of the presence (cf. *Spec.* 2:158–161). In addition, the Passover sacrifice and *tôdâ* – the "thanksgiving sacrifice" – were easily related to one another. In the Jerusalem Talmud, regulations for the *tôdâ* are laid out in the tractate dedicated to the Passover (cf. y. Pesaḥ 1:1). That *tôdâ* and Passover would be grouped together makes sense. Both involve a sacred meal in which the worshipper eats of the sacrifice and of unleavened bread (cf. Exod 12:8; Lev 7:12).

---

[40] See also David E. Garland, *1 Corinthians*, BECNT (Grand Rapids: Baker Academic, 2003), 548; Daniel Harrington, *First Corinthians*, SP 7 (Collegeville, MN: Liturgical Press, 1999), 428.

[41] Cf. also 1QS 2:19; 1Q28a 2:21.

[42] I. Howard Marshall, *Commentary on Luke: A Commentary on the Greek Text* (Exeter: Paternoster, 1978), 804.

[43] Xavier Léon-Dufour, *Sharing the Eucharistic Bread: The Witness of the New Testament*, trans. Matthew J. O'Connell (New York/Mahwah: Paulist, 1982), 109 (emphasis added).

In fact, the rabbis derive specific regulations for the thanksgiving sacrifice from the ordinances of the Passover (cf. m. Menaḥ 7:6). Furthermore, the *tôdâ* was linked to praising God for deliverance (e.g., Jer 33:11). In this, it was like Passover, which celebrated Israel's deliverance from Egypt. Philo, therefore, fittingly describes Passover as "a reminder and *thank-offering*" (*Spec.* 2:146). Given their similarities, it is no wonder that allusions to all three of these offerings – Passover, the bread of the presence, and the *tôdâ* – have been detected in the Last Supper narratives. Since sacrificial categories could be blurred, we need not insist a reference to one excludes the others. In fact, the opposite may be the case.

First, Mary Douglas argues that Jesus's words over the bread and the cup draw from bread of the presence traditions. The Torah's description of the ritual uses many of the key terms that appear in the Last Supper accounts:

- "bread" (*artos*), which is "eaten" (*esthio*; Lev 24:5, 7, 9 LXX; Luke 22:19; cf. 1 Cor 11:26)
- "covenant" (*diathēkē*; Lev 24:8 LXX; Luke 22:20; 1 Cor 11:25)
- "remembrance" (*anamnēsis*; Lev 24:9 LXX; Luke 22:19; 1 Cor 11:25)
- a "table" (*trapeza*; Exod 25:23, 27, 28, 30 LXX; Luke 22:21; cf. 1 Cor 10:21).

The bread of the presence is also associated with drink-offerings (Exod 25:29).[44] It should not be forgotten that earlier in the Synoptics, Jesus compares himself and his disciples with David and his men who were given access to this very same holy bread (cf. Matt 12:3–4//Mark 2:25–26//Luke 6:3–4). Luke's account of this story in particular seems to anticipate the Last Supper narrative. As Joseph Fitzmyer has shown, Jesus recalls how David "took" (*lambanō*) the "bread" (*artos*) and "gave" (*didōmi*) it to his men (Luke 6:4). The same sequence of verbs is repeated in Luke's Last Supper narrative (cf. Luke 22:19).[45]

David's Actions with the Bread of the Presence (Luke 6:4)	Jesus's Actions at the Last Supper (Luke 22:19)
David "took" (*lambanō*)	Jesus "took" (*lambanō*)
"bread" (*artos*)	"bread" (*artos*)
"gave" (*didōmi*) to his men	"gave" (*didōmi*) to his disciples

[44] For further discussion see Mary Douglas, "The Eucharist: Its Continuity with the Bread Sacrifice of Leviticus," *Modern Theology* 15, 2 [1999]: 209–224.

[45] Fitzmyer, *Luke*, 1:609. See also Levine and Witherington, *Luke*, 163.

Within the comparison, the bread of the Last Supper thus functions in the place of the bread of the presence. In Luke, Jesus's account of "what David did" (*poieō*, Luke 6:3) therefore anticipates what Jesus will tell his disciples to "do" (*poieō*, Luke 22:19).

Second, Jesus's use of "remembrance" (*anamnēsis*) is especially fitting given the paschal context of the Last Supper in the Synoptic narratives. In addition, contrary to what some have claimed, there are strong indicators that Paul was aware of the paschal nature of the meal, such as his assertion that it occurred "at night [*en tē nukti*]," (1 Cor 11:23), a peculiar dimension of its observance (cf. Exod 12:8; Deut 16:4–8; 11Q19 17:6–9) and his earlier affirmation of Christ as a paschal sacrifice (1 Cor 5:7).[46] Passover was also associated with a similar term for "remembrance" (*mnēmosynon*, cf. Exod 12:14).[47] In short, that Jesus chooses a Passover meal as the context for his command to repeat his actions over the bread and wine as a "remembrance" (cf. Luke 22:15, 19) would unavoidably be seen as drawing on the imagery of the feast itself. The appearance of "new covenant" terminology from the LXX's account of Jeremiah 31 further reinforces the Passover imagery. In the Septuagint, Jeremiah's new covenant oracle is *explicitly linked to Passover*:

> Behold, I am bringing them from the north,
> and I will gather them from the farthest part of the earth
> *at the feast of Passover* [*phasek*].
> (Jeremiah 38:8 LXX; NETS adapted)

A paschal backdrop is also fitting given the appearance of "covenant" language; the festival is *repeatedly* linked to covenant renewal in Jewish history (Josh 3:7–5:12; 2 Kgs 23:21; 2 Chr 29–30).[48] A Passover background also makes sense of why both Jesus's death and the eucharistic meal are described in cultic terms. In light of the paschal connection, Jesus's act of giving the bread (=his body) to the disciples to be *consumed* is the natural corollary of his role as a sacrificial victim; the Passover lamb was not only sacrificed but also *eaten*.[49] Regev notes: "Mark does not portray Jesus as being anti-sacrificial. It is even possible that the

---

[46] See, e.g., Jane Lancaster Patterson, *Keeping the Feast: Metaphors of Sacrifice in 1 Corinthians and Philippians*, ECL (Atlanta: SBL Press, 2015), 151. For further discussion, see Pitre, Barber, and Kincaid, *Paul, A New Covenant Jew*, 237–238.

[47] See Nolland, *Luke*, 3:1057; Green, *Luke*, 762.

[48] See, e.g., Pitre, *Jesus and the Last Supper*, 415–416; Peter Stuhlmacher, "Das neutestamentliche Zeugnis vom Herrenmahl," *ZTK* 84 (1987): 10–13; Barry Smith, *Jesus's Last Passover Meal* (Lewiston: Edwin Mellen, 1993), 155–156.

[49] See, e.g., Fitzmyer, *Luke*, 2:1392.

description is historical and that Jesus uses a sacrificial metaphor while eating the Paschal lamb."[50]

Third, scholars have also argued that Jesus's words evoke the thanksgiving sacrifice (*tôdâ*).[51] Like Matthew and Mark (cf. Matt 26:27// Mark 14:23), Paul and Luke emphasize Jesus's act of "giving *thanks* [*eucharistēsas*]" (Luke 22:19//1 Cor 11:24). Obviously, by itself the use of this word cannot establish a *tôdâ* reference. Other factors, however, incline the reader to make the connection. For one thing, Jesus alludes to Jeremiah's new covenant prophecy. This prophecy is followed by a vision of the age to come in which the returned exiles offer *tôdâ* sacrifices (cf. Jer 33:11). Given the cultic setting and the appearance of "new covenant" imagery from Jeremiah's vision, an allusion to the *tôdâ* seems fitting, if not even expected. Furthermore, as we have seen, a *tôdâ* connection is plausible given that Jesus's meal takes place during Passover week. As we have seen, Passover and the thanksgiving sacrifice were easily connected.

Some have doubted the dominical origin of Jesus's statement that his actions should be repeated based on the assumption that Jesus would not have used such cultic language. The fact that the report is similar to the community's cultic practice is seen as *itself* proof of its later origin. Consider Jürgen Becker's confident assertion:

> All of the texts that deal with the Last Supper of Jesus reflect the liturgical concerns of the meal celebrations of the various churches. No text reports the historical event. The purpose of each text, rather, is to justify why the church celebrates the Lord's Supper as it does.[52]

Yet the assumption that Jesus could not have used Jewish cultic language is wholly unjustified. Moreover, the logic of dissimilarity can be reversed. That Jesus gave instructions to the disciples to repeat what he had done at table can be supported by the widespread and early practice of the eucharist in the early community. Furthermore, whatever one makes of the precise chronology, Jesus's last meal likely took place against the backdrop of Passover week, a time in which Jews partook of a cultic meal that was to be repeated as a "memorial" (Exod 12:14). The idea that

---

[50] Regev, *The Temple in Early Christianity*, 52.
[51] See, e.g., Richard H. Bell, *Deliver Us from Evil*, WUNT 216 (Tübingen: Mohr Siebeck, 2007), 274–277; Hartmut Gese, *Essays in Biblical Theology*, trans. Keith Crim (Minneapolis: Augsburg, 1981 [1977]), 128–140; Jerome Kodell, *The Eucharist in the New Testament* (Collegeville: Michael Glazier, 1988), 48–50.
[52] Jürgen Becker, *Jesus of Nazareth*, trans. James E. Crouch (Berlin: Walter de Gruyter, 1998), 340. I owe this quotation to Pitre, *Jesus and the Last Supper*, 425.

Jesus anticipated his demise and that he performed actions at his final meal interpreting his death in cultic terms is not hard to believe. That he intended for his actions to be repeated would also make sense against the festival backdrop.[53] Skepticism regarding these early and well-attested traditions is unnecessary.

Does any of this mean that Jesus used the cultic metaphors found in the Last Supper tradition? Here we can begin by asking whether this impression is elsewhere attested. In fact, it is.

OTHER CULTIC IMAGERY IN THE JESUS TRADITION

That Jesus was remembered early on as interpreting his mission through sacrificial categories is attested not only in Matthew but also, as we have seen, as early as Paul's account of the Last Supper. Indeed, Mark and Luke also portray Jesus as alluding to cultic traditions in his words over the bread and the cup. Here we will examine various other passages that indicate Jesus's use of temple and priesthood imagery not only in the Synoptics but also in John. Many of these traditions are viewed as secondary by scholars. This, however, is not universally the case. We will note instances where material seems to have an especially strong claim to reflect impressions Jesus himself made. *Nevertheless, we are not primarily concerned with "authenticating" specific traditions.* What matters most at this stage of the discussion is noting how frequently such imagery is attributed to Jesus.

The Twelve's Task of Judging the Twelve Tribes as Priestly

As we have already mentioned, scholars generally accept the idea that Jesus appointed a group of twelve. Because of that, Jesus's saying regarding the twelve's future task "judging" the twelve tribes in Matthew 19 has long fascinated questers. A similar saying is found in Luke:

And I covenant [*diatithemai*] to you, as my Father has covenanted [*dietheto*] to me, a kingdom, that you may eat and drink at my table in my kingdom, and sit on thrones judging [*krinontes*] the twelve tribes of Israel. (Luke 22:29–30)[54]

---

[53] See, e.g., Joachim Gnilka, *Jesus von Nazaret: Botschaft und Geschichte*, HThKNT (Freiberg: Herder, 1990), 289.

[54] Though English translations regularly render this with words such as "confer" (NRSV) or "assign" (RSV), "covenant" is preferable. The Greek term that appears is the verbal form of the word "covenant [*diathēkē*]," which occurs in the immediate context (cf.

Many scholars believe this teaching – typically viewed as Q material – probably reflects the historical Jesus's actual rationale for gathering twelve apostles.[55] As we have seen, it is probable that Jesus did gather twelve to himself as part of his Jewish eschatological outlook. Though some claim Jesus would not have envisioned his disciples "ruling" over Israel,[56] this position is usually based on the assumption that Jesus did not see himself as playing a central role in the age to come. We have challenged that belief earlier. If Jesus did view himself as the future king, the objection tracing the idea back to Jesus fails. That Jesus said something about the twelve's future place in the kingdom – that is, that he indicated the twelve would have some future role governing Israel – is difficult to dismiss as a later innovation. Still, our argument here does not necessarily depend on "authenticating" this particular tradition.

On a literary level, it is important to look at the Lukan version of the saying within its context. As we saw earlier, judging Israel was a responsibility especially associated with priests. We noted that the saying about the twelve's future role in Matthew 19 occurs within a context in which there seems to be other allusions to Levitical traditions (see pages 000–00). Notably, the parallel in Luke also occurs in a setting where cultic allusions abound – Luke's Last Supper narrative. Among other things, Jesus's statement about the disciples' future role as judges follows shortly on the heels of the dominical command, "*Do* this" (*poieō*, Luke 22:19).[57] The language of this directive evokes the terminology the Torah uses for the priests' performance of the cultic rites (cf. Lev 4:20 LXX; Num 15:11–13 LXX). That Jesus would speak of his disciples as judges, an office that typically belonged to the priests, is only surprising if one has failed to pick up on the cultic motifs already found in Luke 22.

Furthermore, the saying in Luke 22 about the apostles serving as judges brims over with Davidic connotations. Jesus says his "father" has "covenanted [*dietheto*]" a "kingdom" to him (Luke 22:29). The coordination of these three ideas would have called to mind Davidic traditions: (1) the Davidide was God's "son" (cf. 2 Sam 7:14; Ps 2:7; 89:27); (2) the

---

Luke 22:20). The latter is attested in the LXX (e.g., Josh 7:11; 2 Chr 7:18; Ezek 16:30). While the word can have the meaning of making a "testament" or "will," it is perhaps best to see both meanings as in play since the ideas were interrelated in a Jewish outlook. Fitzmyer, *Luke*, 2:1419.

[55] See, e.g., Meier, *A Marginal Jew*, 3:138; Erhman, *Apocalyptic Prophet*, 186; Horsely, *Jesus and the Spiral of Violence*, 206–207.

[56] Bultmann, *History of the Synoptic Tradition*, 158–159.

[57] Cf. also 1QS 2:19; 1Q28a 2:21.

Lord was believed to have established a "covenant" with David (e.g., Ps 89:3–4, 28, 34, 39; 132:12; Isa 55:3; Jer 33:20–21; Sir 47:11; 4Q252 *frag.* 1, 5, II, 1–6); and (3) this covenant was linked to the promise of a kingdom (e.g., Ps 89:3–4, 34–39; Sir 45:25; 47:11; 4Q252 5:1–7). A Davidic echo seems assured due to the combination of themes. It should also be pointed out that David and Solomon were the only two kings to reign over all twelve tribes of Israel – the very scenario Jesus envisions being restored.[58]

There is another feature of David's reign that should not be forgotten: he assigned the tasks of the priests (cf. 1 Chr 15–16; 23–27). Jesus is depicted as the king anticipating his enthronement. It makes sense, therefore, that he is portrayed as having a role in installing the temple officials as David once did. With Jesus's words to Peter in Matthew 16, the sayings about the twelve judging Israel offers corroborating data that he was remembered as indicating that his disciples would have such a position. This reading also aligns with our reading of the Parable of the Wicked Tenants.

The Parable of the Wicked Tenants and the "Cornerstone" Saying

As we have seen, the Parable of the Wicked Tenants suggests Jesus intends to replace the current leaders with new ones (cf. Luke 20:16). The story appears not only in Matthew, but also in the other Synoptic Gospels as well as in the Gospel of Thomas (cf. Mark 12:1–12//Luke 20:9–18//Gos. Thom. §§65–66). In each account, Jesus concludes by applying the cornerstone imagery from Psalm 118 to himself. In addition, as in Matthew's narrative, Mark and Luke have Jesus speak these lines in the temple and couch the scene within the broader backdrop of the controversy created by Jesus's actions there (Mark 11:27//Luke 20:1). Exegetes, therefore, recognize that the cultic connections of Isaiah 5 and Psalm 118 we discussed in our preceding treatment are likely intended in Mark and Luke.[59]

As in Matthew, Jesus's use of Psalm 118 in Luke can also be seen as entailing temple-community imagery. A cultic reading of Jesus's identity as the "cornerstone" is further encouraged by the saying that follows it: "Everyone who *falls* [*pesōn*] on that *stone* [*lithon*] will be broken

---

[58] Jipp, *Messianic Theology*, 95.
[59] See, e.g., Collins, *Mark*, 548; Green, *Luke*, 704n.21.

[*synthlasthēsetai*] to pieces, and when it falls [*pesē*] on anyone, it will crush [*likmēsei*] him" (Luke 20:18). Here Jesus appears to employ the Jewish hermeneutic of *gezerah shavah*, which connects passages based on common words.[60] In this case, interpreters generally agree that Jesus is presented as using Psalm 118 in concert with other "stone [*lithos*]" passages from Isaiah and/or Daniel 2.[61] Remarkably, like Psalm 118, these other texts likely also involve temple allusions. The first is taken from Isaiah 8, where the Lord is said to be both a "sanctuary" and a "stone":

And he will become *a sanctuary* [LXX: *hagiasma*], and a *stone* [LXX: *lithou*] of offense, and a rock of stumbling to both houses of Israel, a trap and a snare to the inhabitants of Jerusalem. And many shall stumble thereupon; they shall *fall* [LXX: *pesountai*] and be broken; they shall be snared and taken. (Isaiah 8:14–15)

In addition to employing the word "stone" (*lithos*), the Greek version of Isaiah also uses the same verb for "crush" (*piptō*) found in Jesus's saying.

Psalm 118 and Isaiah 8 are also brought together in 1 Peter. However, it would be wrong to insist that this constitutes evidence *against* Jesus's use of these traditions (1 Pet 2:7–8). At the very least, 1 Peter could suggest an awareness of the tradition attested in Luke 20. Either way, an allusion to Isaiah 8 on the heels of the stone saying of Ps 118 would further reinforce the impression that the scene portrays Jesus as applying temple imagery to himself.[62]

The other passage often viewed in the backdrop of Jesus's stone imagery in Luke 20 is found in Daniel 2:

And in the days of those kings the God of heaven will set up a kingdom that shall never be destroyed, nor shall this kingdom be left to another people. It shall crush [LXX: *pataxei*] all these kingdoms and bring them to an end, and it shall stand forever; just as you saw that a stone was cut from the mountain not by hands, and that it crushed [*synēloēse*] the iron, the bronze, the clay, the silver, and the gold. (Daniel 2:44–45)

Notably, this scene also contains a likely cultic echo. To catch it, however, we must look at the setting of this prophetic announcement.

---

60 For further discussion, see David Instone Brewer, *Techniques and Assumptions in Jewish Exegesis before 70 C.E.*, TSAJ 30 (Tübingen: Mohr Siebeck, 1992), 17–18.

61 Fitzmyer, *Luke*, 2:1282; John S. Kloppenborg, *The Tenants in the Vineyard: Ideology, Economics, and Agrarian Conflict in Jewish Palestine*, WUNT 195 (Tubingen: Mohr Siebeck, 2006), 213; Snodgrass, *Parable of the Wicked Tenants*, 67–68.

62 Some have also seen a possible reference here to Isa 28:16, which refers to Zion. See Keener, *Matthew*, 516; Nolland, *Luke*, 3:953; Snodgrass, *Parable of the Wicked Tenants*, 98–99.

In Daniel 2, the dawning of the eschatological kingdom is symbolized by "a stone" (*lithos*) that is "cut out by no human hand" and which "breaks into pieces" a statue symbolizing wicked gentile nations (cf. Dan 2:31–45). Especially noteworthy is the description of this stone: the stone that crushes the gentile kingdoms "became *a great mountain and filled the whole earth*" (Dan 2:35). It is almost certain that ancient Jews would have seen the image of "a great mountain" which *grew in size* as a reference to Zion. The language closely mirrors a prophecy of the eschatological temple, which appears in both Isaiah and Micah:[63]

> It shall come to pass in the latter days
> *that the mountain of the house of the Lord*
> shall be established as the highest of the mountains,
> and shall be raised above the hills,
> and all the nations shall stream to it.   (Isaiah 2:2; Micah 4:1)

Not surprisingly, rabbinic tradition interpreted the stone in Daniel 2 as a reference to the temple.[64] Suffice it to say, Luke reinforces the cultic associations of Psalm 118's cornerstone by tying it to other texts that relate temple traditions.

Before moving on, it is worth discussing the historical probability of this material. While many have insisted that neither the parable nor the cornerstone saying can be traced back to Jesus himself, it is worth taking a moment to briefly examine some of the reasons cited for this position. To begin with, various features of the story have been seen as pointing away from "authenticity":

1. The image of the "son" who is killed reflects what happened to Jesus.[65]
2. The son is sent following the sending of the messengers (=the prophets).[66]
3. The destruction of the tenants is seen as reflecting the destruction of Jerusalem.[67]

[63] See, e.g., Winfried Vogel, *The Cultic Motif in the Book of Daniel* (New York: Peter Lang, 2010), 20–48; André Lacocque, *The Book of Daniel*, trans. D. Pellauer (London: SPCK, 1979), 124.
[64] For further discussion, see Snodgrass, *Parable of the Wicked Tenants*, 98–99; Beale, *Temple and the Church's Mission*, 186.
[65] See, e.g., Adolf Jülicher, *Die Gleichnisreden Jesu*, 2 vols., 2nd ed. (Tübingen: Mohr Siebeck, 1910), 2:385–406; Bultmann, *History of the Synoptic Tradition*, 177, 205.
[66] See, e.g., Kloppenborg, *Tenants in the Vineyard*, 67.
[67] See, e.g., Michel Hubaut, *La parabole des vignerons homicides*, CahRB 16 (Paris: Gabalda, 1976), 77–95, 129–130.

4. The handing over of the vineyard to others reflects the belief that
    God has rejected Israel in favor of the church.[68]

Our preceding discussion raises difficulties with these objections. We
have argued: (1) Jesus likely anticipated his own death; (2) Jesus probably viewed himself as the eschatological Davidic figure (and divine sonship was closely linked to Davidic traditions); (3) Jesus most probably
anticipated the coming destruction of the Jerusalem temple; and (4) the
parable does not indicate that God has rejected Israel.

John P. Meier's especially rigorous treatment of the parable must also
be mentioned.[69] He concludes that the versions in Matthew, Luke, and
Thomas are dependent on Mark's account. While he believes part of the
parable can be traced back to Jesus, he rejects the likelihood that all of
it can. A key consideration in his examination is the fact that the story
has two explanations/applications: (1) the coming judgment on the tenants (Mark 12:9); and (2) the cornerstone saying (Mark 12:10–11). The
first ending, he notes, involves a shift in verb tense. Whereas the parable
previously described the actions taken by the owner and the tenants in
the aorist, Jesus goes on to use the future: the owner "will come," "will
destroy" the tenants, and "will give" the vineyard to others (Mark 12:9).
The second conclusion once again involves a shift back to the aorist –
the stone that was "rejected" is said to have "become" the cornerstone
(cf. Mark 12:10). Meier contends that these changes reveal the story's
development. He concludes that the parable can be traced back to Jesus
himself but originally ended with the shocking conclusion of the death
of the son in Mark 12:8. Early believers then affixed to the original story
the explanations of what the vineyard owner did to the tenants and the
cornerstone saying in Mark 12:9–12.

Meier buttresses his argument by making two observations. First, the
conclusion in Mark 12:9 – the idea that the owner will punish the tenants
and lend the vineyard out to others – "sticks out" because nowhere else
in the Synoptic tradition does Jesus's explanation of a parable involve
extending its narrative. The story is completed in Mark 12:8; it originally
ends with the son being killed and his body cast out of the vineyard without a proper burial. For Meier, this allegorized account of the Jesus story
is manifestly "dissimilar" to the early community's proclamation since it

---

[68] See, e.g., C. G. Montefiore, *The Synoptic Gospels*, 3 vols. (London: Macmillan and Co.,
1909), 1:275.
[69] For the following, see Meier, *A Marginal Jew*, 5:240–253.

involves no mention of Jesus's vindication. Moreover, he observes that the use of Psalm 118 as a reference to the resurrection fits comfortably with the tendency of Jesus's followers to interpret scriptural passages about stones as "christological proof texts" (cf. Acts 4:11; Rom 9:33; Eph 2:20; 1 Pet 2:6–8).[70] According to Meier, the "widespread tradition in the early church of using OT prophecies about a stone to refer to Jesus" points away from its origin in Jesus's teaching.[71] Since it fails the test of dissimilarity, it should also be dismissed.

Meier's analysis, while ingenious, is not fully convincing. The allusion to Isaiah 5 is deeply imbedded in the parable and there is little reason to think this echo is only the result of later reshaping.[72] The Isaianic echoes are clearly present in the Markan version, which Meier himself recognizes informs the other accounts.[73] While the allusions to Isaiah 5 are less pronounced in Luke, they are certainly not absent there.[74] It is true that the Thomasine version mutes the scriptural allusion, but that is to be expected given the Gospel's *tendenz*.[75] The parable's use of Isaiah 5, therefore, is unlikely to be due to later redaction. This makes it difficult to think that the message of coming divine judgment is only a later addition to the parable. In fact, *the entire thrust of the Isaianic passage is that divine retribution is coming.* To insist that Jesus told the parable *without* appealing to the notion of divine punishment is unpersuasive. No version of the story omits it. It is a vital element that makes sense of the Isaiah 5 allusion.

Moreover, the emphasis given to the change in verbal tense is overwrought. The tense shift must not just be accounted for diachronically, but within its literary setting. Mark's shifts in tenses are well known.[76] Given that the parable focuses on *future* judgment, the shift in tense is perfectly explicable. While Jesus's death is also in the future, the tense change regarding judgment likely indicates that this is the story's

---

[70] Meier, *A Marginal Jew*, 252.
[71] Meier, *A Marginal Jew*, 253.
[72] See, e.g., Bryan, *Jesus and Israel's Traditions of Judgement and Restoration*, 54n.18; Weren, "The Use of Isaiah 5, 1–7," 1–26; Hooker, *Mark*, 274.
[73] Meier, *A Marginal Jew*, 240–41.
[74] See Green, *Luke*, 704n.21 and the sources cited.
[75] See, e.g., Goodacre, *Thomas and the Gospels*, 144.
[76] See, e.g., the treatment of the shift from present to past in Mark 3:26 and the discussion in Elizabeth E. Shively, *Apocalyptic Imagination in the Gospel of Mark: The Literary and Theological Role of Mark 3:22–30*, BZNW 189 (Berlin: Walter de Gruyter, 2012), 66–67.

particular focus. One also wonders if the preoccupation with tense is informed by the questionable assumption that the gospel writers preserve the *ipsissima verba Jesu*. In addition, as Meier's analysis of other parables shows, Jesus is remembered as varying his use of the medium. One should not, therefore, make too much of the fact that the parable has unique features. To insist Jesus could not have departed from certain formats is unpersuasive.

Finally, Meier's arguments depend on the criterion of dissimilarity, a tool I have argued should be questioned. As we have seen, there are good reasons to believe that some of the early community's beliefs did have their origin in Jesus's teaching. The criterion rules out too much of the material that the community would have been most likely to preserve. In particular, there are no convincing reasons to think that Jesus did not foresee his coming death. To imagine he did not realize his kingdom message had dangerous implications is to attribute to him an implausible naïveté. That Jesus would have anticipated suffering fits too well with his use of apocalyptic traditions to dismiss as a later invention. Furthermore, it is improbable that Jesus simply thought his story would end in disastrous defeat. His eschatological outlook would have entailed an expectation of divine vindication. Resurrection from the dead was very much a part of eschatological hopes (e.g., Dan 12:2–3; 2 Macc 7:14, 23; 1 En. 51:1–5; 4 Ezra 7:32–36; 2 Bar 42:8). There is no reason to believe Jesus could not have entertained such hopes for himself. Jesus's use of Psalm 118 is perfectly explicable in light of this. As we have seen, the use of the cultic imagery of the psalm fits nicely with Isaiah 5, which, we have seen, was associated with the temple in other texts. In fact, Meier's argument should be viewed as reversible – it seems likely that widespread use of stone texts in reference to Jesus emerged out of memories that this was precisely how Jesus taught.

The Temple Charge Made at Jesus's Trial

We would be remiss not to mention the accusation made at Jesus's trial in Mark 14: "We heard him say, 'I will destroy this temple [*naon*] *made by hands*, and within three days I will build another *not made by hands*'" (Mark 14:58). The claim that Jesus affirmed he would destroy and rebuild the temple is repeated by bystanders at Jesus's crucifixion (Mark 15:29). We have already argued that Jesus likely spoke of the temple's future demise. Did he also speak of a future rebuilding of the temple?

In our discussion in Chapter 3, we saw that the phrase "made by hands" should not be used as evidence that Jesus viewed the temple as idolatrous per se. Why the term, then? Some texts indicate that the eschatological temple will be established by God himself (e.g., Ezek 37:26; 1 En. 90:28; Jub 1:17, 27–29), a tradition likely rooted in Exodus:

> You brought them in and planted them on the
>   mountain of your own possession,
> the place, O LORD, that you made your abode,
> the *sanctuary*, O LORD, that *your hands* have established.
> *The Lord will reign* forever and ever.   (Exodus 15:17)[77]

Here the concept of the Lord's definitive reign – the basis for eschatological beliefs in the coming kingdom of God – is linked to a "sanctuary" that is established by God's "hands." The idea of a temple made by the hands of the Lord thus fits well with Mark's message that Jesus proclaimed the coming of the kingdom. In fact, as we have seen, Jesus is also remembered as drawing from sources envisioning an eschatological temple (e.g., Mark 11:17; Isa 56:7).

The other phrase attributed to Jesus in Mark, "not made by hands [*acheiropoiēton*]," bears a resemblance to the picture painted by the Greek version of Daniel 2: "a stone cut without hands [*tmēthēnai lithon aneu cheirōn*]" (Dan 2:45 LXX).[78] The wording in the Greek does not quite match. Nevertheless, the charge that Jesus envisioned a coming new temple, which he identified somehow with himself and/or the community, fits well with an allusion to this prophecy. The use of Daniel's vision about the stone in connection with the message that Jesus is the cornerstone of a new temple being constructed in Luke 20 fits nicely together.

Did Jesus speak of the rebuilding of the temple in reference to his resurrection? The notion that Jesus said something like what is reported by the false witnesses in Mark's trial scene is often ruled out based on the assumption that such an idea necessarily points to a post-Easter setting. This should not be a convincing argument though. That Jesus could have forecasted his death and resurrection is, as we have argued, perfectly consistent with the idea that his message involved imagery taken from Jewish apocalyptic eschatology. The idea that Jesus could have

---

[77] Yet see Allison's caution that Jewish tradition did allow for human temple-builders (*Jesus of Nazareth*, 100n.21 citing 2 Sam 7:10–14; Zech 6:7; Sib. Or. 5:422).
[78] See, e.g., Evans, *Mark 8:27–16:20*, 445.

associated temple imagery with himself is also not inconsistent within a Jewish context: the Qumranites speak of a "temple of man" (4Q174 *frag.* 1, *col.* i, 21, 2:6).

Nevertheless, it would be wrong to conclude that if Jesus referred to himself as a sanctuary, this meant he rejected the Jerusalem temple's holiness. This conclusion does not necessarily follow. Although my argument does not depend upon it, the notion that Jesus made some sort of veiled prediction about his future vindication using temple imagery that was obscure to his original hearers would explain the data quite well. If Jesus did cite Psalm 118's cornerstone in reference to his future vindication, we can begin to see how such an idea could have taken shape.

Priestly Arrangement of the Disciples

Brant Pitre's work on Jesus's arrangement of his disciples also has relevance for our study.[79] Pitre writes, "Although it is widely recognized that Jesus gathered around himself followers in different degrees of relation to him, the symbolic significance of these various circles has often gone unnoticed."[80] He offers an overview of the data:

1. *Peter as the Chief Disciple.* Peter always has preeminence in lists of the twelve and is typically cast in the role of the disciples' spokesperson (cf. Matt 10:2; 16:16–19; Mark 1:36; 3:16; 16:7; Luke 6:14; 9:32; 12:41; 22:31–32; John 1:42; 6:66–69).

2. *The Circle of Three.* Aside from Peter, within the group of the twelve three are typically singled out: Peter, James, and John (cf., e.g., Mark 3:16–17; 5:36; 9:2–8; 14:32–33 and parr.). These three are the only ones ever explicitly said to be renamed by Jesus (Mark 3:14, 16–17 and parr.).

3. *The Circle of the Twelve.* Although the lists of names are often different, as we have seen, that Jesus chose a group of twelve is remarkably well attested.

4. *The Circle of Seventy(-Two).* In Luke we learn that Jesus also appointed seventy "other" (*heterous*) disciples to heal and proclaim the message of the kingdom (cf. Luke 10:1).

Beyond this, Jesus is not remembered for organizing his disciples into other sets or groups.

---

[79] Pitre, *Jesus and the Last Supper*, 139–141.
[80] Pitre, *Jesus and the Last Supper*, 139.

Pitre shows that the pattern that emerges from our sources finds a striking parallel in the text of Exodus 24, a passage we have already seen alluded to in the Last Supper narrative. It is helpful to read the text carefully:

And [the LORD] said to *Moses*, "Come up to the LORD, *you and Aaron, Nadab, and Abihu, and seventy of the elders of Israel,* and worship afar off. Moses alone shall come near to the LORD; but the others shall not come near, and the people shall not come up with him." ... And he [Moses] rose early in the morning, and built an altar at the foot of the mountain, and *twelve pillars, according to the twelve tribes of Israel.* And he sent *young men of the people of Israel, who offered burnt offerings and sacrificed peace offerings of oxen to the LORD.* And Moses took half of the blood and put it in basins, and half of the blood he threw against the altar... And Moses took the blood and threw it on the people, and said, "Behold, *the blood of the covenant* which the LORD has made with you in accordance with all these words." *Then Moses and Aaron, Nadab, and Abihu, and seventy of the elders of Israel went up,* and they saw the God of Israel ... And he did not lay his hand on the chief men of the people of Israel; they beheld God, and ate and drank. (Exodus 24:1–11)

To summarize, here we see the following: (1) the one high priest, Aaron; (2) three priestly figures, which includes the first figure, Aaron (with Nadab, and Abihu); (3) twelve priestly men who offer sacrifice; and (4) seventy elders.

Pitre points out that the arrangement of the leaders at Sinai mirrors what we discover in the gospels. If this is right, then the twelve would correspond to the priestly young men who offer the sacrifice.

Moses and Priestly Hierarchy	*Jesus and His Disciples*
Moses	Jesus
The 1: High Priest, Aaron	The 1: Peter, the Chief Disciple
The 3: Aaron, Nadab, Abihu	The 3: Peter, James, and John
The 12: The Twelve Priestly Young Men at Twelve Pillars	The 12: Twelve Apostles who Judge the Twelve Tribes
The 70: Priestly Elders of Israel	The 70: Appointed and Sent Out[81]

Pitre concludes, "What are we to make of these parallels? Is it possible that the numerical correspondence between Jesus's own disciples and the priestly mediators at Mount Sinai is coincidence? I find this extremely implausible."[82] I agree.

---

[81] Chart taken from Pitre, *Jesus and the Last Supper,* 141.

[82] Brant Pitre, "Jesus and the Messianic Priesthood" (paper presented at the annual meeting of the Society of Biblical Literature. Boston, MA, November 23, 2008), 9.

Is it far-fetched that Jesus would have evoked such traditions? Against that position, Pitre points out that a similar arrangement is also attested at Qumran, where the priests of the eschatological age are also organized into similar numerical groups. Here, besides "one" high priest, the numbers "twelve" and "three" stand out. In 1Q33 2:1–2 we read, *"They shall arrange the chiefs of the priests behind the High Priest and of his second (in rank), twelve chiefs to serve in perpetuity before God."*[83] Furthermore, 4Q164 (4QIsaiah Pesher[d]) 1:4–6 speaks of "the twelve [chiefs of the priests who] illuminate with the judgment of the Urim and the Thummim [... without] any from among them missing, like the sun in all its light."[84] Likewise, in 1QS it is said:

> In the Community council (there shall be) *twelve men and three priests*, perfect in everything that has been revealed from all the law to implement truth, justice, judgment, compassionate love and unassuming behaviour of one to another ... *to atone for sin* by doing justice. (1QS 8:1, 3)[85]

That this group "atones" would seem to underscore their sacerdotal identity.

The gospels' "depictions" of Jesus dividing the disciples into carefully demarcated groups is historically plausible in light of these parallels. Like the Dead Sea Scrolls, it is perfectly reasonable to think that Jesus also envisioned an eschatological leadership patterned on the Sinai model. Furthermore, it is worth noting that in Pitre's scenario, Peter is correlated to Aaron. This coheres with what we saw in the last chapter – Peter is compared to Eliakim in Isaiah 22, a figure described as wearing the high priest's vestments. Whatever one makes of that connection, at the very least, the preceding data would further confirm the impression that Jesus viewed his disciples in terms of eschatological *priestly* leaders.

Jesus's Contagious Holiness and Cultic Traditions

We have already seen that our sources remember that Jesus instructed cleansed lepers to offer the appropriate purification sacrifices at the temple (cf. Matt 8:4//Mark 1:44//Luke 5:14; Luke 17:14). As we explained, these stories indicate that Jesus affirmed the legitimacy of the cult. Nonetheless, they also highlight an idea that receives attention in various

---

[83] *DSSSE* 1:115.
[84] *DSSSE* 1:327.
[85] *DSSSE* 1:89.

ways in our sources, namely, Jesus's power over impurity. The subject has received careful analysis by Matthew Thiessen.[86] As he shows, Jesus is portrayed as a unique source of cleansing holiness. One aspect of his treatment that is pertinent for our study is the way in which Thiessen ties Jesus's contagious holiness to temple traditions. According to the Torah, whatever comes into contact with the sacred elements of the sanctuary is sanctified. Exodus 30 explains:

And you shall anoint with [the holy anointing oil] the tent of meeting and the ark of the covenant, and the table and all its utensils, and the lampstand and its utensils, and the altar of incense, and the altar of burnt offering with all its utensils, and the basin with its stand; you shall consecrate them. And they will be most holy things; *whatever touches them will become holy.* (Exodus 30:26–29)

The holiness of the temple, therefore, can be communicated to whatever touches its most sacred things. Jesus's affirmation of the sanctity of the sanctuary in Matthew 23 shows an awareness of this tradition: "the altar ... makes the gift sacred" (Matt 23:17, 19).

With this in mind, the story of the hemorrhaging woman, an episode that appears in all three Synoptic gospels (cf. Matt 9:20–22//Mark 5:25–34//Luke 8:42–48), is relevant to our conversation. In the story, the woman is cured by simply touching Jesus's garment. Thiessen points out that the depiction of Jesus as a source of purifying holiness reminds the reader of Israel's cultic traditions. He writes:

Just as the tabernacle and its accoutrements exercise no will in sanctifying objects that come into contact with them, Mark portrays Jesus's body as automatically and involuntarily purifying those who touch him in faith.[87]

Later, Thiessen returns to this observation in a section detailing Jesus's frequent conflict with evil spirits – forces connected with impurity; for example, "unclean spirits" (Matt 10:1//Mark 6:7; Matt 12:43//Luke 11:24; Mark 1:23, 26, 27//Luke 4:33, 36; Mark 3:11; Mark 5:2, 8, 13// Luke 8:29; Mark 7:25; Mark 9:25//Luke 9:42; Luke 6:18). Thiessen says:

Jesus's presence on earth introduces a power of holiness within the terrestrial realm that is both radically opposed to and stronger than the demonic. If some contemporaries of the Gospel writers were ascribing this same function to Israel's tabernacle (and by extension to the Jerusalem temple), since it housed the holy God of Israel, then the Gospel writers might have been implying that the holiness

---

[86] Thiessen, *Jesus and the Forces of Death.*
[87] Thiessen, *Jesus and the Forces of Death,* 91.

of Israel's God was housed in the person of Jesus in a way that actualized God's control over the demonic forces that plagued humanity.[88]

Jesus's ability to overcome impurity parallels the power associated with the temple. Yet Jesus's holiness overcomes potential sources of impurity in unprecedented ways. The logion in Matthew 12, "something greater than the temple is here" (Matt 12:6), may take on a new meaning in light of all of this.

In fact, Crispin Fletcher-Louis notes that the story of the woman who is healed by touching Jesus's garment is reminiscent of Ezekiel's account of eschatological priestly vestments in the future temple. Ezekiel speaks of the way in which the priestly garments have the power to transmit holiness:

When [the priests] go out into the outer court to the people, they shall take off the vestments in which they have been ministering, and lay them in the holy chambers; and they shall put on other garments, *so that they may not communicate holiness to the people with their vestments.* (Ezekiel 44:19)

To the best of my knowledge, there is no other ancient Jewish account of *garments* communicating holiness to others. The scene from Ezekiel's vision would thus seem to present the best precedent for explaining how Jesus's clothing is capable of healing the woman, a healing that resolves her impurity issues. Moreover, aside from the story of the hemorrhaging woman, the notion that people were healed by merely touching Jesus's garments is attested elsewhere (cf. Matt 14:36//Mark 6:56). The Ezekiel reference is an apt background for these accounts as well. In this, as Fletcher-Louis observes, Jesus would seem to be described as an eschatological priest.[89]

Cultic Metaphors Broadly in the Johannine Tradition

The use of cultic symbolism in the Fourth Gospel is widely noted.[90] The evangelist's decision to narrate Jesus's temple action early in his narrative is widely seen as having programmatic importance for the overall message of the Gospel. In the episode, Jesus speaks of his body as a temple (John 2:19–21). This is not the last time we encounter this motif in the Fourth Gospel. We have already explored how Jesus apparently borrows

---

[88] Thiessen, *Jesus and the Forces of Death*, 148.
[89] Fletcher-Louis, "Jesus as the High Priestly Messiah: Part 2," 76.
[90] See the sources in n. 113 in Chapter 5.

temple metaphors from the festal imagery associated with the Feast of Tabernacles in John 7 and applies them to himself. Yet this is only the tip of the iceberg. While few if any scholars find such episodes "authentic," they contribute once again to the overall impression that Jesus was remembered as applying cultic imagery to himself.

In John 10, Jesus is portrayed as going up to the temple for the Feast of Dedication. This festival recalled the restoration of the temple at the time of the Maccabees, during which Judas Maccabeus and his companions "consecrated [*hēgiasan*]" the sanctuary (1 Macc 4:48). Jesus uses this precise language in referring to himself as the one "the Father *consecrated* and *sent* [*apesteilen*] into the world" (John 10:36).[91] Here Jesus is depicted as applying the language associated with the sanctuary to himself. Moreover, Jesus goes on to speak of the disciples as "consecrated" in John 17:17–19, extending the temple imagery to them. Jesus is identified as a temple, but the same seems to be true about believers.[92]

In addition, Jesus is clearly identified as the Suffering Servant in the Fourth Gospel (John 3:14; 12:38).[93] Previously we discussed the fact that the Suffering Servant is not merely a sacrificial offering but also seems to be a priestly figure. The Fourth Gospel may be seen as affirming both aspects of this identification. In regard to being a sacrificial victim, John notices that Jesus's bones were not broken after his death thus fulfilling the requirements of the paschal lamb (cf. John 19:36; Ex 12:46).

Yet one also notes texts in John where Jesus seems to be depicted as a priestly figure. For example, the evangelist is careful to observe a detail about Jesus's garment at his crucifixion: "the tunic [*ho chitōn*] was seamless [*araphos*], woven from the top through the whole [*ek tōn anōthen hyphantos di' holou*]" (John 19:23). As others have argued,[94] John's account of Jesus's apparel calls to mind those worn by the high priest. As Jesus's garment is "woven [*hyphantos*]," similar language is used for the high priest's robe and ephod (cf. Exod 28:6, 32 LXX: "woven work [*ergon hyphanton*]"). Jesus's garment is woven "through the whole [*di' holou*]," which corresponds to the way the high priest's garment is said to be woven "wholly [*holon*]" of blue (Exod 28:31 LXX) and was designed "so that it will not tear [*hina mē rēgē*]" (Exod 28:32

[91] Coloe, *God Dwells*, 153.
[92] See, e.g., Kerr, *Temple of Jesus's Body*, 369; Coloe, *God Dwells*, 163.
[93] See, e.g., Brown, *John*, 1:146; Johannes Beutler, S.J. *A Commentary on the Gospel of John*, trans. Michael Tait (Grand Rapids: Eerdmans, 2017 [2013]), 96–97.
[94] See, e.g., John Paul Heil, "Jesus as the Unique High Priest in the Gospel of John," *CBQ* 57, 4 (1995): 741–744.

LXX). That this tradition regarding the high priest's apparel was known is further suggested by Josephus, who similarly describes the high priest's seamless garment (*Ant.* 3.161).[95] Since John 19:36 explicitly describes Jesus in terms of the sacrificial Passover lamb (cf. Exod 12:46), it is difficult to write these parallels off as mere coincidence. John Paul Heil writes, "Thus Jesus's tunic, the undergarment worn under the clothes that the soldiers divided (19:23a), corresponds to the high priestly robe, described as an undergarment ([*hypodytēs*], Exod 28:31; 36:29) worn under the ephod (Exod 36:29)."[96] Finally, Jesus's high priestly role may also be suggested by his earlier statement that he is the Son of Man upon whom the Father has "set his *seal* [*esphragisen*]" (John 6:27) given that a "seal [*sphragidos*]" was associated with the high priest's headpiece (cf. Exod 28:36 LXX).[97]

IMPLICATIONS FOR THE HISTORICAL JESUS

Over the course of the last two chapters, we have examined various traditions in which Jesus is depicted as applying temple and priestly metaphors to himself and to his disciples. Can this be seen as reflecting impressions caused by Jesus himself? We are now in a position to consider this question more fully.

Jesus's Use of Cultic Imagery as Recurrently Attested

In various and sundry ways, our sources indicate that Jesus used imagery associated with the cult in connection with himself and his disciples. Here let us review some of the data we have examined.

Traditions Involving Jesus's Use of Cultic Traditions

1. Jesus Words at the Last Supper Depict His Death as a Sacrifice and the Meal in Cultic Terms
   (1 Cor 11:23–26//Mark 26:26–28//Matt 14:22–24//Luke 22:19–21)
2. Jesus Is the Suffering Servant, a Figure Who Offers Himself as a Sacrifice
   (e.g., Matt 8:17; Matt 8:27; 26:28; Mark 14:24; Luke 22:37; John 3:14; 12:37–38; 1 Cor 11:25)

---

[95] LCL Thackery.
[96] Heil, "Jesus as the Unique High Priest," 733.
[97] Fletcher-Louis, "Jesus as the High Priestly Messiah: Part 2," 60n.6.

3. The Stratification of the Disciples into Groups (One, Three, Twelve, and Seventy) Is Evocative of the Priestly Leaders at Sinai in Exod 24:1–11
(One [e.g., Matt 16:18–19]; the Three [e.g., Mark 5:37]; the Twelve [e.g., Matt 19:28//Luke 22:29–30 [Q?]; and the Seventy [e.g., Luke 10:1])

4. The Twelve Serve as Eschatological Judges, a Role Played by Priests
(Matt 19:28//Luke 22:29–30 [Q?]; cf. Ezek 44:21–24)

5. Jesus Compares Himself and the Disciples to David and His Men Who Enjoyed Priestly Privileges
(Matt 12:1–8//Mark 2:23–28//Luke 6:1–5)

6. Jesus's Garments Communicate Purifying Holiness Like the Temple and Eschatological Priests
(Matt 9:20–22//Mark 5:27–30//Luke 8:44; Matt 14:36//Mark 6:56; cf. Ezek 44:19)

7. The Parable of the Vineyard Indicates Jesus Will Establish New Temple Leaders
(Matt 21:33–41//Mark 12:1–11//Luke 20:9–17)

8. The Disciples Renounce Lands and Kin to "Inherit" Like the Levites
(Matt 19:16, 27–30//Mark 10:17, 28–31//Luke 18:18, 28–30)

9. Jesus Is Like the Cornerstone of the Temple in Psalm 118:22
(Matt 21:42//Mark 12:10//Luke 20:17//Gos Thom §§65–66)

10. Jesus's Disciples Are Like Zion, a City on a Hill
(Matt 5:14)

11. The Disciple Is Compared to a Wise House-Builder, Evoking Solomon as Temple-Builder
(Matt 7:24)

12. Jesus Is the Davidic Temple-Builder and Peter Is Like the Priestly Eliakim
(Matt 16:16–19)

13. Jesus Speaks of His Divine Presence Among the Disciples and Their Cultic Activity in Ways Evocative of the Temple
(Matt 18:20)

14. Jesus Is Identified with the Cultic Stone Imagery
(Luke 20:18; cf. Isa 8:14–15; Dan 2:44–45)[98]

15. Jesus Compares Himself to the Temple (Matt 12:6).

---

[98] See, e.g., Timo Eskola, *A Narrative Theology of the New Testament*, WUNT 350 (Tübingen: Mohr Siebeck, 2015), 65–66.

16. Jesus Connects the Imagery of the Rebuilding of the Temple to Resurrection Imagery
    (John 2:20–21; cf. Mark 14:58)
17. Jesus, Like the High Priest, Is Given a Seal
    (John 6:27)
18. During the Feast of Tabernacles, a Feast That Celebrated the "Consecration" of the Temple, Jesus Speaks of How He Has Been "Consecrated"
    (John 10:36)
19. Jesus Uses Temple Imagery to Describe the Disciples in the Fourth Gospel's Last Supper Narrative
    (e.g., John 17:17–19, 23)
20. Jesus Is the Sacrificial Lamb
    (John 19:36; cf. John 1:29, 36)
21. Jesus Wears a Seamless Garment Like the High Priest Does
    (John 19:23)

Given the history of prejudice against ritual and cult inherited by modern biblical scholarship, it is not surprising that allusions to Israel's liturgical traditions have often been overlooked. In general, one gets the sense that contemporary exegetes have the impression that such imagery occurs sparsely. This, however, is far from the case, as the preceding list demonstrates. Of course, to reiterate, by appealing to recurrent attestation we are not claiming that all of the traditions in our list are historical. Some, however, are harder to dismiss as later inventions than others.

What accounts for this dynamic of the tradition? Should we simply view it as the result of the later community's theology? What points away from this conclusion is that not only is it broadly attested, but that it is also fully consistent with Jesus's identity as a first-century Jewish teacher and that it makes sense in light of his historical effects.

Jesus's Use of Cultic Traditions within a First-Century Jewish Context

It should go without saying that there is nothing un-Jewish about the idea that Jesus would have applied cultic imagery to himself or his disciples. While some have assumed that such traditions must mean that he somehow taught that the temple's sacrifice had been nullified,[99] nothing could

---

[99] See, e.g., Theissen and Merz, *Historical Jesus*, 434–435.

be further from the truth.[100] Here it is important to be reminded of Eyal Regev's work, which shows that the use of cultic metaphors does not necessarily entail a *rejection* of Israel's liturgical rites.[101] A few examples from Jewish literature are worth highlighting.

Psalm 51 compares a broken spirit to sacrifice before going on to commend actual animal sacrifices (cf. Ps 51:17–19):

> The sacrifices of God are a broken spirit;
> a broken and contrite heart, O God, you will not despise.
> Do good to Zion in your good pleasure;
> rebuild the walls of Jerusalem,
> then you will delight in righteous sacrifices,
> in burnt offerings and whole burnt offerings;
> then bulls will be offered on your altar. (Psalm 51:17–19)

Likewise, Psalm 141 speaks of prayer as a sacrifice:

> Let my prayer be set before you as incense,
> and the lifting up of my hands as an evening sacrifice! (Psalm 141:2)

The description of prayer as a sacrifice does not, however, involve a rejection of cultic offerings.

Likewise, Sirach uses cultic metaphors without implying that temple worship is somehow invalid:

> The one who keeps the law makes many offerings;
> the one who heeds the commandments makes a peace offering.
> The one who returns a kindness offers fine flour,
> and the one who gives alms sacrifices a thank offering. (Sirach 35:1–2)

The book goes on to explicitly extol cultic sacrifice:

> The offering of the righteous enriches the altar,
> and its pleasing odor rises before the Most High.
> The sacrifice of the righteous is acceptable,
> and it will never be forgotten.
> Be generous when you worship the Lord,
> and do not stint the first fruits of your hands. (Sirach 35:8–10)

> Fear the Lord and honor the priest,
> and give him his portion, as you have been commanded:
> the first fruits, the guilt offering, the gift of the shoulders,
> the sacrifice of sanctification, and the first fruits of the holy things.
> (Sirach 7:31)

---

[100] See Klawans, "Interpreting the Last Supper," 1–17.
[101] See, e.g., Regev, *The Temple in Early Christianity*, 16.

The author also goes on to speak glowingly of the cultic offerings of Aaron, Samuel, and the high priest Simon (Sir 45:16; 46:16; 50:11–21). Numerous other texts could be mentioned here.

Tobit likewise compares almsgiving to a cultic offering: "for all who practice it charity is an excellent offering in the presence of the Most High" (Tob 4:11). Yet this cannot be read as indicating a rejection of the Jerusalem temple cult. The book looks forward to the rebuilding of the temple after the Babylonian exile (Tob 14:5). The temple is not to be left behind but is part of Israel's future.

Of course, as we have seen, the community of the Dead Sea Scrolls, which did withdraw from the Jerusalem sanctuary, is described as a temple (cf. 1QS 8:4–10). The scrolls even speak of atoning for Israel "without the flesh of burnt offerings and without the fats of sacrifices" speaking of how the community's prayer and good deeds "will be acceptable like a freewill offering" (1QS 9:4–5). Nonetheless, as Timothy Wardle explains, "the offering of animal sacrifices is not denigrated since if it was the analogy would be of little worth."[102] Indeed, 11Q19 envisions the community worshipping at a physical temple, offering burnt offerings and other sacrifices in the future (11Q19 29).

The community-temple imagery in the Scrolls serves us with an extraordinary parallel to passages we have seen where Jesus's disciples are viewed similarly. That the community's leaders are viewed as the foundation of the temple-community offers us a particularly strong parallel with what we find in Matthew 16. It also works well with Jesus's identification of himself as the "cornerstone" of a temple under construction (Matt 21:42//Mark 12:10//Luke 20:17//Gos Thom §§65–66). None of these sayings, however, indicate that Jesus taught that the current temple's sacrifices were invalid. As we have argued, Jesus's probable presence in Jerusalem for the Passover celebration before his death weighs heavily against such a conclusion.

It is also important to note that cultic imagery is applied to the suffering of the righteous in Jewish sources. The *locus classicus* of this concept is the Isaianic Suffering Servant passage (Isa 53:10). While the Servant is certainly described in sacrificial terms, it cannot be argued that this implies the rejection of the temple per se. The book goes on to describe sacrifices being offered in a future temple (Isa 56:7).

---

[102] Timothy Wardle, *The Jerusalem Temple and Early Christian Identity*, WUNT 2/291 (Tübingen: Mohr Siebeck, 2010), 156.

In addition, the Prayer of Azariah identifies the obediential suffering of the righteous in sacrificial terms:

> Yet with a contrite heart and a humble spirit may we be accepted,
>   as though it were with burnt offerings of rams and bulls,
>   and with tens of thousands of fat lambs;
> such *may our sacrifice* be in your sight this day,
>   and may we wholly follow you,
>   for there will be no shame for those who trust in you.
>   (*Prayer of Azariah* 16–17)

Again, nothing here indicates that suffering precludes the need for cultic worship. Other texts could also be mentioned. For example, 4 Maccabees 17 uses the term *hilastērion* – a concept relating to cultic atonement rites (cf., e.g., Exod 25:16; Ezek 43:14, 17, 20) – in reference to the death of the martyrs.[103] Even though this work is written in the post-temple period, one could hardly claim that its use of cultic metaphors reflects the conviction that the temple was somehow illegitimate.

As for the use of cultic imagery in connection with the eucharistic meal, this is also not without precedent. Josephus describes the way the Essenes would purify themselves and then "repair to the refectory, as to some sacred shrine [*kathaper eis hagion ti temenos paraginontai to deipnētērion*]" (*J.W.* 2.129).[104] Philo reports that the Theraputae linked their sacred meals with the priestly meal of the bread of the presence:

> then the young men bring in the table which was mentioned a little while ago, on which was placed that most holy food, the leavened bread, with a seasoning of salt, with which hyssop is mingled, *out of reverence for the sacred table, which lies thus in the holy outer temple; for on this table are placed loaves and salt without seasoning, and the bread is unleavened, and the salt unmixed with anything else*, for it was becoming that the simplest and purest thing should be allotted to the most excellent portion of the priests, as a reward for their ministrations, and that the others should admire similar things, but should abstain from the loaves, in order that those who are the more excellent persons may have the precedence. (*On the Contemplative Life* 81–82).

To find bread of the presence imagery in the Last Supper narrative, then, is not therefore without Jewish precedent.[105] To quote Jonathan Klawans:

---

[103] For a discussion, see Finlan, *Background and Content*, 29–44; McKnight, *Jesus and His Death*, 169–170.
[104] LCL Thackeray.
[105] See Pitre, *Jesus and the Last Supper*, 134–135.

The Last Supper traditions, in their various forms, fit well within the context of ancient Jewish applications of temple significance to non-temple rituals. And thus the historical Last Supper was most likely not an anti-temple symbolic action.[106]

The Problem of Non-Levitical Priests

That Jesus would speak of the disciples in priestly terms is not inherently implausible. Whether he would have actually envisioned them serving as Israel's priests, however, might seem less likely. According to the Torah, the priesthood was reserved for the Levitical descendants of Aaron. Yet the apostles are never said to be Levites. How could non-Levites serve as priests? Three things should be said here.

First, while priestly duties were almost always reserved for Levites after Sinai, there are exceptions. As we have seen, the Davidic king – who was not from the Levitical line – enjoyed priestly prerogatives and David's sons are said to be priests (2 Sam 8:18). Notably, Isaiah announces that God's covenant with David will be extended to all the people (Isa 55:3). Likewise, Elijah's Levitical ancestry is never affirmed in the biblical narrative, yet he is unmistakably presented as performing ritual sacrifice (cf. 1 Kgs 18:30–40). Based on 1 Chronicles 8, later rabbinic tradition would even identify him as a Benjaminite (Gen. Rab. 71.9; cf. 1 Chr 8:27, 40). Despite the lack of clarity over his lineage, Jewish sources nevertheless explicitly identify him as a priest (cf. LAB 48:2; Gen. Rab. 71:9; Tg. Ps.-J. on Deut 30:4).

Second, Jewish expectations for the eschatological age often involve a transcending of the Torah.[107] This is especially evident in texts relating to Israel's cultic life in the future age. For example, in contrast to the restrictions of Deuteronomy 12:13–14, Isaiah foresees sacrifices being offered on an *altar in Egypt* (Isa 19:19).[108] Similarly, Malachi foresees acceptable sacrificial offerings being made among the nations:

I have no pleasure in you, says the LORD of hosts, and I will not accept an offering from your hand. For from the rising of the sun to its setting my name is great among the nations, and in *every place incense is offered to my name, and a pure offering.* For my name my name is great among the nations, says the LORD of hosts. But you profane it when you say that the table of LORD is defiled, and the food for it may be despised. (Malachi 1:10–12)

[106] Klawans, "Interpreting the Last Supper," 17.
[107] For further discussion, see the Appendix.
[108] See John D. Watts, *Isaiah 1–33*, rev. ed., WBC 24 (Dallas: Thomas Nelson, 2005), 315. The passage goes on to describe how the Assyrians will join with the Egyptians in worshiping the Lord (cf. Isa 19:23).

This prophecy has been read by some as contrasting the polluted sacrifices of the corrupt cult with the pure sacrifices of the eschatological age.[109] Either way, acceptable cultic offerings are not restricted to the central sanctuary but are offered "in every place." Something similar can be found in rabbinic texts, which state that in the eschaton certain cultic features of Torah practice will cease – for example, sacrifices – excepting the thank offering (Pesiq. Rab. 12; Lev. Rab. 9.7), or all feasts save Purim and Yom Kippur (Yalqut on Prov 9:2). These texts are late and should not be viewed as expressing ideas necessarily current in Jesus's day. Nonetheless, they do reveal that Jewish sources, following texts like Isaiah, envisioned a transcending of the Torah in the age to come. There is nothing un-Jewish about that principle broadly construed.

What is more, the account of Israel's restoration in Isaiah seems to suggest that the priesthood will be expanded beyond the limits of the Torah. This is evidenced in Isaiah 56, the passage Jesus is said to have quoted in the Synoptic accounts of his temple action, as well as in a vision found in the book's climactic chapter:

And the foreigners who join themselves to the LORD, to *minister* [*ləšārtô*] to him, to love the name of the LORD, and to be his servants, everyone who keeps the sabbath, and does not profane it, and holds fast my covenant—*these I will bring to my holy mountain*, and make them joyful in my house of prayer. Their *burnt offerings and their sacrifices will be accepted on my altar*, for my house shall be called a house of prayer for all peoples. (Isaiah 56:6–7)

And they shall bring all your people from all the nations *as an offering to the LORD*, upon horses, and in chariots, and in litters, and upon mules, and upon camels, to my holy mountain Jerusalem, says the LORD, just *as the Israelites bring their grain offering in a clean vessel to the house of the LORD. And some of them also I will take for priests and for Levites*, says the LORD. (Isaiah 66:20–21)

The expectation in the first passage from Isaiah 56 that foreigners will come "to *minister*" (*ləšārtô*) to the Lord is striking. The verb (*šārat*) is

---

[109] That an eschatological view is likely present is suggested by the similarity of language to the eschatological visions of other prophets contained in the collection of the "Book of the Twelve." See Donald K. Berry, "Malachi's Dual Design: The Close of the Canon and What Comes Afterward," in *Forming Prophetic Literature: Essays on Isaiah and the Twelve in Honor of D. W. Watts*, ed. James W. Watts, John D. W. Watts, and Paul R. House (Sheffield: Sheffield Academic Press, 1996), 277–278; Peter Verhoef, *The Books of Haggai and Malachi*, NICOT (Grand Rapids: Eerdmans, 1987), 228.

used elsewhere to describe priestly activity.[110] That the line was scandalous to some is suggested by the fact that it is absent from the text of the book found at Qumran. The omission is best attributed to discomfort with the apparent suggestion that non-Levites will serve a priestly role.[111] The passage in Isaiah 66 also suggests the bestowal of sacerdotal responsibilities on those who otherwise would not be entrusted with them. Regarding it, Shalom Paul writes:

> In contrast with [the Torah's] ritual hierarchy ... the prophet proposes a revolutionary reform... This means that not only the Levitical priests shall serve in the Temple, but the entire nation of Israel shall minister to the Deity, thus fulfilling the mission of being "a kingdom of priests and a holy nation." (Exodus 19:6)[112]

For the prophet, then, the transcending of the law may be seen as a kind of restoration of Israel's ideal state.

A third observation closely following upon the preceding point should also be made: Jewish eschatology frequently emphasizes the way in which the age to come will involve a return to the state of ideal affairs. For ancient Jews, as Dale Allison explains, "eschatology is protology, a return to the primal state from which humanity fell."[113] With that in mind, it is worth recognizing that, according to the Torah, the priesthood was only restricted to the Levites *after* they alone stood up to those who worshipped the golden calf.[114] Earlier, Moses simply commissions twelve "young men from the people of Israel" (Exod 24:5) to offer sacrifices; in effect, they serve as priests. Conspicuously, there is no mention of their Levitical pedigree. As Jacob Milgrom observes, Numbers 3 suggests the Levites replaced the firstborn (Num 3:11–12).[115] This interpretation is found in the Mishnah and other rabbinic sources (m. Zebaḥ; b. Sabb. 88a). As per Shalom Paul's suggestion, Isaiah, then, would seem

---

[110] See, e.g., Exod 28:35; Num 3:6; 8:26; 18:2; Deut 10:8; 17:12; 1 Kgs 8:11; 2 Chr 5:14; Jer 33:21. Likewise, see Beale, *The Temple and the Church's Mission*, 262n.29.

[111] See Dwight W. Van Winkle, "An Inclusive Authoritative Text in Exclusive Communities," in *Writing and Reading the Scroll of Isaiah*, ed. Craig C. Broyles and Craig A. Evans (Leiden: Brill, 1997), 425.

[112] Shalom M. Paul, *Isaiah 40–66: Translation and Commentary*, Eerdmans Critical Commentary (Grand Rapids: Eerdmans, 2012), 21.

[113] Allison, *End of the Ages*, 91.

[114] See, e.g., A. M. Rodriguez, "Sanctuary Theology in Exodus," *Andrews University Seminary Studies* 24 (1986): 139.

[115] See, e.g., Jacob Milgrom, *JPS Torah Commentary: Numbers* (Philadelphia: Jewish Publication Society, 1990), 432

to envision a scenario in which the priesthood is restored to Israel in its original conception – the nation will truly be a "kingdom of priests" (Exod 19:6).

Is it probable that Jesus thought the eschatological age would involve a return to a situation in which non-Levites would serve at the altar? Our sources do indicate that Jesus's teaching on divorce and remarriage was informed by a desire to restore what was "from the *beginning [apo de archēs]*" (Mark 10:6; cf. Matt 19:8). Jesus was therefore remembered as connecting protology to eschatology. Is there evidence that points in a different direction? Not that I am aware of. It is naturally best to assume that Jesus's eschatology likely involved the same kind of inferences other Jews made – the end would be a return to the beginning. In sum, there would seem to be no reason to think that, in light of his Jewish setting, Jesus could not have envisioned non-Levites serving as priests in the eschatological kingdom.

The Historical Effects of Jesus's Cultic Imagery in Paul

Moreover, as we have seen, cultic associations are already made with Jesus and the community in the letters of Paul, which were written prior to the Jewish War. To reiterate what was said earlier, while Paul obviously speaks of the community as a temple (1 Cor 3:16; 6:19; 2 Cor 6:16), there is no evidence that he rejected the holiness of the Jerusalem temple in the process. Acts, we have already seen, portrays him as *participating* in the temple cult. Indeed, in various ways, what we find in Paul's letters maps nicely onto what we have found in the Jesus tradition.

First, Paul uses cultic metaphors to describe Jesus's death. This coheres with what we found in the Last Supper narrative. Second, Paul explicitly refers to the community as a temple (1 Cor 3:16; 6:19), an idea that our sources also appear to attribute to Jesus. Third, Paul describes himself as having a priestly role (cf. Rom 15:16; 1 Cor 9:13–14). What is interesting here is that Paul was certainly not a Levite; he tells us he was from the tribe of Benjamin (cf. Rom 11:1; Phil 3:5). If Paul could speak of himself, a non-Levite, as having a priestly function, there would seem to be no reason to insist that Jesus could not have likewise used sacerdotal imagery for the disciples. In fact, Paul views his apostolic ministry as equivalent to Peter's (cf. Gal 2:7–8). If Paul saw himself as carrying out a priestly service, there is no reason to think he did not think the same of Peter's ministry.

Moreover, in our preceding analysis of 1 Corinthians 11 we explained that the Pauline account of the Last Supper not only depicts Christ's death in sacrificial terms but also uses cultic language to refer to the eucharistic meal itself. With that in mind, we should highlight the way Paul elsewhere interprets the meaning of the Lord's Supper by means of Israel's sacrificial worship:

The cup of blessing which we bless, is it not a *communion* [*koinōnia*] in the blood of Christ? The bread which we break, is it not a *communion* [*koinōnia*] in the body of Christ? Because there is one bread, we who are many are one body, for we all share of the one bread.[18] Consider Israel according to the flesh: are not they who eat of the sacrifices *partakers* [*koinōnoi*] of the altar? (1 Corinthians 10:16–18)

Paul here explicitly applies the imagery of Israel's cult to the meal Jesus's followers are to celebrate in remembrance of him, an idea we have already detected in the Jesus tradition.

Furthermore, Paul identifies the table of the Lord's Supper as the "table of the Lord [*trapezēs kyriou*]" (1 Cor 10:21). Here Paul uses wording taken from Malachi 1:

in *every place incense is offered to my name, and a pure offering.* For my name is great among the nations, says the LORD of hosts. But you profane it when you say that *the table of the* LORD [LXX: *trapeza kyriou*] is defiled, and the food for it may be despised. (Malachi 1:11–12)

The allusion is not entirely unexpected. Paul has already drawn from this same passage in 1 Corinthians 1:

1 Corinthians 1:2	Malachi 1:11
"those who *in every place* [*en panti topō*] call on the *name* [*to onoma*] of our Lord Jesus Christ."	"in every place [LXX: *en panti topō*] incense is offered to my name [LXX: *tō onomati mou*]."[116]

E. P. Sanders writes, "[Paul] turns to Malachi and Isaiah to contrast the 'table of the Lord' (Mal. 1:7, 12) and 'the table of demons' (Isa. 65:11). The verses in Malachi deal with the 'pollution' or 'defilement' of *the altar* ('the table of the Lord') by *sacrificing* maimed animals."[117]

The apostle's use of Malachi in connection with the Lord's Supper dovetails remarkably well with the idea that the Last Supper tradition

---

[116] Roy E. Ciampa and Brian S. Rosner, *The First Letter to the Corinthians*, PNTC (Grand Rapids: Eerdmans, 2010), 57–58; Roy E. Ciampa and Brian S. Rosner, "1 Corinthians" in *Commentary on the New Testament Use of the Old Testament*, ed. D. A. Carson and G. K. Beale (Grand Rapids: Baker Academic, 2007), 696.

[117] Sanders, *Paul: The Apostle's Life*, 326 (emphasis added).

draws on bread of the presence imagery. Malachi begins by speaking of an offering from the "rising of the sun to its setting," which calls to mind the daily sacrifice of the Tamid, a rite performed every evening and morning. The "pure *offering* [*minha*]" in Malachi 1 would therefore seem connected to this ritual. The bread of the Presence is often described in connection with the *Tamid*.[118] Indeed, Malachi's reference to the Lord's "table" (*trapeza*) uses the precise noun the Septuagint employs for the table of the bread of the presence (e.g., Exod 25:23 LXX).

The Historical Effects of Jesus's Cultic Imagery in Acts

One final piece of relevant data should be mentioned: Acts. In Acts 1, we hear about the disciples' first course of business after the ascension: choosing a successor to Judas. We learn that the apostles narrowed the choice down to two figures who had accompanied Jesus from the beginning. We then read:

Then they prayed and said, "Lord, you know the hearts of all. Show us which one of these two you have chosen to take the place in this ministry and apostleship from which Judas turned aside to go to his own place."And *they cast lots for them* [*edoōkan klērous autois*], and *the lot fell* [*epesen ho klēros*] on Matthias; and he was added to the eleven apostles. (Acts 1:24–26)

At first glance, the whole scene appears strange. Why leave the selection of the next apostle up to lots?

Of course, casting lots could be nothing more than a game of chance. This would seem to be the case with the lot-casting the Roman soldiers engage in at the foot of cross in Luke 23:34. Nevertheless, Luke's Gospel also bears witness to another perspective on casting lots. After the prologue, the very first scene of the Gospel narrative recounts how Zechariah ended up serving in the temple:

Now while he was serving as priest before God when his division was on duty, *according to the custom of the priesthood it fell to him by lot* [*kata to ethos tēs hierateias elache*] to enter the temple of the Lord and burn incense. (Luke 1:9)

Luke's description of lot-casting as "the custom of the priesthood" is consistent with other Jewish texts. That casting lots was associated with determining priestly duties in Israel is clear from numerous sources. For example, we read in 1 Chronicles: "The divisions of the sons of Aaron

---

[118] See Exod 29:38–42; Num 28:3–8; m. Tamid 3:9; 6:1–3; m. Yoma 5:1.

were these. The sons of Aaron: Nadab, Abihu, Eleazar, and Ithamar...
They organized them by lot" (1 Chr 24:1, 5). Numerous other texts
could be mentioned here (cf. 1 Chr 24:7, 31; 25:8, 9; 26:13–14; Neh
10:34; Josephus, *Ant.* 7.367).

The placement of lot-casting at the beginning of Acts, mirrors the
beginning of the Gospel, which opens with the story of Zechariah.
Scholars have long noted the way the material in Acts mirrors the flow of
the narrative of the Gospel.[119] To name a few of the parallels:

- Both works begin with a prologue to Theophilus (Luke 1:1–4; Acts
  1:1–2).
- The commencement of Jesus's ministry in Luke and the apostles' ministry in Acts is described in similar ways. Both begin with an account
  of the descent of the Spirit in visible form: the dove at the baptism of
  Jesus (Luke 3:21–22) and the tongues of fire at Pentecost (Acts 2:1–3
  [described as "baptism" in Acts 1:5]).
- Just as Jesus begins his ministry in Luke with a speech in the Jewish
  place of worship, the synagogue (Luke 4:16–27), Peter launches the
  apostles' ministry in Acts with a speech delivered in the temple (Acts
  2:14–40).
- Near the outset of his Galilean ministry, Jesus heals a man who is
  unable to walk (Luke 5:17–26). Peter's first miracle involves a similar
  figure (Acts 3:1–10).

These parallels run throughout the entirety of Luke-Acts. That Paul
stands accused before rulers *four* times at the end of Acts (Acts 23:
Sanhedrin; Acts 24: Felix; Acts 25: Festus; Acts 26: Agrippa) is hardly a
coincidence; Jesus also appeared before rulers on *four* occasions (Luke
22:54: the high priest and the council; Luke 23:1: Pilate; Luke 23:9:
Herod; Luke 23:11: Pilate). Given this parallel structuring of Luke-
Acts it hardly seems coincidental that both books begin with a scene of
lot-casting.

The lot-casting scene in Acts is only surprising if one has failed to note
the ways the Gospel of Luke has prepared the reader for the idea that the
disciples will be like priests; for example, in the Parable of the Vineyard,
Jesus's instructions that they repeat the eucharistic rite, and judging the
twelve tribes of Israel. Given what comes before it in Luke, the scene in
Acts 1 is almost expected.

---

[119] See, e.g., the classic treatment in Charles H. Talbert, *Literary Patterns, Theological
Themes and the Genre of Luke-Acts*, SBLMS 20 (Missoula: Scholars Press, 1974).

Some may prefer to think that all of these associations should be attributed to the imagination of Jesus's earliest Jewish followers rather than to his own teaching. This, however, would be to ignore all the data before us. Jesus is broadly remembered as using temple and priestly metaphors in his teaching. This makes sense since he appears to have endorsed the temple's rites. At the same time, Jesus was also most probably convinced that the temple would be destroyed. That Jesus therefore spoke of himself and his disciples in terms taken from Israel's liturgical life makes complete sense. That he did so is not only recurrently attested, but also situates him well within his Jewish context *and* makes sense given his historical effects. Moreover, if, as we have argued, Jesus saw himself as the Davidic king in waiting, it makes perfect sense that he would expect to appoint the priestly leaders of the eschatological regime. Is it *possible* that the traditions portraying Jesus as using cultic metaphors only emerged after him in the circle of his very early followers? Yes. Yet the best explanation of all the evidence seems to be that Jesus gave the tradition this shape. Matthew's overall portrait likely brings together themes Jesus's original hearers would have seen as interrelated.

Concluding Thoughts

The quest for an "uninterpreted Jesus" needs to be abandoned – there never was one to be found. In other words, we cannot hope to isolate "uninterpreted" traditions about Jesus – what is typically identified as "authentic" material – from our sources. Memory research has underscored the reality that *all memories are interpreted memories.* Instead of looking for an uninterpreted Jesus *behind* the Gospels, the historian's best way forward is to begin with a different question: *which interpretations* of Jesus likely bring us closest to history? Scholars generally seem to agree that, rather than beginning with a particular saying or tradition, the best place to start is with the big picture. However, we ought also not ignore how our sources arrange their material overall. Matthew, I have argued, offers the Jesus historian much to work with, particularly in understanding Jesus's use of Israel's cultic traditions. We can summarize our findings in four major areas.

JESUS AFFIRMED THE TEMPLE'S HOLINESS

Our preceding analysis has shown that, as many questers agree, it is most likely that Jesus affirmed the temple's legitimacy and participated in its cultic life. This feature of the Jesus tradition is repeatedly affirmed in our sources; it situates Jesus nicely within the first-century Jewish world, and it also explains Jesus's effects, particularly the reports that his early followers continued to worship in the temple after Easter (Luke 24:52; Acts 2:46; 3:1; 21:17–26). In particular, it coheres with the widely attested notion that Jesus was crucified after having gone up to celebrate the Passover festival with his disciples. Jesus, then, would not have counted himself among groups like the Dead Sea community that withdrew from the Jerusalem sanctuary. Jesus went up and participated in the temple's life.

Matthew's portrait confirms this impression. The evangelist has Jesus affirming the sanctity of the temple and its sacrifices (Matt 23:16–22) and instructing others to worship there (e.g., Matt 5:23–24; 8:4; 26:17–19). For Matthew, one way that Jesus's commitment to the law is expressed is in his insistence that cultic obligations should be fulfilled (cf. Matt 8:4). Moreover, within a context regarding the nature of eschatological righteousness, Matthew depicts Jesus teaching about how to offer proper sacrificial worship (Matt 5:23–24). Matthew's general portrait of these matters seems reliable. Even if we conclude that various elements of the Gospel are secondary, Matthew likely preserves an aspect of Jesus's message – the dawning of the eschatological age would not involve repudiation of ritual worship. Moreover, Matthew shows us *what kinds of Jews* were embracing his message. We have yet to find explicit evidence that Essenes found their way into the early Jesus movement. Jesus seems to have attracted the kinds of Jews who were convinced that the temple was holy.

JESUS PREDICTED THE TEMPLE'S COMING RUIN

Given that it is most probable that Jesus affirmed the temple's sanctity, we are confronted by what may seem to be a glaring problem: our sources indicate Jesus also predicted the sanctuary's future destruction. Should this element of the tradition be written-off as the product of post-70 reflection? This is unlikely.

That Jesus predicted the destruction of the temple is widely attested. Without claiming that all of the various traditions in our sources reflect statements made by Jesus himself, it is difficult to insist that they are all the product of later innovation. The way the tradition wrestles with the logion attributed to Jesus by the "false witnesses" (Mark 14:58) points away from an origin in Jesus's later followers. In fact, Jesus would not have been the only figure to speak of coming judgment and the destruction of the temple. Such a tradition also explains the effects of Jesus, particularly, Paul's teaching about Judeans being under a divine indictment (1 Thess 2:14–16), a passage that should not be dismissed as a later interpolation.

Again, Matthew is especially helpful here. In the evangelist's arrangement of the pieces, the demise of the temple is related to a major motif of Jesus's preaching: judgment. Indeed, Jesus's apocalyptic eschatology is on full display in the First Gospel. According to the First Gospel, then, the temple ended up in ruins not because Jesus rejected its sanctity; rather, the Jerusalem leadership is portrayed as having triggered divine judgment. Among other things, the leaders defiled themselves by shedding righteous blood (Matt 23:35). Notably, in Matthew's account of the temple "cleansing," Jesus quotes not only from Jeremiah's prophecy of doom, but also from Isaiah's vision of a future temple (Matt 21:13; cf. Isa 56:7; Jer 7:11), which affirms the existence of temple worship in the eschatological age. In Matthew, Jesus then brings his eschatological healing ministry into the sacred precincts (Matt 21:14). The evangelist's portrait is not simply "Jewish" broadly, but representative of the *kind* of Jewish outlook we would otherwise expect Jesus to express, namely, one rooted in apocalyptic eschatology. As we saw, the temple's desolation is repeatedly emphasized in one of the most influential apocalyptic works of the Second Temple period, namely, the book of Daniel. If Jesus's message was being received by Jews for whom apocalyptic works held sway, it makes sense that he would have spoken of the coming ruin of the sanctuary. *Yet this would not imply that such Jews or Jesus himself believed the temple itself had been desacralized.*

In addition, while apocalyptic works like Daniel recognized that divine retribution would not spare the sanctuary, they nonetheless affirmed the temple's place in the age to come. Matthew's depiction of an apocalyptic Jesus helps us understand why our sources indicate that people concluded that Jesus's predictions of the temple being destroyed also involved a claim that he would *rebuild* the temple. To be sure, the two ideas do not necessarily follow. Jesus ben Ananias was not, for example, said to claim the temple would be *rebuilt*. Why then was Jesus remembered as anticipating some sort of *future* sanctuary? The best explanation of the data is that Jesus, like Daniel, upheld a place for the cult in the eschatological restoration.

JESUS'S TEMPLE CONCERNS AND HIS DAVIDIC ROLE

Moreover, any discussion of Jewish attitudes toward the temple would have to take into account the way in which the sanctuary was associated with Davidic traditions. While it was certainly possible for Jews to think about the temple without making recourse to David and eschatological hopes regarding his line, it seems Jesus's relationship to the temple was in fact shaped by such ideas. We have argued that Jesus likely intentionally said and did things that evoked Davidic expectations. This idea is broadly attested in our gospels and is bound up with features of the tradition difficult to write-off as later inventions: Jesus's preaching of the kingdom, his appointment of twelve, his use of parables, and his crucifixion as "king of the Jews." Moreover, that Jesus triggered Davidic associations situates him well within the first-century Jewish world and explains the way his earliest believers wrote about him (e.g., Paul).

Matthew makes a point of emphasizing the connection between Jesus's Davidic identity and his activity in the temple. Yet Matthew did not create this association. Our other sources repeatedly connect Jesus's teaching about the temple to Davidic traditions. Indeed, this not only makes sense within Jesus's Jewish context, the Davidic-temple matrix can also be seen in the writings of Paul and other early followers of Jesus. Matthew, therefore, amplifies an aspect of the tradition we have good reason to trace back to Jesus. Notably, Matthew especially links Jesus's role as Davidic Messiah to his establishment of the *ekklēsia*, which the evangelist portrays in terms of temple imagery. This raises a final question: Did Jesus apply temple imagery to himself and his disciples?

JESUS'S USE OF TEMPLE IMAGERY FOR HIMSELF AND HIS FOLLOWERS

One point we have repeatedly stressed in this study is that Jesus could both affirm the sanctity of the Jerusalem sanctuary and employ temple metaphors in his teaching. Other Jewish sources like the Psalms or Sirach are able to speak of activities such as almsgiving or righteous suffering as having atoning value without rejecting the holiness of the temple. Jesus, we have argued, likely did something similar.

Matthew portrays Jesus as applying cultic imagery to himself and to his disciples. This need not be viewed as entailing rejection of the Jerusalem temple's holiness per se. It should not be attributed to a post-70 setting since Paul speaks of the community as a sanctuary long before the temple was destroyed. Indeed, although often overlooked – no doubt due to anti-ritual biases that have long permeated the guild – Jesus is often depicted as applying temple and priestly metaphors to himself and to the community. Some of these traditions may be dismissed as secondary, but others are more difficult to view as later inventions.

Once again, it is helpful to pay attention in particular to Matthew's arrangement of the pieces. Though Jesus announces the desolation of the holy place in his account, he never unambiguously affirms in the Gospel that a physical structure will be rebuilt. Jesus is remembered as drawing on eschatological temple traditions, yet the traditions in which he speaks of future temple-building indicate he was speaking of himself and/or the community. Matthew underscores this impression – Jesus is the cornerstone of a sanctuary that is under construction (Matt 21:42) and the one who builds a temple, the *ekklēsia* (Matt 16:18).

That Jesus used temple imagery in reference to his own future vindication and in reference to the disciples without calling into question the sanctity of the temple would explain his effects. On the one hand, as we have seen, the disciples appear to have continued to worship in the temple (Luke 24:52; Acts 2:46; 3:1; 21:17–26). On the other hand, they *also* view themselves as a sanctuary (1 Cor 3:16; 6:19; 2 Cor 6:16). In Acts, the disciples worship in the temple *and* "break bread," a reference that likely includes the idea that they celebrated the eucharist (Luke 22:19; cf. 1 Cor 10:16: "the bread that we break"), following Jesus's directives at the Last Supper: "Do this in remembrance of me" (Luke 22:19).[1] As we have seen, the community understood this meal in cultic terms. Yet somehow participation in it did not rule out continuing to worship at the Jerusalem temple.

Matthew leaves us with a witness to Jesus that must be explained, not written off: Jesus reverenced the temple while also applying its imagery to himself and the community. Matthew, I would argue, embodies the scribe who "brings out of his treasure what is new and what is old" (Matt 13:52). He certainly depends upon traditional material, but his creativity should also not be denied. Nonetheless, what he presents to us is a treasure. *Matthew's overall portrait presents us with a historically plausible picture: Jesus's affirmation of the holiness of the Jewish temple cult served as the basis for the early believers' tendency to view themselves and their practices in terms of it.* The *ekklēsia* was a temple and its leaders were priestly figures. This outlook did not entail a rejection of Jewishness but was an expression of it.

---

[1] See, e.g., Fitzmyer, *Acts*, 270–271; Keener, *Acts*, 2:1002.

Appendix: Matthew within Jewish Partings

Matthew has gained a reputation as a "Jewish" gospel. Here we will look at some of the reasons for this. We will also address arguments from those who have dissented from this position.

THE QUESTION OF AUTHORSHIP

The recognition of Matthew's Jewish character is no late development. The reception of the work as "the Gospel according to Matthew" – a title that, with the possible exception of the incomplete fragment 𝔓¹, is attested in the earliest manuscripts of the Gospel that preserve a title page[1] – indicates that from a very early period it was associated with one of Jesus's Jewish disciples. This is reinforced by ancient ecclesiastical writers. Origen says that Matthew wrote to the "Hebrews" (*Hebraiois*).[2] Various sources quoted by Eusebius agree on this point, with some claiming that it was originally composed in Hebrew:

- Papias' taught that Matthew "collected the words [*ta logia synetaxato*] in the Hebrew language [*dialektō*]."[3]
- Irenaeus believed that Matthew wrote a gospel "among the Hebrews [*en tois Hebraiois*] ... in their own language [*tē idia autōn dialektō*]."[4]

---

[1] For a further discussion, see Simon Gathercole, "The Titles of the Gospels in the Earliest New Testament Manuscripts," *ZNW* 104 (2013): 38–39.

[2] Origen, *Comm. Jo.* 1.22. See also Eusebius, *Hist. Eccl.* 6.25.4.

[3] Eusebius, *Hist. Eccl.* 3.39.16.

[4] Eusebius, *Hist. Eccl.* 5.8.2. *Pace* Robert H. Gundry (*Matthew: A Commentary on His Handbook for a Mixed Church Under Persecution*, 2nd ed. [Grand Rapids: Eerdmans,

- Origen held that the evangelist's audience was "believing people from Judaism [*tois apo Ioudaismou pisteusasin*]."[5]
- Pantaenus of Alexandria is said to have discovered that believers in India had preserved a Hebrew copy of Matthew's Gospel.[6]

Following these earlier writers, later sources would confidently repeat the tradition that Matthew wrote to Jewish believers.[7]

For Jerome, a Hebrew gospel was no mere pious legend; he quotes repeatedly from a text that he says was used by the Ebionites and Nazarenes.[8] He identifies this work as that "which many call the authentic Matthew [*quod vocatur a plerisque Mathei authenticum*]."[9] Jerome does not appear to endorse this view, though. Origen, Pantaenus' Alexandrian heir, appears to have quoted from the same work Jerome knew, though he does not specifically identify it as the work of the apostle Matthew.[10] Notably, quotations from this work involve material not found in canonical Matthew, including Jesus speaking of the holy spirit as "my mother."[11] The relationship, then, of this Hebrew text to canonical Greek Matthew is unclear. What we can say is that the Hebrew Gospel known to Jerome does not appear to be merely a complete Hebrew version of canonical Matthew.

The possibility that there was a pre-canonical source stemming from the apostle Matthew is entertained by some prominent contemporary scholars.[12] That said, contemporary exegetes almost universally reject apostolic authorship of the canonical Gospel.[13] For one thing, its Greek

---

1994], 619–620), the expression does not likely mean that Matthew wrote Greek in a Hebraic way. See D. A. Carson and Douglas A. Moo, *An Introduction to the New Testament* (Grand Rapids: Zondervan, 2005), 145.

5 Eusebius, *Hist. Eccl.* 6.25.4.
6 Eusebius, *Hist. Eccl.* 5.9.3.
7 See John Chrysostom, *Hom. Matt.* 1.3; Jerome, *Prol. Matt.*; Gregory of Nazianzus, *Carmina dogmatica*, 1.12.6–9.
8 See, e.g., *Epist.* 20.5; *Comm. Matt.* 2.5; 6.11; 12:13; 23.35; 27.16; 27:51 (and *Epist.* 120.8.2); *Comm. Isa.* 11:1–3; *Pelag.* 3.2; *Comm. Mich.* 7:7.
9 *Comm. Matt.* 12:13.
10 *Comm. Jo.* 2.12.87; cf. with Jerome, *Comm. Mich.* 7:7; *Comm. Isa.* 40:9; *Comm. Ezech.* 16:13.
11 See, e.g., Origen, *Comm. Jo.* 2.12.87.
12 For further discussion, see David C. Sim, "The Gospel of Matthew, John the Elder and the Papias Tradition: A Response to R. H. Gundry," *HvTSt* 63 (2007): 287–291.
13 A few exceptions exist. See Patrick Schreiner, *Matthew: Disciple and Scribe: The First Gospel and Its Portrait of Jesus* (Grand Rapids: Baker Academic, 2019), 7n.1; France, *Gospel of Matthew*, 15 ("as likely a candidate as any"); Keener, *Matthew*, 40. See also Scot McKnight, *Sermon on the Mount*, SGBC (Grand Rapids: Zondervan, 2013), 47–51 who, despite hesitations, concludes the attribution is "the most likely conclusion we can draw" (51).

does not look like a translation from Hebrew.[14] This observation is admittedly weak since a talented translator might be able to obscure such an origin.[15] A weightier observation is that the Gospel never expressly identifies its author in its main text. Even this, however, is not necessarily decisive. The anonymous style of narration may reflect an attempt to emulate the scriptures of Israel. The narrators of works like 1 Samuel or 2 Kings fail to identify themselves.[16] It must be conceded, then, that its attribution to the apostle is hard to explain.[17] If the work aims at addressing the concerns of Jews, why attribute it to a former tax collector instead of someone else like James, a revered figure in the Jerusalem church?

More than anything else, however, it is the scholarly consensus regarding Markan priority that has undercut support for the First Gospel's apostolic authorship.[18] Why would the apostle depend so heavily on Mark's description of his own conversion (cf. Matt 9:9; Mark 2:14)?[19] If early traditions about the Petrine origins of Mark are accurate,[20] Matthew's deference for Mark might be attributed to the evangelist's respect for Peter, whose unique role among the twelve is emphasized in Matthew's special material (e.g., Matt 16:17–19; 14:28–31; 17:24–27). Nonetheless, such a position would depend upon making a number of assumptions – for example, the reliability of Papias' statement regarding the Petrine origins of Mark's Gospel – which are questioned by many scholars.[21] The vast majority of contemporary scholars therefore reject the notion that Matthew wrote the canonical Gospel of Matthew. This study does not dispute this conclusion and simply refers to the evangelist as "Matthew" in accord with scholarly convention.

---

[14] Sim, "Gospel of Matthew, John the Elder," 287.

[15] Davies and Allison, *Matthew*, 1:12.

[16] See Bart D. Ehrman, *Forgery and Counterforgery* (Oxford: Oxford University Press, 2013), 50; Collins, *Mark*, 41.

[17] See, e.g., Martin Hengel, *The Four Gospels and the One Gospel of Jesus Christ*, trans. John Bowdon (Harrisburg: 2000), 71.

[18] See, e.g., the overview of earlier scholarship in Repschinski, *Controversy Stories*, 15–17.

[19] See, e.g., McKnight, *Sermon on the Mount*, 50.

[20] The most influential defender of this position is Richard Bauckham, *Jesus and the Eyewitnesses: The Gospels as Eyewitness Testimony*, 2nd ed. (Grand Rapids: Eerdmans, 2017).

[21] For a critique of Bauckham's argument, see Stephen J. Patterson, "Can You Trust a Gospel? A Review of Richard Bauckham's *Jesus and the Eyewitnesses*," *JSHJ* 6 (2008): 194–210.

Matthew's Jewish Emphases

Notwithstanding the difficulties involved with identifying the Gospel's author, it is nonetheless true that the "broad consensus" is that the author was Jewish.[22] One of the main reasons for this is that, as we explained in the introduction, the evangelist emphasizes Jesus's Jewishness and appears sensitive to concerns Jews may have had about Jesus's ministry.[23] Without attempting to identify every example of this, we can generally speak of five major areas where this is on display.

1. *Torah Observance*. Matthew includes some of the most forceful sayings of Jesus regarding the permanence of the Torah (Matt 5:17–20). For example, we read:

> Whoever therefore who loosens one of the least of these commandments [*lusē mian tōn entolōn toutōn tōn elachistōn*] and teaches others to do so will be called least in the kingdom of heaven. But whoever does them and teaches them shall be called great in the kingdom of heaven. (Matthew 5:19)

This verse seems to suggest that Jesus kept the Torah in all of its details.[24] Even ancient and medieval writers such as Aquinas caught this implication.[25] As explained in the introduction, Jesus's teaching about the law's importance in Matthew is evident in other ways.

2. *Jesus's Endorsement of Jewish Authorities*. Given the fact that the scribes and Pharisees frequently oppose Jesus in the Gospel, the explicit endorsement of their teaching authority in Matthew 23 is startling:

> The scribes and the Pharisees sit on Moses's seat. Therefore, do and observe whatever they tell you [*panta oun hosa ean eipōsin hymin poiēsate kai tēreite*]. (Matthew 23:2–3)

In addition, the recognition of Jewish authorities is reinforced by the reference to the disciples being punished in synagogues (Matt 10:17). Its readers apparently think they are under synagogue authority and are, therefore, Jewish.[26]

3. *Jesus's Israel-Focused Mission*. Jesus's public ministry in Matthew is especially focused on Israel. Two passages that are indicative of this especially stand out:

---

[22] See Konradt, *Matthew*, 17.
[23] See, e.g., Heinrich Julius Holtzmann, *Die synoptischen Evangelien: ihr Ursprung und geschichtlicher Charakter* (Leipzig: Wilhelm Engelmann, 1863), 377–384.
[24] Zahn, *Das Evangelium nach Matthäus*, 220.
[25] See, e.g., Aquinas, *Summa Theologiae*, III, q. 40, art. 4.
[26] Levine, "Concluding Reflections," 454; Davies and Allison, *Matthew*, 2:183.

Go nowhere among the gentiles, and enter no town of the Samaritans, *but go rather to the lost sheep of the house of Israel.* (Matthew 10:6)

I was sent *only* to *the lost sheep of the house of Israel.* (Matthew 15:24)

As explained in the introduction of this volume, Matthew also appears to downplay Mark's descriptions of Jesus's activity in gentile regions.[27] A formal mission to the gentiles begins only after the resurrection (cf. Matt 28:19–20).

4. *Matthew's Use of Scripture.* Compared with Mark, Anne O'Leary explains, in Matthew, "the use of the Old Testament is much more comprehensive and intensive."[28] Matthew also amplifies the allusions to the Jewish scriptures in his narrative, adjusting features of Mark to better conform to scriptural language.[29] Moreover, while the quotations in Mark follow the Septuagint, the so-called fulfillment quotations which are unique to Matthew (Matt 1:23; 2:15, 17–18, 23; 4:14–16; 8:17; 12:17–21; 13:35; 21:4–5; 27:9) often conform more closely to the Hebrew of the Masoretic Text.[30]

5. *Jesus's Reverence for the Temple.* Our study has underscored Jesus's respect for the Jerusalem temple. As we have seen, he instructs people to participate in the Jerusalem temple cult (Matt 8:4; 5:23–24; 26:17–19) and even proclaims its sanctity (Matt 23:16–21). As we have seen, this is a further expression of Jesus's Jewish piety in Matthew.

Tensions with Jewish Sensibilities in Matthew

Nevertheless, not all have been convinced of the Gospel of Matthew's Jewish character.[31] The first major work to push back against Matthew's Jewishness came from Kenneth W. Clark (1947).[32] Others have followed.[33] Some have argued that while Matthew himself was Jewish, the Gospel largely reflects a primarily gentile rather than Jewish perspective.[34]

---

[27] For the following, see Sim, "Matthew and Jesus of Nazareth," 156–159.
[28] Anne M. O'Leary, *Matthew's Judaization of Mark: Examined in the Context of the Use of Sources in Graeco-Roman Antiquity,* LNTS 323 (London: T&T Clark, 2006), 137.
[29] See O'Leary, *Matthew's Judaization of Mark,* 118–171.
[30] Hüber, "OT Quotations in the New Testament," 4:1099.
[31] See, e.g., Eduard Reuss, *Geschichte der heiligen Schriften, Neuen Testamentes* (Braunschweig: C. A. Schwetschke und Sohn [M. Bruhn], 1860), 182.
[32] Kenneth W. Clark, "The Gentile Bias of Matthew," *JBL* 66 (1947): 165–172.
[33] See, e.g., John P. Meier, *Law and History in Matthew's Gospel,* AnBib 71 (Rome: Biblical Institute Press, 1976); George Strecker, *Der Weg der Gerechtigkeit: Untersuchung zur Theologie des Matthäus,* 3rd ed. (Göttingen: Vandenhoeck & Ruprecht, 1971).
[34] See, e.g., Hare, *Persecution.*

Yet, although John Meier thinks it is more probable than not that the evangelist was a gentile, he nevertheless acknowledges that the evidence is "not so clear-cut."[35] Recent works, in fact, are showing that passages suggestive of tensions with Jewish sensibilities have been misinterpreted. Here let us briefly address the key pieces of evidence often cited.

1. *The Rejection of Jesus by the Crowds in the Passion (Matt 27:25)*. Infamously, Matthew has the Jewish crowd take responsibility for Jesus's death: "His blood be on us and on our children!" (Matt 27:25). This passage has long been used in the service of antisemitism.[36] Yet the verse is best read in reference to 70 CE and cannot be used to signify the wholesale rejection of Israel. In the Gospel, Jesus teaches that his own disciples – *Jewish* followers – will sit on thrones and judge *the twelve tribes* of Israel (Matt 19:28). Jesus seems to think Israel will be restored (more on this later).

It is also worth noting that, when it comes to Jesus's Galilean ministry, the crowds are typically sympathetic to Jesus's preaching.[37] The scene at the end of the Sermon on the Mount is instructive:

> And it happened, when Jesus had completed these words, the crowds were astonished at his teaching, for he was teaching them as one having authority, and not as their scribes. And when he came down from the mountain, great crowds followed him. (Matthew 7:28–8:1)

Here the Galilean "crowds" are distinguished from "their scribes." The former "follow" (*ákoloutheō*) him (cf. Matt 8:1; 13:2; 14:13–14), the latter do not. The crowds repeatedly respond positively to Jesus (and to John the Baptist; cf. 8:1, 18; 13:2; 14:13–14; 19:2, 13; 20:29; 21:8–9, 14–15; 23:1; 26:5). To be sure, it is not simply the case that all Jews accept Jesus in Matthew (e.g., Matt 11:20–24). Nevertheless, the inadequacy of the people's response to him is typically tied to the leaders' rejection of him (cf. Matt 12:38–42; Matt 23:29–36). In Matthew 15, Jesus says of them: "Let them alone: they are blind guides of the blind. And if the blind lead the blind, both will fall into a pit" (Matt 15:14). The leaders are therefore portrayed as in some way responsible for the people's failure to embrace Jesus's message – the people end up in a "pit" because of the blind guides. This is on full display in the passion narrative, where

---

[35] Meier, *Law and History*, 17.
[36] See, e.g., John Kampen, "The Problem of Christian Anti-Semitism and a Sectarian Reading of the Gospel of Matthew: The Trial of Jesus," in *Matthew within Judaism*, 371–397.
[37] See Runesson, *Divine Wrath*, 270–307.

the crowds' rejection of Jesus is explicitly attributed to the instigation of the chief priests and elders (Matt 27:20).

2. *The Parable of the Wicked Tenants (Matt 21:33–46).* Though the parable has long been read as indicating God's "replacement" of Israel, as we explained earlier in Chapter 6, this misinterprets the symbolism of the story – it is the tenants (=leaders) who are replaced, not the vineyard itself.

3. *The "Many" vs. the "Sons of the Kingdom" (Matt 8:11–12).* Much attention has been given to Jesus's statement in Matthew 8: "I tell you, *many [polloi]* will come from east and west and will eat with Abraham and Isaac and Jacob in the kingdom of heaven, while *the sons of the kingdom [huioi tēs basileias]* will be cast out into the outer darkness" (Matt 8:11–12). The description of "many" coming from a distance is often seen as an anticipation of the gentile mission announced at the end of the Gospel (Matt 28:19). Since this group seems to stand in opposition to the "sons of the kingdom," the logion has been thought to teach replacement theology, that is, to depict the gentile church supplanting Israel.[38] This interpretation has also been sharply criticized.

One cannot assume that the "many" who come "from east and west" are necessarily gentiles. The saying is probably best taken as alluding to Jewish hopes for the ingathering of the scattered tribes of Israel.[39] Furthermore, while *"the sons of the kingdom [huioi tēs basileias]"* are *"cast out [ekblēthēsontai],"* this does not mean that Matthew thinks Israel as a whole will be damned. Jesus elsewhere uses the terminology of "sons of the kingdom" to describe those who accept his teaching (Matt 13:38), which would include his Jewish disciples. Jesus's teaching in Matthew 8, therefore, could be taken as a warning that even those in the believing community can put their kingdom status at risk if they ignore the wider mission envisioned by Jesus.[40] Yet even if gentiles are included in the saying about many coming from east and west,[41] to interpret the passage as indicative of a replacement theology reads too much into it. While Matthew certainly does affirm a post-Easter mission to gentiles (Matt 28:19) and frequently previews this with

---

[38] See list of advocates of this reading in Konradt, *Israel, Church, and the Gentiles,* 202n.181.

[39] Pitre, *Jesus, the Tribulation, and the End of the Exile,* 279–283; Dale C. Allison, Jr., "Who Will Come from East and West? Observations on Matt 8:11–12-Luke 13:28–29," *IBS* 11 (1989): 158–170.

[40] See Konradt, *Israel, Church, and the Gentiles,* 207–208.

[41] See, e.g., Allison, *Jesus Tradition in Q,* 191.

examples of non-Jews acknowledging Jesus's identity – for example, the magi (Matt 2:1–12), a Canaanite woman (Matt 15:21–28), the centurion (Matt 27:54) – this does not imply the rejection of Israel as a whole. Other Jewish sources frequently depicted gentile inclusion in the eschatological age (e.g., Isa 42:6; 49:6; 56:7; Zech 14:16; 1 En 48:4–5).[42] Jesus's statement that an unrepentant member of the community ought to be treated like "a gentile and a tax collector" (Matt 18:17) is instructive; the general sinful status of a gentile is affirmed but, as with tax collectors, they too are to be evangelized.

4. *"Their Synagogues" (Matt 4:23; 9:35; 12:9; 13:54; 10:17; cf. Matt 23:34).* As we mentioned in the introduction, the appearance of "their synagogues" has led many to conclude that Matthew's readers had parted ways with "Judaism." Yet, as explained earlier, this must be challenged. The phrase may point to conflict between Jesus's disciples and *certain* Jewish synagogues, probably those especially associated with the Pharisees.[43]

5. *"The Jews" and the Report that Jesus's Body Was Stolen (Matt 28:15).* Matthew reports that the soldiers who were stationed at the tomb of Jesus were paid off by the Jewish leaders and instructed to report that his disciples had stolen his body. According to the evangelist, "this story is still told *among Jews to this day*" (Matt 28:15: *para Ioudaiois mechri tēs sēmeron hēmeras*). This passage is often held up as evidence that Matthew's community views itself as standing "outside" Judaism (*extra muros*).[44] Yet, contrary to what most English Bible translations indicate, no definite article appears in the Greek text of the passage; the evangelist is best seen as asserting that the report circulated "among Jews to this day."[45] It need not be read as implying that it was spread by "all Jews."[46]

6. *Judgment on Israel.* The polemics against the Pharisees and other Jewish leaders is indicative of the kinds of intramural Jewish polemics attested in the Dead Sea Scrolls.[47] There is no reason to insist this dimension of the Gospel's portrait of Jesus reflects an "anti-Jewish" attitude.

---

[42] See, e.g., Paula Fredriksen, *Paul: The Pagan's Apostle* (New Haven: Yale University Press, 2017), 73–77.

[43] See, e.g., Runesson, "Behind the Gospel of Matthew," 460–471.

[44] See, e.g., Nils Dahl, "Die Passionsgeschichte bei Matthäus," *NTS* 2 (1955): 28.

[45] See, e.g. Wesley G. Olmstead, *Matthew 15–28: A Handbook on the Greek Text* (Waco: Baylor University Press, 2019), 410.

[46] Sim, *Gospel of Matthew and Christian Judaism*, 149–150.

[47] Kampen, *Matthew within Sectarian Judaism*, 49–59, 162–164.

7. *Conflating the Pharisees and Sadducees.* Since Jesus speaks of "the teaching of the Pharisees and Sadducees" (Matt 16:11–12), Meier thinks the evangelist is ignorant that the two groups took different positions. Furthermore, Meier analyzes the episode of the Sadducees' question regarding the resurrection (Matt 22:23). According to him, the evangelist is unaware that the Sadducees as a group rejected the notion of resurrection of the dead (Matt 22:23; vs. Mark 12:18; Luke 20:27).[48] In context, however, "the teaching of the Pharisees and Sadducees" (Matt 16:12) likely refers to these groups' rejection of *Jesus* and is not necessarily a reference in general to other beliefs.[49] Furthermore, it must not be overlooked that Matthew only has *Sadducees* questioning the resurrection, which fits what we know about them.

8. *"Whitewashed Tombs" (Matt 23:27).* Some have observed that Jesus's description of "white-washed tombs [*taphois kekoniamenois*] that outwardly appear beautiful [*hoitines exōthen men phainontai hōraioi*]" betrays a lack of familiarity with Jewish sensibilities since such a practice does not cohere with Jewish purity concerns (cf. b. B. Qam. 69a).[50] Yet there are various ways to read the logion that resolve this difficulty. It could be a reference to monuments that had been erected.[51]

9. *"I Desire Mercy Not Sacrifice" (Matt 9:13; 12:7).* These verses, which quote from Hosea, are treated in this study. As we explained, those who take an anti-cultic reading of them must ignore the way the passage was understood in other Jewish sources. They also must disregard the thrust of sayings such as Jesus's words about the holiness of the temple and its altar (Matt 23:16–23), which could hardly have been included if the evangelist was set on portraying Jesus as rejecting the temple's legitimacy.

Jesus and the Law in Matthew

One of the perennial difficulties of interpreting Matthew's Gospel is explaining Jesus's relationship to the Torah. His forceful insistence that he has not come to abolish the law at the beginning of the Sermon on the Mount (Matt 5:17–20) has seemed to clash with the so-called "six antitheses" that follow (Matt 5:21–48). In these sayings, Jesus cites a

---

48 See Meier, *Law and History*, 16–19.
49 Repschinksi, *Controversy Stories*, 33–34; Davies and Allison, *Matthew*, 1:31–32; 2:592.
50 Luz, *Matthew*, 1:48; 3:130.
51 See Cohen, *Matthew and the Mishnah*, 144n.24; Davies and Allison, *Matthew*, 301–302.

passage from the Torah and then offers a teaching which begins, "but I say to you [*egō de legō hymin*]" (5:22, 28, 32, 34, 39, 44). While many of these statements can be read as intensifications of the law's requirements, others are more difficult to explain along these lines. Among other things, the Torah's sanctioning of divorce and remarriage is said to amount to "adultery" (Matt 5:31–32). Jesus, then, appears to explicitly forbid what the law upholds.[52] Similar tensions with Jesus's endorsement of the law are also held to be found later in the gospel (e.g., the question of the temple tax in Matt 17:24–27, a story we have examined). To these claims a few points need to be made.

First, tensions with the Torah would hardly constitute clear evidence against Matthew's Jewish character. There are tensions within the Pentateuch itself. For example, whereas Leviticus prohibits the killing of animals outside of the sanctuary (Lev 17:1–4), Deuteronomy explicitly allows the practice (Deut 12:15–24).[53] Furthermore, discontinuity abounds in other Jewish scriptures. According to the Chronicler, David redefined the duties of the priests and Levites from what their task had been in the Torah (cf. 1 Chronicles 15–16; 23–27; cf. e.g., Exod 29–30).[54] Furthermore, Jewish texts from the first-century exhibit departures from the Torah as well. To give one example, while the Torah permits polygamy and divorce, the Dead Sea Scrolls take a different stand (11Q19 57:17–18; CD 4:19–21; 5:1–2).[55] Simon Joseph remarks: "the authors of CD [Damascus Document] and 11QT [11QTemple] seem to have assumed the scribal and exegetical freedom to *revise* Torah."[56]

Second, drawing on the work of Hindy Najman, John Kampen explains that ancient Jews viewed authoritative texts outside the Torah as "seconding Sinai."[57] In other words, the "law" could refer to material not found in the books of the Pentateuch. To name a few examples:

---

[52] See Paul Foster, *Community, Law and Mission in Matthew's Gospel*, WUNT 2/177 (Tübingen: Mohr Siebeck, 2004), 106–114.

[53] Attempts to harmonize the two laws have been unconvincing. See, e.g., Christophe Nihan, *From Priestly Torah to Pentateuch: A Study in the Composition of the Book of Leviticus*, FAT 2/25 (Tübingen: Mohr Siebeck, 2007), 411.

[54] See, e.g., Schweitzer, *Reading Utopia*, 142.

[55] Whether the scrolls permit divorce is debated, but they clearly prohibit polygamy. See Joseph, *Jesus and Temple*, 51–53.

[56] Joseph, *Jesus and the Temple*, 53.

[57] Kampen, *Matthew within Sectarian Judaism*, 88–90; Hindy J. Najman, *Seconding Sinai: The Development of Mosaic Discourse in Second Temple Judaism*, JSJSup 77 (Leiden: Brill, 2003).

- Ezra is said arrange the temple service of the priests and Levites according to their divisions, following what was "written in the book of Moses" (Ezra 6:18). Yet these divisions are never mentioned in the Pentateuch. Notably, 2 Chronicles attributes the origin of these divisions to David and Solomon (cf. 2 Chr 35:2–5).
- In the Dead Sea Scrolls, the term "law of Moses" is used to refer to the oath sworn by the sect, not just to the so-called five books of Moses (cf. CD 15:8–9; 1QS 8:1–27).
- Jubilees, as mentioned earlier, reinterprets certain laws, presenting its understanding as essentially the law of Moses.

In sum, the "law" need not be limited strictly to "texts of the Pentateuch" but could refer to passages that were believed to offer authoritative interpretation of what Moses had received at Sinai. These works were viewed as continuing the Mosaic discourse.[58]

Third, as we show in our discussion in Chapter 7, tensions with the Torah are often found in texts involving eschatological scenarios. As Simon Joseph shows, the teaching on marriage in the Dead Sea Scrolls also appears governed by this eschatological outlook.[59] Indeed, some Qumran texts suggest that the eschaton will entail a change in the law.[60] For example, 1QRule of the Community (1QS) 9:9–11 says:

They should not depart from any counsel of the law in order to walk in complete stubbornness of their heart, but instead shall be ruled by the first directives which the men of the Community began to be taught *until* the prophet comes, and the messiahs of Aaron and Israel.[61]

Here the "counsel of the law" is equated with the "first directives." These are said to remain in place "until" the future prophet comes. A tension seems to exist between these precepts and the eschatological age. Joseph writes, "the laws described in CD [Damascus Document] only apply to observing the Sabbath during the *current* age of wickedness."[62]

The preceding discussion is relevant for interpreting Matthew. First, in Matthew 5, Jesus's words, "but I say to you [*egō de legō hymin*]," root

---

[58] For further discussion, see John Kampen, "Torah's Authority in the Major Sectarian Rules Texts from Qumran," in *The Scrolls and Biblical Traditions: Proceedings of the Seventh Meeting of the IOQS in Helsinki*, ed. George J. Brooke, Daniel K. Falk, Eibert J. C. Tigchelaar, and Molly M. Zahn, STDJ 104 (Leiden: Brill, 2012), 231–254.

[59] Joseph, *Jesus and Temple*, 53–54.

[60] Joseph, *Jesus and Temple*, 53–54.

[61] Translation slightly adapted from *DSSSE* 1:91–93.

[62] Joseph, *Jesus and the Temple*, 51.

his teaching about the law in his *own* authority.[63] The antitheses, then, are closely tied to the important Christological assertion in the preceding lines about Jesus's fulfillment of the law: Jesus – the "Christ" (Matt 1:1) – has come not to "abolish [*katalysai*]" the law and the prophets but so that they may be "fulfilled [*plērōsai*]" (Matt 5:17). In Matthew, Jesus is presented as the authoritative teacher of the law par excellence. While various features of the narrative reinforce this, the point is made most dramatically in his sweeping declaration at the end of the gospel: "All authority in heaven and on earth has been given to me" (Matt 28:18). For the evangelist, Jesus is the final authority on how Torah must be interpreted.

Second, the language of "fulfillment" is inextricably bound up with the notion of prophecy in Matthew – Jesus is understood as the one who realizes what the prophets described (e.g., Matt 1:23; 2:6; 2:23). In context, this prophetic "fulfillment" involves the dawning of the eschatological age, the "new world [*palingenesia*]" (Matt 19:28). Here we see Matthew's strong indebtedness to Jewish apocalyptic works,[64] which often involve eschatological expectations.[65] As Runesson writes, "the eschatological character of Matthew's Gospel cannot be ignored."[66] Jesus's transcending of the law in Matthew, then, is hardly un-Jewish; given its eschatological dimension, it is perfectly coherent with a Jewish outlook. To that end, Matthew reveals that, according to Jesus, not everything permitted in the Torah meets the level of the eschatological "surpassing righteousness" (cf. Matt 5:20) that he teaches. Specifically, the provisions made for divorce and remarriage in Deuteronomy are understood as involving concessions to Israel's sinfulness: "For your hardness of heart Moses allowed you to divorce your

---

[63] See, e.g., Morna D. Hooker, "Creative Conflict: The Torah and Christology," in *Christology, Controversy, & Community: New Testament Essays in Honour of David R. Catchpole*, ed. D. G. Horrell and C. M. Tuckett (Leiden: Brill, 2000), 125–126; Samuel Byrskog, *Jesus the Only Teacher: Didactic Authority and Transmission in Ancient Israel, Ancient Judaism, and the Matthean Community*, ConBNT 24 (Stockholm: Almqvist & Wiksell, 1994), 294–296; Robert A. Guelich, "The Antitheses of Matthew v. 21–48: Traditional and/or Redactional?," *NTS* 22 (1976): 455–457.

[64] See, e.g., David C. Sim, *Apocalyptic Eschatology in the Gospel of Matthew*, SNTSMS 88 (Cambridge: Cambridge University Press, 1996), 44.

[65] For a carefully nuanced discussion of the distinctions regarding the different meanings of "apocalyptic" and "eschatology," see especially, Daniel Gurtner, "Interpreting Apocalyptic Symbolism in the Gospel of Matthew," *BBR* 22, 4 (2012): 525–545.

[66] Runesson, *Divine Wrath*, 24. See also Paul Foster, "The Eschatology of the Gospel of Matthew," in *"To Recover What Has Been Lost": Essays on Eschatology, Intertextuality, and Reception History in Honor of Dale C. Allison Jr.*, ed. Tucker S. Ferda, Daniel Frayer-Griggs, and Nathan C. Johnson, NovTSup (Leiden: Brill, 2021), 77–103.

wives, but from the beginning it was not so" (Matt 19:8). As Patrick Schreiner puts it, this passage suggests that Jesus aims at explaining the "original intention" of the law.[67]

Finally, a follow-up point must be registered here. As W. D. Davies and Dale Allison observe, while Jesus transcends the law in Matthew, Jesus does not specifically advocate *breaking* the law. For example, no text of the Pentateuch insists that one must divorce and remarry or swear oaths. Davies and Allison explain, "The contrast [implied in Matt 5:21–48] involves not contradiction but transcendence. The OT does not command divorce or the taking of oaths ... Thus 5:31–2 and 33–7 cannot be said to overthrow OT *commandments*."[68] Allison also points out elsewhere that Deuteronomy says, "if you refrain from vowing, it shall be no sin in you" (Deut 23:22).[69] The other antitheses should also not be construed as advocating behavior that directly contradicts the Torah.[70]

Matthew and Hebraisms

John Meier highlights certain linguistic features of the Gospel that, in his estimation, weigh against the likelihood of Jewish authorship. For example, the Gospel sometimes avoids Semitic expressions and generally improves Mark's Greek.[71] In addition, Meier focuses on one particular episode in Matthew that he views as betraying the author's ignorance of Hebrew: Jesus's "triumphal" entry into Jerusalem (Matt 21:1–11).

Unlike Mark, Meier points out that Matthew indicates that *two* animals were present: a donkey and a colt (Matt 21:2, 7).[72] According to Meier, Matthew's depiction misreads the Hebrew of the oracle from Zechariah the evangelist quotes, which names both animals in a parallel literary construction:

> Behold, your king comes to you,
> meek and sitting on *a donkey* [*epi onon*]
> and on a colt, the foal of a beast of burden [*epi pōlon huion hypozygiou*].
> (Matthew 21:5 citing Zechariah 9:9)

---

[67] Schreiner, *Matthew, Disciple and Scribe*, 143.

[68] Davies and Allison, *Matthew*, 1:507.

[69] Dale C. Allison, Jr., *The Sermon on the Mount: Inspiring the Moral Imagination* (New York: Herder & Herder, 1999), 88.

[70] See, e.g., Allison, *Sermon on the Mount*, 93–94.

[71] Meier, *Law and History*, 16–19.

[72] Meier, *Law and History*, 17.

Meier explains that the original Hebrew parallelism indicates a single animal is in view, not two separate ones. The evangelist's ignorance of the Hebrew forces him into an "unimaginable" scene: the two animals are brought to Jesus and he is said to have "sat upon *them* [*epekathisen epanō autōn*]" (Matt 21:7). Yet Jesus could not have straddled both animals. Matthew thus reveals his ignorance of Hebrew and betrays his gentile identity.

Meier's reading, however, has been subject to critique. For one thing, his argument that Matthew must have misinterpreted the Hebrew is questionable. Davies and Allison point out that Jewish rabbis understood the passage as signifying two animals like Matthew did.[73] This was certainly not because of their ignorance of Hebrew. In addition, that Matthew intends readers to think that Jesus somehow balanced himself on the two animals is also unnecessary. It is certainly possible that the phrase "he sat upon them" (Matt 21:7) refers not to Jesus sitting upon *two* animals but, rather, to the *garments* spread over both animals.[74]

Finally, the charge that the evangelist simply misunderstands the Hebrew of Zechariah 9 faces other difficulties. In quoting it, Matthew actually departs from the Septuagint, rendering *a more literal translation* of the Hebrew.[75] Since Matthew works with Greek and Hebrew not only here but also elsewhere, the idea that the evangelist simply fails to comprehend Hebrew appears prima facie unlikely.[76] While it is true that Matthew omits Semitisms found in Mark, this should be tempered by other indications of his knowledge of Hebrew.[77] The evangelist also offers glosses that reveal a Hebraic mindset. For example, in the first chapter of his Gospel, the evangelist provides a genealogy that stresses Jesus's Davidic pedigree. It revolves around the number fourteen, which is the numeric value of David's name in Hebrew gematria. David's name is also the *fourteenth* name in the genealogical list (Matt 1:6). Furthermore, Matthew observes that Jesus's name in Hebrew literally refers to the notion of salvation (Matt 1:21), an etymological explanation for the name found in another Greek work written by a Jew, Sirach (Sir 46:1). Davies and Allison thus conclude that "the evidence that our author was a bilingual or even trilingual Jew is compelling."[78]

---

[73] Davies and Allison, *Matthew*, 1:28.
[74] See, e.g., Luz, *Matthew*, 3:8; Olmstead, *Matthew 15–28*, 410.
[75] Keener, *Matthew*, 491.
[76] See also Evans, *Matthew*, 359; Repschinski, *Controversy Stories*, 33.
[77] See the analysis in Nolland, *Matthew*, 29–33.
[78] Davies and Allison, *Matthew*, 3:124–125; cf. 1:7–58; 72–73.

Acknowledgments

This study has its origins in my doctoral dissertation, but it is far more than a revision of that work. Although my thesis also dealt with the question of the historical Jesus's relationship to the temple, I have changed my mind on several important matters, not least of which is my approach to historical methodology. The lengthy path from that work to this one has, I hope, led me to become a more careful thinker and scholar. Of course, I have not made that journey alone. I would therefore like to thank some of the key people who have walked that road with me and helped me think through the questions at the heart of this project. Of course, it should be stressed that the weaknesses of this work are my own. Nonetheless, had it not been for the following people, this project would have been greatly diminished.

I must begin with Anthony Le Donne. Shortly before my doctoral dissertation was due, I read his monograph *The Historiographical Jesus: Memory, Typology, and the Son of David* (Baylor University Press, 2009). This book was simultaneously exhilarating and depressing: exhilarating because the study was brilliant, depressing because I recognized that much of what I was doing in my dissertation would need to be rethought. I will forever be thankful to Anthony for his outstanding study and for the kind encouragement he has offered me over the past decade.

Unfortunately, before I had a chance to fully digest Anthony's work, I had to submit my thesis to fulfill the requirements of my doctoral degree. Nevertheless, to the initial disappointment of my wonderful Doktorvater, Colin Brown, I resisted publishing it. I simply did not feel I could publish it with integrity until I had thought through methodological questions – and their implications – more carefully. No one came to appreciate that conviction more than Colin. He was always amazed by – I might even say suspicious of – scholars who never reversed themselves. I would continue to have long conversations with him about Jesus studies until his death in 2019. It is a great sorrow for me that he did not live to see this study in print. Yet I am immensely grateful for the privilege I had of studying under him, that I counted him a friend, and that he taught me the value of being willing to change one's mind.

I also must make special mention of Dale Allison. From reading Le Donne, I knew that I would have to change my approach, but I did not see *how* I could proceed until I read Dale Allison's now-classic book *Constructing Jesus: Memory, Imagination, and History* (Eerdmans, 2010). This book was a watershed for me. It should go without saying that besides its important methodological insights, this monograph also made major contributions to our material understanding of the historical Jesus. Jesus's likely understanding of his own eschatological role, his use of extended discourses, and his probable anticipation of a violent end all immediately spring to mind. Along with the landmark studies of Albert Schweitzer, E. P. Sanders, and John Meier, I firmly believe *Constructing Jesus* will be remembered as one of the most important books ever written on Jesus. The study presented here, while drawing widely from the insights of numerous scholars, is especially indebted to Dale's body of work. Given my admiration of his scholarship, I cannot adequately express how grateful I am that he wrote a Foreword to this book. The generosity he has shown to me is, to borrow from George Harrison, "all too much for me to take."

Other scholars deserve mention as well. Chris Keith's seminal monograph, *Jesus's Literacy* (T&T Clark, 2011), further drove home for me the implications of memory research for Jesus studies. The book he co-edited with Anthony Le Donne, *The Demise of the Criteria of Authenticity* (T&T Clark, 2012), was especially important for my own thought. Likewise, Rafael Rodríguez's study *Structuring Early Christian Memory* (T&T Clark, 2010) further convinced me of the need for Jesus scholars to interact with memory research. Here, I also wish to add a personal word of thanks to both Chris and Rafael. Their kind words helped spur me on to persevere in times of discouragement. Many are not willing to rethink the project of Jesus research; I honor their courage.

In addition, I owe a word of thanks to Amy-Jill Levine. Her publications are a reservoir of insight. Among other things, she has helped me to become more acutely aware of the complexities involved in locating Jesus within his first-century Jewish environment. I have also greatly benefited from observing her graceful and thoughtful interactions with colleagues at academic conferences. I look back with some embarrassment at positions she has heard me take in conference papers and in casual conversations. What redeems those memories is the recollection of her charitable forbearance. Rather than burying me in discouragement with humiliating questions, her thoughtful responses enabled me to grow as a scholar.

Special gratitude is due to my dear friend Brant Pitre. Brant has made important contributions of his own to the field, particularly his two monographs: *Jesus, the Tribulation, and the End of the Exile* (Mohr Siebeck, 2005) and *Jesus and the Last Supper* (Eerdmans, 2015). I have learned much from these works and the reader will find them cited at key points in this study. Even more important, however, has been what I have learned from him through countless conversations. For close to twenty years, amid the highs and lows of our lives, we have talked at length about virtually every aspect of historical Jesus research, "sparring," as he would say, as we have tested the cogency of different arguments. His friendship has incalculably improved my scholarship. Even more important, it has made me a better man. He generously devoted time to carefully reading through this study and offering substantial feedback. His input greatly enhanced the book in countless ways.

I must also thank John Kincaid. For over a decade, John and I have shared a deep bond of friendship. His support has helped to sustain my work on this project and has made me a more virtuous person than I otherwise would be. He also carefully read this work and helped me strengthen it by asking important questions. Moreover, Brant, John, and I coauthored a study of Paul – *Paul, A New Covenant Jew* (Eerdmans, 2019). Having come to grips with the implications of memory research for historiography, I became convinced that I needed to plunge myself into a deeper study of the reception of the Jesus tradition in the Apostle's letters. Working on that book with Brant and John was a gift and a joy. It helped me clarify important issues related to this project.

Furthermore, I must express my gratitude to two other dear friends who, like Brant, are professors with me at the Augustine Institute Graduate School: John Sehorn and Jim Prothro. John carefully pored over every word of this manuscript. His input was simply invaluable and significantly improved this book. Jim also offered important observations about my argument, specifically in areas related to Pauline studies.

On to other scholarly colleagues. Rafael Rodríguez and I served as coconveners of a Continuing Seminar on the historical Jesus at the Catholic

Biblical Association. Those discussions helped me think through the way I presented issues in the final form of the manuscript. I thank those who participated in those conversations, especially Michael Cover, Tucker Ferda, Darrell Bock, and Jennifer Guo. I also wish to thank those I have served with on the steering committee for the Matthew Study Unit of the Society of Biblical Literature: Nathan Eubank, Daniel Gurtner, Anders Runesson, Catherine Sider Hamilton, David Sim, and Joel Willitts. Other friends are also owed mention for clarifying and/or encouraging conversations: Jonathan Bernier, Michael Bird, David Burnett, Anthony Giambrone, O.P., Michael Gorman, Nijay Gupta, Tom Harmon, Leroy Huizenga, Joshua Jipp, Simon Joseph, Craig Keener, Seyoon Kim, Matthew Levering, Aaron Lockhart, Curtis Mitch, David Moffitt, Isaac Morales, O.P., Lidija Novakovic, Jonathan Pennington, O.P., Matt Peterson, Camilla Raymond, Jordan Ryan, Christopher Skinner, Joshua Smith, Jason Staples, Gregory Tatum O.P., Matthew Thomas, Chris Tilling, R. Jarrett Van Tine, Danny Yencich and Andrew Younan. Thanks also to Paula Fredriksen, Mark Goodacre, John Kampen, John P. Meier, Matthew Thiessen, and to the late James D. G. Dunn. I have learned much from their impressive scholarship and I am grateful for the kind interactions I have had with them, limited though they have been.

I must say a further word of thanks to others at my institution: President Timothy C. Gray (whose study on the temple in Mark made an important impression on me as a graduate student) and our provost, Christopher Blum. Their leadership has enabled me to have the time and resources necessary to engage in serious research and scholarship, and I am grateful for their friendship. In addition, I thank my other colleagues on the faculty: Mark Giszczak, Scott Hefelfinger, Elizabeth Klein, Lucas Pollice, Ben Akers, Sean Innerst, and Fr. Daniel Moloney. I also thank my students, particularly those who studied the Gospel of Matthew and Luke-Acts with me.

I am very grateful to Beatrice Rehl at Cambridge University Press for her work in bringing this book into print, and to the blind reviewers whose comments pushed me to refine my arguments. I also thank copy-editor Jan Baiton for saving me from multiple errors and improving the manuscript.

My parents Patrick and Theresa have supported and encouraged me over the years. I can never repay them or thank them enough for their unfailing, selfless generosity. I also wish to thank my uncle, Fr. G. Peter Irving III, who gave me my first book on biblical Greek when I was only a teenager, and who has remained a constant source of support.

Finally, I thank my beloved wife, Kim, and our wonderful children, Michael, Matthew, Molly, Thomas, Susanna, and Simon Peter for the countless ways they have given of themselves to allow me to complete this project. Kim, who holds a graduate degree in Theology from Fuller Theological Seminary, has been my constant conversation partner over the years, never losing enthusiasm for this project. She has been by my side since I first began thinking about Jesus's relationship to the temple. Moreover, she has carefully read through these pages, pointing out problems and suggesting solutions. Without her love, patience, and encouragement, this project would never have been completed. I dedicate it to her.

Bibliography

Ådna, Jostein. "Jesus and the Temple." Pages 2635–2675 in vol. 3 of *Handbook for the Study of the Historical Jesus*. 4 vols. Edited by Tom Holmén and Stanley E. Porter. Leiden: Brill, 2010.

Jesu Stellung zum Tempel: Die Templaktion und das Tempelwort als Ausdruck seiner messianischen Sendung. Wissenschaftliche Untersuchungen zum Neuen Testament 2/119. Tübingen: Mohr Siebeck, 2000.

"Jesus' Symbolic Act in the Temple (Mark 11:15–17): The Replacement of the Sacrificial Cult by His Atoning Death." Pages 461–475 in *Gemeinde ohne Tempel = Community without Temple: Zur Substituierung und Transformation des Jerusalemer Tempels und seines Kults im Alten Testament, antiken Judentum und frühen Christentum*. Edited by B. Ego, A. Lange, and P. Pilhofer. Tübingen: Mohr Siebeck, 1999.

Ahearne-Kroll, Stephen P. *The Psalms of Lament in Mark's Passion: Jesus's Davidic Suffering*. Society for New Testament Studies Monograph Series 142. Cambridge: Cambridge University Press, 2007.

Allen, Brian Louis. "Removing an Arrow from the Supersessionist Quiver: A Post-Supersessionist Reading of Colossians 2:16–17." *Journal for the Study of Paul and His Letters* 8 (2018): 127–146.

Allison, Dale C., Jr. "Cyprus and Early Christianity: Did Everybody Know Everybody?" Pages 127–146 in *Cyprus within the Biblical World: Are Borders Barriers?* Jewish and Christian Texts in Context and Related Studies 32. Edited by James H. Charlesworth and Jolyon G. R. Pruszinksi. London: T&T Clark, 2021.

The Resurrection of Jesus: Apologetics, Polemics, History. London: T&T Clark, 2021.

"Memory, Methodology, and the Historical Jesus: A Response to Richard Bauckham." *Journal for the Study of the Historical Jesus* 14 (2016): 13–27.

"Response to Rafael Rodríguez, 'Jesus as his Friends Remembered Him: A Review of Dale Allison's Constructing Jesus.'" *Journal for the Study of the Historical Jesus* 12 (2014): 245–254.

"It Don't Come Easy: A History of Disillusionment." Pages 186–199 in *Jesus, Criteria, and the Demise of Authenticity*. Edited by Chris Keith and Anthony Le Donne. London: T&T Clark, 2012.

Constructing Jesus: Memory, Imagination, and History. Grand Rapids: Baker Academic, 2010.

"How to Marginalize the Traditional Criteria of Authenticity." Pages 3–30 in vol. 1 of *Handbook for the Study of the Historical Jesus*. 4 vols. Edited by Tom Holmén and Stanley E. Porter. Leiden: Brill, 2010.

The Historical Christ and the Theological Jesus. Grand Rapids: Eerdmans 2009.

Resurrecting Jesus: The Earliest Christian Tradition and Its Interpreters. London: T&T Clark, 2005.

Studies in Matthew: Interpretation Past and Present. Grand Rapids: Baker Academic, 2005.

The Intertextual Jesus: Scripture in Q. Harrisburg: Trinity Press International, 2000.

"Behind the Temptations of Jesus: Q 4:1–13 and Mark 1:12–13." Pages 195–214 in *Authenticating the Activities of Jesus*. Edited by Bruce Chilton and Craig A. Evans. New Testament Tools and Studies 28/2. Leiden: Brill, 1999.

"Jesus and the Victory of Apocalyptic." Pages 126–141 in *Jesus and the Restoration of Israel: A Critical Assessment of N. T. Wright's "Jesus and the Victory of God."* Edited by Carey C. Newman. Downers Grove: InterVarsity Press, 1999.

The Sermon on the Mount: Inspiring the Moral Imagination. New York: Herder & Herder, 1999.

Jesus of Nazareth: Millenarian Prophet. Minneapolis: Fortress Press, 1998.

The Jesus Tradition in Q. Harrisburg: Trinity, 1997.

The New Moses: A Matthean Typology. Minneapolis: Fortress Press, 1993.

"Who Will Come from East and West? Observations on Matt 8:11–12-Luke 13:28–29." *Irish Biblical Studies* 11 (1989): 158–170.

The End of the Ages Has Come: An Early Interpretation of the Passion and Resurrection of Jesus. Minneapolis: Fortress Press, 1985.

"The Pauline Epistles and the Synoptic Gospels: The Pattern of the Parallels." *New Testament Studies* 28 (1982): 1–32.

Andersen, Francis I. and David Noel Freedman. *Hosea: A New Translation with Introduction and Commentary*. Anchor Yale Bible 24. New Haven: Yale University Press, 2008.

Anderson, A. A. *2 Samuel*. Word Biblical Commentary 11. Dallas: Word Books, 1989.

Anderson, Janice Capel. *Matthew's Narrative Web: Over, and Over, and Over Again*. Journal for the Study of the New Testament Supplement Series 91. Sheffield: JSOT Press, 1994.

Armerding, C. E. "Were David's Sons Really Priests?" Pages 75–86 in *Current Issues in Biblical and Patristic Interpretation*. Edited by G. Hawthorne. Grand Rapids: Eerdmans, 1975.

Atkinson, Kenneth. *A History of the Hasmonean State: Josephus and Beyond*. London: Bloomsbury T&T Clark, 2016.

Aune, David E. and Eric Stewart. "Restoration in Jewish Apocalyptic Literature." Pages 147–178 in *Restoration: Old Testament, Jewish, and Christian Perspectives*. Edited by James H. Scott. Supplements to the Journal for the Study of Judaism 72. Leiden: Brill, 2001.

Aune, David E. "Oral Tradition and the Aphorisms of Jesus." Pages 211–265 in *Jesus and the Oral Gospel Tradition*. Edited by Henry Wansbrough. Journal for the Study of the New Testament Supplement Series. Sheffield: JSOT, 1991.

Prophecy in Early Christianity and the Ancient Mediterranean World. Grand Rapids: Eerdmans, 1983.

Barber, Michael Patrick. "Did Jesus Anticipate Suffering a Violent Death? The Implications of Memory Research and Dale C. Allison's Methodology." *Journal for the Study of the Historical Jesus* 18, 3 (2020): 191–219.

"Jesus as the Davidic Temple Builder and Peter's Priestly Role in Matthew 16:17–19." *Journal of Biblical Literature* 132, 4 (2013): 935–953.

Barber, Michael P. and John A. Kincaid. "Cultic Theosis in Paul and Second Temple Judaism." *Journal for the Study of Paul and His Letters* 5, 2 (2015): 237–256.

Barbour, Robert Stewart. *Traditio-Historical Criticism of the Gospels: Some Comments on Current Methods*. London: SPCK, 1972.

Barclay, John M. G. *Jews in the Mediterranean Diaspora: From Alexander to Trajan (323 B.C.E.–117 C.E.)*. Edinburgh: T&T Clark, 1996.

Barker, James. *John's Use of Matthew*. Minneapolis: Fortress Press, 2015.

Baron, Lori Jill Hicks-Keeton, and Matthew Thiessen, eds. *The Ways That Often Parted: Essays in Honor of Joel Marcus*. Early Christianity and Its Literature. Atlanta: SBL Press, 2018.

Barrett, C. K. *The Second Epistle to the Corinthians*. Black's New Testament Commentary. London: Continuum, 1973.

Bauckham, Richard. *Jesus and the Eyewitnesses: The Gospels as Eyewitness Testimony*, 2nd ed. Grand Rapids: Eerdmans, 2017.

"The General and the Particular in Memory: A Critique of Dale Allison's Approach to the Historical Jesus." *Journal for the Study of the Historical Jesus* 14 (2016): 28–51.

ed. *The Gospels for All Christians: Rethinking the Gospel Audiences*. Grand Rapids: Eerdmans, 1998.

"Jesus' Demonstration in the Temple." Pages 72–89 in *Law and Religion: Essays on the Place of the Law in Israel and Early Christianity*. Edited by Barnabas Lindars. Cambridge: James Clark & Co., 1988.

"The Coin in the Fish's Mouth." Pages 219–252 in *Gospel Perspectives, vol. 6: The Miracles of Jesus*. Sheffield: JSOT Press, 1986.

Baxter, Wayne S. "Healing and the 'Son of David': Matthew's Warrant." *Novum Testamentum* 48, 1 (2006): 36–50.

Beale, G. K. *The Temple and the Church's Mission: A Biblical Theology of the Dwelling Place of God*. New Studies in Biblical Theology 17. Downers Grove: InterVarsity Press, 2004.

Beasley-Murray, George R. *Jesus and the Kingdom of God*. Grand Rapids: Eerdmans, 1986.

Becker, Eve-Marie, Chris Keith, and Helen Bond, eds. *John's Transformation of Mark*. London: T&T Clark, 2021.

Becker, Jürgen. *Jesus of Nazareth*. Translated by James E. Crouch. Berlin: Walter de Gruyter, 1998.

Bell, Richard H. *Deliver Us from Evil*. Wissenschaftliche Untersuchungen zum Neuen Testament 216. Tübingen: Mohr Siebeck, 2007.

Bernier, Jonathan. The Quest for the Historical Jesus after the Demise of Authenticity: Toward a Critical Realist Philosophy of History in Jesus Studies. The Library of New Testament Studies 540. London: Bloomsbury, 2016.

Berry, Donald K. "Malachi's Dual Design: The Close of the Canon and What Comes Afterward." Pages 269–302 in *Forming Prophetic Literature: Essays on Isaiah and the Twelve in Honor of D. W. Watts*. Edited by J. W. Watts, J. D. W. Watts, P. R. House. Sheffield: Sheffield Academic Press, 1996.

Betz, Hans Dieter. *The Sermon on the Mount: A Commentary on the Sermon on the Mount, Including the Sermon on the Plain (Matthew 5:3–7:27 and Luke 6:20–49)*. Edited by Adela Yarbro Collins. Minneapolis: Fortress Press, 1995.

Betz, Otto. "*Die Frage* nach dem messianischen Bewusstsein Jesu." *Novum Testamentum* 6 (1963): 20–48.

Beutler, Johannes, S.J., *A Commentary on the Gospel of John*. Translated by Michael Tait. Grand Rapids: Eerdmans, 2017.

Bird, Michael F. *Jesus and the Origins of the Gentile Mission*. Library of Historical Jesus Studies 331. New York: T&T Clark, 2007.

Bockmuehl, Markus. *The Ancient Apocryphal Gospels*. Interpretation. Louisville: Westminster John Knox, 2017.

Bodnar, John. *Remaking America: Public Memory, Commemoration, and Patriotism in the Twentieth Century*. Princeton: Princeton University Press, 1992.

Bond, Helen K. *The First Biography of Jesus: Genre and Meaning in Mark's Gospel*. Grand Rapids: Eerdmans, 2020.

The Historical Jesus: A Guide for the Perplexed. London: T&T Clark, 2012.

Borg, Marcus J. *Conflict, Holiness, and Politics in the Teachings of Jesus*. Harrisburg: Trinity Press International, 1998.

Boring, M. Eugene. *Mark: A Commentary*. New Testament Library. Louisville: Westminster John Knox Press, 2006.

Botner, Max. *Jesus Christ as the Son of David in the Gospel of Mark*. Society for New Testament Studies Monograph Series 174. Cambridge: Cambridge University Press, 2019.

Brewer, David Instone. *Techniques and Assumptions in Jewish Exegesis before 70 c.e.* Texte und Studien zum antiken Judentum 30. Tübingen: Mohr Siebeck, 1992.

Broadhead, Edwin K. *Naming Jesus: Titular Christology in the Gospel of Mark*. Journal for the Study of the New Testament Supplement Series 175. Sheffield: Sheffield Academic Press, 1999.

"Christology as Polemic and Apologetic: The Priestly Portrait of Jesus in Mark." *Journal for the Study of the New Testament* 47 (1992): 21–34.

Brooke, George J. "4Q500 1 and the Use of Scripture in the Parable of the Vineyard." *Dead Sea Discoveries* 2 (1995): 268–294.

Exegesis at Qumran: 4QFlorilegium in Its Jewish Context. Journal for the Study of the Old Testament Supplement Series 29. Sheffield: JSOT Press, 1985.

Brown, Jeanine K. *The Disciples in Narrative Perspective.* Leiden: Brill, 2002.

Brown, Raymond E., S.S. *Death of the Messiah: From Gethsemane to the Grave, A Commentary on the Passion Narratives of the Four Gospels.* Anchor Bible Reference Library. New York: Doubleday, 1994.

Birth of the Messiah: A Commentary on the Infancy Narratives in the Gospels of Matthew and Luke. Rev. ed. Anchor Bible Reference Library. New Haven: Yale University Press, 1993.

The Virginal Conception and Bodily Resurrection of Jesus. New York: Paulist Press, 1973.

The Gospel According to John. 2 vols. Anchor Bible 29–29A. New York: Doubleday, 1966.

Brunson, Andrew C. *Psalm 118 in the Gospel of John: An Intertextual Study on the New Exodus.* Wissenschaftliche Untersuchungen zum Neuen Testament 2/158. Tübingen: Mohr Siebeck, 2003.

Bryan, Steven M. "Jesus and Israel's Eschatological Constitution." Pages 2835–2853 in vol. 3 of *Handbook for the Study of the Historical Jesus.* 4 vols. Edited by Tom Holmén and Stanley E. Porter. Leiden: Brill, 2010.

Jesus and Israel's Traditions of Judgement and Restoration. Society for New Testament Studies Monograph Series 117. Cambridge: Cambridge University Press, 2002.

Bultmann, Rudolph. *Theology of the New Testament.* 2 vols. Translated by Kendrick Grobel. Waco: Baylor University Press, 2007.

The Gospel of John: A Commentary. Translated by George R. Beasley-Murray, Rupert W. N. Hoare, and John K. Riches. Philadelphia: Westminster Press, 1971.

History of the Synoptic Tradition. Rev. ed. Translated by John Marsh. Peabody: Hendrickson, 1963.

"Die Frage nach dem messianischen Bewusstsein Jesu und das Petrus-Bekenntnis." *Zeitschrift für die neutestamentliche Wissenschaft und die Kunde der älteren Kirche* 19 (1919–20): 165–174.

Burkitt, F. C. *The Gospel History and Its Transmission.* 3rd ed. Edinburgh: T&T Clark, 1911.

Burns, Joshua Ezra. "Essene Sectarianism and Social Differentiation in Judaea after 70 C.E." *Harvard Theological Review* 99, 3 (2006): 247–274.

Burridge, Richard. *What Are the Gospels? A Comparison with Graeco-Roman Biography.* 2nd ed. Cambridge: Cambridge University Press, 1995.

Byrskog, Samuel. *Jesus the Only Teacher: Didactic Authority and Transmission in Ancient Israel, Ancient Judaism, and the Matthean Community.* Coniectanea Biblica New Testament Series 24. Stockholm: Almqvist & Wiksell, 1994.

Campbell, Douglas A. *The Deliverance of God: An Apocalyptic Rereading of Justification in Paul.* Grand Rapids: Eerdmans, 2009.

Carroll, John T. *Luke: A Commentary.* New Testament Library. Louisville: Westminster John Knox Press, 2012.

Carson, D. A. and Douglas A. Moo. *An Introduction to the New Testament.* Grand Rapids: Zondervan, 2005.

Carter, Warren. *Matthew and the Margins: A Socio-Political and Religious Reading*. London: T&T Clark, 2004.

Cassidy, R. J. "Matthew 17:24–27: A Word on Civil Taxes." *Catholic Biblical Quarterly* 41 (1979): 571–580.

Catchpole, David R. "The 'Triumphal Entry.'" Pages 319–334 in *Jesus and the Politics of His Day*. Edited by Ernst Bammel and C. F. D. Moule. Cambridge: Cambridge University Press, 1984.

Chae, Young S. *Jesus as the Eschatological Davidic Shepherd*. Wissenschafltliche Untersuchungen zum Neuen Testament 2/216. Tübingen: Mohr Siebeck, 2006.

Charlesworth, James H. "Jesus and the Temple." Pages 145–181 in *Jesus and Temple: Textual and Archaeological Explorations*. Edited by James H. Charlesworth. Minneapolis: Fortress Press, 2014.

"The Temple and Jesus's Followers." Pages 183–212 in *Jesus and Temple: Textual and Archaeological Explorations*. Edited by James H. Charlesworth. Minneapolis: Fortress Press, 2014.

The Old Testament Pseudepigrapha. New York: Doubleday, 1985.

Chávez, Emilio G. *The Theological Significance of Jesus' Temple Action in Mark's Gospel*. Toronto Studies in Theology 87. Lewiston: Edwin Mellen Press, 2002.

Chilton, Bruce D. "Temple Restored, Temple in Heaven: Isaiah and the Prophets in the Targumim." Pages 335–362 in *Restoration: Old Testament, Jewish, and Christian Perspectives*. Edited by James M. Scott. Leiden: Brill, 2001.

"Shebna, Eliakim and the Promise to Peter." Pages 319–352 in *Jesus in Context: Temple, Purity, Restoration*. Edited by B. Chilton and C. A. Evans. Leiden: Brill, 1997.

"Caiaphas." Pages 803–806 in vol. 1 of *Anchor Bible Dictionary*. Edited by D. N. Freedman. 6 vols. Anchor Bible Reference Library. New York: Doubleday, 1992.

The Temple of Jesus: His Sacrificial Program within a Cultural History of Sacrifice. University Park: Pennsylvania State University Press, 1992.

The Isaiah Targum. Aramaic Bible 11. Collegeville: Liturgical Press, 1987.

God in Strength: Jesus' Announcement of the Kingdom. Studien zum Neuen Testament und seiner Umwelt 1. Freistadt: Plöchl, 1979.

Cho, Bernardo. *Royal Messianism and the Jerusalem Priesthood in the Gospel of Mark*. The Library of New Testament Studies 607. London: T&T Clark, 2019.

Ciampa, Roy E. and Brian S. Rosner. *The First Letter to the Corinthians*. Pillar New Testament Commentary. Grand Rapids: Eerdmans, 2010.

"1 Corinthians." Pages 695–752 in *Commentary on the New Testament Use of the Old Testament*. Edited by D. A. Carson and G. K. Beale. Grand Rapids: Baker Academic, 2007.

Clark, Kenneth W. "The Gentile Bias of Matthew." *Journal of Biblical Literature* 66 (1947): 165–172.

Cohen, Akiva. *Matthew and the Mishnah: Redefining Identity and Ethos in the Shadow of the Second Temple's Destruction*. Wissenschaftliche Untersuchungen zum Neuen Testament 418. Tübingen: Mohr Siebeck, 2016.

Cohen, Shayne J. D. *From the Maccabees to the Mishnah.* 3rd ed. Louisville: Westminster, 2014.

"'Those Who Say They Are Jews and Are Not': How Do You Know a Jew in Antiquity When You See One?" Pages 1–45 in *Diasporas in Antiquity.* Brown Judaic Studies 288. Edited by S. J. D. Cohen and E. S. Frerichs. Atlanta: Scholars Press, 1993.

"The Significance of Yavneh: Pharisees, Rabbis, and the End of Jewish Sectarianism." *Harvard Union College Annual* 55 (1984): 27–53.

Collins, Adela Yarbro. *Mark.* Hermenia. Philadelphia: Fortress Press, 2007.

"Finding Meaning in the Death of Jesus." *Journal of Religion* 78, 2 (1998): 175–196.

Collins, John. *The Apocalyptic Imagination: An Introduction to Jewish Apocalyptic Literature.* 2nd ed. Grand Rapids: Eerdmans, 1998.

The Scepter and the Star: The Messiahs of the Dead Sea Scrolls and Other Ancient Literature. Anchor Bible Reference Library. New York: Doubleday, 1995.

Coloe, Mary L. *God Dwells with Us: Temple Symbolism in the Fourth Gospel.* Collegeville: Liturgical Press, 2001.

Conzelmann, Hans. *1 Corinthians.* Translated by James W. Leitch. Hermeneia. Philadelphia: Fortress Press, 1975 (orig. 1969).

Crook, Zeba. "Collective Memory Distortion and the Quest for the Historical Jesus." *Journal for the Study of the Historical Jesus* 11, 3 (2013): 53–76.

"Memory Distortion and the Historical Jesus." Paper presented at the annual meeting of the Society of Biblical Literature. Baltimore, MD, 25 November 2013.

Crossan, John Dominic. *The Birth of Christianity: Discovering What Happened in the Years Immediately after the Execution of Jesus.* San Francisco: HarperCollins, 1998.

Crossley, James G. "Matthew and the Torah: Jesus as Legal Interpreter." Pages 29–52 in *Matthew within Judaism: Israel and the Nations.* Early Christian Literature. Edited by Anders Runesson and Daniel M. Gurtner. Atlanta: SBL Press, 2019.

Jesus and the Chaos of History: Redirecting the Life of the Historical Jesus. Oxford: Oxford University Press, 2015.

The Date of Mark's Gospel. Journal for the Study of the New Testament Supplement Series 266. London: T&T Clark, 2004.

Dahl, Nils Alstrup. "The Crucified Messiah." Pages 10–36 in *Jesus the Christ: The Historical Origins of Christology Doctrine.* Edited Donald H. Juel. Minneapolis: Fortress Press, 1991.

"Die Passionsgeschichte bei Matthäus." *New Testament Studies* 2 (1955): 17–32.

Daly-Denton, Margaret. *David in the Fourth Gospel: The Johannine Reception of the Psalms.* Leiden: Brill, 2000.

Danby, Herbert, trans. *The Mishnah: Translated from the Hebrew with Introduction and Brief Explanatory Notes.* Oxford: Oxford University Press, 1933.

Davenport, Gene L. "The 'Anointed of the Lord' in Psalms of Solomon 17." Pages 67–92 in *Ideal Figures in Ancient Judaism: Profiles and Paradigms.* Edited by John J. Collins and George W. E. Nickelsburg. Society of Biblical Literature Septuagint and Cognate Studies 12. Chico: Scholars Press, 1980.

Davies, W. D. and Dale C. Allison. *The Gospel According to St. Matthew*. International Critical Commentary. 3 vols. London: T&T Clark, 1988–1997.

De Vries, Simon J. "Moses and David as Cult Founders in Chronicles." *Journal of Biblical Literature* 107, 4 (1988): 619–639.

Dinkler, Erich. "Peter's Confession and the 'Satan' Saying': The Problem of Jesus's Messiahship." Pages 169–192 in *The Future of Our Religious Past: Essays in Honor of Rudolf Bultmann*. Edited by James M. Robinson. Translated by Charles E. Carlston and Robert P. Scharlemann. London: SCM, 1971.

Dodd, C. H. *The Founder of Christianity*. London: Collins, 1971.

History and the Gospel. New York: Scribner's, 1938.

Doering, Lutz. *Schabbat: Sabbathalacha und -praxis im antiken Judentum und Urchristentum*. Texte und Studien zum antiken Judentum 78. Tübingen: Mohr Siebeck, 1999.

Douglas, Mary. "The Eucharist: Its Continuity with the Bread Sacrifice of Leviticus." *Modern Theology* 15, 2 (1999): 209–224.

Dunn, James D. G. *Christianity in the Making*. Vol. 1: *Jesus Remembered*. Grand Rapids: William B. Eerdman's Publishing, 2003.

Galatians. Black's New Testament Commentary. London: A&C Black, 1993.

Romans 1–8. Word Biblical Commentary 38A. Dallas: Word Books, 1988.

Dvořáček, Jiří. *The Son of David in Matthew's Gospel in the Light of Solomon as Exorcist Tradition*. Wissenschafltliche Untersuchungen zum Neuen Testament 2/415. Tübingen: Mohr Siebeck, 2016.

Ehrman, Bart. *How Jesus Became God: The Exaltation of a Jewish Preacher from Galilee*. New York: HarperCollins, 2014.

Forgery and Counterforgery. Oxford: Oxford University Press, 2013.

Jesus: Apocalyptic Prophet of the New Millennium. Oxford: Oxford University Press, 1999.

Elledge, Roderick. *Use of the Third Person for Self-Reference by Jesus and YHWH: A Study of Illeism in the Bible and Ancient Near Eastern Texts and Its Implications for Christology*. The Library of New Testament Studies 575. London: T&T Clark, 2017.

Emerton, J. A. "Binding and Loosing—Forgiving and Retaining." *Journal of Theological Studies* 13 (1962): 325–331.

Eppstein, Victor. "The Historicity of the Gospel Account of the Cleansing of the Temple." *Zeitschrift für die neutestamentliche Wissenschaft und die Kunde der älteren Kirche* 55 (1964): 42–58.

Ernst, Josef. *Das Evangelium nach Lukas*. Regensburger Neues Testament. Regensburg: Pustet, 1977.

Eskola, Timo. *A Narrative Theology of the New Testament*. Wissenschafltliche Untersuchungen zum Neuen Testament 350. Tübingen: Mohr Siebeck, 2015.

Messiah and the Throne: Jewish Merkabah Mysticism and Early Christian Exaltation Discourse. Wissenschafltliche Untersuchungen zum Neuen Testament 2/142. Tübingen: Mohr Siebeck, 2001.

Evans, Craig A. *Matthew*. New Cambridge Biblical Commentary. Cambridge: Cambridge University Press, 2012.

The Historical Jesus: Critical Concepts in Religious Studies. New York: Routledge, 2004.

"Zechariah in the Markan Passion Narrative." Pages 64–80 in *Biblical Interpretation in Early Christian Gospels: The Gospel of Mark*. The Library of New Testament Studies 304. Edited by T. R. Hatina. London: T&T Clark, 2004.

"Jesus and Zechariah's Messianic Hope." Pages 373–88 in *Authenticating the Activities of Jesus*. Edited by Bruce D. Chilton and Craig A. Evans. Leiden: Brill, 2002.

"The Misplaced Jesus: Interpreting Jesus in a Judaic Context." Pages 11–39 in *The Missing Jesus: Rabbinic Judaism and the New Testament*. Edited by Bruce David Chilton, Craig A. Evans, and Jacob Neusner. Leiden: Brill, 2002.

"Daniel in the New Testament: Visions of God's Kingdom." Pages 490–527 in vol. 2 of *The Book of Daniel: Composition and Reception*. 2 vols. Edited by John J. Collins and Peter W. Flint. Leiden: Brill, 2001.

Jesus and His Contemporaries: Comparative Studies. Leiden: Brill, 2001.

Mark 8:27–16:20. Word Biblical Commentary 34B. Nashville: Thomas Nelson Publishers, 2001.

"Qumran's Messiah: How Important Is He?" Pages 135–149 in *Religion in the Dead Sea Scrolls*. Edited by John J. Collins and Robert A. Kugler. Grand Rapids: Eerdmans, 2000.

"From 'House of Prayer' to 'Cave of Robers': Jesus' Prophetic Criticism of the Temple Establishment." Pages 417–422 in *The Quest for Context and Meaning: Studies in Biblical Intertextuality in Honor of James A. Sanders*. Edited by C. A. Evans and S. Talmon. Leiden: Brill, 1997.

"Authenticity Criteria in Life of Jesus Research." *Christian Scholar's Review* 19 (1989): 6–31.

Eve, Eric. *Behind the Gospels: Understanding the Oral Tradition*. Minneapolis: Fortress Press, 2014.

Farrer, Austin. "On Dispensing with Q." Pages 55–88 in *Studies in the Gospels: Essays in Memory of R. H. Lightfoot*. Edited by D. E. Nineham. Oxford: Blackwell, 1955.

Fee, Gordon D. *The First Epistle to the Corinthians*. New International Commentary on the New Testament. Grand Rapids: Eerdmans, 1987.

Finegan, Jack. *Die Überlieferung der Leidens- und Auferstehungsgeschichte Jesu*. Giessen: Töpelmann, 1934.

Finlan, Stephen. *The Background and Context of Paul's Cultic Atonement Metaphors*. Atlanta: Society of Biblical Literature, 2004.

Fitzmyer, Joseph A., S.J. *First Corinthians: A New Translation with Introduction and Commentary*. Anchor Yale Bible 32. New Haven: Yale University Press, 2008.

Acts of the Apostles. Anchor Bible 31. New Haven: Yale University Press, 1998.

The Gospel According to Luke. 2 vols. Anchor Bible 28–28A. Garden City: Doubleday, 1981, 1985.

Fletcher-Louis, Crispin H. T. "Jesus as the High Priestly Messiah: Part 1." *Journal for the Study of the Historical Jesus* 4, 2 (2006): 155–175.

"Jesus as the High Priestly Messiah: Part 2." *Journal for the Study of the Historical Jesus* 5, 1 (2006): 57–79.

"Jesus Inspects His Priestly War Party (Luke 14:25–33)." Pages 126–143 in *The Old Testament in the New Testament. Essays in Honour of J.L. North*.

Edited by S. Moyise. Journal for the Study of the New Testament Supplement Series 189. Sheffield: Sheffield Academic Press, 2000.

Foster, Paul. "The Eschatology of the Gospel of Matthew." Pages 77–103 in *"To Recover What Has Been Lost": Essays on Eschatology, Intertextuality, and Reception History in Honor of Dale C. Allison Jr.* Edited by Tucker S. Ferda, Daniel Frayer-Griggs, and Nathan C. Johnson. Supplements to Novum Testamentum. Leiden: Brill, 2021.

"Memory, Orality, and the Fourth Gospel: Three Dead-Ends in Historical Jesus Research." *Journal for the Study of the Historical Jesus* 10 (2012): 191–227.

Community, Law and Mission in Matthew's Gospel. Wissenschaftliche Untersuchungen zum Neuen Testament 2/177. Tübingen: Mohr Siebeck, 2004.

France, R. T. *The Gospel of Matthew.* New International Commentary on the New Testament. Grand Rapids: Eerdmans, 2007.

Franklyn, Paul N. "The Cultic and Pious Climax of Eschatology in the Psalms of Solomon." *Journal for the Study of Judaism in the Persian, Hellenistic, and Roman Periods* 18 (1987): 1–17.

Fredriksen, Paula. *When Christians Were Jews: The First Generation.* New Haven: Yale University Press, 2018.

Paul: The Pagan's Apostle. New Haven: Yale University Press, 2017.

"Arms and the Man: A Response to Dale Martin's 'Jesus in Jerusalem: Armed and Not Dangerous.'" *Journal for the Study of the New Testament* 37, 3 (2015): 312–325.

Augustine and the Jews: A Christian Defense of Jews and Judaism. New Haven: Yale University Press, 2008.

"Gospel Chronologies, the Scene in the Temple, and the Crucifixion of Jesus." Pages 246–82 in *Redefining First-Century Jewish and Christian Identities: Essays in Honor of Ed Parish Sanders.* Edited by Fabian E. Udoh, Susannah Heschel, Mark Chancey, and Gregory Tatum. Notre Dame: University of Notre Dame Press, 2008.

From Jesus to Christ. 2nd ed. New Haven: Yale Nota Bene, 2000.

Jesus of Nazareth: King of the Jews. New York: Vintage Books, 1999.

Frey, Jorg. "Der historische Jesus und der Christus der Evangelien." Page 273–336 in *Der historische Jesus: Tendenzen und Perspektiven der gegenwärtigen Forschung.* Edited by Jens Schröter and Ralph Brucken, Beihefte zur Zeitschrift für die neutestamentliche Wissenschaft 114. Berlin: Walter de Gruyter, 2002.

Friebel, Kelvin G. *Jeremiah's and Ezekiel's Sign Acts: Rhetorical Nonverbal Communication.* Journal for the Study of the Old Testament Supplement Series 283. Sheffield: Sheffield Academic Press, 1999.

Frühwald-König, Johannes. *Tempel und Kult: Ein Beitrag zur Christologie es Johannesevangeliums.* Biblische Untersuchungen 27. Regensburg: Friedrich Pustet, 1998.

Furnish, Victor Paul. *II Corinthians.* Anchor Bible 32A. New York: Doubleday, 2008.

Garland, David E. *1 Corinthians.* Baker Exegetical Commentary on the New Testament. Grand Rapids: Baker Academic, 2003.

"Matthew's Understanding of the Temple Tax." Pages 69–98 in *Treasures New and Old: Contributions to Matthean Studies*. Society of Biblical Literature Symposium Series. Edited by David R. Bauer and Mark A. Powell. Atlanta: Scholars Press, 1996.

Gaston, Lloyd. *No Stone on Another: Studies in the Significance of the Fall of Jerusalem in the Synoptic Gospels*. Novum Testamentum Supplements 23. Leiden: Brill, 1970.

Gathercole, Simon. "The Titles of the Gospels in the Earliest New Testament Manuscripts." *Zeitschrift für die neutestamentliche Wissenschaft und die Kunde der älteren Kirche* 104 (2013): 33–76.

The Composition of the Gospel of Thomas: Original Language and Influences. Society for New Testament Studies Monograph Series 151. Cambridge: Cambridge University Press, 2012.

Geddert, Timothy J. *Watchwords: Mark 13 in Markan Eschatology*. Sheffield: JSOT, 1989.

Gerdmar, Anders. *Roots of Theological Anti-Semitism: German Biblical Interpretation and the Jews: From Herder and Semler to Kittel and Bultmann*. Leiden: Brill, 2009.

Gese, Hartmut. *Essays in Biblical Theology*. Translated by Keith Crim. Minneapolis: Augsburg, 1981.

Gillihan, Yonder Moynihan. "Sectarianism." Pages 718–721 in vol. 2 of *T&T Clark Encyclopedia of Second Temple Judaism*. Edited by Daniel M. Gurtner and Loren T. Stuckenbruck. 2 vols. London: T&T Clark, 2019.

Gnilka, Joachim. *Jesus von Nazaret: Botschaft und Geschichte*. Herders Theologischer Kommentar zum Neuen Testament. Freiberg: Herder, 1990.

Goldsmith, D. "Acts 13:33–37: A Pesher on 2 Samuel 7." *Journal of Biblical Literature* 87 (1968): 321–324.

Goodacre, Mark. "Criticizing the Criterion of Multiple Attestation: The Historical Jesus and the Question of Sources." Pages 152–169 in *Jesus, Criteria, and the Demise of Authenticity*. Edited by Chris Keith and Anthony Le Donne. London: T&T Clark, 2012.

Thomas and the Gospels: The Case for Thomas's Familiarity with the Synoptics. Grand Rapids: Eerdmans, 2012.

The Case Against Q: Studies in Markan Priority and the Synoptic Problem. Harrisburg: Trinity Press International, 2002.

Synoptic Problem: A Way through the Maze. London: T&T Clark, 2001.

Goodacre, Mark and Nicholas Perrin, eds. *Questioning Q: A Multidimensional Critique*. Downers Grove: InterVarsity Press, 2005.

Goulder, Michael. *Midrash and Location in Matthew*. London: SPCK, 1974.

Gray, Timothy C. *Temple in the Gospel of Mark: A Study in Its Narrative Role*. Wissenschaftltliche Untersuchungen zum Neuen Testament 2/242. Tübingen: Mohr Siebeck, 2008.

Green, H. Benedict. *Matthew, Poet of the Beatitudes*. Sheffield: Sheffield Academic Press, 2001.

Green, Joel B. "The Death of Jesus." Pages 2383–2408 in vol. 3 of *Handbook for the Study of the Historical Jesus*. 4 vols. Edited by Tom Holmén and Stanley E. Porter. Leiden: Brill, 2010.

The Gospel of Luke. New International Commentary on the New Testament. Grand Rapids: Eerdmans, 1997.

Gregg, Brian Han. *The Historical Jesus and the Final Judgment Sayings in Q.* Wissenschafltliche Untersuchungen zum Neuen Testament 207. Tübingen: Mohr Siebeck, 2006.

Grossberg, Daniel. "Judges." Page 752 in *Eerdmans Dictionary of the Bible.* Edited by David Noel Freedman, Allen C. Myers, and Astrid B. Beck. Grand Rapids: Eerdmans, 2000.

Grundman, Walter. *Das Evangelium nach Matthäus.* 3rd ed. Theologischer Handkommentar zum Neuen Testament 2. Berlin: Evangelische Verlagsanstalt, 1972.

Das Evangelium nach Lukas. Theologischer Handkommentar zum Neuen Testament. Berlin: Evangelische Verlagsanstalt, 1966.

Guelich, Robert A. "The Antitheses of Matthew v. 21–48: Traditional and/or Redactional?" *New Testament Studies* 22 (1976): 444–457.

Gundry, Robert H. *Matthew: A Commentary on His Handbook for a Mixed Church under Persecution.* 2nd ed. Grand Rapids: Eerdmans, 1994.

Gurtner, Daniel M. *Introducing the Pseudepigrapha of Second Temple Judaism: Message, Content, and Significance.* Grand Rapids: Baker Academic, 2020.

"Interpreting Apocalyptic Symbolism in the Gospel of Matthew." *Bulletin of Biblical Research* 22, 4 (2012): 525–545

"Matthew's Theology of the Temple and the 'Parting of the Ways.'" Pages 128–153 in *Built upon the Rock: Studies in the Gospel of Matthew.* Edited by Daniel M. Gurtner and John Nolland. Grand Rapids: Eerdmans, 2008.

The Torn Veil: Matthew's Exposition of the Death of Jesus. Society for New Testament Studies Monograph Series 139. Cambridge: Cambridge University Press, 2007.

Haenchen, Ernst. *John.* Hermeneia. 2 vols. Translated by Robert Funk. Edited by Robert W. Funk with Ulrich Busse. Minneapolis: Fortress Press, 1984.

Hägerland, Tobias. *Jesus and the Forgiveness of Sins: An Aspect of His Prophetic Mission.* Society for New Testament Study Monograph Series 150. Cambridge: Cambridge University Press, 2011.

Hagner, Donald A. "Matthew: Christian Judaism or Jewish Christianity." Pages 263–282 in *The Face of New Testament Studies: A Survey of Recent Research.* Edited by Scot McKnight and Grant R. Osborne. Grand Rapids: Baker Academic, 2004.

Matthew. 2 vols. Word Biblical Commentary 33A–B. Dallas: Word, 1993–1995.

Hahn, Ferdinand. *Der urchristliche Gottesdienst.* Stuttgarter Bibelstudien 41. Stuttgart: Katholisches Bibelwerk, 1970.

Ham, Clay Alan. *The Coming King and the Rejected Shepherd: Matthew's Reading of Zechariah's Messianic Hope.* New Testament Monographs 4. Sheffield: Sheffield Phoenix Press, 2005.

Hamilton, Catherine Sider. *The Death of Jesus in Matthew: Innocent Blood and the End of the Exile.* Society for New Testament Studies Monograph Series 167. Cambridge: Cambridge University Press, 2017.

Hamm, Dennis, S.J. "The Tamid Service in Luke-Acts: The Cultic Background Behind Luke's Theology of Worship (Luke 1:5–25; 18:9–14; 24:50–53; Acts 3:1; 10:3, 30)." *Catholic Biblical Quarterly* 25 (2003): 215–231.

Hare, Douglas R. *The Theme of Jewish Persecution of Christians in the Gospel According to St. Matthew.* Cambridge: Cambridge University Press, 1967.

Harrington, Daniel J., S.J. *First Corinthians.* Sacra Pagina 7. Collegeville: Liturgical Press, 1999.

The Gospel of Matthew. Sacra Pagina 1. Collegeville: Liturgical Press, 1991.

Harris, Murray J. *The Second Epistle to the Corinthians.* New International Greek Testament Commentary. Grand Rapids: Eerdmans, 2005.

Harris, Sarah. *The Davidic Shepherd King in the Lukan Narrative.* The Library of New Testament Studies 558. London: T&T Clark, 2016.

Hay, David M. *Glory at the Right Hand: Psalm 110 in Early Christianity.* Nashville: Abingdon Press, 1973.

Hays, Richard. *Echoes of Scripture in the Gospels.* Waco: Baylor University Press, 2016.

First Corinthians. Interpretation. Louisville: John Knox, 1997.

Heil, John Paul. "Jesus as the Unique High Priest in the Gospel of John." *Catholic Biblical Quarterly* 57, 4 (1995): 729–745.

"Ezekiel 34 and the Narrative Strategy of the Shepherd and Sheep Metaphor in Matthew." *Catholic Biblical Quarterly* 55 (1993): 698–708.

Hengel, Martin. "Jesus, the Messiah of Israel: The Debate about the 'Messianic Mission' of Jesus." Pages 329–349 in *Authenticating the Activities of Jesus.* Edited by B. Chilton and C. A. Evans. Leiden: Brill, 2002.

The Four Gospels and the One Gospel of Jesus Christ. Translated by John Bowden. Harrisburg: Trinity Press International, 2000.

Studies in Early Christology. Edinburgh: T&T Clark, 1995.

Hill, David. *The Gospel of Matthew.* New Century Bible. London: Oliphants, 1972.

Hofius, Otfried. "The Fourth Servant Song in the New Testament Letters." Pages 163–188 in *The Suffering Servant: Isaiah 53 in Jewish and Christian Sources.* Edited by Bernd Janowski and Peter Stuhlmacher. Grand Rapids: Eerdmans, 2004.

Holladay, William. *Jeremiah.* Edited by Paul D. Hanson. 2 vols. Hermeneia. Philadelphia: Fortress Press, 1986.

Holmén, Tom. *Jesus and Jewish Covenant Thinking.* Biblical Interpretation Series 55. Leiden: Brill, 2001.

"Doubts about Double Dissimilarity: Restructuring the Main Criterion of Jesus-of-History Research." Pages 47–80 in *Authenticating the Words of Jesus.* Leiden: Brill, 1999.

Holmgren, Frederick Carlson. *Israel Alive Again.* Grand Rapids: Eerdmans, 1987.

Holowchak, M. Andrew. *Thomas Jefferson's Bible: With Introduction and Critical Commentary.* Berlin: Walter de Gruyter, 2019.

Holtzmann, Heinrich Julius. *Die synoptischen Evangelien: ihr Ursprung und geschichtlicher Charakter.* Leipzig: Wilhelm Engelmann, 1863.

Hooker, Morna D. "Foreword: Forty Years On." Pages xiii–xvii in *Jesus, Criteria, and the Demise of Authenticity*. Edited by Chris Keith and Anthony Le Donne. London: T&T Clark, 2012.

"Creative Conflict: The Torah and Christology." Pages 137–156 in *Christology, Controversy, & Community: New Testament Essays in Honour of David R. Catchpole*. Edited by David G. Horrell and Christopher M. Tuckett. Leiden: Brill, 2000.

The Signs of a Prophet: The Prophetic Actions of Jesus. Harrisburg: Trinity Press International, 1997.

The Gospel According to St. Mark. Black's New Testament Commentaries. Peabody: Hendrickson, 1991.

"Traditions about the Temple in the Sayings of Jesus." *Bulletin of the John Rylands University Library of Manchester* 70 (1988): 7–19.

"On Using the Wrong Tool." *Theology* 75 (1972): 570–581.

"Christology and Methodology." *New Testament Studies* 17 (1970–1971): 480–487.

Horbury, William. "The Temple Tax." Pages 265–286 in *Jesus and the Politics of His Day*. Edited by Ernst Bammel and C. F. D. Moule. Cambridge: Cambridge University Press, 1984.

Horsely, Richard. *Jesus and the Spiral of Violence: Popular Jewish Resistance in Roman Palestine*. Minneapolis: Fortress Press, 1993.

Hoskins, Paul M. *Jesus as the Fulfillment of the Temple in the Gospel of John*. Paternoster Biblical Monographs. Carlisle: Paternoster, 2006.

Hubaut, Michel. *La parabole des vignerons homicides*. Cahiers de la Revue biblique 16. Paris: Gabalda, 1976.

Hüber, Hans. "OT Quotations in the New Testament." Pages 1096–1104 in vol. 4 of *Anchor Bible Dictionary Anchor Bible Dictionary*. Edited by D. N. Freedman. 6 vols. Anchor Bible Reference Library. New York: Doubleday, 1992.

Huizenga, Leroy. *The New Isaac: Tradition and Intertextuality in the Gospel of Matthew*. Supplements to Novum Testamentum 131. Leiden: Brill, 2009.

Hultgren, Arland J. *The Parables of Jesus: A Commentary*. Grand Rapids: Eerdmans, 2000.

Ingolfsland, Dennis. "The Historical Jesus According to John Meier and N.T. Wright." *Bibliotheca sacra* 155 (1998): 460–473.

Ishida, Tomoo. *The Royal Dynasties in Ancient Israel: A Study on the Formation and Development of Royal-Dynastic Ideology*. New York: Walter de Gruyter, 1977.

Jackson-McCabe, Matt A. *Jewish Christianity: The Making of the Christianity-Judaism Divide*, Anchor Yale Bible Reference Library. New Haven: Yale University Press, 2020.

Jamieson, R. B. *Jesus's Death and Heavenly Offering in Hebrews*. Society for New Testament Studies Monograph Series 172. Cambridge: Cambridge University Press, 2018.

Jaubert, Annie. *The Date of the Last Supper*. Translated by I. Rafferty. Staten Island: Alba House, 1965.

Jensen, Matthew. "The (In)authenticity of 1 Thessalonians 2.13–16: A Review of the Arguments." *Currents in Biblical Research* 18, 1 (2019): 59–79.

Jeremias, Joachim. *New Testament Theology: The Proclamation of Jesus.* Translated by John Bowden. New York: Scribner's, 1971.

Jewett, Robert. *Romans.* Hermeneia. Minneapolis: Fortress Press, 2007.

Jipp, Joshua W. *The Messianic Theology of the New Testament.* Grand Rapids: Eerdmans, 2020.

Johansson, Daniel. "'Who Can Forgive Sins but God Alone?' Human and Angelic Agents and Divine Forgiveness in Early Judaism." *Journal for the Study of the New Testament* 33, 4 (2011): 351–374.

Johnstone, William. *1 and 2 Chronicles.* 2 vols. Sheffield: Sheffield Academic Press, 1997.

Jonge, Henk Jan de. "The Cleansing of the Temple in Mark 11.15 and Zechariah 14.21." Pages 87–100 in *The Book of Zechariah and its Influence: Papers of the Oxford-Leiden Conference.* Aldershot: Ashgate, 2003.

Joseph, Simon J. "Exit the 'Great Man': On James' Crossley's Jesus and the Chaos of History." *Journal for the Study of the Historical Jesus* 16 (2018): 3–22.

Jesus and the Temple: Crucifixion in its Jewish Context. Society for New Testament Studies Monograph Series 165. Cambridge: Cambridge University Press, 2016.

The Nonviolent Messiah: Jesus, Q, and the Enochic Tradition. Minneapolis: Fortress Press, 2014.

Juel, Donald. *Messiah and Temple.* Society of Biblical Literature Dissertation Series 31. Missoula: Scholars Press, 1977.

Jülicher, Adolf. *Die Gleichnisreden Jesu.* 2 vols. 2nd ed. Tübingen: Mohr Siebeck, 1910.

Kahl, Brigitte. *Galatians Re-Imagined: Reading with the Eyes of the Vanquished.* Minneapolis: Fortress Press, 2010.

Kampen, John. "The Problem of Christian Anti-Semitism and a Sectarian Reading of the Gospel of Matthew: The Trial of Jesus." Pages 371–397 in *Matthew within Judaism: Israel and the Nations.* Early Christianity and Its Literature. Edited by Anders Runesson and Daniel M. Gurtner. Atlanta: SBL Press, 2019.

Matthew within Sectarian Judaism. Anchor Yale Bible Reference Library. New Haven: Yale University Press, 2019.

"Torah's Authority in the Major Sectarian Rules Texts from Qumran." Pages 231–254 in *The Scrolls and Biblical Traditions: Proceedings of the Seventh Meeting of the IOQS in Helsinki.* Edited by George J. Brooke, Daniel K. Falk, Eibert J. C. Tigchelaar, and Molly M. Zahn. Studies on the Texts of the Desert of Judah 104. Leiden: Brill, 2012.

Kapic, K. M. "Receiving Christ's Priestly Benediction: A Biblical, Historical, and Theological Exploration of Luke 24:50–53." *Westminster Theological Journal* 67 (2005): 247–260.

Kazen, Thomas. "The Coming of the Son of Man Revisited." *Journal for the Study of the Historical Jesus* 5, 2 (2007): 155–174.

Keener, Craig S. *Christobiography: Memory, History, and the Reliability of the Gospels.* Grand Rapids: Eerdmans, 2019.

Acts: An Exegetical Commentary. 4 vols. Grand Rapids: Baker Academic, 2012–2015.

The Historical Jesus of the Gospels: Jesus in Historical Context. Grand Rapids: Eerdmans, 2009.

A Commentary on the Gospel of Matthew. Grand Rapids: Eerdmans, 1998.

Keith, Chris and Anthony Le Donne, eds. *Jesus, Criteria, and the Demise of Authenticity.* London: T&T Clark, 2012.

Keith, Chris. "The Narratives of the Gospels and the Historical Jesus: Current Debates, Prior Debates and the Goal of Historical Jesus Research." *Journal for the Study of the New Testament* 38, 4 (2016): 426–455.

"Social Memory Theory and Gospels Research: The First Decade (Part One)." *Early Christianity* 6 (2015): 3347–76.

"Social Memory Theory and Gospels Research: The First Decade (Part Two)." *Early Christianity* 6 (2015): 517–542.

"The Indebtedness of the Criteria Approach to Form Criticism and Recent Attempts to Rehabilitate the Search for an Authentic Jesus." Pages 3–37 in *Jesus, Criteria, and the Demise of Authenticity.* Edited by Chris Keith and Anthony Le Donne. London: T&T Clark, 2012.

Jesus's Literacy: Scribal Culture and the Teacher from Galilee. The Library of New Testament Studies 413. London: T&T Clark, 2011.

Kelber, W. H. "Jesus and Tradition: Words in Time, Words in Space." *Semeia* 65 (1995): 139–167.

Kerr, Alan. *The Temple of Jesus's Body: The Temple Theme in the Gospel of John.* Journal for the Study of the New Testament Supplement Series 220. Sheffield: Sheffield Academic, 2002.

Kilpatrick, George D. *The Origins of the Gospel according to Matthew.* Oxford: Clarendon, 1946.

Kinman, Brent. *Jesus's Entry into Jerusalem in the Context of Lukan Theology and the Politics of His Day.* Leiden: Brill, 1995.

Kirk, Alan. *Memory and the Jesus Tradition.* The Reception of Jesus in the First Three Centuries. London: Bloomsbury T&T Clark, 2018.

Kirk, J. R. Daniel. *A Man Attested by God: The Human Jesus of the Synoptic Gospels.* Grand Rapids: Eerdmans, 2016.

Klawans, Jonathan. "Imagining Judaism after 70 c.e." Pages 201–215 in *Companion to Ancient Jews and Judaism: Third Century BCE to Seventh Century CE.* Edited by Naomi Koltun-Fromm and Gwynn Kessler. Hoboken: Wiley Blackwell, 2020.

"Josephus, the Rabbis, and Responses to Catastrophes Ancient and Modern." *Jewish Quarterly Review* 100 (2010): 278–309.

Purity, Sacrifice, and the Temple: Symbolism and Supersessionism in the Study of Ancient Judaism. Oxford: Oxford University Press, 2006.

"Interpreting the Last Supper: Sacrifice, Spiritualization, and Anti-Sacrifice." *New Testament Studies* 48 (2002): 11–17.

Kloppenborg, John S. *The Tenants in the Vineyard: Ideology, Economics, and Agrarian Conflict in Jewish Jewish Palestine.* Wissenschaftliche Untersuchungen zum Neuen Testament 195. Tubingen: Mohr Siebeck, 2006.

The Formation of Q: Trajectories in Ancient Wisdom Collections. Studies in Antiquity and Christianity. Harrisburg: Trinity Press International, 2000.

Kodell, Jerome. *The Eucharist in the New Testament*. Collegeville: Michael Glazier, 1988.

Koester, Craig. *Symbolism in the Fourth Gospel: Meaning, Mystery, Community*. 2nd ed. Minneapolis: Fortress Press, 2003.

Konradt, Matthias. *The Gospel according to Matthew: A Commentary*. Translated by M. Eugene Boring. Waco: Baylor University Press, 2020.

Israel, Church, and the Gentiles in the Gospel of Matthew. Baylor-Mohr Siebeck Studies in Early Christianity. Translated by Kathleen Ess. Waco: Baylor University Press, 2014.

Korner, Ralph. *The Origin and Meaning of Ekklēsia in the Early Jesus Movement*. Arbeiten zur Geschichte des antiken Judentums und des Urchristentums 98. Leiden: Brill, 2017.

Köstenberger, Andreas. "The Destruction of the Second Temple and the Composition of the Fourth Gospel." Pages 69–108 in *Challenging Perspectives on the Gospel of John*. Edited by John Lierman. Wissenschaftliche Untersuchungen zum Neuen Testament 2/219. Tübingen: Mohr Siebeck, 2006.

Kraus, Hans-Joachim. *Psalmen*. 2 vols. Biblischer Kommentar, Altes Testament. Rev. ed. Neukirchen-Vluyn: Neukirchener, 1978.

Kreitzer, Larry. *2 Corinthians*. New Testament Guides. Sheffield: Sheffield Academic Press, 1996.

Kupp, David D. *Matthew's Emmanuel: Divine Presence and God's People in the First Gospel*. Society for New Testament Studies Manuscript Series 90. Cambridge: Cambridge University Press, 1996.

Kvalbein, Hans. "The Authorization of Peter in Matthew 16:17–19: A Reconsideration of the Power to Bind and Loose." Pages 145–176 in *The Formation of the Early Church*. Edited by Jostein Ådna. Wissenschaftliche Untersuchungen zum Neuen Testament 183. Tübingen: Mohr Siebeck, 2005.

Kwon, JongHyun. *The Historical Jesus' Death and 'Forgiveness of Sins'*. Wissenschaftliche Untersuchungen zum Neuen Testament 2/467. Tübingen: Mohr Siebeck, 2018.

Laato, Antti. *A Star is Rising: The Historical Development of the Old Testament Royal Ideology and the Rise of the Jewish Messianic Expectations*. Atlanta: Scholars Press, 1997.

Lacocque, André. *The Book of Daniel*. Translated by D. Pellauer. London: SPCK, 1979.

Lamerson, Samuel. Review of *Constructing Jesus: Memory, Imagination, and History,* by Dale C. Allison, Jr. *Journal of the Evangelical Theology Society* 54 (2011): 839

Lanier, Gregory R. "A Case for the Assimilation of Matthew 21:44 to the Lukan 'Crushing Stone' (20:18), with Special Reference to $\mathfrak{P}^{104}$." *TC: A Journal of Biblical Textual Criticism* 21 (2016): 1–21.

Le Donne, Anthony. "The Rise of the Quest for an Authentic Jesus: An Introduction to the Crumbling Foundations of Jesus Research." Pages 3–21 in *Jesus, Criteria, and the Demise of Authenticity*. Edited by Chris Keith and Anthony Le Donne. London: T&T Clark, 2012.

The Historiographical Jesus: Memory, Typology, and the Son of David. Waco: Baylor University Press, 2009.

Lee, Aquila H. I. *From Messiah to Preexistent Son: Jesus' Self-Consciousness and Early Christian Exegesis of Messianic Psalms*. Wissenschafltliche Untersuchungen zum Neuen Testament 2/192. Tübingen: Mohr Siebeck, 2005.

Légasse, S. "Aproche de l'episode préévangélique des Fils de Zébédée (Marc X.35–40 par.)." *New Testament Studies* 20 (1974): 161–177.

Leim, Joshua E. *Matthew's Theological Grammar: The Father and the Son*. Wissenschafltliche Untersuchungen zum Neuen Testament 2/402. Tübingen: Mohr Siebeck, 2015.

Léon-Dufour, Xavier. *Sharing the Eucharistic Bread: The Witness of the New Testament*. Translated by Matthew J. O'Connell. New York and Mahwah: Paulist Press, 1982.

Levine, Amy-Jill. *Sermon on the Mount: A Beginners Guide to the Kingdom of Heaven*. Nashville: Abingdon Press, 2020.

"Concluding Reflections: What's Next in the Study of Matthew?" Pages 449–466 in *Matthew within Judaism: Israel and the Nations*. Early Christian Literature. Edited by Anders Runesson and Daniel M. Gurtner. Atlanta: SBL Press, 2019.

"Matthew's Portrayal of the Synagogue and Its Leaders." Pages 177–193 in *The Gospel of Matthew at the Crossroads of Early Christianity*. Edited by Donald Senior, C.P.. Leuven: Peeters, 2011.

"Introduction." Pages 1–39 in *Jesus in Context: Princeton Readings in Religion*. Edited by Amy-Jill Levine, Dale C. Allison, Jr., and John D. Crossan. Princeton: Princeton University Press, 2006.

A Misunderstood Jew: The Church and the Scandal of the Jewish Jesus. San Francisco: HarperOne, 2006.

The Social and Ethnic Dimensions of Matthean Social History. Lewiston: Edwin Mellen, 1988.

Levine, Amy-Jill and Ben Witherington III. *Luke*. New Cambridge Bible Commentary. Cambridge: Cambridge University Press, 2018.

Levine, Lee I. "The Sages and the Synagogue in Late Antiquity: The Evidence of the Galilee." Pages 201–222 in *The Galilee in Late Antiquity*. Edited by Lee I. Levine. New York: Jewish Theological Seminary, 1992.

Liver, Jacob. "The Half-Shekel Offering in Biblical and Post-Biblical Literature." *Harvard Theological Review* 56 (1963): 173–189.

Lohmeyer, Ernst. *Lord of the Temple*. Translated by Stewart Todd. Richmond: John Knox Press, 1962.

Das Evangelium nach Markus. Kritisch-exegetischer Kommentar über das Neue Testament I/2. Göttingen: Vandenhoeck & Ruprecht, 1937.

Loofs, Friedrich. *What Is the Truth about Jesus Christ? Problems of Christology*. New York: Charles Scribner's Sons, 1913.

Loos, Hendrik van der. *The Miracles of Jesus*. Leiden: Brill, 1965.

Luckensmeyer, David. *The Eschatology of First Thessalonians*. Göttingen: Vandenhoeck & Ruprecht, 2009.

Lüdemann, Gerd. *Jesus after 2000 Years*. Translated by John Bowden. London: SCM; Amherst: Prometheus Books, 2001.

Luz, Ulrich. "Matthew's Interpretive 'Tendencies' and the 'Historical' Jesus." Pages 577–99 in *Jesus Research: New Methodologies and Perceptions, The Second Princeton-Prague Symposium on Jesus Research*. Edited by James H. Charlesworth with Brian Rhea and Petr Pokorný. Grand Rapids: Eerdmans, 2014.

Matthew. Hermeneia. 3 vols. Translated by James E. Crouch. Minneapolis: Fortress Press, 2001–2007.

Mack, Burton L. *A Myth of Innocence: Mark and Christian Origins*. Philadelphia: Fortress Press, 1988.

Mackay, Ian D. *John's Relationship with Mark: An Analysis of John 6 in Light of Mark 6–8*. Wissenschaftliche Untersuchungen zum Neuen Testament 2/182. Tübingen: Mohr Siebeck, 2004.

Malherbe, Abraham J. *The Letters to the Thessalonians*. Anchor Yale Bible 32B. New Haven: Yale University Press, 2008.

Magness, Jodi. "Sectarianism Before and After 70 CE." Pages 69–89 in *Was 70 CE a Watershed in Jewish History?: On Jews and Judaism before and after the Destruction of the Second Temple*. Edited by Daniel R. Schwartz, Zeev Weiss, and Ruth A. Clements. Leiden: Brill, 2012.

Manson, Thomas W. *The Teaching of Jesus*. Cambridge: Cambridge University Press, 1963.

"The Son of Man in Daniel, Enoch, and the Gospels." *Bulletin of the John Rylands University Library of Manchester* 32 (1950): 171–195.

Marcus, Joel. *Mark*. 2 vols. Anchor Bible 27–27A. New York: Doubleday, 2000, 2009.

The Way of the Lord: Christological Exegesis of the Old Testament in the Gospel of Mark. Louisville: Westminster/John Knox Press, 1992.

Marguerat, Daniel. *Le Jugement dans l'Évangile de Matthieu*. 2nd ed. Geneva: Labor et Fides, 1995.

Marshall, I. Howard. *Last Supper and Lord's Supper*. Exeter: Paternoster, 1980.

Commentary on Luke: A Commentary on the Greek Text. Exeter: Paternoster, 1978.

Martin, Troy W. "Pagan and Judeo-Christian Time-Keeping Schemes in Gal 4:10 and 2:16." *New Testament Studies* 42 (1996): 105–119.

Martínez, Florentino García and Eibert J. C. Tigchelaar. *The Dead Sea Scrolls Study Edition*. 2 vols. Leiden: Brill, 1997/1998.

Martyn, J. Louis. *Galatians*. Anchor Bible 33A. New York: Doubleday, 1997.

Mason, Eric. *'You Are A Priest Forever': Second Temple Jewish Messianism and the Priestly Christology of the Epistle to the Hebrews*. Studies on the Texts of the Desert of Judah 74. Leiden: Brill, 2008.

Mason, Steve. *Josephus and the New Testament*. 2nd ed. Grand Rapids: Baker Academic, 2003.

Matson, Mark. *In Dialogue with Another Gospel? The Influence of the Fourth Gospel on the Passion Narrative of the Gospel of Luke*. Society of Biblical Literature Dissertation Series 178. Atlanta: Society of Biblical Literature, 2001.

McCarthy, Dennis J. *Treaty and Covenant: A Study in Form in the Ancient Oriental Documents and in the Old Testament*. Analecta Biblica 21. Rome: Biblical Institute Press, 1981.

McGuckin, John A. "Sacrifice and Atonement: An Investigation into the Attitude of Jesus of Nazareth towards Cultic Sacrifice." Pages 648–661 in vol. 1 of *Remembering for the Future*. 3 vols. Edited by Y. Bauer et al. Oxford: Pergamon, 1989.

McKnight, Scot. *Sermon on the Mount*. Story of God Bible Commentary. Grand Rapids: Zondervan, 2013.

———. "The Jesus We'll Never Know." *Christianity Today* 54, 4 [2010]: 22–26.

———. *Jesus and His Death: Historiography, the Historical Jesus, and Atonement Theory*. Waco: Baylor University Press, 2005.

———. "Jesus and Prophetic Actions." *Bulletin for Biblical Research* 10, 2 (2000): 197–232.

Meier, John P. *A Marginal Jew: Rethinking the Historical Jesus*. Anchor Yale Bible Reference Library. 5 vols. New Haven: Yale University Press, 1991, 1994, 2001, 2009, 2016.

———. "From Elijah-Like Prophet to Royal Davidic Messiah." Pages 45–83 in *Jesus: A Colloquium in the Holy Land*. Edited by Doris Donnelly. New York: Continuum, 2001.

———. "Jesus, the Twelve and Restoration." Pages 365–404 in *Restoration: Old Testament, Jewish, and Christian Perspectives*. Edited by James M. Scott. Leiden: Brill, 2001.

———. "The Present State of the 'Third Quest' for the Historical Jesus: Loss and Gain." *Biblica* 80 (1999): 459–487.

———. "Dividing Lines in Jesus Research Today: Through Dialectical Negation to a Positive Sketch." *Interpretation* 50, 4 (1996): 355–372.

———. *Matthew*. New Testament Message 3. Wilmington: Michael Glazier, 1980.

———. *The Vision of Matthew: Christ, Church, and Morality in the First Gospel*. New York: Paulist Press, 1979.

———. *Law and History in Matthew's Gospel*. Analecta Biblica 71. Rome: Biblical Institute Press, 1976.

Meyer, Ben F. "The Expiation Motif in the Eucharistic Words." Pages 11–33 in *One Loaf, One Cup: Ecumenical Studies of 1 Cor 11 and other Eucharistic Texts*. Edited by B. F. Meyer. The Cambridge Conference on the Eucharist August 1988. New Gospel Studies 6. Macon: Mercer, 1993.

———. *Christus Faber: The Master-Builder and the House of God*. Allison Park: Pickwick Publications, 1992.

———. *The Aims of Jesus*. London: SCM, 1979.

Milgrom, Jacob. *JPS Torah Commentary: Numbers*. Philadelphia: Jewish Publication Society, 1990.

Miller, Stuart S. "The Rabbis and the Non Existent Monolithic Synagogue." Pages 57–70 in *Jews, Christians, and Polytheists in the Ancient Synagogue: Cultural Interaction during the Greco-Roman Period*. Edited by Steven Fine. London: Routledge, 1999.

Miura, Yuzuru. *David in Luke-Acts*. Wissenschafltliche Untersuchungen zum Neuen Testament 2/232. Tübingen: Mohr Siebeck, 2005.

Moloney, Francis J., S.B.D. "Revisiting the Temple: Mark 11:15–16 and 13:2." Pages 61–75 *The Figure of Jesus in History and Theology: Essays in Honor of John Meier*. Edited by Vincent T. M. Skemp and Kelley Coblentz Bautch. CBQI 1. Washington, DC: CBA, 2020.

Montefiore, C. G. *The Synoptic Gospels*. 3 vols. London: Macmillan and Co., 1909.

Najman, Hindy J. *Seconding Sinai: The Development of Mosaic Discourse in Second Temple Judaism*. Supplements to the Journal for the Study of Judaism 77. Leiden: Brill, 2003.

Nanos, Mark. *The Irony of Galatians: Paul's Letter in First-Century Context*. Minneapolis: Fortress Press, 2002.

Nanos, Mark D. and Magnus Zetterholm. *Paul within Judaism: Restoring the First-Century Context to the Apostle*. Minneapolis: Fortress Press, 2015.

Neirynck, Frans. "John and the Synoptics: 1975–1990." Pages 3–62 in *John and the Synoptics*. Leuven: Leuven University Press, 1992.

"APO TOTE ERKXATO and the Structure of Matthew." Pages 141–182 in *Evangelica II 1982–1991: Collected Essays by Frans Neirynck*. Edited by F. Van Segbroeck. Leuven: University Press, 1991.

"John and the Synoptics." Pages 73–106 in *L'évangile de Jean: Sources, redaction, théologie*. Edited by M. De Jonge. Bibliotheca Ephemeridum Theologicarum Lovaniensium 45. Leuven: Leuven University Press, 1977.

Neusner, Jacob. "Money Changers in the Temple: The Mishna's Explanation." *New Testament Studies* 35 (1989): 287–290.

Newport, Kenneth G. C. *The Sources and Sitz im Leben of Matthew 23*. Journal for the Study of the New Testament Supplement Series 117. Sheffield: Sheffield Academic Press, 1995.

Nihan, Christophe. *From Priestly Torah to Pentateuch: A Study in the Composition of the Book of Leviticus*. Forschungen zum Alten Testament 2/25. Tübingen: Mohr Siebeck, 2007.

Nolland, John. *The Gospel of Matthew*. New International Greek Text Commentary. Grand Rapids: Eerdmans, 2005.

Luke. 3 vols. Word Biblical Commentary 35A–C. Dallas: Word, 1989–1993.

Novakovic, Lidija. *Messiah, the Healer of the Sick: A Study of Jesus as the Son of David in the Gospel of Matthew*. Wissenschafltliche Untersuchungen zum Neuen Testament 2/170. Tübingen: Mohr Siebeck, 2003.

Novenson, Matthew V. *The Grammar of Messianism: An Ancient Political Idiom and Its Users*. Oxford: Oxford University, 2017.

O'Brien, Peter Thomas. *The Epistle to the Philippians: A Commentary on the Greek Text. New International Greek Testament Commentary*. Grand Rapids: Eerdmans, 1991.

O'Leary, Anne M. *Matthew's Judaization of Mark: Examined in the Context of the Use of Sources in Graeco-Roman Antiquity*. Library of New Testament Studies 323. London: T&T Clark, 2006.

Olmstead, Wesley G. *Matthew 15–28: A Handbook on the Greek Text*. Waco: Baylor University Press, 2019.

Overman, J. Andrew. *The Church and Community in Crisis: The Gospel According to Matthew*. London: Bloomsbury, 1996.

Pascut, Beniamin. *Redescribing Jesus's Divinity Through a Social Science Theory: An Interdisciplinary Analysis of Forgiveness and Divine Identity in Ancient Judaism and Mark 2:1–12*. Wissenschafltliche Untersuchungen zum Neuen Testament 2/438. Tübingen: Mohr Siebeck, 2017.

Patterson, Jane Lancaster. *Keeping the Feast: Metaphors of Sacrifice in 1 Corinthians and Philippians.* Early Christianity and Its Literature. Atlanta: SBL Press, 2015.

Patterson, Stephen J. "Can You Trust a Gospel? A Review of Richard Bauckham's *Jesus and the Eyewitnesses.*" *Journal for the Study of the Historical Jesus* 6 (2008): 194–210.

Paul, Shalom M. *Isaiah 40–66: Translation and Commentary.* Eerdmans Critical Commentary. Grand Rapids: Eerdmans, 2012.

Perrin, Nicholas. *Jesus the Priest.* London: SPCK, 2018.

Perrin, Norman. *Rediscovering the Teaching of Jesus.* New York: Harper & Row, 1967.

Pesch, Rudolf. *Das Markusevangelium.* Handkommentar zum Neuen Testament 2. 2 vols. Freiburg: Herder, 1977.

Piotrowski, Nicholas G. *Matthew's New David at the End of Exile: A Socio-Rhetorical Study of Scriptural Quotations.* Supplements to Novum Testamentum 170. Leiden: Brill, 2016.

Pitre, Brant. "Beyond the Criteria of Authenticity: Where Do We Go from Here?" Paper presented at the Annual Meeting of the Society of Biblical Literature. San Diego, CA, 23 November 2015.

Jesus and the Last Supper. Grand Rapids: Eerdmans, 2015.

"Jesus and the Messianic Priesthood." Paper presented at the annual meeting of the Society of Biblical Literature. Boston, MA, 23 November 2008.

Jesus, the Tribulation, and the End of the Exile. Wissenschaftliche Untersuchungen zum Neuen Testament 2/205. Tübingen: Mohr Siebeck, 2005.

Pitre, Brant, Michael P. Barber, and John A. Kincaid. *Paul, A New Covenant Jew: Rethinking Pauline Theology.* Grand Rapids: Eerdmans, 2019.

Poirier, John C. and Jeffrey Peterson, eds. *Marcan Priority without Q: Explorations in the Farrer Hypothesis.* The Library of New Testament Studies 455. London: T&T Clark, 2015.

Polkow, Dennis. "Method and Criteria for Historical Jesus Research." Pages 336–356 in *Society of Biblical Literature 1987 Seminar Papers.* Edited by K. H. Richards. Atlanta: Scholars Press, 1987.

Porter, Stanley E. *The Criteria for Authenticity in Historical-Jesus Research: Previous Discussion and New Proposals.* London: T&T Clark, 2000.

Porter, Stanley E. and Bryan R. Dyer. "What Have We Learned regarding the Synoptic Problem, and What Do We Still Need to Learn?" Pages 165–178 in *The Synoptic Problem: Four Views.* Edited by Stanley E. Porter and Bryan R. Dyer. Grand Rapids: Baker Academic, 2016.

Prothro, James B. *Both Judge and Justifier.* Wissenschaftliche Untersuchungen zum Neuen Testament 2/461. Tübingen: Mohr Siebeck, 2018.

Reeves, Rodney. "The Gospel of Matthew." Pages 275–296 in *The State of New Testament Studies: A Survey of Recent Research.* Edited by Scot McKnight and Nijay K. Gupta. Grand Rapids: Baker Academic, 2019.

Regev, Eyal. *The Temple in Early Christianity: Experiencing the Sacred.* Anchor Yale Bible Reference Library. New Haven: Yale University Press, 2019.

Repschinski, Boris. *The Controversy Stories in the Gospel of Matthew: Their Redaction, Form and Relevance for the Relationship Between the Matthean Community and Formative Judaism.* Forschungen zur Religion und Literatur des Alten und Neuen Testaments 189. Göttingen: Vadenhoeck & Ruprecht, 2000.

Reuss, Eduard. *Geschichte der heiligen Schriften, Neuen Testamentes.* Braunschweig: C. A. Schwetschke und Sohn (M. Bruhn), 1860.

Richardson, Peter. "Why Turn the Tables? Jesus's Protest in the Temple Precincts." Pages 507–523 in *Society of Biblical Literature Seminary Papers 1992.* Edited by E. H. Lovering. Atlanta: Scholars Press, 1992.

Robinson, Bernard P. "Peter and His Successors: Tradition and Redaction in Matthew 16:17–19." *Journal for the Study of the New Testament* 21 (1984): 85–104.

Rodriguez, A. M. "Sanctuary Theology in Exodus." *Andrews University Seminary Studies* 24 (1986): 127–145.

Rodríguez, Rafael. "Jesus as His Friends Remembered Him: A Review of Dale Allison's Constructing Jesus." *Journal for the Study of the Historical Jesus* 12 (2014): 224–244.

———. *Structuring Early Christian Memory: Jesus in Tradition, Performance and Text.* Library of New Testament Studies 407. London: T&T Clark, 2010.

———. "Authenticating Criteria: The Use and Misuse of a Critical Method." *Journal for the Study of the Historical Jesus* 7 (2009): 152–167.

Rollmann, Hans and Werner Zager, "Unveröffentlichte Briefe William Wredes zur Problematisierung des messianischen Selbstverständnisses Jesu." *Zeitschrift für neuere Theologiegeschichte* 8 (2001): 274–317.

Row, Robert D. *God's Kingdom and God's Son: The Background to Mark's Christology from Concepts of Kingship in the Psalms.* Leiden: Brill, 2002.

Rubin, David C. *Memory in Oral Traditions: The Cognitive Psychology of Epic Ballads, and Counting-out Rhymes.* Oxford: Oxford University Press, 1995.

Runesson, Anders. *Divine Wrath and Salvation in Matthew: The Narrative World of the First Gospel.* Minneapolis: Fortress Press, 2016.

———. "Behind the Gospel of Matthew: Radical Pharisees in Post-war Galilee?" *Currents in Theology and Mission* 37 (2010): 460–471.

———. "Rethinking Early Jewish-Christian Relations: Matthean Community History as Pharisaic Intragroup Conflict." *Journal of Biblical Literature* 127 (2008): 95–132.

———. *The Origins of the Synagogue: A Socio-Historical Study.* Stockholm: Almqvist International, 2001.

Runesson, Anders, Donald Binder, and Birger Olsson. *The Ancient Synagogue from Its Origins to 200 C.E.: A Source Book.* Ancient Judaism and Early Christianity 72. Leiden: Brill, 2008.

Runesson, Anders and Daniel M. Gurtner, eds. *Matthew within Judaism: Israel and the Nations.* Early Christian Literature. Atlanta: SBL Press, 2019.

Ryan, Jordan J. *The Role of the Synagogue in the Aims of Jesus.* Minneapolis: Fortress Press, 2017.

Saldarini, Anthony J. *Matthew's Christian-Jewish Community.* Chicago: University of Chicago Press, 1994.

Sanders, E. P. *Paul: The Apostle's Life, Letters, and Thought.* Minneapolis: Fortress Press, 2015.

———. *The Historical Figure of Jesus.* London: Penguin Books, 1993.

———. *Judaism: Practice and Belief, 63 BCE – 66 CE.* London: SCM Press, 1992.

Jesus and Judaism. Philadelphia: Fortress Press, 1985.

Sanders, E. P. and Margaret Davies. *Studying the Synoptic Gospels.* London: SCM Press, 1989.

Schäfer, Peter. "Tempel und Schöpfung. Zur Interpretation einiger Heiligtumstraditionen in der rabbinischen Literatur." Pages 122–133 in *Studien zur Geschichte und Theologie des rabbinischen Judentums.* Arbeiten zur Geschichte des antiken Judentums und des Urchristentums 15. Leiden: Brill, 1978.

Scharlemann, Martin. *Stephen: A Singular Saint.* Analecta Biblica 34. Rome: Biblical Institute, 1968.

Schniedewind, William M. *Society and the Promise to David: The Reception History of 2 Samuel 7:1–17.* Oxford: Oxford University Press, 1999.

Schreiner, Patrick. *Matthew: Disciple and Scribe: The First Gospel and Its Portrait of Jesus.* Grand Rapids: Baker Academic, 2019.

Schudson, Michael. "Dynamics of Distortion in Collective Memory." Pages 346–364 in *Memory Distortion: How Minds, Brains, and Societies Reconstruct the Past.* Edited by Daniel L. Schachter. Cambridge, MA: Harvard University Press, 1995.

Schwartz, Barry. *Abraham Lincoln and the Forge of National Memory.* Chicago: University of Chicago Press, 2000.

Schwartz, Daniel R. "Introduction: Was 70 CE a Watershed in Jewish History? Three Stages of Modern Scholarship, and a Renewed Effort." Pages 1–19 in *Was 70 CE a Watershed in Jewish History?: On Jews and Judaism before and after the Destruction of the Second Temple.* Edited by Daniel R. Schwartz, Zeev Weiss, and Ruth A. Clements. Leiden: Brill, 2012.

Studies in the Jewish Background of Christianity. Wissenschafltliche Untersuchungen zum Neuen Testament 60. Tübingen: Mohr Siebeck, 1992.

Schweizer, Eduard. *Das Evangelium nach Matthäus.* Das Neues Testament Deutsch 2. 3rd ed. Göttingen: Vandenhoeck & Ruprecht, 1981.

Schweitzer, Steven. *Reading Utopia in Chronicles.* The Library of Biblical Studies. London: T&T Clark, 2007.

Scott, R. B. Y. *The Relevance of the Prophets.* New York: Macmillan Company, 1960.

Senior, Donald, C.P. "Viewing the Jewish Jesus of History through the Lens of Matthew." Pages 81–95 in *Soundings in the Religion of Jesus: Perspectives and Methods in Jewish and Christian Scholarship.* Edited by Bruce Hilton, Anthony Le Donne, and Jacob Neusner. Minneapolis: Fortress Press, 2012.

Matthew. Abingdon New Testament Commentary. Nashville: Abingdon, 1998.

Sherwin-White, A. N. *Roman Society and Roman Law in the New Testament.* Oxford: Clarendon Press, 1963.

Shively, Elizabeth E. *Apocalyptic Imagination in the Gospel of Mark: The Literary and Theological Role of Mark 3:22–30.* Beihefte zur Zeitschrift für die neutestamentliche Wissenschaft 189. Berlin: Walter de Gruyter, 2012.

Sim, David C. "Matthew: The Current State of Research." Pages 33–51 in *Mark and Matthew, Comparative Readings I: Understanding the Earliest Gospels in their First Century Settings.* Edited by Eve-Marie Becker and Anders Runesson. Tübingen: Mohr Siebeck, 2011.

"Matthew and Jesus of Nazareth." Pages 155–176 in *Matthew and His Chris-tian Contemporaries*. Edited by David C. Sim and Boris Repschinski. The Library of New Testament Studies 333. New York: T&T Clark, 2008.

"The Gospel of Matthew, John the Elder and the Papias Tradition: A Response to R. H. Gundry." *Hervormde teologiese studies* 63 (2007): 283–299.

"The Gospels for All Christians? A Response to Richard Bauckham." *Journal for the Study of the New Testament* 84 (2001): 3–27.

The Gospel of Matthew and Christian Judaism. Edinburgh: T&T Clark, 1998.

Small, Jocelyn Penny. *Wax Tablets of the Mind: Cognitive Studies of Memory and Literacy in Classical Antiquity*. Abingdon: Routledge, 1997.

Smallwood, E. Mary. *The Jews under Roman Rule: From Pompey to Diocletian: A Study in Political Relations*. 2nd ed. Studies in Judaism in Late Antiquity 20. Leiden: Brill, 1981.

Smith, Barry. *Jesus' Last Passover Meal*. Lewiston: Edwin Mellen, 1993.

Smith, Daniel Lynwood and Zachary Lundin Kostopoulos. "Biography, History and the Genre of Luke-Acts." *New Testament Studies* 62 (2017): 390–410.

Smith, Ian K. *Heavenly Perspective: A Study of the Apostle Paul's Response to a Jewish Mystical Movement at Colossae*. London: T&T Clark, 2006.

Snodgrass, Klyne R. *Stories with Intent: A Comprehensive Guide to the Parables of Jesus*. 2nd ed. Grand Rapids: Eerdmans, 2018.

Parable of the Wicked Servants: An Inquiry into Parable Interpretation. Wis-senschaftliche Untersuchungen zum Neuen Testament 27. Tübingen: Mohr Siebeck, 1983.

Soares, George M. Prabhu. *The Formula Quotations in the Infancy Narrative of Matthew: An Inquiry into the Tradition History of Mt 1–2*. Rome: Biblical Institute Press, 1976.

Staples, Jason. *The Idea of Israel in Second Temple Judaism: A New Theory of Peo-ple, Exile, and Israelite Identity*. Cambridge: Cambridge University Press, 2021.

"'Lord, Lord': Jesus as YHWH in Matthew and Luke." *New Testament Studies* 64 (2018): 1–19.

Stein, Robert H. "The 'Criteria' for Authenticity." Pages 225–263 in *Studies of History and Tradition in the Four Gospels*. Gospel Perspectives 1. Sheffield: JSOT Press, 1980.

Strauss, Mark L. *The Davidic Messiah in Luke-Acts: The Promise and its Ful-fillment in Lukan Christology*. Journal for the Study of the New Testament Supplement Series 110. Sheffield: Sheffield Academic Press, 1995.

Strecker, George. *Der Weg der Gerechtigkeit: Untersuchung zur Theologie des Matthäus*. 3rd ed. Göttingen: Vandenhoeck & Ruprecht, 1971.

Stuart, Douglas. *Hosea–Jonah*. Word Biblical Commentary 31. Dallas: Word, Incorporated, 1987.

Stuhlmacher, Peter. "Das neutestamentliche Zeugnis vom Herrenmahl." *Zeitschrift für Theologie und Kirche* 84 (1987): 1–35.

Sumney, Jerry L. *Steward of God's Mysteries: Paul and Early Church Tradition*. Grand Rapids: Eerdmans, 2017.

Svartvik, Jesper. *Mark and Mission: Mark 7, 1–23 in its Narrative and Historical Contexts*. Coniectanea Neotestamentica or Coniectanea Biblica: New Testa-ment Series 32. Stockholm: Almqvist and Wiksell, 2000.

Talbert, Charles H. *Literary Patterns, Theological Themes and the Genre of Luke-Acts.* Society of Biblical Literature Monograph Series 20. Missoula: Scholars Press, 1974.

Talmon, Shemaryahu. "'Exile' and 'Restoration' in the Conceptual World of Ancient Judaism." Pages 107–146 in *Restoration: Old Testament, Jewish, and Christian Perspectives.* Edited by James M. Scott. Leiden: Brill, 2001.

Tan, Kim Huat. *The Zion Traditions and the Aims of Jesus.* Society for New Testament Studies Monograph Series 91. Cambridge: Cambridge University Press, 1997.

Tannehill, Robert C. "The Disciples in Mark: The Function of a Narrative Role." *Journal of Religion* 51 (1977): 386–405.

Tellbe, Mikael. "The Temple Tax as Pre-70 c.e. Identity Marker." Pages 19–44 in *The Formation of the Early Church.* Edited by Jostein Ådna. Wissenschafltliche Untersuchungen zum Neuen Testament 183. Tübingen: Mohr Siebeck, 2005.

Thate, Michael J. *Remembrance of Things Past? Albert Schweitzer, the Anxiety of Influence, and the Untidy Jesus of Markan Memory.* Wissenschafltliche Untersuchungen zum Neuen Testament II/251. Tübingen: Mohr Siebeck, 2013.

Theissen, Gerd. "From the Historical Jesus to the Kerygmatic Son of God: How Role Analysis Contributes to the Understanding of New Testament Christology." Pages 235–260 in *Jesus Research: New Methodologies and Perceptions, The Second Princeton-Prague Symposium on Jesus Research.* Edited by James H. Charlesworth with Brian Rhea and Petr Pokorný. Grand Rapids: Eerdmans, 2014.

Theissen, Gerd and Annette Merz. *The Historical Jesus: A Comprehensive Guide.* London: SCM, 1998.

Thiessen, Matthew. *Jesus and the Forces of Death: The Gospels' Portrayal of Ritual Impurity within First-Century Judaism.* Grand Rapids: Baker Academic, 2020.

Thompson, Marianne Meye. *The Promise of the Father: Jesus and God in the New Testament.* Louisville: Westminster John Knox Press, 2000.

Thompson, William G. *Matthew's Advice to a Divided Community: Mt. 17,22–18,35.* Analecta Biblica 44. Rome: Biblical Institute Press, 1970.

Trilling, Wolfgang. *Das Wahre Israel: Studien zur Theologie des Matthäusevangeliums.* 3rd ed. Munich: Kösel, 1964.

Trocmé, Étienne. *The Childhood of Christianity.* Translated by John Bowden. London: SCM Press, 1977.

Tuckett, Christopher. "Jesus Tradition in Non-Markan Material Common to Matthew and Luke." Pages 1853–1874 in vol. 3 of *Handbook for the Study of the Historical Jesus.* 4 vols. Edited by Tom Holmén and Stanley E. Porter. Leiden: Brill, 2010.

Turner, David L. *Matthew.* Baker Commentary on the New Testament. Grand Rapids: Baker Academic, 2008.

Twelftree, Graham. *Paul and the Miraculous: A Historical Reconstruction.* Grand Rapids: Baker Academic, 2013.

"Sanhedrin." Pages 728–732 in *Dictionary of Jesus and the Gospels.* Edited by Joel B. Green, Scot McKnight, and I. Howard Marshall. Downers Grove: InterVarsity Press, 1992.

Um, Stephen T. *The Theme of Temple Christology in John's Gospel.* The Library of New Testament Studies 312. Sheffield: Sheffield Academic, 2006.

Van der Wal, A. "Themes from Exodus in Jeremiah 30–31." Pages 559–566 in *Studies in the Book of Exodus: Redaction, Reception, Interpretation.* Edited by Marc Vervenne. Bibliotheca Ephemeridum Theologicarum Lovaniensium 126. Louven: Leuven University Press, 1996.

Varkey, Mothy. *Salvation in Continuity: Reconsidering Matthew's Soteriology.* Emerging Scholars. Minneapolis: Fortress Press, 2017.

Verhoef, Peter. *The Books of Haggai and Malachi.* New International Commentary on the Old Testament. Grand Rapids: Eerdmans, 1987.

Verseput, Donald J. *The Rejection of the Humble Messianic King: A Study of the Composition of Matthew 11–12.* New York: Peter Lang, 1986.

Viviano, Benedict T., O.P. "John's Use of Matthew: Beyond Tweaking." *Revue biblique* 111, 2 (2004): 209–237.

"A Woman's Quest for Wisdom and the Adoration of the Magi as Part of Matthew's Program of Solomonic Sapiential Messianism." Pages 683–700 in *The Gospel of Matthew at the Crossroads of Early Christianity.* Edited by Donald Senior, C.P.. Bibliotheca Ephemeridum Theologicarum Lovaniensium. Leuven: Peeters, 2011.

Vogel, Winfried. *The Cultic Motif in the Book of Daniel.* New York: Peter Lang, 2010.

Waetjen, Herman C. *Matthew's Theology of Fulfillment, Its Universality and Its Ethnicity: God's New Israel as the Pioneer of God's New Humanity.* London: Bloomsbury, T&T Clark, 2017.

A Reordering of Power: A Socio-Political Reading of Mark's Gospel. Minneapolis: Fortress Press, 1989.

Walck, Leslie W. *The Son of Man in the Parables of Enoch and in Matthew.* Jewish and Christian Texts Series 9. New York: T&T Clark, 2011.

Index of Primary Sources

Index

For EU product safety concerns, contact us at Calle de José Abascal, 56–1°,
28003 Madrid, Spain or eugpsr@cambridge.org.

www.ingramcontent.com/pod-product-compliance
Ingram Content Group UK Ltd.
Pitfield, Milton Keynes, MK11 3LW, UK
UKHW040621240426
470322UK00011B/243